10 -

Organic

wine guide

Organic

wine guide

MONTY WALDIN

FRIENDS *of the*
earth
for the planet for people

Thorsons

Thorsons
An Imprint of HarperCollins*Publishers*
77–85 Fulham Palace Road,
Hammersmith, London W6 8JB

The Thorsons website address is:
www.thorsons.com

First published 1999
10 9 8 7 6 5 4 3 2 1

A catalogue record for this book
is available from the British Library

ISBN 0 7225 3833 2

Printed and bound in Great Britain by
Caledonian International Book Manufacturing Ltd, Glasgow

Contents

Foreword

Organic wine fascinates drinkers. There are no questions I am more regularly posed than those which concern organic wine. What is it? Where can you get it? How does it differ from ordinary wine? Is it as good? Is it better?

This is unsurprising. Wine, after all, has a psychological value as well as a nutritive one; it arouses our emotional interest as well as stimulating our taste buds and denting our purses. Most wine drinkers regard wine as a friend, albeit an enigmatic one. We want to trust it.

Yet wine is also a processed product. It is often sourced from a foreign country; its producer may be identified by no more than initials and a post code. Sealed up in a bottle, wine resists any sort of inspection; once poured, it offers little more scope for visual assessment. There are no evident wrinkles, no tell-tale waxy film on its surface. You can't wash it before you consume it. Back labels are generally richer in flowery adjectives or bland food-matching suggestions than in hard, factual descriptions of vine cultivation and winemaking; the full listing of a wine's ingredients is, regrettably, not mandatory. If organic wine exists, most drinkers reason, then there must be an explanation as to why the overwhelming majority of wines do not claim to be organic. What exactly is in there?

This is not an easy question to answer. Wine producers relish the distance and obscurity in which they work, and are rarely keen to describe exactly what they have used at every stage of the vine growing and winemaking process. Journalists ask questions, but have no way of verifying answers. Even where strict production rules exist, they are hard to police and to enforce.

Wine, moreover, is intrinsically anarchic. It is produced by tens of thousands of individuals and companies worldwide; each growing season presents different problems and challenges; no winemaker ever duplicates his or her previous work exactly. This chaos defeats the normal mechanisms of consumer selection, which is why many wine-purchasers rely either on familiar, branded names or on recommendations from writers or retailers. It may also be a reason why the organic badge is less widely seen on wine bottles than it now is on bags of onions or carrots.

These are just some of the reasons why this book is so welcome. Monty Waldin explains exactly what 'organic' means in the wine context – he also tells us what may be in those bottles which do not claim to be organic. Biodynamics is an exceptionally important variant on organic production in the wine world: we discover why. A sceptic by nature, Monty Waldin also has the advantage of having worked in vineyards and wineries in both hemispheres; he knows at first-hand, as few other journalists do, the kind of compromises and ruses which go on there. Most usefully, perhaps, he has bloodhounded his way through all the world's major wine-producing regions in search of organic growers. He's talked to them and tasted their wines. When those wines are good, he tells us; when they aren't, he tells us too. Organic status cannot redeem a poor wine, and incompetent organic producers damage the ideal they should serve.

My own belief is that organic cultivation is the hard and difficult goal for which all of those involved in agriculture should strive; in the long run, it is best for human health, best for human taste buds, and the only option for a future in which we cease to exploit and deplete our environmental patrimony. Wine producers, it is true, have been laggardly in addressing these issues, and why? Because drinkers, browbeaten by wine's complexities, do not demand a quality organic alternative in the same way that we are now doing for bread, for vegetables, for fruit and for meat.

I like to imagine a future in which all good wine will be organic. Use this book, support the world's most skilled organic and biodynamic wine-growers, and it may happen.

Andrew Jefford

Introduction

What is Organic Wine?

Organic wine is wine made from grapes grown without the help of synthetic fertilisers, weed-killers or insecticides. All of these things damage the soil and can end up in the wine as residue. The legal definition of organic wine is somewhat more complicated and varies according to where the vineyard is, where the grapes from it are fermented into wine and, finally, in which market the wine is sold. In all cases in order for a vineyard to be classed as organic the owner must be able to prove which vineyard the grapes came from, which officially recognized body certified the vineyard as organic and from what date certified organic practices began.

DEFINITIONS

Within Europe, organic wine is defined as 'wine made from organically grown grapes'. Wines sold within the European Union from organic vineyards are labelled according to a single standard. This is laid out in EU Directive 2092/91, which came into effect with the 1992 vintage. It recognizes agricultural crop products as organic only when they are in an unprocessed (raw) state, i.e. wine grapes, carrots, tomatoes and cabbages. Thus it applies to the grapes from which the wine was made but *not* to the wine itself. Hence wines promoted as organic must be labelled only as 'made from organically grown grapes', not 'organic wine'. In the same way you can buy loose, raw 'organic carrots' and 'carrot juice made from organically grown carrots', but not 'organic carrot juice'!

Outside Europe, organic wine can be defined as 'wine made from organically grown grapes' as well as 'organic wine'. Wines sold outside Europe will defer to whatever national law is in place in the country the wine is sold in. The level of strictness varies from area to area. For example, in California wine which is bottled without preservatives can be called 'organic'. The main preservative which must be avoided for wine to be labelled as 'organic' in California is sulphur dioxide (what the Americans call 'sulfite'). However because America is a federal country, the regulations vary from state to state – unlike in Europe where there is only one set of standards.

European organic winegrowers who use no sulphur during winemaking have a ready market in California. There they can label their wines 'Château X, organic wine', whereas on their own doorstep they can label it only as 'Château X, wine made from organically grown grapes'. In Europe they are not even allowed to add to the label terms like 'sulphur free' or 'low in sulphur'.

Organic Vineyards

Organic vineyard owners have the same goal as non-organic (conventional) vineyard owners – to produce grapes from which to make wine profitably. The only difference is that on organic vineyards no herbicides and no synthetic pesticides or fertilisers are used. The idea is that making wine from grapes grown without man-made chemicals is better both for the planet *and* for the wine drinker, because there are no chemical residues to end up either in the vineyard soil or in the wine. The owners of organic vineyards point out that what they do is more than just not using certain chemical sprays – leaving the sprays in the shed will not, in itself, produce a healthy crop of grapes. This is why organic vineyard owners promote the fertility of the soil – its structure and content – by using natural compost, which they describe as dead matter brought back to life by worms; the worms provide the oxygen the vines need below ground, something which wormless, man-made chemical fertilisers in plastic sacks are unable to provide.

Organic vineyards promote polyculture (biodiversity) by allowing plants other than vines to grow in and around the vineyard. These other plants may be plain weeds – remember organic growers cannot use herbicides/weed-killers. Or, these other non-vine plants may be flowers, herbs, vegetables and clovers that the winegrower sows between the rows of vines as 'cover crops' (*see Appendix 2*). This sort of biodiversity helps regulate the vineyard soil, by giving the worms below ground something to chew on as the cover crops establish roots, and by giving insects above the ground a choice of habitats when the cover crops flower. In vineyards which contain nothing but vines (monocultures), insect pests have a field day, every day – just like a greedy child would in a supermarket full of nothing but ice-cream (and hence the need for ever increasing doses of chemical pesticides). Having extra habitats creates the biodiversity in vineyards that encourages the insects to regulate each other naturally, because no single species of insect – whether pest or benefical insect – can dominate. Therefore the winegrower has more time to spend on pampering the vines and the grapes they produce to make better wine, rather than spending all day frantically preparing sprays in a vicious circle of chemical dependency. Chemical pesticides are very good at eliminating a single pest, but they also wipe out beneficial insects too, and the vineyard quickly loses its natural balance as a result. And because the vine is a perennial plant – the same vine in the same piece of ground produces grapes year after year, perhaps for over a century before replanting – the need for natural balance is paramount if the wine produced is to be of optimum quality every vintage. Farmers who mess up an annual crop (like corn) one year can get it right the following year by re-seeding: vinegrowers do not have that option.

Organic vineyards are not perfect. There are contradictions. For example not using herbicides to kill weeds may mean hoeing the weeds out with a tractor-mounted plough to create the space for cover crops. Non-organic growers make one pass through the vines with the herbicide tractor during the year. Organic growers will have to plough the weeds down as many as four times a year. As a result they burn more tractor diesel (few organic growers use horse-drawn ploughs as labour costs are now so high), and risk compacting the soil more, which is bad news for vine roots and soil worms. And there are bad organic growers just as there are bad conventional ones – ploughing the weeds just after it has rained, rather than waiting for the soil to dry, will compact the soil perhaps irrevocably – and not all organic growers always have the time or inclination to wait. This is why the chemical community argues that the term 'organic' is a misnomer, and an example of 'quaint anti-scientism' dreamt up by a chemophobic world.

As wine drinkers you must decide whether to drink wine that may contain traces of pesticides, or herbicides, such a Round-Up (which is claimed by its manufacturer to break down in the soil into harmless substances but which may, according to a study published in *Environmental and Molecular Mutagensis* (Vol 31, 1998, pp 55–9), cause cancer). Contact pesticides that are sprayed on the grape skins to protect them from disease end up as residue in the wine by being washed from the grapes as they are pressed or put in the vat. Systemic pesticides are sprayed on the ground to be sucked up by the vine roots, and end up in the grape pulp (which inevitably means residues end up in the wine). The alternative is to take the organic option, despite its occasional contradictions. Any traces of chemical residue found in wine made from organic grapes will be there because of background contamination from spray drift or from the atmosphere – not through the actions of the winegrower. And if we want this background contamination caused by the wine industry to go away, then the only way we'll do it is to support and drink wines from those who eschew chemicals in the first place.

HOW ARE GRAPES GROWN ORGANICALLY?

For organic growers the soil and its natural fertility is paramount. The intensive agricultural practices adopted more and more in the past 50 years have stripped the minerals essential for healthy crops from the soil, necessitating the increasing use of artificial help to replace what has been lost. Conventional vineyards use chemical fertilisers. Organic and biodynamic growers apply compost.

Composted fertiliser is the most natural form of fertiliser and it is where organic growing begins. Compost is made by letting manure (horse, sheep and cow rather than human) rot down with dry matter (e.g., straw bedding used for animals, grape stalks, prunings, etc.). Once compost is spread in the vineyard worms drag it into the ground where it is broken down into humus by bacteria in the soil, which attach themselves to the vine roots and draw in the nutrients the vine needs.

Again, the conventional answer to the problem of weeds, is to use chemical weed-killers. The organic alternative is to allow the weeds to grow, and mow them periodically so that the cut weeds rot back into the ground (thus providing organic fertiliser). However, self-propagating weeds do not always produce soil nutrients of such quality as cereals and legumes. Organic growers have learnt to plant what are called 'cover crops' between the vines. Not only do these help keep down weeds, they also provide more desirable nutrients and in greater quantity than weeds. A list of cover crops is given in Appendix 2.

Disease control is more of a problem. The majority of the world's wine is made from grape varieties that belong to the disease-susceptible European vine species rather than the more resistant non-European ones. The main diseases to which the European vines (Chardonnay, Merlot, etc.) are vulnerable include:

- Downy mildew – treatable with the contact spray Bordeaux Mixture (a mixture of copper sulphate and lime)
- Powdery mildew – treatable with sulphur
- Grey Rot – treatable with anti-rot sprays like ground marine algae (for organic vinegrowers), but really only countered by farming scrupulously so that the rot never takes hold in the first place, for example, by attracting warmth and light into the vineyard.

Pests that attack the vine or the grapes (including spiders, hoppers, caterpillars, insects and mites, as well as birds) can be controlled organically through the use of naturally occurring plant or mineral extracts which leave no residues in the soil (e.g., Rotenone and Pyrethre (pyrethroids) to counter unwanted aphids and caterpillars); or through paraffin oil and potassium soap (soft soap); or cultures of naturally occurring bacteria like Bacillus Thuringiensis (Bt) that paralyse and kill grape caterpillars when sprayed on the vine-leaves) may also be used. An alternative, especially when cover crops attract a range of bird and insect life to the vineyard, is to rely on natural predators to control aphids, etc.

Many of the smaller organic vineyards hand pick their grapes, rather than use mechanical pickers. Hand picking is the only way to get the grapes off the vine without damaging the vine, the grapes or the soil. It is, however, slow to do and expensive to organize. French growers, for example, have to fill out seven forms for each picker employed!

Hand picking allows only the healthiest and ripest bunches to be picked – even the best managed vineyards will have bunches with bird pecks in them. Only with the best grapes can the winemaker hope to have natural yeasts in great enough quantity to ferment the wine without recourse to packets of yeast and fining agents. Hand picking is also the only way of picking the same vine in stages, as for late picked sweet white wines (produced in the Loire region, and in Austria and Germany). With mechanical picking it is all or nothing, although mechanized picking is up to 40 times quicker than picking by hand.

What is Biodynamic Viticulture?

Biodynamic vineyards have the same goal as organic vineyards – to produce grapes from which to make wine profitably without using synthetic additives. The only difference between organic and biodynamic vineyards is that on biodynamic ones the work in the vineyard is timed to coincide with the earth's natural rhythms so that the vine is receptive to what the winegrower is asking it to do. These natural rhythms are determined by the position of the sun, the moon and the planets as well as the earth. So whereas organic growers spend most of their time preoccupied with what is beneath their feet – the soil – biodynamic growers are as preoccupied with what is going on above their heads. They ask you to think of what a vine looks like in winter after it has just been pruned (the vine has to be pruned to produce a crop). The vine is a bare stump; by summer it is thick and bushy with considerable shoot growth and leaves upon it, as well as the emerging grapes. Only 10 per cent of the bushy growth and the grape bunches created by the vine between the winter pruning and summer is provided by the roots drawing matter (i.e., mineral elements) up from the soil. The other 90 per cent is created by the atmosphere – think of sunlight, without which photosynthesis would not occur.

An example of working with natural earth rhythms is the timing of planting. A vineyard plot maybe planted once only every 100 years, so biodynamists feel that choosing the right day on which to plant is critical if a vine plot is to remain productive and healthy for those 100 years, and not need to be ripped up and replaced after just 15 or 20 years; or sprayed constantly because the vines are weak. This is why biodynamists plant near the new moon, when the earth's gravitational rhythms are downwards – the direction the baby vine's roots must first go if it is subsequently to survive and prosper and then grow up towards the sun. New moon days are sometimes called 'root' days, because that is when this part of the plant is 'working' or favoured. By combining the downward movement of the vine root with the downward gravitational pull exerted by the new moon on the earth, a biodynamic grower hopes to give all his baby vines and their roots the best possible start in life. The vine will grow quickly and strongly – and will be less susceptible to disease for its 100-year lifespan – and that saves an awful lot of potential spraying. (*See Appendix 3 for further details on biodynamic growing principles.*)

Many people think biodynamics is all hocus pocus, because growers are constrained to do certain tasks in the vineyard only on certain days, when the planetary influences are right. However, no one seems to think organic growers are crazy because they plant new vines in spring, harvest their grapes in autumn and prune the vines in winter. The organic (and conventional) farming calendars are broadly divided into four seasons per year; the biodynamic calendar is precisely divided into 365 days per year. Vine treatments – which are sprayed on the leaves, usually in the form of homoeopathic, plant-based biodynamic teas – are timed for 'leaf days', when the passage of the moon through certain constellations is such as to make the leaves receptive; harvesting of the grapes is timed for 'fruit days' – to capture or pick the grapes at the moment they are in harmony with natural forces, and so on.

Biodynamics is sometimes as imperfect as organic when the ideology meets practical reality. Biodynamic vineyards are supposed to be as self-sufficient as possible – which means, for example, that all the compost must be made on site, rather than bought in. The idea is that each vineyard becomes an individual, unique place – the opposite of the conventional approach where all the vineyards in a village may buy the same brand of fertiliser, the same brands of sprays and the same brands of fermentation yeast from a single supplier. However, many biodynamic vineyards could do more to create this 'individuality' – for example by getting rid of tractors and re-adopting horse-drawn ploughs, so as to have a ready supply of natural manure to build the compost piles. They can usually get compost (from a neighbouring farmer or rancher), but delivering the dung in a truck burns fossils fuels and goes against the biodynamic idea of the vineyard as a self-sustaining entity.

Vineyards claiming to make wines from biodynamically grown grapes are certified by a regulatory body called Demeter, and bear the Demeter seal which is an international trademark. (Demeter was the

Greek goddess of agriculture and protector of the fruits of the earth.) The whole vineyard must be converted to biodynamics for the wine from it to be marketed with the Demeter seal.

Why Should Wine Drinkers Care About Organics and Biodynamics?

Whether wines from organic or biodynamic grapes taste better than those from conventional sources is a contentious point. More and more consumers and critics are begining to think that they do taste better, and most people accept that even if not all organic or biodynamic vineyards produce perfect wines, they are trying to make their wine by using more sustainable methods. This means reducing the level of unnatural and external inputs (sprays and chemicals) in the growing and production processes and increasing the reliance on materials local to the vineyard. Examples for the future might include planting beneficial trees around vine plots that can be coppiced every year to provide vineyard supporting posts – most of the growers cited in this book buy in metal support posts. Vineyards could also begin planting wicker trees, which can be used to tie the vines to the supporting posts rather than using plastic or metal ties. Cover crops like herbs and lavender can become cash-crops or food sources as well as introducing the biodiversity mentioned above.

Many wine merchants specializing in organic wines talk of organics as a way of rediscovering 'wines our grandfathers might have drunk'. Perhaps we should look even further back to the ancients, for they could read the movements of the moon and planets against the background of the fixed stars to time agricultural work (like biodynamic theory), and they made use of local and natural materials (like the organic idea of planting more than just vines in a vineyard), because they had to – airfreight didn't exist. Think of Greek and Roman vineyards, when the vines were trained up fruit or olive trees giving two crops, not just one, in the same space. To use these ancient techniques in the most sustainable way growers must first rediscover them, and then apply them. As the human population increases and the pressure on land and resources becomes ever more strained, organic vineyards may become the harbingers of a new agriculture in which wine is one of a number of crops in biodiverse vinegardens. Then wine and food may once again be produced in the way they are meant to be consumed – with each other.

Wine Buying Tips

Wine is a living product; its taste changes over time as it ages. The best wines age the longest, which is why they are 'cellared'. However, our convenience culture means we want our wines ready right now, not in 10 or 20 years' time. One side effect of this is that houses are no longer designed with cool, underground cellars for ageing wine (or for curing meat for that matter). In the UK for example, it is estimated that 98 per cent of all wine is consumed with 48 hours of purchase: we grab a bottle on the way home from work and crack it open later that night when the food comes out of the oven. The problem with this smash-and-grab approach is that, because wine is a living product, it responds poorly to movement. Try to buy your wine a few days (preferably a week or two) ahead to let it settle down before opening. This way it can get used to the temperature of your house for example, and it will taste better too.

If your lifestyle precludes such a 'planned' approach to wine buying and wine drinking, don't worry. You can still improve your wine buying, and thus the taste of the wine you pay for, by being more alert in the wine shop.

WHERE TO BUY ORGANIC WINE
You wouldn't buy fresh fish from a fishmonger who ran out of ice, so don't shop from wine merchants who store and display wine incorrectly. This is the way it should be done:

- bottles of wine should lie horizontally so the cork is always wet

- bottles of fortified wine should be stored vertically to stop the higher level of alcohol decomposing the cork
- sparkling wines should be displayed in an area of the store with very subdued lighting (ideally with no light at all, i.e., still in the case it was delivered in). If you are buying an expensive Champagne, select the brand name you want from the shelf but *insist* on getting a bottle taken from an unopened case in the store room. You are the customer after all – so why take a risk?
- the temperature and humidity of the store should not be subject to huge variations because this kills the wine's taste, making it dull and lifeless.

Many high street wine shops seem poorly equipped for storing wine correctly (with bright lights, big front windows that act as a magnifying glass for the wines stored within, wines that are stood cork up on vertical racks, and cramped backroom storage areas where cases of wine get kicked about like footballs by overwrought staff). The merchants argue that their turnover of stock is rapid, thus the wine is not in the store long enough to deteriorate. If you are unconvinced by this, try the independent merchants who generally work to a smaller scale and have better storage facilities (because they are often sited out of town on cheaper rent sites with more space). They also tend to have a more substantial selection of organic wines because the people who run them buy direct from the wine producers, not through brokers like the chains.

Visiting a Wine Shop – Minimizing your Risk

- Avoid wines displayed on the top shelf of wine stores, where levels of heat and light, two things which adversely affect wine, are at their greatest.
- Take the bottle you want to buy off the shelf (better still, get the shop assistant to do it for you so you don't have to pay if it gets dropped!) and stand the bottle upright. Then push your thumb down onto the cork, to see if this is loose (caused by poor bottling practice at the winery or too much heat in the shop, which will make the cork dry out and shrink). If it is, tell the shop assistant, because chances are the wine within will have been turned to vinegar due to prolonged contact with the air (wine + air = water + vinegar).

- Check that the wine has a good 'fill level', i.e., that there is no empty head space in the neck of the bottle caused by leakage or evaporation resulting from a loose cork. To check this you'll need to hold the bottle up against the light at eye level. Again, get the shop assistant to do this for you if you are worried about breaking it.

If you find when you get home that your wine has small bits of cork floating in it you probably do *not* need to take it back to the shop. Although inconvenient, bits of cork do not mean a wine is 'corked', and they rarely adversely affect the taste of the wine. Wine shop assistants simply *love* people who take back wines with bits of cork floating in them – because they get to taste (or sample) an opened and perfectly good bottle of wine without having to pay for it (once the wine is opened, they reason, it will spoil before it can be sent back to head office for analysis, 'so someone might as well drink it').

Complaining

If you are really not satisfied with your purchase – and just because you feel you know nothing about wine there's no reason you should be – have the courage of your convictions. If you think a wine is faulty, take it back.

You'll have more chance of success with the merchant if you describe what you thought was wrong instead of adopting the 'this wine is off' approach. Did it taste 'fizzy' when it should have been still? (A sign of re-fermentation in bottle caused by stray yeast.) Did it taste bitter and sharp when the label promised 'ripe fruit flavours'? (Perhaps a sign of bad storage – or of bad winemaking.) Establish a dialogue with your merchant – they are not all 'wine snobs'. In fact, most wine shop staff love talking about wine with the customers and exchanging tasting notes, even on what may be faulty bottles.

If you think a wine is good, write down the name on the label before you take the empty bottle to the bottle bank, and tell your friends about it – but make sure you buy enough of it for yourself first. Many wines are 'batch bottled' over a period of days and the wine in each day's bottling will be slightly different, even though the wine label on each batch will be identical. (This is the advantage of buying wine in a case lot as all the bottles in the case will contain identical wine.)

Serving Organic Wine

In most cases, decanting benefits both the appearance and the taste of the wine. Decanting helps the appearance by leaving any sediment in the wine at the bottom of the bottle the wine came in, rather than in your glass. Remember that organic and biodynamic wines are often bottled without any fining treatments (to brighten the wine's appearance) or filtration (to remove sediment), so they are more likely to contain sediment than conventional wine. In the overwhelming majority of cases, wine sediment is a good sign in a wine, and is harmless if consumed.

Decanting also helps the taste of the wine by aerating it, allowing it to breathe. Just as people like to limber up for a bracing walk by taking a few deep breaths, so wine likes to find its feet by being poured a bit of time before reaching your glass. Many organic and biodynamic growers feel their wines are stronger and more robust since converting to organic methods, and they recommend decanting. The best part about decanting is it allows you to see the colour of the wine – impossible otherwise if the wine comes in a coloured or smoked bottle.

Decanting need not be a hassle. You can use a clean, empty wine bottle as a decanter instead of buying one. Practise pouring with water first, or use a funnel. Remember – decanting is not obligatory. The only rule to remember about decanting is: if you don't want to decant, don't.

All but the lightest red wines can be decanted a few hours before you intend to drink them. This allows the dry structure of the wine, the tannin, to soften, while leaving the soft body of the wine, the black and red fruits, to thicken out and thus flatter your tongue.

For dry white and pink wines (rosés), remove the cork and place in the fridge for chilling. Decant once the wine is ready for serving. It is better to chill a white wine gradually in the refrigerator during a morning or afternoon than to do it too quickly by shoving it in the freezer compartment half an hour before your guests arrive. (Another reason for trying to plan your wine purchases a day or two ahead.) Chill medium dry white wines slightly less than bone-dry whites to preserve their aromas. Champagne and other sparkling wines often suffer from a lack of aroma and texture, due either to over-chilling or because the person opening the bottle has allowed it to go 'pop' and foam.

Sweet white wines can be decanted, but sometimes it is better to keep this style of wine in its original bottle and let the wine 'breathe' in the glass for up to half an hour. Opened bottles of the finest sweet white wines can be kept in the refrigerator for nearly a fortnight, so you can dip in for a glass when you need a pick-me-up! Sweet white wines suit savoury things like nuts and cheese rather than sweet desserts.

Sparkling wines do not benefit from decanting, because they lose their fizz.

If you are serving more than one wine at a time, the typical order for serving is dry before sweet, white before red, good before better, and better before best.

How to use this Book
Contact Details

The contact details (address, telephone, fax and email) given under each producer are the ones to use if you want to contact a particular winery for more information – about receiving newsletters, putting yourself on the mailing list for winery events (tastings, concerts, food and wine evenings, releases of new vintages, special bottlings, etc.) or to keep abreast of the vegetarian or vegan status of the wines in future vintages.

Visiting a vineyard is one of the best ways to buy your wine because you buy direct from the producer, rather than through a third party. A visit to a vineyard is also the best way to appreciate how vines are grown and wine is made, and to learn about organic production methods (you may even get to meet livestock – sheep and cows – on the more polycultural vineyards, which is great for children who can't usually taste or consume the wine). However, bear in mind that because on most 'green' vineyards humans rather than machinery do the bulk of the work, the number of people given over to receiving visitors may be somewhat limited. This means it is absolutely essential to make an appointment in advance to avoid the disappointment of there being nobody to show you and your family around the vineyard once you arrive. Otherwise look for the visitor or farm shop information given under each producer's address and contact details. (Note: the address given under the name of the producer may not necessarily be where visits will be to, as some vineyards have separate areas and buildings for visits and winery tours; it pays to make an appointment to confirm arrangements.)

Price Rating Codes

The price of a wine is determined by many factors, most obviously the costs of production: planting costs for the vineyard (vines, posts and wires), the wages of those who prune and pick the vines, equipment for the cellar like fermenting tanks and, lastly, the bottles, corks and wine labels. The most fundamental aspect to how high production costs are in the vineyard is the site the vineyard is on — flat vineyards (Bordeaux) are far cheaper and quicker to work than those on steep hillsides (Burgundy).

The price of wine is also influenced by how much it costs to transport it to the marketplace, be that a local farmers' market in the same village as the vineyard, or a supermarket located on another continent. Also, as restaurant-goers are aware, the price of the same bottle of wine can triple between the local off-licence and the local restaurant. Finally wine is taxed more in some countries than in others (duty on wine is around one hundred times less in France than in the UK for example). This makes pricing every wine featured in this book impossible, so a price code is used for each, from 🍾 to 🍾🍾🍾, with 🍾 the lowest and 🍾🍾🍾 the highest in terms of price. Where a producer is given an 'Overall Price Rating' all the wines featured in the notes are priced in the same band.

The symbols 🍾 – 🍾🍾🍾 are awarded according to how each producer's wine(s) compare to those produced locally in the regional section it is found in. So, for example, if a red Côtes du Rhône is rated 🍾, then this wine is competitively priced against all other Côtes du Rhônes, whether organic (and thus featured in this book) or non-organic. If a red Côtes du Rhône carries a 🍾🍾🍾 rating however, then you can be sure that this is a wine priced at the top end of all the Côtes du Rhônes. This should help those of you choosing between a non-organic Côtes du Rhône which you really like, and a similarly priced organic Côtes du Rhône you're thinking about trying — you, the reader/taster, decides whether the wine offers 'value' — so you can close your eyes and pretend to be the wine buyer for your favourite restaurant or wine shop.

Note too that two wines from the same producer with the same price code may carry different prices in the same shop or restaurant: for example a Riesling from an Alsace producer rated 🍾 and a Grand Cru Riesling rated 🍾🍾 from the same grower. The Grand Cru wine would be more expensive in the shops because French law says Grand Cru Alsace Riesling is subject to greater restrictions (notably lower yields) than non-Grand Cru Alsace Riesling.

Wines from some regions – Champagne is the obvious example – are always expensive to buy, but the way the 🍾–🍾🍾🍾 scale works in this book means that not every Champagne listed here automatically carries a 🍾🍾🍾 or 'expensive' rating. In fact, none of the Champagne producers in this book get a 🍾🍾🍾 rating for any of their wines, because none of them price their wines at the top end of the scale as the famous (and without exception non-organic) Champagne houses tend to do. This is because all of the organic Champagne producers featured here do not need to recoup large sums of money spent paying for glossy advertisements (such as those which adorn wine and style magazines for example). (It is estimated than one-third of the price of a bottle of Champagne from any one of the 20 or so big name or 'grandes marques' houses – like the ones handed to victorious racing drivers at the end of grand prix – goes on marketing, rather than on maintaining the vineyards.)

This is one way of thinking about what the symbols mean:

- 🍾 wines which are as inexpensively priced for their style and region as you are likely to find. Such wine represent 'everyday value' (the Americans rather unkindly call these 'jug' wines). Look out for 🍾 wines from producers who keep costs down and still remain 'organic in spirit, organic in practice' by retaining sustainable traditions like picking the grapes by hand, for example by involving friends and family at harvest time. Be careful of 'everyday' value if it means the producer has saved money by dispensing with human pickers in favour of machine harvesters which, although allowed under organic rules, pollute the environment, damage the soil through compaction, and can weaken the vines.

- 🍾🍾 wines priced slightly above average for their region and style. They are mid-range wines where the higher price results ideally from extra attention being paid to keep yields down, to give more concentration of flavour in the wine. One example of this is tougher pruning of the vine in winter. This reduces the number of grapes on the vine but (of course) means less wine overall is produced – hence the higher price. (Vines which are asked to yield less are stronger, more resistant to disease, and thus less reliant on chemicals.)

- ♙♙ wines priced above average for their region and style. They can be considered 'premium' or special occasion wines. Here the extra money should be justified by really meticulous selection of the grapes by the grower at picking for example, so that only the ripest and most flavoured bunches are used for the wine. The idea is not to make a 'blockbuster wine', merely one which is balanced and with more complex flavours than if slightly underripe grapes were thrown in the vat without some thought.

- ♙♙♙ wines priced as expensively for their style as you are likely to find. They are 'super premium' wines ('ultra premium' in the USA), which, because they are labelled 'organic', should be hand grown, hand picked and hand made to justify the extra expense. Hopefully there are enough clues in the profiles of the ♙♙♙ wines below for readers to work out which of them justify their high price rating, and which are out to make a buck. Super premium should mean a quality-at-all-costs approach that begins with total commitment to the vineyard, the soil and the vines. This entails ploughing the soil at the right moment, turning and applying the compost when nature demands (even at weekends for example), rather than when it suits the grower. At the other end of the wine production scale it means respecting what goes into the bottle – bottling slowly by gravity rather than quickly by machine and using the finest corks so the wine can age. The super premium price should encourage you to get some more detailed advice from the supplier before you part with your money: 'Was the vintage a good one?' is the first question to ask, followed by, 'Was it also a good vintage for this producer?' One theory is that organic vineyards tend to perform better in poor vintages than non-organic ones, because the vines have more natural resistance to poor weather or pestilence.

Stockists

The names of stockists are given where possible, but the changing nature of supply means that such information as is given may change at short notice. As traders go, wine merchants are a pretty friendly bunch, and the stockists mentioned should be happy to point you in the right direction if they no longer list a particular wine or producer, by giving you the name of the new stockist.

Note: The stockists listed under each producer are UK stockists, unless otherwise indicated. For a full list of stockists see Appendix 1.

MAIL ORDER SUPPLIES

For mail order details contact the producers direct. In the USA mail order can be problematic because each state has its own rules about crossborder shipments of alcohol. In France, on the other hand, wine deliveries are straightforward, cheap and efficient – if you are lucky enough to have a French address of course. For mail order from the stockists listed in Appendix 1, contact them direct.

Vegetarian and Vegan Suitable Wines

Awareness about vegetarian and vegan issues in the UK in particular has increased in the light of BSE or 'mad cow disease'. Animal products are used by both organic and non-organic winemakers during production, to clear or 'fine' the wine to keep it from turning cloudy for example, or to remove 'off' tastes and flavours. For this reason wines included in the producer profiles which are suitable for vegetarians and vegans are marked as such. However it must be noted that just because a wine is certified organic or biodynamic it is not automatically suitable for vegetarians or vegans.

It should also be noted that while a wine may be suitable for vegetarians in one vintage or year, the following vintage the same producer may decide to use an animal fining. For instance in 1990 the red Bordeaux wines were really ripe after a hot year, so some producers did not fine their wine with egg whites. In 1991 the red Bordeaux wines were underripe or slightly bitter, so many producers did fine the wines to make them softer tasting. So, only wines from those producers who never use animal-based fining agents will always be suitable for vegetarian and vegan wine drinkers. However, even then, it always pays to check first – with the retailer or directly with the producer – if you are in any doubt about the vegetarian or vegan status of wine you wish to drink. For more details and a factsheet on 'Alcohol', contact:

The Vegetarian Society
Parkdale, Dunham Road, Altrincham, Cheshire WA14 4QG
Tel:+44 161 928 0793
Fax:+44 161 926 9182
Internet:www.vegsoc.org/.uk

Appendix 4 contains more details on fining agents and their suitability for vegetarian and vegan wine drinkers.

Europe: France
Alsace

Alsace is a predominantly white wine region in north-eastern France. The region was once part of Germany though, and as a result the locals speak their own dialect – neither French nor German – so those of you thinking of harvesting grapes here should leave the dictionaries at home. Alsace's other particularity is its climate. The region's steeply sloping vineyards are protected to the west by the Vosges mountain range, so that despite the northerly location these are some of the driest vineyards in France. As a result the wines have high levels of alcohol and plenty of body. In addition, the mineral elements present in the Alsace soils mean that the region's white wines take on a spicey note. Dry, bodied and spicy white wines like Alsace's match oriental and 'fusion' food perfectly.

Alsace growers leave more fruiting buds on their vines per square metre than any other French vine growers and their average yields are the highest in France. It stands to reason that, because the crop of grapes taken off the Alsace vines every vintage is huge – bigger than anywhere else in France – a host of core nutrients from the soil are lost every time a truck load of grapes disappears into one of Alsace's Hansel and Gretel-style wineries. Organic winegrowers in Alsace are worried that the Alsace soils are becoming impoverished. They look to replace these lost nutrients with animal manures or green compost. Compost is applied by burying it in small doses in clay balls in holes bored into the vineyards. It has to be applied in this way because much of the Alsace vineyards lie on steep, sometimes terraced slopes from which topsoil and fertiliser are washed away each time it rains.

The organic and biodynamic vineyards listed below accounted for 45 hectares out of a possible total of 12,500 hectares in Alsace in 1998, a relatively minor proportion. It seems that they will soon be joined by a considerable number of growers in the process of conversion to organic and biodynamic methods. Many of these vineyards are founder members of a 60-strong network who have coordinated their own composting programme. Cooperation can involve one grower supplying animal manure from sheep that he might own, while another grower loans a sheltered piece of vineyard where tonnes of compost can decompose slowly.

ALSACE STYLE TERMS

Vendanges Tardives: late harvested grapes, which give extra alcohol and richer body. Vendanges Tardives wines are sweet all over the world, and are sweet in Alsace too, but they can be made in a drier style. This produces some of the most intense white wines, with alcohol levels up to 15 per cent. Gewurztraminer and Pinot Gris are comparatively drier than Riesling or Muscat.

Sélection de Grains Nobles: late picked from berries affected by 'noble rot'. This makes the wines intensely sweet. Usually 'SGN' works best from Riesling and Tokay-Pinot Gris.

Grand Cru: this means the grapes came from one of 50 top named sites. Only Riesling, Muscat, Gewurztraminer and Tokay-Pinot Gris grapes allowed. Expect to pay a premium for Grands Crus, especially when made as Vendanges Tardives or Sélection de Grains Nobles.

Crémant d'Alsace: sparkling wine made by the traditional method (*see Champagne, page 72 for details of this*). Underrated, piercing style, in contrast to the richer one of the Loire.

ALSACE LABELLING

Don't be put off by Alsace wines' presentation – green fluted bottles and labelling more reminiscent of Germany than France. Alsace white wines are generally dry and full of body, unlike German Mosels, for example, which are off-dry and light. The majority of Alsace output is still white wine made 100 per cent from a single grape variety, such as:

- Auxerrois: big yielder, can taste like Viognier, fat and tropical, but in a minor key.
- Chardonnay: increasing in popularity and used in sparkling Alsace wine – see Crémant d'Alsace, above.
- Gewurztraminer: a spicy full white smelling of rose petals and Turkish delight. The best examples are made during vintages when the buds

are nipped slightly by spring frost – this reduces the yield and makes for concentrated wines. Allowed for Grand Cru, used for Vendanges Tardives and Sélection de Grains Nobles.

- Muscat: shows a grapey character that can tire quickly once in the wine is in the bottle, so store in a cool and dark part of the house or cellar. Drink regularly to check on its evolution. Allowed for Grand Cru, Vendanges Tardives and Sélection de Grains Nobles.
- Pinot Blanc: subdued, lean, crisp – a variety to start rather than finish the evening with?
- Pinot Gris: still labelled as Tokay-Pinot Gris despite EU regulations to the contrary (Tokay is also the name of the sweet Hungarian wine). See Tokay-Pinot Gris below.
- Riesling: a chameleon on Alsace's varied mountain topography. Allowed for Grand Cru, Vendanges Tardives and Sélection de Grains Nobles.
- Sylvaner: unfashionable earthy white grape; generally drink the latest vintage available.
- Tokay-Pinot Gris: always full bodied and usually nutty tasting. Allowed for Grand Cru, Vendanges Tardives and Sélection de Grains Nobles.

Red wines are also made from one variety:

- Pinot Noir: made into a red wine but more often pressed as a white base-wine to be used for Crémant d'Alsace.

Spirits

Many of the producers listed below also make fruit brandies (*eaux-de-vie*) from William pears (*poire William*), cherries and Mirabelle plums, as well as grape brandies (*fine d'Alsace* – distilled from wine and *marc d'Alsace* – distilled from washing the marc left after pressing). Such fruits flourish here because Alsace's climate is warm and dry. The region is protected from rain-laden clouds appearing from the west by the mountains of the Vosges, which stretch north across the German border into the Pfalz, where similar style spirits are made (*see page 210*).

Eugène Meyer

21a rue de Bergholtz-Zell, 68500 Bergholtz

Tel:+33 389 76 13 87

Fax:+33 389 83 03 94

Visits/Farm Gate sales: every day 8.30–11.30 and 14.00–18.30 (except Sundays and Public Holidays)

Accomodation: Holiday flats (4 to 6 people)

Stockist: Vinceremos

This family domaine consists of nearly 10 hectares of vines and was an original member of France's Demeter association when this was founded in April 1980. The Meyers converted to biodynamic methods in 1969 when members of the family suffered asthma attacks caused by the sprays they were using on the vines. Both the family and the vines appear to have gained new strength from the change. The Meyer vines now descend deeper into the hillside than before. This is significant because vines owned by Meyer's non-organic neighbours stop at a depth of one metre, at the point where the clay topsoil ends and the earth's bedrock begins. Penetrating the bedrock allows Meyer's vines more chance of finding complex micro-nutrients no longer present in the topsoils – adding to the health of the plant and the complexity of the wine. The grapes are picked by hand and they ferment with natural (not added) yeast. The wines contain minimal sulphur dioxide preservative.

- Crémant Brut, Cuvée de la Cave Dîmière méthode champenoise: dry white sparkling wine made by the traditional method, shows clean and persistent bubbles with a lovely aftertaste of lime and butter. ♦♦
- Sylvaner: dry white, full rather than flavoured, not for keeping. ♦
- Edelzwicker: dry white, a blend of several white grapes, fruity, pleasant to drink every day, and especially with starters at meals. ♦
- Pinot Blanc: dry white, fine fruit, intense example. ♦
- Pinot Noir: dry red, fruity rather than tannic. ♦♦
- Riesling: dry white, oily. ♦♦
- Riesling, Sélection de Grains Nobles Spiegel: sweet white, even texture, warm, inviting. ♦♦

- Tokay-Pinot Gris: dry, full, slightly coarse on its own, needs a creamy sauce. ▮
- Tokay-Pinot Gris, Schwarzberg (doux): sweet white from a named vineyard (but not one with a Grand Cru designation). ▮▮▮
- Tokay-Pinot Gris, Vendanges Tardives: sweet white, from over-ripe grapes, heady. ▮▮
- Tokay-Pinot Gris, Sélection de Grains Nobles: sweet white, 'noble rot' grapes, intense. ▮▮
- Muscat d'Alsace: dry white, simple, effective grapey fruit. ▮▮
- Gewurztraminer: dry white, full, broad, commanding style. ▮▮
- Gewurztraminer, Grand Cru Spiegel: dry white, shows 'flowers and spices' to the proprietor. ▮▮▮
- Gewurztraminer, Vendanges Tardives: sweet white, heady in 1989, refined in 1994, benchmark style for this part of the Alsace region. ▮▮
- Gewurztraminer, Sélection de Grains Nobles: sweet white, lots of weight, can appear clumsy in youth. ▮▮

Pierre Frick & Fils
5 rue de Baer, 68250 Pfaffenheim
Tel:+33 389 49 62 99
Fax:+33 389 49 73 78
Sales: Monday to Friday 8.00–11.30 and 13.30–18.30; vineyard visits
Stockist: Vinceremos
Overall Price Rating: ▮▮

Pierre Frick & Fils is the domaine of Jean-Pierre Frick and his wife Chantale. There are 9.5 hectares of vines, certified organic since the 1970s. Some biodynamic preparations such as oak bark and valerian (*see Appendix 3*) are used and the Fricks make their own compost. Even though the vines occupy soils and slopes which vary considerably, the style of wine made here is consistent and unvarying – big, upfront, approach-able, enjoyable. White wines are made from Gewurztraminer, Muscat, Pinot Blanc, Riesling, Sylvaner and Tokay-Pinot Gris, and all are suitable for vegans.

Marc Kreydenweiss

12 rue Deharbe, 67140 Andlau

Tel:+33 388 08 95 83

Fax:+33 388 08 41 16

Cellar Door Sales: by appointment only

This domaine comprises just over 10 hectares of Demeter-certified biodynamic vineyards centred on Andlau. Marc Kreydenweiss succeeded his father in 1971 and is not given much to talking. He is, however, most animated during the harvest, when he ensures that each variety from each vineyard site is picked at full maturity. Older vines are tagged so the pickers keep their grapes separate from younger vines, and there may be as many as 40 separate pressings for each vintage. (Contact the producer for details, particularly of the late picked wines, i.e., Vendanges Tardives and Sélection de Grains Nobles – both styles 🍾🍾🍾.) The wines produced share a neatness of aroma and compactness of texture that makes them easy to miss first time around. You have to give them time to breathe in the glass to get the full effect. Wines made include:

- Kritt Pinot Blanc: dry white with a touch of sweetness; expressive. 🍾🍾🍾
- Kritt Klevner: dry white, made from Pinot Blanc picked over-ripe; this shows how rich this sometimes lean variety can become. 🍾🍾
- Andlau, Pinot Noir: dry red, shows moderate colour, cherry fruit; stylish. 🍾
- Clos du Val d'Eléon: dry white blend of Riesling and Pinot Gris, vines planted in 1987. 🍾
- Clos Rebgarten Muscat: dry white, with ripeness and delicacy; shows the value of pressing slowly. 🍾🍾🍾
- Riesling, Grand Cru Kastelberg: dry white, powerful example from mature vines, lots of extract – you can feel the fruit all the way round your mouth. 🍾🍾🍾🍾
- Pinot Gris, Grand Cru Moenchberg, Vendanges Tardives: sweet white, shows over-ripe tropical fruit which retains its freshness. 🍾🍾🍾🍾
- Pinot Gris, Grand Cru Moenchberg, Sélection de Grains Nobles: sweet white, with a steady succession of minerals and fruit. 🍾🍾🍾🍾

André Stentz

2 rue de la Batteuse, 68920 Wettolsheim

Tel:+33 389 80 64 91

Fax:+33 389 79 59 75

Sales: every day except Sundays, please call in advance

Stockists: Organic Wine Company; Vintage Roots

André Stentz is a fastidious organic grower. He applies his compost to the soil just before the rains fall so it will be assimilated more easily. The soil is lightly scratched beforehand to create channels for the water. Stentz's wine style is understated, but in the last few years has gained some punch. The late picked wines (Vendanges Tardives and Sélection de Grains Nobles) are well thought out:

- Gewurztraminer: dry white, turkish-delight texture, rosehip taste (1997 vintage, Organic Wine Company, 🍾).
- Gewurztraminer, Vendanges Tardives, Steingrubler Grand Cru: late picked selection of over-ripe bunches; firm, lush white wine from the Steingrubler Grand Cru. This vineyard is ideally exposed (south-east facing) and contains Gewurztraminer's preferred soil of compacted clay limestone (1992 vintage, Organic Wine Company, 🍾🍾🍾).
- Gewurztraminer Sélection de Grains Nobles, Steingrubler Grand Cru: later picked than the above and from an individual berry selection; sweeter than the above, slightly more intense, but no loss of balance. 🍾🍾🍾
- Muscat: clean and grapey, no bitterness, good signs for Alsace Muscat (1996 vintage, Organic Wine Company, 🍾).
- Pinot Noir: red wine. Alsace Pinot Noir tends to be lighter coloured than its red wine counterparts in Burgundy, and this one is typical (1997 vintage, Organic Wine Company, 🍾).
- Riesling: refined, unique full style for this variety (1996 vintage, Organic Wne Company, 🍾).
- Tokay d'Alsace: more sophisticated than Frick's (see above), possibly the pick of the Stentz varieties (1997 vintage, Organic Wine Company, 🍾).
- Tokay-Pinot Gris Vendanges Tardives, Steingrubler Grand Cru: sweet white; full, steamroller style (1992 vintage, Organic Wine Company, 🍾).

Armand Weber
14 rue de Colmar, 68420 Eguisheim
Tel:+33 389 41 35 56
Fax:+33 389 41 35 56
Sales: from the domaine every day
Market: St Louis, Saturday mornings

Armand Weber is a family-run domaine, owned by sisters Odile and
Danielle Weber. The vineyards were certified organic in 1996 and are
located on a relatively high part of the Vosges foothills where the soils are
very warm. As a result the flavours in the wines are buried beneath considerable levels of alcohol.

● Gewurztraminer: the most consistent of Weber's white wine varieties. ▮

ALSACE – USEFUL ADDRESSES
**Organisation Professionnelle de l'Agriculture Biologique en Alsace
(OPABA)**
Maison de l'Agriculture, 103, route de Hausbergen, 67309 Shiltigheim Cedex
Tel:+33 388 19 17 91
Fax:+33 388 81 27 29

A list of organic and biodynamic winegrowers in Alsace is contained in
Guide de la Bio en Alsace, (FF20), published by OPABA.

Organic Wine Fair
Foire Européenne du Pain, Vin et Fromage Eco-Biologique de Rouffach
Information: Tel:+33 389 49 62 54/+33 389 49 62 99
Syndicat d'Initiative (Rouffach): Tel:+33 389 78 53 15

The European Organic Bread, Wine and Cheese Fair takes place during
five days every Ascension weekend (May) in the Hotel de Ville Rouffach.
It is the biggest fair of its type in Europe.

Bordeaux

The port of Bordeaux in south west France gives its name to the world's biggest fine wine region. The vineyards here dominate the landscape. Often they surround turreted châteaux inhabited by wealthy, aristocratic owners. Thus for many wine drinkers, Bordeaux fits the classic image of where wine comes from. The vineyards tend to be large in size, and generally are sited on flat land, two factors which combine to make winegrowing relatively easy to manage. By far and away the most important style of Bordeaux wine is red claret – but dry and sweet wines are made here too. All the wines made here are blends of several varieties, but the exact blend for each wine will change according to the year or vintage (some varieties do better in some years than others). This is why Bordeaux buffs spend hours noting and discussing the blends from their favourite châteaux and comparing vintages. Bordeaux benefits from a temperate, Atlantic-influenced climate, and as a result the wines are characterized by their elegance. They match any food, except spicy dishes. As far as prices go, the region is so large that there is something for everyone.

To get a sniff of organic wine in Bordeaux you will have to forgo the air-conditioned tasting galleries favoured by the region's 100 or so top châteaux and scrabble over barrels in more homespun surroundings. None of the top châteaux even really bother to claim or pretend they are organic. Some will admit to having joined lower input spray programmes (*la lutte raisonée*), and the biggest have even produced for public show flocks of sheep which, they claim, manure all of their vines! However, the truth is that Bordeaux sells very well without having to play the 'green' trump card. According to CIVAM BIO, the Syndicat des Vignerons Agrobiologistes, at St Emilion in Bordeaux, the vineyards which are certified organic in that region in 1998 amounted to just 1,260 hectares out of 112,000 hectares planted.

The majority of the most famous Bordeaux vineyards were replanted relatively recently in the last decade, to replace unproductive, older plots. The château owners welcome young, vigorous vines and the very high yields they give because red Bordeaux is worth a lot of money at the moment. High yields and silly prices help repay the replanting costs. The owners know that if the wines taste too light this defect can be masked using certain techniques during the winemaking process. The first step is an extra hot alcoholic fermentation of the red wine while on the grape skins to deepen its colour. Then a secondary fermentation of the wine in new oak barrels adds a toast-like, vanilla smell. A bit of sugar to boost the alcohol by at least a degree and a half doesn't go amiss either, to make the fruit taste riper than it actually is (*flatteur* is how the French describe it). The result is an anonymous style of wine exhibiting what one leading American critic calls (approvingly!) 'gobs of fruit, black color, oaky smell'. Real Bordeaux aficionados despair. They know that Bordeaux should display refined fruit, integrated or unobtrusive oak aroma and moderate claret colour.

Another reason why the top Bordeaux wines are so light is that the vines are appallingly pruned, so much so that some of the top château owners have been asked to go back to wine school to learn how to do it correctly. Some of them appear to spend more time entertaining than inspecting the work of those paid to prune. The cheap way to prune is to pay part-timers on a 'the more you prune the more you are paid' basis. The cane pruning system which must be used for the top Bordeaux red wine châteaux is, however, slow. Those paid to prune have been pruning to the quicker spur system common in the Midi (where many of them are from) to earn more money, but this affects the yield and quality of the grapes. One château owner couldn't work out why the yield of part of his vineyard was so high. After four years he clambered into his four-wheel-drive jeep and drove off to the high yielding plots, and the penny dropped. The yields, however, did not; they are still just as high, as a visit to the mayor's office in St Estèphe (where the yields of this particular vineyard are declared) shows.

Despite the entertaining, most of the top château owners claim to have lived lives of technical bankruptcy for the majority of the 20th century, and want to cash in on high yields, big profits and critical acclaim from our American friend noted above before anybody notices. For the moment at least, it seems putting the name of the château on the label is worth far more in Bordeaux than any organic stamp. (This contrasts with

Burgundy, where vines in several of the top or 'grand cru' vineyards are certified organic – see Lalou Bize Leroy of the Domaine d'Auvenay for example.)

BORDEAUX STYLES AND TERMS

All Bordeaux wines are blends ('assemblages') of different grape varieties. Red Bordeaux, or claret, is blended from Merlot, Cabernet Sauvignon and Cabernet Franc, with smaller amounts of Malbec, Petit Verdot and Carmenère. Red wines now account for four out of every five bottles of Bordeaux, and are taking over from Bordeaux's white wines, which comprised 50 per cent of production until the early 1970s. White Bordeaux is blended from Sauvignon Blanc, Sémillon and Muscadelle, and can be made in dry, medium dry and fully sweet styles. A small amount of sparkling wine is made, generally to use up excess stocks of dry white wine, which sells rather more slowly than Bordeaux's reds. These sparkling wines generally contain base wines made from crisp, neutral and high yielding white varieties like Colombard and Ugni Blanc. They are labelled Crémant de Bordeaux.

Clairet – Pink Bordeaux or How Red Bordeaux Became Known as Claret

The English have been buying Bordeaux wines since 1152 when Aliénor of Aquitaine married Henry Plantagenet of England, the future Henry II. In Aquitaine they made a dark style of rosé called 'clairet' – the Middle Age precursor of what the English call 'claret' or red Bordeaux. Originally 'clairet' was made when both dark skinned and fair skinned grapes were fermented together. This left wine of pale 'clairet' colour – light red at the rim of the glass (the wine's meniscus). Contemporary claret is made only from dark-skinned grapes these days, by law.

Bordeaux is the biggest fine wine region in the world and it is divided into two halves – the left bank and the right bank.

LEFT BANK

The left bank is the side of Bordeaux closest to the Atlantic. It consists of three regions – from north to south: Médoc, Graves and Sauternes. Each of these regions is further sub-divided into more precise appellations. Only those containing certified organic vineyards have been highlighted (thus the four most famous left bank red wine villages – St Estèphe, Pauillac, St Julien and Margaux – do not feature here).

THE MÉDOC REGION

The vineyards directly north of the city of Bordeaux run parallel with the Gironde estuary and are collectively known as the Médoc. They form a peninsula, divided into two halves. The lower half is entitled to the Haut Médoc appellation and the half furthest from Bordeaux is entitled to the Médoc AC.

Haut Médoc AC

The Haut Médoc covers 4,500 hectares. Its Cabernet Sauvignon-dominated red wines are regarded as some of the most aristocratic in the world.

Château Haut Gouat

33180 Vertheuil
Tel:+33 556 41 97 98
Fax:+33 556 41 98 53
Accommodation: bed and breakfast
Visitors: direct sales by appointment
Stockists: Vintage Roots; Organic Wine Company; Vinceremos

Château Haut Gouat was converted to organic methods from 1995 and was certified in 1997. Owner Mme Nicole Lépine makes two wines from 7.5 hectares of Cabernet Sauvignon, Cabernet Franc and Merlot grapes.

- Château Haut Gouat, Bordeaux Clairet AC: dry pink wine, dark salmon pink in colour, cleans the palate but needs drinking very chilled and quickly. 👭
- Château Haut Gouat, Haut-Médoc AC: dry red, crimson in colour, smells slightly oaky, tight fruit, medium weight, attractive claret to drink 3–6 years. 👭

Listrac AC

Listrac covers 700 hectares of flat ground in the centre of the highest part of the Médoc peninsula. The commune has its own AC and one 'unofficial' organic producer worth noting.

Domaine du Haut Brugas

33480 Médrac-Listrac
Tel:+33 556 58 03 13

Domaine du Haut Brugas is an organic minded estate which finds itself technically lying beyond the margins of the organic certification bodies currently in existence. Its owner, Jean Pierre Bispalie, describes the single red wine he makes as 'un vin nature', a natural wine. Putting such terms on labels without the blessing of an official certifying body invites prosecution, as Bispalie has discovered. He was challenged by the French Fraud Squad. So far his defence has been successful and the term 'un vin nature' remains on the Domaine du Haut Brugas wine label.

Bispalie uses no synthetic weed-killers or pesticides on his three-hectare vineyard and he enriches the soil with animal manure rather than chemical fertiliser. This would be enough to qualify Domaine du Haut Brugas as organic under EU rules, but Bispalie sees no reason why he should pay a certification or joining-up fee for doing what he does and telling people about it. In addition (and unlike a majority of organic growers) he picks the grapes by hand and then ferments them with natural yeast and in wooden, rather than stainless steel, vats. He also refrains from adding any sugar or yeast to the wine during fermentation to boost the wine's alcohol ('chaptalization') to make it taste fuller. The preservative sulphur dioxide is added to the wine at the same levels certified organic growers use, except Bispalie adds milk with it 'as my grandfather did' to make it more effective. The milk is from a dairy which, like Domaine du Haut Brugas, could be described as producing 'lait nature' rather than 'certified organic'. However its presence does mean that this wine is not suitable for vegans.

- Domaine du Haut Brugas, Listrac AC: dry red, bright healthy cherry colour, shows the directness and concentration of low yielding, old vines. ♙♙

In 1996 Bispalie produced a good wine in a year when it was hard to make a bad red wine in the Médoc region, and in 1997 he produced an exceptional wine when it was difficult to make a good one.

Médoc AC

The Médoc AC is the same size as the Haut Médoc, except that it lies further from Bordeaux. The soils are heavier and there are few really famous 1855 châteaux to spot, although there are still plenty of turrets. There is one vineyard here of interest which practises natural farming methods and natural winemaking, but which is not certified organic.

Château Tour Haut Caussan

33340 Blaignan
Tel:+33 556 09 06 26
Fax:+33 556 09 06 24
Stockist: Bibendum

This château's current owner, Philippe Courrian, is the youngest of four brothers and represents the fourth generation of his family to farm here. He practises organic but non-certified viticulture based partly on *la méthode cousinié*. This method is named after Jean-Christophe Cousinié, a soil specialist from southern France. He adopts a 'treat the cause rather than the symptom' attitude when it comes to addressing problems in the vineyard. It is common practice for example for conventional winegrowers to treat a case of magnesium deficiency in the vine by adding magnesium-rich chemical fertiliser to the soil. Cousinié has discovered that often they do not need to do this. The soil had enough magnesium – it just wasn't getting to the vine. This may be because it was being blocked by a third chemical element in the soil. That is the one that Cousinié addresses directly. The method is considered non-organic under EU rules because Cousinié sprays the vine leaves with nutrients (foliar feeds). The vine must get these from the soil alone under organic rules.

- Château La Tour Haut Caussan, Médoc AC: very pure, scented claret combining ripe but fresh Merlot with persistent Cabernet, sourced from a vineyard which surrounds the only remaining 18th-century windmill in the Médoc (the area was colonized by the Dutch who drained it and planted corn). Fermented with natural yeast, unchaptalized, unfined, unfiltered. Reminiscent of the style of wine made by H Coturri & Sons in Sonoma, California (which is also organic but not certified). ♙

THE GRAVES REGION

The Graves is the mirror of the Médoc, located to the south of Bordeaux rather than to the north. The reputation of the Graves has waned since its 12th-century heyday because its wines are seen as slightly old fashioned and understated. Yet some of the organic wines produced here show irresistible fruit in comparison to the more laboured efforts of their non-organic peers. Cabernet Sauvignon-dominated red wines feature strongly in the northern part of the Graves, now known as Pessac-Léognan AC. White wines made from Sémillon and Sauvignon Blanc are more common in the southern part, which is called Graves AC.

Pessac-Léognan AC

The northern part of the Graves, nearest the city of Bordeaux, has been called Pessac-Léognan since 1987. It is where a Celtic tribe called the Biturges planted Bordeaux's first vineyards, possibly bringing the Cabernet Sauvignon grape to Bordeaux in the process. Most of these vineyard sites are now under housing, playing fields and schools. The remaining vineyards encroach into the southern suburbs of the city of Bordeaux itself, and surround Pessac-Léognan's one organic producer.

Château Haut Nouchet

33650 Martillac
Tel:+33 556 72 69 74
Sales: from the château by appointment
Stockist: Vintage Roots

Louis Lurton, Château Haut Nouchet's owner, was one of twelve children, each of whom were given a château by their father. Only Haut Nouchet espouses certified organic practices, however. Since converting to organic methods in 1994 Louis Lurton has changed the way he makes his red wines. 'The skins are thicker on my grapes since becoming organic, so I can leave the fermenting wine in contact with the skins for longer to extract more flavour and colour.' Louis Lurton's wines are growing in stature with each vintage as the winemaking improves and the vines age. The wines are picked by hand and pressed slowly to extract the best quality of juice. The two principal wines are:

- Château Haut-Nouchet, Pessac-Léognan Blanc Sec AC: dry white, light to medium-bodied. Made predominantly from the aromatic Sauvignon Blanc variety, with around one third of the buttery Sémillon. Shows clean, creamy, stone fruit flavours; barrel fermentation adds to rather than detracts from the texture. Suitable for vegans, it requires at least two to four years in the bottle before drinking to be near its optimum (1996 vintage, 🍷). The second label of this wine is Domaine du Milan. 🍷

- Château Haut-Nouchet, Pessac-Léognan Rouge AC: red brick colour, refreshing taste of thick blackcurrants, suitable for vegans. Made from a blend of Cabernet Sauvignon (70 per cent) and Merlot (30 per cent). (1996 vintage, 🍷; this and the previous 1995 vintage much improved on the anaemic 1994.) The second label is Domaine du Milan. 🍷

Graves AC

The southern part of the Graves region has the most inviting air of all those regions on this side of Bordeaux. Unlike the barren and wind-swept Médoc to the north, which is exposed to the Atlantic Ocean, this more southerly part of the left bank is protected from it by the forests of the Landes. These run south down to the Gers and Armagnac, and play an important part in shaping the entire Bordeaux weather pattern. The forests are state owned but run by private contractors, who also come here looking for gravel to be used by the construction industry. There are several fine organic vineyards planted on the famous gravel soils (*les graves*) here.

Le Druc de Perran
33720 Landiras
Tel:+33 556 62 40 37
Fax:+33 556 62 40 37
Overall Price Rating: 🍷

This certified organic Graves domaine belongs to Gérard Labuzan. He is the son of the co-owner of Domaine de Moulin à Vent and brother of the owner of Château Monbazan, both of which are also certified organic Graves estates (*see below*). There are 20 hectares of vines producing dry white Graves Blanc Sec AC, dry red Graves AC and medium sweet white Graves Blanc Supérieurs AC.

Château St Hilaire

Castres, 33640 Portets
Tel:+33 556 67 12 12
Fax:+33 556 67 53 23
Cellar Door Sales: daily (0800–2000)
Markets: Bordeaux St Pierre (Thursday)
Stockist: Organic Wine Company
Overall Price Rating: ♙

The commune of Portets is often overlooked because it is where the Pessac Léognan AC ends and the supposedly inferior Graves AC begins. Sand is mixed in with the gravel in the soil here, which brings a lighter tone to the fruit. Château St Hilaire's owner, Gabriel Guerin, compensates for this during winemaking – seeking to extract as much colour from the fruit as possible in his red wine. This sort of technique works only if the grapes are fully ripened, so pick your vintage.

- Château St Hilaire, Graves Blanc Sec AC: dry white, suitable for vegans (although crisp enough to suit the local Arcachon oysters well too). Second label is Clos de la Perichère.
- Château St Hilaire, Graves Rouge AC: red, inky right to the rim of the glass, leafy, herbaceous fruit due to a high Merlot content, suitable for vegans (although thick and brutal enough to suit the local wild venison). Second label is Clos de la Perichère.

Château Méric

Chante l'Oiseau, 33650 La Brède
Tel:+33 556 78 45 05
Fax:+33 556 20 22 20

Sales: from the château, weekdays (0900–1200 and 1500–1900), Saturday mornings. Own grown organic table grapes and apples are available to callers in the farm shop.

Overall Price Rating: ◢ (for both labels)

La Brède's one organic enterprise consists of two vineyards: Chante l'Oiseau and Château Méric. They belong to François and Sylvie Barron who produce moderate dry Graves Blanc Sec AC and dry red Graves Rouge AC. The commune of La Brède provides a cautionary tale for potential vineyard agri-tourists. It is named after its majestic château, Château La Brède. This contains the library of the writer Charles de Segondat, Marquis de la Brède et de Montesquieu (1689–1755), who was born here. Château La Brède hit the French headlines in 1996 when it failed to open its doors to the public as it was supposed to on French culture day as an historical monument. The then tenant, an elderly lady whose republican spirit deserted her momentarily, raised the drawbridge, leaving coach-loads of would-be visitors perplexed on the wrong side of the moat.

Château Monbazan

Place de l'Eglise, 33720 Landiras
Tel:+33 556 62 42 82
Fax:+33 556 62 41 22
Sales: direct by appointment; grape juice also available
Accommodation: three to four persons in a gîte

Château Monbazan is a family domaine created in the late 1990s by Pierre and Béatrice Labuzan. The wines are made at Château du Moulin à Vent (*see below*) which is owned by Pierre's mother Paulette. The Monbazan vineyard is certified organic and covers 20 hectares, with two hectares in rotation always kept fallow. This allows an extra year between replanting, which is important to allow the new vines to go into a soil given the time to purge itself of virus-transmitting worms like nematodes.

- Château Monbazan, Graves Blanc Sec AC: dry white, clean, satisfying, made from 70 per cent Sémillon, 15 per cent Sauvignon Blanc and 15 per cent Muscadelle. This is an example of a modern dry white Bordeaux made with cool temperature fermentation (to preserve the gooseberry aroma of the Sauvignon Blanc grape) and skin contact (to preserve body and maximize flavour from the Sémillon grape). ♦♦♦ Second label is Tertre Chanteau. ♦♦

- Tertre Chanteau, Graves Blanc Supérieures AC: medium white with matching body, crisp sweetness and creamy texture. Wines made with the Graves Blanc Supérieures AC of this quality are rarely seen. Most contain only the paltry amount of minimum sweetness stipulated by the appellation regulations and are made specifically for supermarkets in the Low Countries where price rather than quality comes first. This wine ages partially in big oak tuns, which help it age once in the bottle (1997 vintage, ex-château, ♦♦).

- Château Monbazan, Graves Rouge AC: red, medium weight, elegant, made from vineyards planted with 50 per cent Merlot, 45 per cent Cabernet, 5 per cent Malbec. The fermentation for these grapes is slow (10 days of active fermentation of the grapes and skins and two to three weeks of soaking the wine on the skins). To do this you must have really healthy fruit but you get a richer wine. This is a clear, tasty, insistent example of better than everyday Graves from a producer worth following. ♦♦♦. Second label is Tertre Chanteau. ♦♦

Domaine du Moulin à Vent
33720 Landiras
Tel:+33 556 62 50 66
Fax:+33 556 62 41 22
Sales: direct by appointment
Accommodation: available
Overall Price Rating: ♦♦

Mme Paulette Labuzan and her son Pierre (of Château Monbazan, *see above*) are the latest in a family line dating back to the 17th century to have farmed Domaine du Moulin à Vent. The Labuzans have never used synthetic products on the vines here, and their vineyards are the perfect place to study insects. Natural populations of tiny hoppers called typhlodromes are abundant here, and they are natural predator insects of the red spider mite. Bordeaux's Institut Technique de la Vigne (ITV) is using Domaine du Moulin à Vent's typhlodromes to try to repopulate other vineyards where numbers have been lowered by poor practices. The wines are:

- Domaine de Moulin à Vent, Graves Blanc Sec AC: dry white, made from four hectares of Sémillon (70 per cent), Sauvignon Blanc (20 per cent) and Muscadelle (10 per cent). They are pressed and the juice fermented naturally (without added yeast) to produce a healthy smell of warm pulpy apple juice. Consume within two years to catch the fruit; somewhat inconsistent but always worth trying.

- Domaine de Moulin à Vent, Graves Rouge AC: dry red made from 26 hectares of Merlot (60 per cent) and the two Cabernets (40 per cent). Shows a very natural style of red, late autumn fruit – the result of old vines, healthy grapes and a natural fermentation. Shows the untamed grace of the southern Graves. The 1990 vintage showed a broad range of fruit and cedar flavours and remarkable freshness in such a hot year. The 1998 showed a solid frame, but needs to 2002 to soften. The 1997 was a success when other red Graves were anaemic. 1996 was one to miss.

THE SAUTERNES REGION

The left bank's most southerly vineyards produce the late-picked ('noble rot') sweet white wines of Sauternes AC. One of the five communes allowed this appellation is Preignac, home to one organic producer and a fine sandy soil. This is said to produce the most floral style of Sauternes. It lends itself well to tilling by horse, a practice discontinued in Preignac in 1993 when the commune's most senior grower, Claude Larrue, gave up his vines on account of ill health. His white horse was sent to another Bordeaux vineyard (Château la Madeleine, a Premier Grand Cru Classé or 'first growth' St Emilion). Aerating the soil by ploughing with a horse is said to be especially good for young vines, which have their roots impeded when heavy tractors are used for the work.

Château la Garenne

La Garenne, 33210 Preignac
Tel:+33 556 63 27 22
Sales: direct from the château by appointment
Stockists: Organic Wine Company; Vintage Roots; Vinceremos

Château la Garenne is owned by Christian and Nicole Ferbos and has been certified organic since 1996. The vineyard covers six hectares and is planted with the traditional three Sauternes grape varieties, in the usual proportions: Sémillon (70 per cent), Sauvignon Blanc (20 per cent) and Muscadelle (10 per cent). One wine is made:

● Château la Garenne, Sauternes AC: sweet white made from grapes affected by 'noble rot'. The aroma of this wine shows how well the sweet vegetable flavour the 'noble rot' brings can merge with the 'noble' sweetness created by the shrivelling of the grapes (1996 vintage, ᛗ).

Note: Sauternes, like all French vineyard regions, is a name protected by appellation law. Only those wines made in the five Sauternes communes can use the name. The locals get very agitated when producers like Robinvale in Australia (*see page 372*) describe their sweet white wines as 'Sauternes'. However, the growers here are throwing stones from glasshouses when they object to anyone else pinching their brand name. What you taste in the château of a Sauternes and what you get in the bottle can be markedly different, as the Sauternes growers allow themselves the luxury of tankering their wines around in bulk. They say the journey is usually only a short one (true, a 25-minute long walk) to the town of Langon, and that the cellar facilities here of the merchants are convenient for fining and bottling. What they forget to mention is that the merchant warehouses are also home to sweet white wines trucked in from other châteaux and merchants from nearly everywhere else in Bordeaux. The way the merchants here are connected means that might as well be the world. So why shouldn't the Australians call their sweeties Sauternes?

THE RIGHT BANK

The eastern half of Bordeaux is called the right bank because it lies to the right of the Garonne. Soils here are less gravelley and more fertile than on the left bank. This suits the early ripening varieties like Merlot and Cabernet Franc for red wines, as well as all the white grape varieties used in Bordeaux for dry whites. The wine regions of Blaye, Bourg, Fronsac, Lalande de Pomerol, St Emilion, Côtes de Castillon and Côtes de Francs all lie north of the Dordogne river, which divides the right bank in two.

Côtes de Blaye AC

Blaye is a broad, rather flat and invariably sandy area between the Bordeaux region's northern border with the Charentes (*see Cognac*) and Côtes de Bourg (*see below*) to the south. The region produces dry white and red wines labelled as Premières Côtes de Blaye.

Domaine des Allants

Le Bourg, 33920 Saint Vivien de Blaye
Tel:+33 557 42 58 75
Fax:+33 557 42 56 39
Cellar Door Sales: by appointment
Overall Price Rating: ▮

Domaine des Allants is a certified organic domaine owned by Nelly and Hervé Meynard, who produce an unpretentious range of dry white, dry pink and red wines from one of Bordeaux's lesser known communes.

Domaine du Grand-Loup

Domaine de Jullouc, Les Augirons
33820 St Ciers dur Gironde
Tel: +33 557 32 72 89
Fax: +33 557 32 69 54
Sales: cellar door, in the market at Lacanau-Océan on the Atlantic Coast
(Wednesdays mid-June to mid-September)
Stockist: Vintage Roots
Overall Price Rating: ▮

In Blaye, the growers to try to ensure huge quantities of grapes are ready to be picked come harvest. They use cordon rather than cane pruning to increase the number of fruitful buds per vine and thus its potential yield. Domaine du Grand-Loup's owner, Didier Eymard, is no exception. The fact that his vines yield so generously allows him to offer what are arguably Bordeaux's finest value organic wines. What separates Eymard from his conventional peers is he fertilises the soil with green manure by mulching in cover crops. These keep the vines much healthier and produce better quality juice than if chemical fertilisers were used.

- Domaine du Grand-Loup, Blaye Blanc AC: dry white, blend of Ugni Blanc and Colombard showing delicate green fruit, suitable for vegetarians and vegans.
- Domaine du Grand-Loup, Premières Cotes de Blaye Rouge AC: dry red, made with a dominance of Cabernet Sauvignon but tastes more like Merlot, no nasty surprises; consume within a year or two, suitable for vegetarians and vegans.

Château Grand Renard

1 Côtes des Renauds, 33820 St Ciers sur Gironde
Tel: +33 557 32 96 75
Fax: +33 557 32 74 54
Cellar Door Sales: by appointment
Markets: Tremblade in Charentes-Maritimes (Wednesdays to Sundays during July and August)
Overall Price Rating: ▮

This domaine comprises 18.5 hectares and has been certified organic since 1987. Owner François Joubert produces dry white sparkling Crémant de Bordeaux AC, dry white Bordeaux Blanc AC and Premières Côtes de Blaye Blanc AC, dry pink Bordeaux Rosé AC, dry red Bordeaux Rouge AC and Premières Côtes de Blaye Rouge AC.

Château la Grave à Blaye

33620 Saint Mariens
Tel:+33 557 68 13 20
Fax:+33 557 68 18 07
Cellar Door Sales: by appointment
Markets: Montalivet et Oloron in the Gironde during July and August
Overall Price Rating: ▮

This small domaine is run by Patrick Pouvreau and is located on a good patch of ground in an unfashionable commune. Wines available for fair prices and fairly immediate drinking. This domaine is not to be confused with the biodynamic domaine belonging to the Barre family in Fronsac.

- Premières Côtes de Blaye Blanc, AC: dry white, heavy, simple fruit.
- Premières Côtes de Blaye Rouge, AC: dry red, shows open plum-skin fruit over a hard, dry core.

Château la Mirandole

Les Allains, 33820 Braud et St Louis
Tel:+33 557 32 61 47/+33 557 32 77 33
Fax:+33 557 32 61 47
Cellar Door Sales: every day (0800–1900), plus tasting
Overall Price Rating: ♦

This certified organic domaine belongs to the Berjon family. There are 8.66 hectares of vines producing dry white sparkling Crémant de Bordeaux AC and still dry white and red wines under the Bordeaux and Premières Côtes de Bordeaux appellations.

Côtes de Bourg AC

The Côtes de Bourg is a broad chain of hills (*côtes*) which begins south of Blaye and which locally is called 'little Switzerland'.

Château Falfas

33710 Bayon
Tel:+33 557 64 80 41
Fax:+33 557 64 93 24
Sales: direct from the château by appointment
Stockists: contact Vintage Roots for details

Château Falfas has been certified biodynamic by Demeter since 1989 when it was purchased by an American lawyer based in Paris, John Cochran III, and his French wife Véronique. The Cochrans purchase their biodynamic preparations and composts from Véronique's father, Monsieur François Boucher, who makes them. He is considered one of the leading advisers on biodynamic viticulture in France. He has been involved in a number of prestigious conversion projects, and was also one of the founders of Nature et Progrès, France's first organic grower association.

Château Falfas covers 22 hectares of vines overlooking the east bank of the Gironde estuary from south-west facing slopes. There are three distinct plots planted overall with Merlot (55 per cent), Cabernet Sauvignon (25 per cent), Malbec (15 per cent) and Cabernet Franc (5 per cent). Two red wines are produced and both are suitable for vegetarians and vegans:

- Château Falfas, Côtes de Bourg AC: dry red, has been hand picked since 1994 and since 1995 has begun to benefit from the full seven years of conversion to biodymanics. The wine spends some time in large oak tuns (of 400 litres) to encourage the fruit and tannins to soften. These oak tuns require considerable maintaining to stop the wooden staves from rotting, but they do allow a bottled wine to age with lower levels of sulphur preservative (they allow the wine to become accustomed to the effects of oxygen). This wine shows incisive blackberry fruit and well-constructed wine tannins. The presence of glycerol from a slow, natural fermentation (detectable in the 'mouth-feel'), adds to the impression of richness. ♣♣
- Château Falfas, 'Le Chevalier', Côtes de Bourg AC: dry red, hand picked from the oldest vines, fermented and macerated in cement tanks, basket pressed, aged in new French oak barrels (225 litres). The debut vintage was 1995. Shows very clear fruit, natural freshness, strong enough to perfume the room if allowed the time. Shows positive potential for development over 6–12 years at least. ♣♣♣

See also Domaine du Château Gaillard in Anjou-Saumur in the Loire for the activities of Véronique Cochran's brother, Mathieu Boucher.

Château Pillot
33710 Bourg sur Gironde
Tel:+33 557 68 24 29
Sales: from the château by appointment

Jean-Marc Grenier's domaine directly overlooks the point where the Dordogne meets the Garonne to become the Gironde estuary. (The name of the commune is a misnomer because the Gironde begins only at St Seurin de Bourg, the commune directly to the north-west.) The best vineyards in this commune lie on a limestone crust (*croûte*) which endows piercing aromas to the grapes, the Merlot variety in particular. One red wine is made:

- Château Pillot, Côtes de Bourg Rouge AC: dry red, light, crisp, refreshing; drink within 3–5 years, but allow half an afternoon to breathe. ▲

Organic Wines from the Edge of the Côtes de Bourg

St German la Rivière lies at the eastern edge of the Côtes de Bourg and is also the most westerly of those seven communes entitled to the AC for Fronsac. There are two certified organic growers here with vines that lie in part of the commune entitled only to the generic Bordeaux appellation for red wines.

Bernard Dumas de la Roque

Le Grand Bordieu, 33240 St Germain la Rivière
Tel:+33 557 84 40 27
Fax:+33 557 84 49 75
Visits: by appointment
Overall Price Rating: ♙

Bernard Dumas de la Roque makes red and dry white Bordeaux from vineyards within a stone's throw of the Dordogne. This area is neglected because the soil is muddy and alluvial (*le palus*) because it lies so close to the river. However it was covered in vines during the late 19th-century phylloxera crisis when desperate growers from more prestigious sites arrived. Phylloxera could never take hold in vineyards right next to the river because the soil is too wet, and can flood in winter. Vines can even survive here without the need for grafting onto phylloxera tolerant American rootstocks. Some organic growers argue that ungrafted vines are less reliant on chemical sprays because they are growing on their own roots. Although planting ungrafted vines is forbidden in Bordeaux (for fear of encouraging the louse – even though it is present already to a greater or lesser extent in every Bordeaux vineyard), wines made from such vineyards do exist. Examples of these wines come from along the left bank of the Garonne in the Graves region, rather than on the banks of the Dordogne in St Germain la Rivière. They are a revelation for the smoothness and depth of their fruit. Bernard Dumas de la Roque produces kiwi fruit as well as wine, and protects the crops from frost with windbreaks.

Château Fayol

Les Chevaliers de Bellevue, Le Bourg
33240 Saint Germain La Rivière
Tel:+33 557 84 81 47
Overall Price Rating: ▮

This domaine has been certified organic since 1989 and produces an honest range of dry red wines under the Bordeaux Rouge AC, Bordeaux Supérieur and Premières Côtes de Bourg ACs.

Fronsac AC

Fronsac today is considered very much the poor relation of the wine regions in the Libournais, the district which also comprises Pomerol and St Emilion, even though it possesses some of the finest limestone slopes for vineyards anywhere in south-west France. These slopes have been cultivated as vineyards since 769, when Charlemagne, King of the Franks, built a castle here. Within the last 20 years however, the topsoil on some of the slopes has begun to erode so seriously that the slopes may never be able to support vines again. Greedy Libourne merchants, who do all their work in the vineyards they rent or own with heavy tractors, rather than with hands borne by lighter human feet, are to blame. Fronsac has one grower certified by Demeter as biodynamic. He and his family own two vineyards overlooking the Dordogne east of Côtes de Bourg.

Château la Fleur Cailleau and Château la Grave

33126 Fronsac
Tel:+33 557 51 31 11
Fax:+33 557 25 08 61
Sales: direct from the château by appointment
Stockist: Vintage Roots

Château la Fleur Cailleau and Château la Grave belong to a small family led by Paul Barre. His mother, Madame Maryse Barre, was responsible for converting Château Pavie-Macquin in St Emilion to biodynamic methods in the 1980s (*see page 34*). Paul Barre gained his own wine experience by working in the vineyards of châteaux in the Libournais district. He purchased his in the 1980s. Both vineyards lie within walking distance of each other and both are planted at a high density (6,000 vines/hectare). High vine densities augur well for deep colours and flavours in the wine, especially on Fronsac's soft limestone soils (called *molasse*). The roots are forced down, making for strong, healthy vines. This is a producer to watch because both Barre and his vineyards are coming into their prime. Three red wines are made:

- Château Esterling, Bordeaux Rouge AC: dry red, always agreeable in taste if marked by inconsistencies of vintage; made from the left overs from the two bottlings below, suitable for vegetarians and vegans. ♦
- Château la Grave, Fronsac AC: dry red, comes from a three-hectare vineyard on the south-east facing slopes below Fronsac's L'Eglise St Martin planted with Merlot (45 per cent), Cabernet Sauvignon (40 per cent) and Cabernet Franc (5 per cent). It displays a range of clear, damson-style fruits, all with firm skins but tender hearts, suitable for vegans (1996 vintage, ♦♦).
- Château la Fleur Cailleau, Canon Fronsac AC: dry red, comes from a 4.39 hectare vineyard in a south facing bowl below the site of Charlemagne's castle. The sun-trap there is one of the best sites in the AC, and is planted with Merlot (about 90 per cent), Cabernet Franc (roughly 10 per cent) with a little Cabernet Sauvignon. The 1990 vintage showed intricately woven black and red fruit, intense, very forceful in tone yet refined. 1993 was disappointing in a difficult year, 1994 was tight in the year that almost brought wines of dramatic intensity (but were spoiled by rain), while 1995 and 1996 show potential for evolution over 8–12 years. ♦♦♦

Lalande de Pomerol AC

Lalande de Pomerol is divided from Fronsac by the river Isle which flows into the Dordogne at Libourne. It produces dry red wines similar to but generally lighter than its more famous neighbour, Pomerol, immediately to the south. There is one certified organic producer (although one lady in the prestigious western part of Pomerol claims to be organic, but the name of her château is not on any current official list of organic Bordeaux producers).

Château la Rose Haut Musset
33500 Lalande de Pomerol
Tel:+33 556 41 97 98
Sales: direct from the château by appointment

When Jean-Baptiste Abbadie inherited Château la Rose Haut Musset in 1982 it consisted of a small plot of 1,000 vines, about a sixth of a hectare. Another two hectares of vines were purchased, and the whole converted to organic cultivation. In 1996 the total was reduced back to under one hectare when the current owner divorced.

- Château la Rose Haut Musset, Lalande de Pomerol AC: dry red; little evidence of flavour, unclear direction, lack of harmony; fined with egg white so suitable for vegetarians rather than vegans. 🍾🍾

St Emilion AC

St Emilion is Bordeaux's prettiest wine town and knows it. Its thousand-year-old stone streets cover some of France's best preserved chalk cellars, home to succulent red wines. The dominant two varieties are always Merlot and Cabernet Franc rather than the later ripening Cabernet Sauvignon. There are a number of vineyards certified as organic or biodynamic but they account for less than 1 per cent of St Emilion's total of 5,000 hectares. Soil types vary widely and this affects in which proportion the grapes are planted. It also means that St Emilion is the hardest Bordeaux region to pin down in terms of style. It may be Bordeaux's prettiest wine town, but tread carefully if you want wines from it which are pretty.

Château Barrail des Graves

Château Renaissance, Port de Branne, 33330 St Sulpice de Faleyrens
Tel:+33 557 74 94 77
Fax:+33 557 74 97 49
Sales: direct from the château 0800–1900
Accommodation: available
Stockist: Vinceremos
Overall Price Rating: ♟♟

Château Barrail des Graves lies on St Emilion's broad fertile plain where vines finally give way to maize fields. The vineyard is in the lee of an iron river bridge designed by Georges Eiffel. This bridge takes you across the Dordogne river to the town of Branne in rural Entre Deux Mers (*see also the wines of Château Large Malartic, page 42*). Château Barrail des Graves has been farmed organically since the 1950s by the Descrambe family. Current incumbent, Gérard Descrambe, uses irreverent cartoon-style labels for some of his red wines. These appeal to Parisian café society unconcerned with political correctness. Unfortunately, for me the packaging is more of a talking point than the product. I find Descrambe's reds suffer uncomfortably from over-strenuous winemaking. This involves trying to extract more colour, tannin and flavour from the grapes than is present in them at picking.

Château Chouteau

3570 Petit Palais (Lussac)
Tel:+33 557 74 65 85
Fax:+33 557 74 58 76
Cellar Door Sales: by appointment
Stockist: Organic Wine Company
Overall Price Rating: ♟

Château Chouteau lies north of St Emilion outside the small satellite town of Lussac. The landscape here is less open and the vineyards tumble around woodland. This is as close as Bordeaux gets to be Burgundian. The soils are heavier in clay here too than they are nearer St Emilion town, and this endows more colour and sharpness of flavour to the grapes. Château Chouteau is planted with a predominance of Merlot, because this

Friends of the Earth **Organic Wine Guide**

variety buds and ripens best on clay. Château Chouteau produces two red wines and a white:

- Château Chouteau, Bordeaux Blanc Sec AC: dry white, made in vineyards around north-east St Emilion where Merlot Blanc or 'white Merlot', a very minor variety, survives from the 19th century. Its soft, squashy grapes taste of little, a twist of bitter limes perhaps. May stage a comeback due to its famous namesake, Merlot.
- Clos le Mas, Bordeaux Superieur AC: the junior relation to the wine below, simple, thick, amenable, with leafy character typical of right bank claret.
- Château Chouteau, Lussac St Emilion AC: crisp claret that benefits from decanting to allow the fruit to open and prevent it from tasting pinched.

Château Franc-Pourret
SCEA Vignobles Ouzoulias, 17 rue de General Picot, BP93, 33500 Libourne
Tel:+33 557 51 07 55
Sales: from the château by appointment
Stockist: Organic Wine Company

Château Franc-Pourret has belonged to the Ouzoulias family since 1956 and forms one of a number of vineyards owned by them in the St Emilion region. They also own other, non-organic vineyards in Fronsac and the Médoc. Franc-Pourret's is located where St Emilion's western slopes begin. Trenches dug by the Romans into the limestone soil survive in one corner of the vineyard. Into these trenches fruit trees and vines were put, but now they are given to scrub. The wines here have jumped several notches since 1994 and show thicker, riper fruit. This is partly due to better management in the vineyards (not even organic growers always get it right!), with particular emphasis on more balanced pruning. This has steadied yields. Once the grapes arrive in the winery better selection is evident – meaning the best grapes are not mixed up with less good ones. This allows the winemaker to keep his options open.

- Domaine de Haut Patarabet, St Emilion Grand Cru AC: the earliest maturing wine in this range. Showed well in 1990 when Bordeaux (like the rest of France) had a remarkably ripe year. ♦♦
- Château Franc-Pourret, St Emilion Grand Cru AC: medium weight, can show some of the Christmas cake fruit associated with St Emilion in a hot vintage, but not a keeper either. ♦♦
- Clos Chante l'Alouette, St Emilion Grand Cru AC: benefits from ageing in oak allowing the fruit to breathe and rendering this the most expensive, but most dynamic, wine in the range. ♦♦♦

Château Jacques Blanc
33330 St Etienne de Lisse
Tel:+33 557 40 18 01
Fax:+33 557 40 01 98
Sales: from the château direct by appointment on weekdays (0830–1200 and 1330–1730)
Stockist: Vintage Roots

Château Jacques Blanc has been certified biodynamic since 1989, but was certified organic for seven years before that too. The vines face south across the Bordeaux–Bergerac railway line to the Dordogne beyond. The vines are in a single block so the application and management of biodynamic preparations is made easier. Château Jacques Blanc's owners, the Chouet family, occasionally supplement hand picking of the vines with a machine. Three red wines are made:

- Domaine de Jacques Blanc, St Emilion AC: dry red, shows basic, crisp fruit, medium weight, harmonious finish, suitable for vegetarians (1996 vintage, ♦).
- Château Jacques Blanc, Cuvee Aliénor, St Emilion AC: dry red, deep colour, medium weight, shows the influence of a winemaking technique called hyper-oxidation (*le microbullage*). This is designed to make wines to please the 'international' market. A fine stream of oxygen is bubbled through the red wine as it rests in the tank to make it taste more appealing and plump (the oxygen makes the small jagged bits of the wine, the tannins, stick to each other to make bigger, smoother bits). It works, but only for part of the wine because it has no effect on

the wine acid. This tastes more tart once the tannins have been made softer, and becomes out of place. The vines at Château Jacques Blanc could, I believe, produce much more dramatic and more diversely flavoured St Emilion than this. ♙

- Château Jacques Blanc, Cuvée du Maître, St Emilion AC: thicker texture than the other wines above – the result of oak ageing, new French barrels; a crowd pleaser which does its job. ♙/♙♙

Château Meylet

La Gomerie, 33330 St Emilion
Tel:+33 557 24 68 85
Visits: by appointment
Accommodation: bed and breakfast accommodation available

Château Meylet lies on St Emilion's sandy western slopes below the vineyard of Château Franc-Pourret (above) and thus closer to Libourne. The vineyard amounts to just 1.6 hectares and is worked entirely by hand. Its owners, Michel and Marie-France Favard, became interested in biodynamic methods gradually through Michel's maternal grandfather. Since 1987 the vines have been Demeter certified. At picking each bunch is sorted by hand twice, first in the vineyard, and again in the winery. This 'pick bunches like they were apples' approach is unusual in Bordeaux where the majority of grapes are trucked about like cattle. The care which Monsieur Favard and his team of family and friends take at picking means only the finest quality bunches enter the cement fermenting vats. Those pecked by the birds are put to compost. A policy of 'healthy fruit only' stems protects the bloom (and yeast spores) on the berries so they ferment spontaneously, rather than with the addition of a yeast culture. The wine is run off from the skins into new oak barrels (made by hand at a rate of just four barrels a day, by Pierre Darnajou, the only true *artisan* cooper left in the Bordeaux region). Most of Darnajou's casks end up with French winemakers rather than in those of Bordeaux's most earnest imitators in Chile, Tuscany or California – he sells them only to producers whose wines he knows he will respect.

After 12–18 months' maturing in the Darnajou barrels, Château Meylet is bottled by gravity. No liquid sulphur dioxide, fining or filtration is used, although sulphur wicks are burnt in the barrels, much to the chagrin of barrel maker Darnajou.

- Château Meylet, St Emilion Grand Cru AC: dry red wine with a crimson colour to brighten cheeks; the presence of concentrated and ripe Cabernet Franc is indicated by an airy smell of summer hedgerow fruits, and the fuller presence of Merlot is indicated by the smell of moist undergrowth. Made from such clean fruit that it will age happily for a decade, the most natural tasting red wine in Bordeaux. Suitable for vegetarians and vegans. 🍶

Other St Emilion domaines

Other St Emilion domaines, which are sometimes described as biodynamic but which have never been certified either as organic or biodynamic, include:

- Château Laroze in the commune of St Emilion, adjacent to Château Meylet, which has practised non-certified biodynamic methods since 1990 when Guy Meslin took over from his father. In 1996 two treatments not authorized by Demeter – one to counter leaf hopper and the 'Bt' bacteria to counter grape worm – were used. Meslin admits to be a natural non-risk taker, although he himself has taken homoeopathic treatments for 20 years. **Overall Price Rating:** 🍶🍶🍶
- Château Moulin du Cadet – under green-minded vineyard consultant Philippe Garde, a biodynamic treatment trial was started in this 3.5 hectare estate in November 1995. One hectare of 8–10-year old Merlot, and 2.5 hectares of Merlot and Cabinet Franc, were converted. **Overall Price Rating:** 🍶
- Château Pavie-Macquin covers seven hectares of lighter ground immediately east of St Emilion town. Under its previous owner, Madame Maryse Barre, Château Pavie-Macquin was run biodynamicially (her son Paul owns Château La Fleur Cailleau et Château la Grave, Fronsac, *see page 27*). It produced some remarkable wines, fleshy and intense, especially in the three great Bordeaux vintages of 1988, 1989 and 1990. They owed their denseness in part to Madame Barre's policy of low yields. Pavie-Macquin lies in a frost pocket and when a

severe frost struck in 1991, Madame Barre was forced to sell her vineyard. The new owners dispensed with some of the biodynamic preparations, and Demeter status has lapsed. **Overall Price Rating:** ♦

- Château Quercy in the commune of Vignonet, the poorest sited commune in St Emilion of the seven allowed the AC. Quercy's owner, Monsieur Appelbaum, is advised by Philippe Garde, the independent vineyard consultant who also works at Château Moulin du Cadet, above. Note that Garde is working in direct competition with biodynamic advisers like François Boucher, whose clients invariably are certified to Demeter standards – see Château Falfas in Côtes de Bourg (*page 24*) and Clos du Château Gaillard in the Loire (*page 97*). Quercy produces wines in such small quantities that the bulk of production is reserved for private clients.

Côtes de Castillon AC

The town of Castillon la Bataille lies east of St Emilion on the same chain of hills (these go all the way to Bergerac), and makes red wines from the same grape varieties. There are three organic vineyards, all producing creditable red Bordeaux. These wines are labelled Côtes de Castillon AC or as Bordeaux and Bordeaux Supérieur. Dry white and pink Bordeaux wines also made here.

Château Brandeau

33350 Les Salles de Castillon
Tel:+33 557 40 65 48
Fax:+33 557 40 65 65
Sales: direct from the château by appointment
Overall Price Rating: ♦

Located near a Gallo-Roman villa in the hills above the Dordogne, Château Brandeau has been certified organic since 1993. Like a number of châteaux in this region its owners, Andrea Gray and Anthony King, are not French. They form part of a growing non-native community in this part of France which has its own networks and cliques – and even cricket tournaments in the case of the English.

- Château Brandeau, Côtes de Castillon AC: dry red, dominated by Merlot, shows inky colour, appealing fruit, popular and smooth style of wine.

Château Moulin de St Magne
33350 St Magne de Castillon
Tel:+33 557 40 21 92
Fax:+33 557 40 09 41
Sales: from the château by appointment
Accommodation: available
Stockist: Organic Wine Company
Overall Price Rating: 👖

Jean-Gabriel Yon produces a range of value for money wines from his base in Castillon la Bataille's flat south-west suburbs. The grapes come from certified organic vineyards in both the northern and southern parts of the right bank.

- Cuvée la Croix Simon, Crémant de Bordeaux AC: dry sparkling white made by the traditional method (*see page 72 for details*) from Semillon and Sauvignon Blanc, and released in small volumes. Easy drinking, pleasant tasting, early maturing sparkler sourced from vines grown in the commune of Doulezon, Entre Deux Mers (*see also the wines of GFA Leclerc, Entre Deux Mers, page 42*).
- Château Moulin de St Magne, Côtes de Castillon AC: dry red, shows fresh cherry fruit and a firm bed of tannin; suitable for vegans.

Château de Prade
33350 Belvès de Castillon
Tel:+33 557 47 99 73
Fax:+33 557 47 91 39
Sales: every day from 0800–2030
Stockists: Vinceremos; Co-op
Overall Price Rating: 👖

Château de Prade is located in the commune of Belvès where the recon-struction of the 1453 Battle of Castillon takes place each year with a spectacular son-et-lumière show, which is held between 21 July and 14 August (Fridays and Saturdays only) at Château Castegens in Belvès de Castillon. Dry white and pink Bordeaux wines are made here, in addition to:

● Château de Prade, Bordeaux Supérieur AC: dry red, shows crisp cedar-like wine tannins; a good standard claret, suitable for vegetarians.

Côtes de Francs AC

Côtes de Francs forms Bordeaux's hilly, north east boundary and is the driest region in Bordeaux. It is named after the Frankish warriors who settled here and in Fronsac after the Dark Ages. The area produces red wines which show fuller body than Côtes de Castillon, and which have more depth of taste often too, perhaps because of the extra dryness here.

Château du Puy

33570 St Cibard
Tel:+33 557 51 24 28
Fax:+33 557 51 31 37
Sales (domestic): direct by appointment
Stockist: Organic Wine Company
Overall Price Rating: ♦♦♦

Château du Puy's proprietor, Robert Amoreau, began farming organically in 1945. Such is his reputation that his wines are sold to the French Parliament, and it seems ironic that politicians could have spent such a large part of the post-war period drinking organic without thinking organic. (Only recently has France made it easier for vineyards to take on casual labour during the growing season without masses of paperwork or tax problems. This benefits labour-intensive organic vineyards whose greatest need is spare hands.) Robert Amoreau makes two red wines:

● Château Rocher du Puy, Bordeaux Supérieur AC: dry red, the junior relation to the wine below; fuller than most clarets bearing this AC, with an appealing thick quality to the tannin, somewhat tighter fruit, well-knit with no rough edges.

- Château du Puy, Bordeaux Supérieur AC: dry red, smells and looks cedary, tastes dry and crisp – and thus a claret with 'grip'; medium bodied, well-toned. Bottled with a wax capsule.

The area south of the Dordogne is known as Entre Deux Mers, or 'between two seas'. The 'seas' in question are the Dordogne river to the north, and the Garonne river to the west. At roughly 50 miles wide and 15 miles deep, Entre Deux Mers is the biggest geographic area in Bordeaux and it has the biggest number of organic growers. It covers several large ACs so making generalized statements about vintage conditions is haphazard. Pick the producer rather than the appellation on the bottle or the vintage. The following designated wine regions lie within the geographical Entre Deux Mers.

Entre Deux Mers AC

Entre Deux Mers AC covers the bulk of the area between the Garonne and the Dordogne but refers only to dry white wines, slightly herbaceous, nervy, thirst-quenching and uncomplicated. They are made from Sauvignon Blanc, Semillon and Muscadelle. Look for the most recent vintage you can find. Red wines made within this area contain around 70 per cent Merlot and 30 per cent Cabernet and Malbec mix. They sell under the Bordeaux AC or Bordeaux Supérieur AC and are direct clarets with simple structure.

Château la Blanquerie
La Blanquerie, 33350 Mérignas
Tel:+33 557 84 10 35
Stockist: Vinceremos

This certified organic domaine is located in wooded hills some distance south of the Dordogne. Owner Serge Rougier makes a solid range.

- Château la Blanquerie, Entre Deux Mers AC: bone dry white, clean green fruit, suitable for vegans. ▮
- Château la Blanquerie, Bordeaux Supérieur Rosé AC: dry pink, light to medium bodied, clean tastes of simple redcurrants with waxy skins, suitable for vegans. ▮

- Château la Blanquerie, Bordeaux Supérieur Rouge AC: dry red, unoaked, suitable for vegans. ♦

Château de Chavrignac
Chavrignac, 33190 Fossés et Baleyssac
Tel:+33 556 61 70 50
Fax:+33 556 61 72 70
Visits: by appointment
Accommodation: available
Overall Price Rating: ♦♦

This domaine has been certified organic since 1964, and the consistency this length of organic farming gives to the wines seems clear. Never spectacular, but better than merely solid.

- Château de Chavrignac, Bordeaux Blanc Sec AC: dry white, clean modern style, pineapple fruit, chalky, made with Semillon and Sauvignon Blanc, suitable for vegans. The owners could use the Entre Deux Mers AC for this white wine but opt for the Bordeaux AC instead. They feel Entre Deux Mers has become associated in consumers' minds with Sauvignon Blanc-dominated dry white wines exhibiting pungent gooseberry aromas, more suited to New Zealand Sauvignon Blanc than Bordeaux. (*See also Château Fourton la Garenne, below*).
- Château de Chavrignac, Bordeaux Rosé AC: dry pink, simple style, clean, suitable for vegans.
- Château de Chavrignac, Bordeaux Rouge AC: dry red, shows light, clean Cabernet Franc-dominated blue fruit in the 1997 vintage; in the 1998 it is more Merlot dominated, with thicker plum-skin texture. Well made, suitable for vegans.

Château les Dauphins
33450 Saint Loubès
Tel:+33 556 20 41 08
Cellar Door Sales: every day (0900–2000)

This certified organic domaine belongs to Yves Noel and overlooks the city of Bordeaux from across the Garonne.

- Château les Dauphins, Bordeaux Supérieur Rouge AC: dry red, simple taste but layered texture, which makes this a generous basic claret. 🍷

Château Fourton la Garenne
5 Hourton, 33750 Nérigean
Tel:+33 557 24 55 24
Fax:+33 557 24 05 72
Cellar Door Sales: by appointment; weekends 1500–2000
Markets: Montpon, Dordogne (Wednesdays); Neuvic, Dordogne (Tuesdays); La Teste, Gironde (Fridays)

This certified organic vineyard is typical of many in Entre Deux Mers that are slowly reconverting their vineyards to higher vine densities, i.e., with more vines to the hectare. In the 1960s Entre Deux Mers growers decided to save on labour costs by ripping out every other row of vines. Yields remained the same. This meant that each vine in the new, lower density vineyards produced proportionately double the amount of grapes as before. This left each vine weaker and more prone to disease, and the resultant wines lacked concentration. Replanting the vineyards at 4,500 vines per hectare (as opposed to maintaining them at 2,500 vines per hectare), should make for healthier vines. However, for Fourton la Garenne's owners Bernard and Martine Richard, it means adapting the vineyard machinery to suit the narrower distance between the vine rows.

Two red wines are made from their vineyards planted with Merlot 70 per cent, Cabernet Sauvignon 15 per cent and Cabernet Franc 15 per cent.

- Château Damanieu, Bordeaux Rouge AC: dry red, the non-oak aged version of the wine below. Its name, Damanieu, refers to a house owned by the Richard family in one of the family vineyards. 🍷
- Château Fourton la Garenne, fût de chêne Cuvée Damanien, Bordeaux Rouge AC: dry red, oak aged, showed interesting, delicate fruit in 1997. 🍷🍷

La Grange du Roy

33350 Pujols

Tel:+33 557 40 50 71

Cellar Door Sales: daily 1000–2000. Grape juice sold.

Markets: Marché du Boulevard Raspail, Paris (third Sunday of every month); Boulogne Billancourt (third Saturday of every month).

Overall Price Rating: ▮

La Grange du Roy ('the King's Barn') consists of a small certified organic vineyard near Château Moulin de Peyronin (see below). Owner Bernard Bouillon used to keep a vine nursery but gave up because the French state insists soil used for the propagation of vines grafted to phylloxera-resistant rootstocks must first be disinfected with a chemical. This is to prevent virus diseases being transmitted by microbes in the soil (such as nematodes). One of the recommended chemical treatments used was manufactured at Bhopal, India, until the disaster in the 1980s. The compulsory use of this chemical means that organic rootstock growing is not possible in France (in contrast to Ceãgo Vinegarden in the US for example, *page 304*). The bigger vine nurseries in Bordeaux line up their rows of grafted plants by laser beam; Bouillon used to mark out his ground by riding a bicycle up and down the rows in line with a string after the ground had first been ploughed.

- La Grange du Roy, Bordeaux Rouge AC: dry red, about as raw as claret gets. Tastes better if you shut your eyes first!

Château la Hage

33420 Saint Aubin de Branne

Tel:+33 557 84 55 51

Cellar Door Sales: by appointment

Markets: Marché de Montalivet (Gironde) (every day July to September)

Overall Price Rating: ▮▮

This certified organic Entre-Deux-Mers estate lies directly south of the last big loop taken by the Dordogne as it feeds into the Garonne to become the Gironde. Owner Jean-Jacques Favereau makes three wines:

- Château la Hage, Crémant de Bordeaux: dry white sparkling wine made by the traditional method; quite frothy, clean earth rather than unwashed soil taste.
- Château la Hage, Bordeaux Blanc Sec AC: dry white, nutty taste, a contrast to the tropical fruit dry whites made by Favereau's neighbours in this part of Entre Deux Mers.
- Château la Hage, Bordeaux Rouge AC: dry red, contains a kernel of older Cabernet vines.

Château Large Malartic

Guillac, 33420 Branne
Tel:+33 557 84 57 87
Cellar Door Sales: 0900–1800 Monday to Saturday
Stockist: Vintage Roots
Overall Price Rating: ♙

Château Large Malartic is certified organic and lies in the hills above Branne. This town is the gateway to St Emilion if coming from the south across the Dordogne river (*see Château Barrail des Graves in St Emilion, page 30*). Château Large Malartic is due for full organic certification in 1999 under its owner, Bernard Large and his family. They also release wines under the Château Canet label. This could be a domaine to watch if your taste is for clean rather than shockingly modern Bordeaux.

- Château Large Malartic, Entre Deux Mers AC: dry white, clean, well structured, appley, blend of Semillon and Sauvignon Blanc.
- Château Large Malartic, Bordeaux Rouge AC: dry red, tight, crisp Merlot dominated fruit, suitable for vegetarians.

Leclerc (GFA)

Château Lagnet, Doulezon, 33350 Pujols
Tel:+33 557 40 51 84
Fax:+33 557 40 55 48
Cellar Door Sales: weekdays (0900–1200 and 1400–1700) except public holidays

GFA Leclerc is the name given to a group of three certified organic vineyards covering 50 hectares in the central part of Entre Deux Mers. This group is owned by Hélène Levieux, the daughter of Edouard Leclerc, the entrepreneur who was responsible for bringing supermarket-style shopping to France in the 1960s. Products labelled organic are unusual in French supermarkets but demand for them is growing. The branch of 'Leclerc' just outside Castillon la Bataille (*see page 35*) provides a selection of Madame Levieux's organic wines, priced just above those from non-organic sources. There is a feel of 'styled for supermarket' about Madame Levieux's wines and, with the reputation of French supermarkets for wine buying mediocre at best, especially in the eyes of Anglo-Saxons, this cannot be a good omen.

- Château Roques Mauriac, Bordeaux Blanc Sec AC: dry white, light, frosty pineapple, drink within 18 months. ▮
- Château Labatut, Bordeaux Supérieur AC: dry red, the most basic wine in the range, machine picked, lacks definition with the presence of young vines. ▮▮
- Château Lagnet, Bordeaux Supérieur AC: dry red, middle quality level, machine picked; some potential for 2–4 years ageing. ▮▮
- Château Roques Mauriac, Bordeaux Supérieur AC: dry red, hand picked, but rather green. ▮▮▮
- Château Roques Mauriac, Cuvée Hélène, Bordeaux Supérieur AC: dry red, hand picked and oak aged; still rather green, but the oak adds some warmth. ▮▮▮

Château Moulin de Peyronin

33350 Pujols sur Dordogne
Tel:+33 557 40 54 92
Fax:+33 467 90 66 07
Cellar Door Sales: by appointment
Stockists: Vinceremos; Chartrand Imports (USA)
Overall Price Rating: ▮▮

Moulin de Peyronin is located near Pujols where the French troops gathered before their victory at the Battle of Castillon in 1453. Two solid red wines from certified organic vines feature here:

- Château Moulin de Peyronin, Bordeaux Supérieur AC: dry red, suitable for vegetarians; a sound, modern-style red Bordeaux – a bright red body and a little bit of perfume.
- Château Moulin de Peyronin, Cuvée Capucine, Bordeaux Supérieur AC: dry red, spends 10 months in oak which slightly overawes the fruit (a higher than usual percentage of the lighter Malbec grape variety used here); suitable for vegetarians.

Château Pouchaud-Larquey

Morizès, 33590 La Réole
Tel:+33 556 71 44 97
Cellar Door Sales: by appointment
Fairs: Andernos lès Bains (Gironde) every day in July and August, and Hergnies Sundays and Mondays during Pentecost
Stockist: Vinceremos
Overall Price Rating: ▲

Château Pouchaud-Larquey has been certified organic since 1980 under ower Jean-Luc Piva. It lies in south-western Entre Deux Mers outside La Réole. This town's strategic position above the Garonne allowed it the chance to check the passage of red wines grown in the hilly regions upstream and inland. These '*haut pays*' or high country wines would steal Bordeaux's market unless they were prevented from entering the Port of Bordeaux – at least until Bordeaux had sold its own wine for the year.

- Château Pouchaud-Larquey, Entre Deux Mers AC: dry white; the presence of some older vines means this Entre Deux Mers is fuller than most.
- Château Porchaud-Larquey, Bordeaux Rouge AC: dry red; flat, compact style of red Bordeaux.

Château la Salle

33540 Castelvieil

Tel:+33 556 61 96 16

Cellar Door Sales: by appointment; visits and tasting possible in the 12th cellar (contact Jean-Marie Jaumain)

Overall Price Rating: 🍾

This certified organic domaine lies in one of the higher parts of Entre Deux Mers where the soils are dark and clay rich. These should give colour and body to the red wines produced here under the generic Bordeaux Rouge AC.

Bordeaux Haut Benauge AC

Bordeaux Haut Benauge forms a sub-region at the heart of Entre Deux Mers. The area has two organic estates making contrasting styles of dry white, red and medium dry white wines. The wines are labelled Bordeaux Haut Benauge AC if dry or medium dry whites, and as Bordeaux or Bordeaux Supérieur AC if red. Haut Benauge's fine topsoil is rich in small, fossilized oysters, the shells of which are bright enough to reflect the sun's light onto the ripening grapes. This gives the white wines added intensity, and the reds distinctive richness. The area covers nine communes and 750 hectares.

Vignobles Boudon

Le Bourdieu, 33760 Soulignac

Tel:+33 556 23 65 60

Fax:+33 556 23 45 58

Sales: weekdays (0800–1200 and 1400-1800), weekends by appointment

Stockist: Vinceremos

This family business is run by Patrick and Maryse Boudon, a couple with a combined total of 70 years' winegrowing experience. The wines are made from 27 hectares of certified organic vines divided evenly between red and white. The Boudons have inherited, bought and replanted vine-yards at low density (2,500 vines per hectare). They avoid the thinness associated with low vine densities (*see Château Fourton la Garenne above*) by making the vine work for its nutrients through careful natural manuring. This allows the vine plenty of leeway but never any slack.

- Le Bourdieu Brut, Crémant de Bordeaux AC: dry white sparkling wine made by the traditional method from Sauvignon Blanc (70 per cent) and Ugni Blanc (30 per cent); shows fine and persistent bubbles (*mousse*), whereas most of its sparkling Bordeaux peers are limp and frothy. 🍾🍾
- Domaine du Bourdieu, Entre Deux Mers AC: dry white wine, a blend of Semillon, Sauvignon Blanc and Muscadelle. The Muscadelle has little actual 'Muscat' flavour and is underrated by Bordeaux growers; it crops very reliably, and at high sugar levels too. 🍾
- Château Haut-Mallet, Bordeaux Haut Benauge Sec AC: dry white, oak aged, predominantly Semillon; with structure and flavour. Shows why Haut-Benauge merits its own appellation at the heart of Entre Deux Mers. 🍾
- Domaine du Bourdieu, Bordeaux Blanc Moelleux AC: medium dry white made in 1995 from Semillon (85 per cent) and Sauvignon Blanc (15 per cent) vines grown at Capian in the Premières Côtes de Bordeaux. 1995 a good vintage for this style. 🍾🍾🍾
- Domaine du Bourdieu, Bordeaux Rouge AC: dry red, non-oak aged, clean. 🍾
- Domaine Ste Anne, Bordeaux Rouge AC: dry red (as above). 🍾
- Château Mallet, Bordeaux Supérieur AC: dry red, with oak ageing used to good effect. 🍾🍾🍾
- Premières Côtes de Bordeaux Liquoreux AC: sweet white, more initial richness than some sweet white wines from the famous Sauternes region (*see page 20*). This wine is made only occasionally, in years when the picking of the Semillon grapes can be delayed. It is barrel fermented, which adds structure. 🍾🍾🍾

Château Mourlin Tuilière
33760 St Pierre de Bat
Tel:+33 556 23 94 86
Fax:+33 556 23 65 05

Visits: by appointment
Overall Price Rating: 🍾

Château Mourlin Tuilière has been certified organic under its owners, the Simonneau family, since 1975 and has never been treated with weed-killers. Pierre-Abel Simonneau is a Professor of Oenology (wine science) at the renowned Bordeaux University.

The growing importance of red wine grapes being planted rather than whites is reflected at Château Mourlin Tuilière. There are 25 hectares but only eight are given to white wine varieties like Semillon and Muscadelle. This red wine dominance reflects the historical importance of red wine to Haut Benauge, even though red wines produced here may only use the generic Bordeaux AC.

- Château Mourlin Tuilière, Bordeaux Clairet AC: deep pink; made by running juice off early from the red wine skins before it picks up too much colour; shows cherry fruit, clean tannin, good style.
- Bordeaux Haut Benauge Blanc Sec/Entre Deux Mers AC: dry white with broad appeal. In 1997 had thick quince fruit, showing the Semillon grape variety influence when given warm, well-drained soils; in 1998 the fruit was leaner, greener, more vibrant and Sauvignon Blanc influenced. Contains Ugni Blanc, Sauvignon Blanc, Muscadelle and Semillon.
- Château Mourlin Tuilière, Bordeaux Haut Benauge Moelleux/Entre Deux Mers AC: medium dry white, medium bodied. In 1997 the sweet-ness was creamy and the presence of only 11.5 per cent alcohol means this sweetness is autumnal rather than festive. Semillon dominated.
- Château Mourlin Tuilière, Bordeaux Supérieur AC: dry red made from Merlot, Cabernet Sauvignon and Cabernet Franc; aged partially in large wooden *foudres* to soften the tannins. Has changed in style from the positive 1997, where the blend was better than the sum of its parts, to a more extracted, much deeper coloured style in 1998.

Bordeaux Ste Foy AC

The Bordeaux Ste Foy region forms the eastern wing of the Entre-Deux-Mers and is centred around the medieval town of Ste Foy la Grande. This occupies a strategic position on the south side of Dordogne river between

Bordeaux and Bergerac (*see page 165*). Ste Foy has a high concentration of organic growers, and is an appellation to watch – more of the smaller growers have guarded their old vines here, especially for white varieties, than in the rest of the Entre-Deux-Mers. Most of the organic growers leave grapes in the oldest parcels of Semillon hanging late into the season to concentrate their sugars. The style of wine made from these grapes is called Bordeaux Ste Foy Liquoreux AC. They can provide some of Bordeaux's most original and natural tasting sweet white wines. Dry whites sell as Bordeaux Blanc Sec AC.

Château la Chapelle Maillard

33220 St Quentin de Caplong
Tel:+33 557 41 26 13
Fax:+33 557 41 25 99
Cellar Door Sales: by appointment
Markets: Bordeaux St Pierre (Thursdays)

Château la Chapelle Maillard was sold in 1984 to Jean-Luc and Renée Devert. The previous owner, Monsieur Maillard, had never used herbicides or insecticides on the vines here during half a century, so when the Deverts applied for organic vineyard certification it was granted immediately (the usual conversion period is three years). In 1997 this vineyard became the first (and, so far, only) one in Bordeaux Ste Foy to gain Demeter biodynamic status. The Deverts manure the vines using their own flock of sheep. The wines are well made in a no frills, no spills style.

- Château La Chapelle Maillard, Crémant de Bordeaux AC: dry white sparkling wine made by the traditional method from Semillon, Muscadelle and a small percentage of dark-skinned Cabernet Franc grapes pressed as white. Softer fruit style to that of Vignobles Boudon (*see Haut Benauge, page 45*). ♙♙
- Château La Chapelle Maillard, Bordeaux Blanc Sec AC: dry white Bordeaux, clean, crisp but easy on the gums; shows best after a couple of years in the bottle, in comparison to most Entre Deux Mers dry whites which fade within 18 months. ♙
- Château La Chapelle Maillard, Bordeaux Clairet AC: dry deep pink wine, lots of positive flavour for 3–4 years' ageing. ♙

- Château La Chapelle Maillard, Bordeaux Supérieur AC: dry red, fer- ments in cement tanks with no oak ageing to allow Cabernet Franc's liquorice influence aromatic autonomy. ▟
- Château La Chapelle Maillard, Ste Foy Rouge AC: dry red, as above only ages in wood as part of a rotation, i.e., not all of the wine is in wood all of the time. This approach brings more of the wine's body out, making this a good style for entertaining with. ▟▟

Château Coursou
Gensac, 33890 Pessac sur Dordogne
Tel:+33 557 47 40 27
Fax:+33 557 47 47 10
Stockists: Vintage Roots; Vinceremos
Overall Price Rating: ▟

This certified organic estate lies in the first area in Bordeaux to be affect- ed by the insect that transmits a vine stunting disease called '*la flaves- cence dorée*'. The French government tried to stop its spread elsewhere by spraying farms from the air by helicopter. Departmental prefects were given the right to authorize treatments anywhere and without prior notice. One grower in the Aude claims these sprays rendered the organic status he had enjoyed on his vineyard for 12 years null and void. 'I only just had time to get the dogs in,' he was quoted as saying.

- Château Coursou, Bordeaux Blanc AC: dry white, fermented and aged in stainless steel, pithy, hard pressed, suitable for vegans.
- Château Coursou, Bordeaux Supérieur AC: dry red, simple fruit, twist in the aftertaste, drink within 2–3 years of the vintage, suitable for vegans.

Château des Hautes Combes
Jacquineau, 33220 St Avit de Soulège
Tel:+33 557 41 07 91
Fax:+33 557 41 08 90

Cellar Door Sales: yes
Stockists: contact Organic Wine Company for details
Overall Price Rating: 🍾

The proprietor of this certified organic vineyard, Ramon Garcia, is one of those characters who seem to have a bewildering number of activities, both public and private, to keep him occupied.

- Château des Hautes Combes, Crémant de Bordeaux AC: dry sparkling wine made in both white and pink forms with the pink showing most texture.
- Château des Hautes Combes, Bordeaux Blanc Sec AC: dry white, moderate body, crisp citrus fruit.
- Château des Hautes Combes, Bordeaux Ste Foy Rouge AC: dry red, softens slowly; also available as an easier drinking Bordeaux Supérieur.

Château Moulin de Romage

33220 Les Lèves-et-Thoumeyragues
Tel:+33 557 46 45 99
Fax:+33 557 46 58 66
Cellar Door Sales: by appointment
Stockists: Vintage Roots; Vinceremos

This certified organic estate covers 10 hectares and has been certified organic since 1969. The health quality of grapes picked here each harvest by owner Alain Piroux seems to be consistent.

- Château Moulin de Romage, Bordeaux Ste Foy Sec AC: dry white made with Semillon, Sauvignon Blanc and Muscadelle, suitable for vegans. Shows appealing clean mineral texture to the fruit typical of this region. Drink within a year of the vintage if possible. Good value. 🍾
- Château Moulin de Romage, Bordeaux Ste Foy Rouge AC: dry red. The 1995 was made with 80 per cent Merlot, 20 per cent Cabernet Sauvignon and Cabernet Franc combined. The wine is fermented with natural yeast. Shows very fine fruit and natural body, the result of older vines and slower fermentation. 🍾

- Château Moulin de Romage, Bordeaux Ste Foy Moelleux AC (Bordeaux Supérieur Blanc): medium sweet white made from late picked, Semillon vines, a proportion of which date from the 1960s; characterful as well as refined (Vinceremos, ♦).

Château Le Peyrail
33220 Les Lèves-et-Thoumeyragues
Tel:+33 557 41 23 09
Fax:+33 557 41 22 21
Cellar Door Sales: daily 0900–1800
Overall Price Rating: ♦♦

Château Le Peyrail belongs to Jean-Michel and Marie-Céline Chort. There are nine hectares of vines certified organic since 1987. They produce probably the most consistent range of dry white, medium dry and red wine in the appellation.

- Château le Peyrail, Bordeaux Ste Foy Sec AC: dry white, has a delicate, clean aroma of straw, the result of a natural yeast fermentation and a dose of mature Semillon. All the elements integrate to form a complex wine from seemingly ordinary ground.
- Château le Peyrail, Bordeaux Ste Foy Moelleux AC: medium sweet white, made from mature Semillon vines grown on one hectare of warm sandy soils. Shows ripe, clear honey and stone fruit sweetness, the most naturally layered white wine in the AC.
- Château le Peyrail, Bordeaux Rouge AC: dry red, non-oak aged, direct style, shows the lean side the Cabernet varieties present in the blend. Demands patience.
- Château le Peyrail, Bordeaux Ste Foy Rouge AC: dry red, oak aged, reliable, even in lesser years this has real weight and finesse. Made from mature Merlot and Cabernet vines.

Château Rait
33220 Les Lèves-et-Thoumeyragues
Tel:+33 557 41 22 29
Fax:+33 557 41 26 00

Cellar Door Sales: by appointment
Stockist: Vintage Roots
Overall Price Rating: 🍷

This certified organic vineyard is a useful source of dry white and red wines which exhibit the best of Bordeaux Ste Foy. The winemaking is straightforward, leaving the natural weight of the flavour in the grapes untouched.

- Château Rait, Bordeaux Sec AC: dry white, clean, citrus fruit style, suitable for vegans. Drink within 18 months of the vintage. Made from a vineyard planted Semillon 60 per cent, Sauvignon Blanc 25 per cent and Muscadelle 15 per cent.
- Château Rait, Bordeaux Ste Foy Bordeaux Supérieur AC: dry red. The 1996 vintage reflected the benefits of a later than usual season, and showed complex, country fruits. Suitable for vegans. Made from a vineyard planted Merlot 65 per cent, Cabernet Sauvignon 20 per cent, Cabernet Franc 15 per cent.

Domaine des Côtes de Caris

bis 8 Aux Caris, 33220 St André et Appelles
Tel:+33 557 46 16 25
Fax:+33 557 46 47 63
Cellar Door Sales: by appointment
Stockist: Organic Wine Company
Overall Price Rating: 🍷

This domaine has been certified organic since 1988. There appeared to have been some ups and downs in the winemaking in the mid-1990s. These now seem to have been resolved. The wines may be labelled with either the Bordeaux or Bordeaux Ste Foy appellations.

Premières Côtes de Bordeaux AC

The slopes rising from the eastern bank of the Garonne are known as the Premières Côtes de Bordeaux ('first hills of Bordeaux'). Vineyards here enjoy an excellent range of soils, good south-western exposure to the sun, and warm Atlantic breezes brought via the Gironde estuary into which the Garonne flows.

Château les Jésuites

12 route de Bas, 33490 Saint Maixant
Tel:+33 556 63 17 97
Fax:+33 556 63 17 46
Cellar Door Sales: by appointment

This certified organic Premières Côtes de Bordeaux estate lies near the Garonne on fairly flat ground. Owners Claudine and Guy Lucmaret produce a small amount of dry red wine under the Bordeaux Rouge AC (🍶), Bordeaux Supérieur AC (🍶🍶) and Premières Côtes de Bordeaux AC (🍶🍶) in ascending order of price. The Premières Côtes red is aged in a small collection of mostly older barrels. It shows crisp, satisfying fruit for drinking within two to four years.

Château Tour du Bourdieu

33410 Monprimblanc
Tel:+33 556 62 64 21
Fax:+33 556 65 95 27
Cellar Door Sales: by appointment
Overall Price Rating: 🍶🍶

Château Tour du Bourdieu is a family domaine located at the southern end of the Premières Côtes, just north of St Macaire (see below). This high hinterland is the source of the sweet white wine style for which the Premières Côtes (and near neighbours like Ste Croix du Mont and Loupiac) is renowned. Pick carefully here and you might find something of interest in what is a sensibly sized range made from certified organic grapes. Wines include dry and medium sweet whites, plus dry pinks and dry reds.

Côtes de Bordeaux St Macaire AC

The southern end of the Premières Côtes clusters about the medieval town of St Macaire on the Garonne. Medium dry white wines can be made, but (in common with many other local growers), the two certified organic growers featured below concentrate on dry whites and dry reds.

Château Barrail-Haut

33490 St Pierre d'Aurillac
Tel:+33 557 63 03 09
Fax:+33 557 63 03 09
Cellar Door Sales: by appointment
Stockist: Vinceremos
Overall Price Rating: ⚑

This certified organic vineyard comprises six hectares of Cabernet Sauvignon (40 per cent); Cabernet Franc (20 per cent); Merlot (35 per cent) and Malbec (5 per cent). Its owner, Olivier Raynal, picks by hand and uses oak judiciously.

- Château Barrail-Haut, Bordeaux Supérieur Rouge AC: dry red, usually shows a consistent balance of fruit and tannin that evolves quickly, can be light, good example of a Cabernet-dominated claret from the south of Bordeaux.

Château Vieux Georget

33540 St Laurent du Bois
Tel:+33 556 76 44 44
Fax:+33 556 76 45 98
Cellar Door Sales: by appointment (not Sundays)
Stockist: Vinceremos
Overall Price Rating: ⚑

This St Macaire domaine lies just off the main St-Macaire–Libourne road (N 672). It has been certified organic since 1964. Owner Jean da Fré produces two everyday wines:

- Château Vieux Georget, Bordeaux Blanc Sec AC: dry white 1996 blend of Semillon (50 per cent), Sauvignon Blanc and Muscadelle; suitable for vegans.
- Château Vieux Georget, Bordeaux Rouge AC: dry red blend of Merlot and Cabernet Sauvignon with some Cabernet Franc and Malbec.

Burgundy

Burgundy is a long, thin strip of vineyard in eastern France roughly between Dijon and Lyon. Burgundy rivals Bordeaux as the greatest of France's wine regions. All the best Burgundy vineyards lie on a single slope or ridge above the flat valley of the river Sâone. The sloping terrain makes working the vineyards difficult and costly – one reason why even basic quality Burgundy tends to be relatively expensive. However, the slopes generally allow the vines to catch the best of the sun – hence the heart of the region is called the Côte d'Or – the 'golden slope'. The effect the sun has on the grapes is to ripen them into producing intense, almost overpowering wines with velvety texture. They are described as seductive, in contrast to Bordeaux wines, which tend to be more austere. Many people think Burgundies succeed best with simple food rather than with complex menus – because the wines are often so complex as to be meals in themselves.

Burgundy produces some of France's heartiest organic wines from some of its heartiest winemakers. To produce good wine here requires good organization because holdings are so sub-divided. Napoleonic inheritance laws have produced a patchwork of vine holdings and organic growers rely on cooperation between each other and with non-organic neighbours to minimize any impact of spray drift.

The type of soil the vines grow on is everything for a Burgundian, for it will largely determine the wine's status:

- Grand Cru for the best sites with the finest exposure to the sun on warm and well-drained soils.
- Premier Cru for the best of the rest.
- Village for wines from several plots located in the same village or commune and bottled together under the communal name. Sometimes these plots may also have their own *lieu-dit* or name.
- Bourgogne (French for 'Burgundy') for the generic wines; common to see the grape variety on the label.

Burgundy's organic growers are conscious of the damage done here during the 1960s to the soil with machinery, chemical sprays and super-phosphate fertilisers. The fertilisers adversely affected the vigour of the vines, which is best summed up as plenty of desire but not a lot of performance, or (put another way) high yields and low quality. One former government soil expert, Claude Bourguignon, who lives in the Burgundy region, has compared soil from Grand Cru Burgundy vineyards to the sand in the Sahara in terms of its capacity for life. This is why many wine lovers baulk when they hear Burgundies from conventional vineyards described as 'vivacious' (or 'alive with fruit' by the clown school of wine tasting). Especially galling when they are some of the most expensive wines around! So, buyer beware.

Buying Tip

Bear in mind that the rule in Burgundy is 'Pick the grower, not the name of the vineyard or village' when selecting wine. A poor grower will make nothing of a Grand Cru site, whereas a good grower will produce a wonderful wine with a mere 'Villages' designation. To find these growers is one thing; to be guaranteed a source of their wine is another, as some are made in single barrel lots only (300 bottles) — the result of the Napoleonic patchwork vineyard-holding effect. So unless you plan on visiting the area direct for cellar tastings it is wise to strike up a relationship with your wine merchant to keep up to date.

The main grapes are Chardonnay for white and Pinot Noir for red. Both of these consider Burgundy their spiritual home. A third grape, the Aligoté, produces dry white wines which are similar to Chardonnay but more obviously flavoured and less suited to ageing. The red Gamay grape is found in southern Burgundy or Beaujolais.

Chablis

Chablis is famous for a steely, bone dry white wine made from the Chardonnay grape. The region lies some way to the north of the main Burgundy region, the Côte d'Or, and experiences appreciably cooler weather in spring and autumn. The most noticeable seasonable blot on the sustainable landscape as far as vinegrowing here is concerned occurs in spring, when oil burners are placed (at a rate of 40 per hectare) in the vineyards to protect them against frost. This strikes hard on young

Chardonnay buds and can wipe out the entire potential crop in a morning. The other anti-frost system used here is activated electronically by sensors when the temperature drops. Fine jets of water are sprayed on the buds to encase them in ice which (in case you didn't know) gives off heat as it freezes to keep the buds alive. The following two producers are located on the west (left) bank of the river Serein, which cuts the Chablis region in two.

Domaine Jean Goulley
22 vallée des Rosiers, 89800 La Chapelle Vaupelteigne
Tel:+33 386 42 40 85
Fax:+33 386 42 81 06
Stockists: Vintage Roots; Vinceremos
Overall Price Rating: 👭

Jean Goulley's son Philippe has now taken over the winemaking at this certified organic domaine. The style is for clean and accessible Chablis for drinking within 2–3 years of purchase. All are suitable for vegans.

- Petit Chablis AC: dry white, shows very green fruit which makes it a good base for 'kir' – mixed with *crème de cassis* (see Alain Verdet's in Nuits St Georges below).
- Chablis AC: dry white, as above but a touch richer.
- Chablis Premier Cru Montmains AC: dry white, sourced from a single vineyard with its own Premier Cru designation, which gives the wine its characteristic chalky feel.
- Chablis Premier Cru Fourchaume AC: dry white, as above but from a different vineyard source; shows waxier fruit, not one I would cellar.

Catherine Moreau
Préhy, 89800 Chablis
Tel:+33 386 41 43 78
Fax:+33 386 41 47 73
Overall Price Rating: 👭

Catherine Moreau's vines were planted in 1990 on land that had been used since her grandmother's time for cereals. The three main biodynamic preparations (*see Appendix 3*) supplement certified organic practices in the vineyard.

- Chablis AC: dry white, stocks of 1994 and 1996 available at the château in 1999 (the prized 1995 vintage wines having been sold).

Côte de Nuits

The Côte de Nuits begins immediately south of Dijon and continues to Beaune (*see Côte de Beaune, below*). It forms the northern half of the Côte d'Or, the 'golden hillside' at the heart of Burgundy. The Côte de Nuits produces powerful, mouthfilling red wines made from Pinot Noir, and a richer style of dry white Chardonnay compared to Chablis above.

Domaine Leroy and Domaine Auvenay

15 rue de la Fontaine, 21700 Vosne-Romanée
Tel:+33 380 61 10 82
Fax:+33 380 21 63 81
Stockists: Farr Vintners; Seckford (brokers and auction houses rather than wine shops)
Overall Price Rating: 𝄞𝄞𝄞

These two Demeter-certified biodynamic domaines belong to a formidable lady with a powerful background: Madame Lalou Bize-Leroy. There are less than nine hectares in all, in tiny parcels both owned and rented, along the Côte d'Or. One of the key features here is the concentration obtained in the wines through a policy of low yields. Concentrated Burgundy can be the most seductive of all wines, whether red or white, and Bize-Leroy's are no exception. Such is the demand for them that they achieve some of the highest prices paid for any wines in France. However, there is an argument which says that concentration and elegance do not always coincide, and these Burgundy wines may well provide examples of that. However if you are one of those seduced by a concentrated style, then you'll find these the most irresistible wines in this book. They include:

- Auxey Duresses, red and white.
- Bonnes Mares, Grand Cru red from Chambolle Musigny.
- Chambertin, Grand Cru red from Gevrey-Chambertin.
- Chambolle Musigny, red village wine.
- Chevalier Montrachet, Grand Cru white from Puligny-Montrachet.
- Clos de la Roche, Grand Cru red from Chambolle-Musigny.
- Clos de Vougeot, Grand Cru red from Vougeot.
- Corton Charlemagne, Grand Cru white from Pernand-Vergelesses.
- Corton Renardes, Grand Cru red from Aloxe-Corton.
- Criots Batard Montrachet Grand Cru, white from Chassagne-Montrachet.
- Gevrey Chambertin, red village wine.
- Latrichières Chambertin, Grand Cru red from Gevrey-Chambertin.
- Mazis Chambertin, Grand Cru red from Gevrey-Chambertin.
- Meursault Les Gouttes d'Or, white.
- Musigny, Grand Cru red from Chambolle-Musigny.
- Nuits St Georges, red village wine.
- Pommard, red village wine.
- Puligny Montrachet Premier Cru Les Folatières, white premier cru from Puligny Montrachet.
- Richebourg, Grand Cru red from Vosne Romanée.
- Volnay, red village wine.
- Vosne Romanée, red village wine.

The 1990s have brought a generally successful string of vintages to Burgundy. The only one to skip here is 1993.

Domaine Alain Verdet

Arcenat, 21700 Nuits St Georges
Tel:+33 380 61 08 10
Fax:+33 380 61 08 10
Stockists: Organic Wine Company; Vintage Roots
Overall Price Rating: ♦♦

Alain Verdet's domaine is found in the hilly backwoods above Nuits St Georges. The Verdet vines have been certified organic since 1971 but the scrub they are surrounded by is home to wild boar which can rampage among the vines. The fruit trees, which are trained higher than the vines, fare better, and provide a concentrated range of liqueurs. Note that these, however, are made using non-organic sugar.

- Crémant de Bourgogne AC: dry white sparkling wine made by the traditional method, from white grapes (Aligoté and Chardonnay) and red grapes (Pinot Noir) pressed as white wine.
- Hautes Côtes de Nuits AC: dry red, sees some oak ageing, similar in style to the wines of the Couchois (*see below*), showing tight tannin.
- Crème de Cassis de Bourgogne: blackcurrant fruit liqueur containing 18 per cent alcohol, more aromatic than the version made in Pineau des Charentes (70 cl bottle).
- Crème de Framboise de Bourgogne: raspberry fruit liqueur containing 18 per cent alcohol (70 cl bottle).
- Crème de Mûre de Bourgogne: blackberry fruit liqueur containing 18 per cent alcohol (70 cl bottle).
- Crème de Pêche de Bourgogne: peach fruit liqueur containing 18 per cent alcohol (70 cl bottle).

Côte de Beaune

Vineyards in the southern half of the Côte d'Or centre on Beaune. The style of red wine here is generally softer and more open than in the Côte de Nuits. The white wines have a creamy, milk tooth quality from limestone-rich soils.

Emmanuel Giboulot

Combertault, 21200 Beaune
Tel:+33 380 26 52 85
Fax:+33 380 26 53 67
Stockists: Vinceremos; Vintage Roots

This certified organic domaine is run by two brothers and offers a balanced range. The 'one takes the vineyard while the other one takes the winery' approach seems to work well (*see also the two Italian brothers at La Capuccina in Soave, page 259*).

- Bourgogne Blanc AC: dry white, crisp, no nonsene Chardonnay; suitable for vegetarians. ▮
- Beaune Blanc AC: dry white, sourced from a *lieu dit* called 'La Grande Chatelaine'; shows the overbearing character typical to Beaune Chardonnay; suitable for vegetarians. ▮▮
- Bourgogne Rouge AC: dry red, light, catch it young. ▮
- Hautes Côtes de Nuits Rouge: dry red, sometimes slightly green. ▮▮

Jean-Claude Rateau
Chemin des Mariages, 21200 Beaune
Tel:+33 380 22 52 54
Fax:+33 380 22 46 16
Stockists: Vintage Roots; Vinceremos

This Demeter-certified biodynamic domaine is another key source for punchy and sometimes seductive reds from nearly eight hectares around Beaune. Rateau converted to organic methods in 1979 and had adopted biodynamic treatments fully within ten years.

- Bourgogne Aligoté: dry white, full style, warm, in contrast to the wine below. ▮
- Côtes de Beaune Blanc: dry white, cool marble feel, grown on higher ground than the wine above. ▮
- Hautes Côtes de Beaune Blanc: dry white, the most intense white Rateau makes. ▮▮
- Hautes Côtes de Beaune Rouge: dry red, crisp out front, with softness in the background. ▮▮
- Beaune AC: dry red, sourced from the *lieu dit* Les Coucheries. ▮▮
- Beaune Premier Cru AC Les Reversées: dry red, more open style of fruit to the wine below, from a lighter soil. ▮▮▮
- Beaune Premier Cru AC Bressandes: dry red, sourced from a Premier Cru site noted for its blackcherry style Pinot Noir. ▮▮

Thierry Guyot

Rue de la Pierre Ronde, 21190 St Romain
Tel:+33 380 21 27 52
Fax:+33 380 21 67 59
Stockists: contact Vinceremos for details

Thierry Guyot is one of the old guard biodynamists in this part of Burgundy, having converted in 1986. The vineyards cover nearly seven hectares and stretch south from Beaune to Puligny Montrachet.

- Bourgogne Aligoté AC: dry white, nervy, representative example of this variety. ♦
- Beaune Rouge AC: dry red, sourced from a *lieu-dit* called Les Bons Feuvres, shows a core of Beaunish black plum fruit. ♦♦
- St Romain Blanc AC: dry white, from Guyot's home patch so it is assured and not overpriced, suitable for vegans. ♦♦
- St Romain Rouge AC: dry red; illustrates the contrast between the Beaune (grown on open landscape) and St Romain, where the sharper terrain makes for a more prickly wine, suitable for vegans. ♦♦
- Puligny Montrachet AC: dry white, steely when young but appealing with it, a good sign for Puligny, suitable for vegetarians. ♦♦

Jean Javillier

6 rue Charles Giraud, 21190 Meursault
Tel:+33 380 21 24 61
Fax:+33 380 21 24 61
Stockists: contact Vintage Roots or Organic Wine Company
Overall Price Rating: ♦

Burgundy throws up family rivalries in abundance and the Javillier domaine is no exception. Jean Javillier produces a reliable range of wines from his certified organic vines in Meursault, while his cousin Patrick does pretty much the opposite from a non-organic standpoint just a couple of doors away.

- Bourgogne Blanc AC: dry white; a good entry level white Burgundy.
- Meursault AC: dry white, buttery Meursault suitable for vegetarians (Organic Wine Company).
- Volnay Santenots Premier Cru AC: dry red, auburn colour, firm tasting style typical of this Premier Cru; have to look hard to find the soft fruit associated with the Côte de Beaune but it is there.

Dominique and Catherine Derain

L'Ancienne Cure, 21190 St Aubin
Tel:+33 380 21 35 49
Fax:+33 380 21 94 31
Overall Price Rating: 🍷

St Aubin is one of those Burgundy villages capable of throwing up a real 'find' in the odd year or two, and this Demeter-certified biodynamic domaine is a good place to start. It consists of five hectares, mostly low lying around St Aubin, and thus entitled to the Bourgogne AC. A small amount of St Aubin Premier Cru is made.

Côte Châlonnaise

The golden slope of the Côte d'Or becomes less pronounced once south of St Aubin, and is called the Côte Châlonnaise. This, comparatively, is more marginal ground for wine growing (the vines are later ripening, and there is more risk of frost), and this can be reflected by hardness in the wines. This is the kind of area where organic growers should gain that extra half degree of ripeness in their grapes come picking.

Domaine Musso

Dracy, 71490 Couches
Tel:+33 385 58 97 62
Fax:+33 385 58 97 62
Overall Price Rating: 🍷

This domaine has been certified organic since 1979, and is located at the heart of the Couchois, a developing area in the south west of the Côte de Beaune. The wines are picked by hand, and are suitable for vegans. White wines are hard and include Bourgogne Aligoté AC and Bourgogne Côte

Châlonnaise. Red wines are light and include Bourgogne Passetoutgrain AC, Bourgogne Pinot Noir AC, Bourgogne Hautes Côtes de Beaune AC and Santenay AC. The best wine made here is the sparkling white Crémant de Bourgogne AC.

Domaine d'Heilly Huberdeau

1254 Cercot, 71390 Moroges
Tel:+33 385 47 95 27
Fax:+33 385 47 98 97
Stockist: Vintage Roots

This certified organic domaine lies in the middle of the Côte Châlonnaise and belongs to Martine Huberdeau and Pierre d'Heilly. The wines are made in a clean modern style, but retain their earthiness and charm. Manuring here is from a local source.

- Crémant de Bourgogne AC: dry white sparkling wine made by the traditional method from white grapes (Aligoté and Chardonnay) and red grapes (Pinot Noir); slightly bready smell, suitable for vegans. ♙♙♙
- Bourgogne Aligoté AC: dry white, full, balanced, creamy example, enriched by being left on its fine lees in barrel after fermentation. ♙♙
- Bourgogne Rouge AC: dry red, shows an invigorating style of Pinot Noir, direct, suitable for vegetarians. ♙♙♙
- Bourgogne Passetoutgrain AC: dry red, blend of Pinot Noir (70 per cent) and Gamay (30 per cent); mouthfilling and suitable for vegetarians; serve chilled. ♙
- Côte Châlonnaise Rouge AC: dry red, a step up from the basic Bourgogne Rouge; cherry fruit indicative of Pinot Noir on limestone (white soil + dark Pinot grape skins = dapple coloured cherry blossom which fruits in wine as you swirl it). ♙♙

Guy Chaumont

Le Montroy, 71390 Rosey
Tel:+33 385 47 94 70
Fax:+33 385 47 97 24
Stockist: Chartrand Imports (USA)

Guy Chaumont took over the family vineyards from his father Henri in 1976. There are 5.5 hectares, certified organic since 1965 – the year Chaumont père first took over the vines. Wines made are: Crémant de Bourgogne AC in both white and pink forms (🍾); Bourgogne Aligoté AC (🍾); Bourgogne Passetoutgrain AC (🍾); and Bourgogne Côte Châlonnaise Rouge AC (🍾). He also has vines in the commune of Givry for both red and white wines (🍾).

The Mâconnais

Mâcon forms the southern end of Burgundy and is famed for dry white wines made from Chardonnay. The contrast in richness between the white wines of Mâcon and those of Chablis at the northern end of Burgundy is striking. There are three very strong producers here, all worth visiting (and buying from) direct.

GAEC du Domaine Guillot-Broux
Sagy le Bas, 71260 Cruzillé
Tel:+33 385 33 21 89/+33 385 33 29 74
Fax:+33 385 33 01 94
Stockist: Wine Society
Overall Price Rating: 🍾

This large (16 hectare) domaine shows how successful organic wine growing can be if you get the basics right. The vines are planted at high density (9,500 vines per hectare, 2,000 more than the Mâcon norm) to encourage competition between the roots. This makes for stronger vines and stronger wines (each vine yields proportionately fewer grapes). One red wine is made from Pinot Noir (labelled as Mâcon Cruzillé Rouge AC, Beaumont). The mainstays here are the dry white wines, though. Each picked lot of Chardonnay grapes is pressed separately, and the juice fermented in the barrel with no yeast addition. Each juice lot is kept separate so that each can ferment apart. Most winemakers put all the juice in one tank to settle overnight, and then rack the clear juice into barrel, but this method means each barrel contains the same juice, and makes for a blander fermentation. Here each barrel is different so each can ferment at its own pace. It is more work but makes for a much more complex blend once the contents of the barrels are assembled.

Note also that the juice is put direct into cask without first being allowed to settle clear overnight as is usual. A few cloudy solids help regulate the fermentation in the barrel and allow the wine to retain all of its natural texture. As a result it tastes richer and ages better in bottle. The style of wine made here reflects the chalkiness of the soils the vines grow on. A lot of organic growers bang on about the importance of the soil. Here is a domaine expressing the importance of the soil through its wine. The white wines are sold under the following designations:

- Mâcon Chardonnay AC, Les Combettes.
- Mâcon Cruzillé AC.
- Mâcon Cruzillé AC, Les Perrières.
- Mâcon Cruzillé AC, La Croix.
- Mâcon Grévilly AC, Les Genevrières.

Alain Guillot
Sagy le Bas, 71260 Cruzillé
Tel:+33 385 33 23 51
Fax:+33 385 33 01 91
Overall Price Rating: 👜

Alain Guillot is the brother of Jean-Gérard Guillot of Domaine Guillot-Broux, above. His vines have been certified organic since 1954. Yields in the vineyard are checked by grassing over between the rows. This forces the vine roots deeper in search of moisture. The wines are traditionally made, using a wooden press and wooden vats, and are similar to those made above but more earthy.

Domaine Guillemot-Michel
SCEA de Quintaine, Quintaine, 71260 Clessé
Tel:+33 385 36 95 88
Fax:+33 385 36 91 50
Stockist: Haynes, Hanson & Clark

This Demeter-certified biodynamic Mâcon domaine belongs to Marc Guillemot and Pierrette Michel. The wines ferment with natural yeast, mainly but not entirely in cask (in contrast to Domaine Guillot-Broux, above). The style is rich, forceful Mâcon with the emphasis on fruit rather than mineral.

- Mâcon Clessé Quintaine: dry white, ripe style of mineral-rich Chardonnay. ♨
- Mâcon Clessé Quintaine, Sélection de Grains Nobles: sweet late picked white, made from berries dried by the autumn wind and then shrivelled further by 'noble rot'; made in 1990, 1992 (50 cl bottles) and 1996; combines exotic, apricot sweetness with a fresh aftertaste, makes the sweetness more appealing. ♨

Beaujolais

Beaujolais, the sickly red picnic wine, commands little respect these days but is still made from a unique red grape in a unique way. The grape is the Gamay Noir à Jus Blanc. The unique winemaking method involves putting a majority of the grape bunches into the vat uncrushed. The fermentation begins inside the berries as the yeast gets to work fermenting the pulp. The skins do break but only gradually (1–4 days), meaning the contents of the vat become a slush only over time, rather than from the start as in Bordeaux (or in the Douro for Port). The technique is called carbonic maceration, and it is used here because this is the way the local grape – Gamay – produces rich wines which are simple to drink and great to look at. The best Beaujolais villages like Morgon and Regnié have their own appellations or 'crus'.

Gérard and Christine Belaïd
Les Farjuts, 69430 Marchampt
Tel:+33 474 69 00 56
Stockist: Vintage Roots
Overall Price Rating: ♦

This organic team make their Beaujolais and Beaujolais Villages in a firm style. The Belaïds also make a Morgon. The soils in this Beaujolais cru are rich in manganese, which is said to give the wines a distinct aroma, akin to old Burgundy. All the wines are suitable for vegans.

Château de Boisfranc

69640 Jarnioux
Tel:+33 474 68 20 91
Fax:+33 474 65 10 03
Stockist: Vinceremos
Overall Price Rating: ▲

This domaine belongs to Thierry Doat and has been certified organic since 1982. Both the Gamay Noir à Jus Blanc (11.3 hectares) and the Chardonnay (0.7 hectares) varieties are planted, for dry red and white wines respectively. All the wines are suitable for vegans.

- Château de Boisfranc, Beaujolais Supérieur Blanc AC: dry white made from Chardonnay. Crisp enough to dilute with some blackcurrant juice or fizzy water (or both) for a summer 'spritzer'.
- Château de Boisfranc, Beaujolais Supérieur Rosé AC: dry pink made from Gamay Noir à Jus Blanc; fades quickly, so catch it young.
- Château de Boisfranc, Beaujolais Supérieur Rouge AC: dry red made from Gamay Noir à Jus Blanc, which exibits crisp green rather than red fruit. Also released as a 'Beaujolais Nouveau' or *primeur* style on the third Thursday in November. It provides fruity drinking until into the New Year, so don't listen to your friends who'll think you're mad to hang onto it that long (cover the label up and give them a glass on Christmas Day – they'll never know).

Christian Ducroux

Thulon, 69430 Lantignié
Tel:+33 474 69 20 47
Fax:+33 474 69 28 88
Stockist: Vintage Roots
Overall Price Rating: ▲

Christian Ducroux owns just over five hectares of vines in Regnié, the youngest of Beaujolais' crus. This producer was recommended to me by

Michel Favard of Château Meylet in St Emilion in Bordeaux, and the style of red wine is the same as his: purity of fruit, comfortable to smell and taste, refreshing effect.

- Regnié AC: dry red, smells of bilberries rather than bubblegum like its conventionally made peers, weighty fruit, long aftertaste, suitable for vegans.

Champagne

The Champagne region produces the world's most famous sparkling wine. As Champagne is the most northerly winegrowing region in France, its climate is only just warm enough for the grapes to ripen come September and the harvest. The Champagne producers (the 'Champenois') have turned this marginal climate to their advantage however, because they know it gives grapes which are ripe but crisp tasting (the crispness comes from high levels of fruit acids, due to the northerly latitude). When the grapes are crushed and the juice fermented into a still base wine, this acidity would be unbearable for most people's palates. However, once these still base wines are made to re-ferment in bottle, as all Champagnes have to do by law (see 'Making Champagne – the "Traditional Method"' below), the wine produced has a soft taste and the finest bubbles or 'mousse'.

A famous monk called Dom Pérignon is said to have discovered this secret in the 17th century, but in all probability the way Champagne is made was discovered by accident. As the still base wines warmed up again in April, when spring came, they began to re-ferment naturally. Leaving them in bottle – with a strong cork of course – allowed the magic sparkle to be captured. When wine buffs talk of a Champagne 'with a fine mousse' they are referring to the sparkle. The best Champagne should have a 'persistent' mousse, rather than be 'frothy' as if the wine had been made fizzy with a bicycle pump.

Champagnes bearing organic and biodynamic certification stamps originate from smaller growers rather than from the household name Champagne houses. These big Champagne houses buy up grapes from smaller growers to make the base wines needed to furnish their bulk brands. These brands are advertised as exclusive products but privately the houses boast that 'a bottle of our Champagne is opened somewhere in the world every 12 seconds'. And one of the reasons why Champagne is so expensive is the advertising!

Champagne does not lend itself easily to organic farming. The climate is only just warm enough for the three grape varieties authorized here to ripen. The vines have to be planted low to the ground to keep warm. This augments costs because low-trained vines take longer to be pruned in winter and tucked in during summer. The costs are even higher for an organic Champagne grower who makes extra visits to the vines – repositioning the shoots, for example – to avoid having to spray.

MAKING CHAMPAGNE – THE 'TRADITIONAL METHOD'

Champagne is a sparkling wine made by the 'traditional method'. The 'traditional method' refers to a secondary fermentation that occurs in the bottle the wine is sold in. It is this secondary, in-bottle fermentation that provides Champagne and all other traditional method wines with their sparkle or 'fizz'. All the wines listed in this book described as 'sparkling wine made by the traditional method' follow this process. All the French wines in this book described as 'Crémant' use this method, as do Spanish wines described as 'Cava'.

The Traditional or Champagne Method is as follows:

1   The grapes are picked. In Champagne this must be by hand (no machine harvesting is allowed), but in other areas of the world machines are often used.

2   The grapes are pressed, and the juice collected and settled clear. Dark-skinned varieties like Pinot Noir and Pinot Meunier in Champagne, or Cabernet Franc in Bordeaux, must be pressed carefully to avoid the pick-up of colour and tannin from the skins if the sparkling wine is to be white.

3   The juice is fermented for 3–10 days to leave a dry, raw and slightly cloudy white wine containing 10–12 per cent alcohol by volume. The potential alcohol level of the juice may be boosted with sugar (this procedure is called 'chaptalization').

4   The fermented wines are left in tank for three to four months after harvest. During this time the wine settles clear but remains nonfizzy. The different tanks are assembled into house blends (*les cuvées*). For example a 'Blanc de Blancs' would be blended only from white grapes, i.e., Chardonnay only in Champagne, or Riesling and Chardonnay in Alsace. In Bordeaux the blend will probably

involve black and white grapes. The key is to give the base wine as much complexity before it goes into bottle as possible – once bottled the rules for the traditional method say that this is the bottle the wine must be sold in.

5   The dry base-wine blends are bottled. The bottles are sealed with temporary stoppers – these will be removed and replaced with the real cork before bottling. Before the bottles are sealed with the temporary stoppers, a liquid mixture containing sugar, yeast and wine is added (*liqueur de tirage*). This provokes the secondary in-bottle fermentation that gives all traditional method sparkling wines like Champagne their sparkle.

6   The secondary, in-bottle alcoholic fermentation occurs as the yeast reacts with the sugar added in the *liqueur de tirage*. This fermentation does two things: it adds another degree of alcohol to the wine and produces carbon dioxide gas, which gives the wine its sparkle. The secondary fermentation takes between three weeks and three months, depending on how cold the cellars are where the bottles are stored. The longer the fermentation, the finer the 'mousse' of the wine.

7   Once this second alcoholic fermentation ends the wine is cloudy and fizzy – even if the bubbles cannot be seen (you need to open the bottle first to get air into it, like a fizzy drink). The cloudiness is caused by the presence of the fermentation yeasts still in the bottle. They add flavour to the wine when they decompose in it. The longer the yeasts remain as sediment in the wine, the more toasty, oaty, biscuit flavours they give it. This sediment has to be removed by disgorging.

8   To disgorge the sediment it must first be positioned in the neck of the bottle. This is done by placing the bottle in an upside down position (usually by putting it in a special rack or cage) and shaking or 'riddling' it gently every day. When the sediment is positioned in the neck of bottle, the neck is frozen in brine. The bottle is turned upright and its temporary seal – usually a crown cap – removed. The sediment is forced out of the bottle by the pressure of the bubbles within the bottle.

9   Removing the sediment causes the level of sparkling wine in the bottle to fall. This is made up with a bottling liqueur or 'dosage'. This usually contains wine, sugar and preservative (sulphur dioxide).

10   The bottle is sealed with a permanent cork. This bottle is the same
      one that the 'blend' was put into originally. Hence the term 'made
      sparkling in the same bottle the wine was sold in' is used for this
      style by producers in the New World.

Note that with Champagne the final cork must be natural rather than
plastic and it must bear the Champagne name and be positioned so it
touches the surface of the wine, i.e., the bit that touches the table when
you stand a pulled cork up on it. Champagne is the only French wine
region to forbid bulk wine from other wine regions to be trucked in for
bottling, so the cork stamp does mean something. The downside of this is
that the Champenois then stick everything they produce into bottles under
the Champagne label, and not all of it is good or even average in quality.

LABELLING

One thing to note from the above is that Champagne can have sugar
added on three separate occasions:

- to the juice to boost the potential alcohol (step 3)
- to the wine once fermented to make it sparkle (step 5)
- to make the sparkling wine palatable (step 7).

The level of sugar added in (step 7) will affect the sweetness of the wine
when sold because this sugar does not referment – so it is important to
know your labels. The level of sweetness is given in grammes per litre (g/l).

- Extra Brut: the driest style of Champagne (*see Yves Ruffin et Fils,
  page 81*) which must not exceed 6 g/l residual sugar and may incorpo-
  rate no bottling liqueur or 'dosage' (see step 9 above)
- Brut: the most common style of Champagne. Note that '*brut*' means
  crude or raw in French, hence the only moderate level of dosage: Brut
  Champagne must contain no more than 15 g/l
- Extra Sec: a confusing term which means 'off-dry' rather than 'extra
  dry'. It contains between 12 and 20 g/l
- Sec: another confusing term meaning 'medium dry' rather than 'dry';
  containing between 17 and 35 g/l
- Demi-Sec: medium sweet; contains between 35 and 50 g/l

● Doux: sweet; contains more than 50 g/l.

Without this sugar, and the bubbles, Champagne would be just another green, dry white wine from the north of France.

CHAMPAGNE STYLE CHECK

● Non-vintage – wine made from a blend of grapes grown in several years; the youngest wine in the blend must be 18 months old at least when the wine is sold (*see Régis Poirrier, below*). When bottled too young, Champagne tastes 'green', and this is a major shortcoming of supermarket brands. The cheapest juice plus the shortest ageing time equals a runt of a wine.
● Vintage – wine made from the grapes of a single year or vintage; the youngest wine in the blend must be 36 months old at least when the wine is sold.
● Blanc de Blancs – white Champagne made from white grapes only, i.e., Chardonnay.
● Blanc de Noirs – white Champagne made from red grapes only, i.e., Pinot Noir or Pinot Meunier. Tends to be full-bodied (*see Champagne Fleury below*).

CHAMPAGNE STATUS CHECK

The price of your Champagne is dependent mostly on the amount of money spent on marketing it. The minority of what you pay goes on the cost of the grapes. Their price is determined in the region by the status of the village the grapes were grown in:

● Grand Cru – made from grapes grown in Premier Cru villages rated 100 per cent by the Champagne authorities; such as Ambonnay.
● Premier Cru – made from grapes grown in Premier Cru villages rated 90 to 99 per cent by the Champagne authorities; such as Cumières.
● Champagne AC – made from grapes grown in villages rated at the bottom: 80 to 90 per cent.

From looking at the vines whilst visiting the region during the harvest in 1995, I noted high yields on the 80 per cent vineyards, due to fertile sites, and high yields on the 100 per cent villages, because producers were looking to sell the maximum amount of grapes they are allowed by the authorities each year. It is a form of economic balance, and everyone makes lots of money from it. This money has to be spent – and the Champenois spend a good deal on tractors and trailers and tankers for moving the grapes, base wines and bottled Champagnes around. Those who move the grapes and wine around least are the grower-winemakers or *récoltants-manipulants* ('RM' on the bottle label). All of the growers below are RMs except for Jean-Pierre Fleury. He buys grapes and so is a merchant-winemaker or *négoçiant-manipulant* ('NM'). He just does this on a smaller scale (and using much better grapes) than the big Champagne houses.

André and Jacques Beaufort

1 rue de Vaudemanges, 51150 Ambonnay
Tel:+33 326 57 01 50
Fax:+33 326 52 83 50
Stockist: Organic Wine Company

The brothers Beaufort have put their vineyards back into the conversion process for organic status, having decided to drop out of the fully certified programme for a number of years. Their vineyard comprises two main plots in the separate villages of Ambonnay – which is classified as a Grand Cru or 100 per cent rated village – and the more minor Polisy. The winery is one of the more rudimentary in Champagne, consisting of a couple of outbuildings. However the wines are far from unprepossessing. They include:

- Ambonnay Rouge: still red wine made from Pinot Noir; a curiosity but a good one. 🍷🍷
- Brut NV: non-vintage, dry white Champagne, with fruit very much in evidence. 🍷
- Demi-Sec NV: non-vintage, off-dry white Champagne, lighter style than the above. 🍷
- Brut Millesimé: vintage dry white Champagne, serious and weighty. 🍷🍷

Jean Bliard

41 rue de Buttes, Hautvilliers

Tel:+33 326.59.40.38

Stockist: Organic Wine Company

Jean Bliard's domaine is next door but one to the Abbey at Hautvilliers where Dom Pérignon lived and is buried. Bliard's vineyard has remained the same size since it was first certified organic in 1970. This contrasts with the Champagne region in general which has exploded in size since then (from around 13,000 hectares in 1970 to 35,000 today). Many of the new vineyards were planted with over-productive clones, especially of Pinot Noir. These are due to be grubbed up and replaced after the Millennium sales boom has subsided.

Bliard's range includes:

- Brut NV, 'Cuvée des Trois Cépages': non-vintage dry white Champagne, made from a blend of the three Champagne varieties – Chardonnay, Pinot Noir and Pinot Meunier – hence the name; solid style, with twist in the taste at the finish, it needs food and patience. A slightly less complex example of this wine is sometimes called 'Cuvée de la Marne'. ◖◗

- Brut NV, Blanc de Blancs AC: non vintage dry white Champagne made from white grapes alone, i.e., Chardonnay here in Champagne; light, elegant, more approachable than the Blanc de Blancs made below by Fleury. ◖

Champagne Faust and Champagne Ardinat

rue de la Galichetterie, 51700 Vandières

Tel:+33 326 58 36 07

Stockists: Organic Wine Company; Vintage Roots; Chartrand Imports (USA) (Faust); Vinceremos (Ardinat)

Overall Price Rating: ◖

This family domaine has been certified organic since 1971. José Ardinat has succeeded his father-in-law Serge Faust, but the family tradition of ageing the base wines in wooden vats remains. Such ageing softens the wines before they are bottled ready for the secondary fermentation from which they get their sparkle. The extra softness from the wood makes them drinkable earlier once they are sold. It also helps impurities in the wines to settle better, which minimizes the need for fining treatments. (However, the wooden vats are not used to give the wines an oaky taste.)

The wines are sold under two lables: Champagne Ardinat and Champagne Faust – reflecting the joint ownership of the domaine.

- Brut NV, 'Carte d'Or': non-vintage dry white Champagne, smells of pastry, with apple filling; suitable for vegans.
- Brut Rosé NV, 'Carte d'Or': non-vintage dry pink Champagne; Pinot Meunier provides the body, Pinot Noir the backbone; suitable for vegans.

Fleury Père et Fils

43 Grande Rue, 10250 Courteron
Tel:+33 325 38 20 28/+33 325 38 23 54
Fax:+33 325 38 24 65
Stockists: Booths; Vintage Roots

Jean-Pierre Fleury is the only source of Champagne made from certified biodynamic grapes. Half the grapes used here are from Fleury's own 12.95 hectares of vineyard, and the rest are purchased from two other Demeter-certified biodynamic growers. All the grapes are grown in the Aube sub-region south west of the main Champagne growing towns of Epernay and Reims. The Pinot Noir grape variety ripens early here due to the Aube's relatively warm summers and its limestone soil, which is of a different type to that of Epernay and Reims. The ripeness Pinot Noir achieves at Fleury's produces powerful sparkling wines with forceful, strong flavours. Some of them achieve over 13.5 per cent alcohol, whereas most Champagne is nearer 12.5 per cent.

- Brut NV, 'Carte Rouge': non-vintage dry white Champagne made from 100 per cent Pinot Noir; savoury fruit, woven into the bubbles (*la mousse*) rather than around it, which gives the wine a lift; it needs lots of time in the glass to open fully; resist over chilling. 👭
- Demi-Sec NV, 'Carte Rouge': as above except off-dry. 👭

- Brut NV, 'Fleur de l'Europe': non-vintage dry white Champagne, 100 per cent Pinot Noir; a touch more refined than 'Carte Rouge' but still with a thick, malt-like texture. ♙♙
- Rosé Brut NV 'de Saignée': non-vintage, dry pink Champagne, made from 100 per cent Pinot Noir using the 'de saignée' method. This means the colour comes from careful pressing of clear juice from dark-skinned grapes rather than from simply adding a little red wine to a white Champagne (which is allowed in Champagne – the only French pink wine allowed to be made in this way). ♙
- Brut Millésimé: vintage dry white Champagne, made from 100 per cent Pinot Noir (so it could be called 'Blanc de Noirs'); serious in the great year of 1990, classic in 1993 when the Aube pipped the rest of Champagne. ♙♙
- Blanc de Blancs Millésimé: vintage dry white Champagne made from white grapes alone, i.e., Chardonnay; the non-biodynamic but now mature 1982 (labelled 'Collection Fleury') is a definitive example of Aube Chardonnay. ♙♙

(The Aube is viewed with disdain by the 20 top Champagne houses (*les grandes marques*) who are based near the smart cafés of Reims and Epernay. Yet the grandes marques houses still send trailers and tankers down to the Aube to pinch grapes and wine each year when their own blends need beefing up!)

Champagne Fransoret
Hameau Alancourt, Mancy
Tel:+33 326 59 71 57
Overall Price Rating: ♙

Roger Fransoret decided to become certified organic because he and his father were affected by chemical spray drift from a neighbouring vineyard (see also Eugène Meyer in Alsace (*page 4*) and Bill Powers of Badger Mountain Vineyard, Washington State (*page 347*) amongst others). Fransoret is a hard man to wrest from his organic lunch, which he takes with him as he disappears into his gently sloping vineyard for the day. Fransoret is most noted for:

- Champagne Rosé Brut NV: non-vintage dry pink Champagne, made in a very approachable, soft sherbet style.

Champagne Georges Laval
ruelle de Carrefour, 51480 Cumières
Tel:+33 326 51 73 66
Fax:+33 326 57 80 87
Stockist: Vintage Roots
Overall Price Rating: 🍾🍾

Georges Laval owns a small Chardonnay, Pinot Meunier and Pinot Noir vineyard in Cumières. This commune has Premier Cru status (it rates 93 per cent) and has a core of unofficial organic producers promoting more sustainable methods. These include using natural predators against red spider and grape moth hazards, or using wooden presses and vats as opposed to stainless steel ones. Laval's wines are suitable for vegans. They include:

- Brut NV, Premier Cru, 'Réserve Spéciale': non-vintage, dry white premier cru Champagne; floral and light, elegant, worth finding.

Régis Poirrier
1 rue d'Eglise, 51480 Venteuil
Tel:+33 326 58 49 61
Overall Price Rating: 🍾

Régis Poirrier first gained organic certification for his vines in 1969. He dropped out of the organic programme for a while, after a disagreement with the Champagne authorities rather than the organic certification bodies. It appears that this disagreement concerned the minimum length of time Champagne ready for sale (i.e., bottled with its permanent cork) must age prior to sale (currently this is set at 18 months).

Poirrier's vines are once again certified organic. He is one of a small band of Champenois to have plantings of Petit Meslier. This golden skinned grape variety is being replaced by Chardonnay which produces higher yields. Poirrier's Champagnes include:

- Champagne Rosé Millésimé: pink vintage Champagne which, when made from the three main Champagne varieties, is the style of Champagne which best epitomizes the Champagne region: colour, history, sparkle.

Champagne Yves Ruffin et Fils

6 bld Jules Ferry, 51160 Avenay Val d'Or
Tel:+33 326 52 32 49
Fax:+33 326 52 34 40
Overall Price Rating: 👛👛

This domaine comprises nearly three hectares. The vines have been certified organic since 1971. The Ruffin style is for powerful wine that becomes succulent with age.

- Extra Brut NV: non-vintage, bone dry white Champagne; thick colour and fruit, full-bodied, forceful, the antithesis in style of the over-sugared mainstream brands.
- Brut NV: non-vintage dry white Champagne; biscuity, medium bodied, classic flavour rendered in a simple way.
- Demi-Sec NV: non-vintage medium dry white Champagne with butterscotch fruit; what the French might drink before Sunday lunch.

Cognac

The Cognac region lies south of the Loire river and north of the Bordeaux region in western France. Although world famous for its brandy, Cognac has suffered recently after a bout of overproduction. This was caused by declining demand in traditional markets – such as the Far East – as brandy drinkers there switched from spirits to wine. Cognac is made by taking a base wine and distilling it – separating and concentrating the alcohol present in the wine from the water (wine is 80 per cent water) to make the spirit. European rules do not allow any wine – even base wines for spirits like Cognac – to be called 'organic wine', and because of this there are no organic grape-based spirits in the EU. (For a grain-based one, see Dà Mhìle Millennium Malt whisky, *page 282*.)

Even though organic vineyards in Cognac cannot produce 'organic Cognac', they can still use their grapes to produce 'wine made from organically grown grapes', like their neighbours in the Loire or Bordeaux. The wines are dry, and either red, white or pink. They carry the country wine designation of Vin de Pays Charentais because the Cognac region lies in the departments of the Charentes and Charentes-Maritime. In addition, a style of wine known as Pineau des Charentes is made. This is a sweet aperitif made when unfermented (thus still sweet) grape juice is fortified with the local brandy or Cognac. The mix – known as a *mistelle* or *mistella* – is aged in old American oak casks in long warehouses, just like those used for Cognac. The proportion of three parts grape juice to one part brandy leaves the Pineau des Charentes with a final content of 17–18 per cent alcohol. The alcoholic effect of these wines can be limited by drinking them as the locals do – with lots of fresh melon. (The same style of wine was drunk by Roman lawyers before signing important papers and was known as 'ratafia' – see Domaine de la Grande Grange, *page 161*, for another example.)

The spirit used in Pineau des Charentes must be at least one-year-old cognac rather than a neutral grape spirit. As a result the wines are known under French law as *Vins de liqueur* rather than *Vins doux naturels*, like Muscat de Rivesaltes in the Midi/Roussillon (*page 131*).

The producers listed below own or have access to certified organic vineyards. Even though they are not allowed to call their Cognacs 'organic', these spirits are listed as well as their light wines (Vins de Pays Charentais) and their *mistelles* (Pineau des Charentes). The grape juices made here are some of the best in France.

Jacques & Dany Brard Blanchard

Boutiers, 16100 Cognac
Tel:+33 545 32 19 58
Fax:+33 545 36 53 21

Jacques and Dany Brard Blanchard own 16 hectares of vineyards in the heart of the Cognac region, which have been certified organic since 1972. Their grapes are hand picked. The full range is:

- Jus de Raisin: grape juice bottled during harvest without additives. ▮
- Vin de Pays Charentais Blanc: dry white, fairly neutral, but softer than Muscadet made not far to the north. ▮▮
- Vin de Pays Charentais Rouge: dry red, best drunk within 18 months of the vintage. ▮▮
- Cuvée de la Boissière Brut: dry white sparkling wine made by the traditional method, with an appealing smell of celery. ▮▮
- Pineau des Charentes Blanc: white *vin de liqueur* made from Ugni Blanc grape juice mixed with Cognac; shows marzipan style sweetness and clean fruit (Vintage Roots and Organic Wine Company, ▮▮).
- Pineau des Charentes Rosé: pink *vin de liqueur* made from Merlot grape juice, although any of the red Bordeaux varieties may be used here, and shows a typically deep colour; a crowd pleaser with sherbet and liquorice (Organic Wine Company, ▮▮).
- Cognac: complex brandies worth tracking down; available in three styles, youngest to oldest:

  a *** (Organic Wine Company, ▮▮▮)
  b VSOP, Grande Champagne (Organic Wine Company, ▮▮▮)
  c Napoleon (Vintage Roots, ▮▮).

Guy & Georges Pinard

Foussignac, 16200 Jarnac
Tel:+33 545 35 87 57

This certified organic domaine offers an interesting philosophy on wine-making. Some producers swear the juice from the first pressing is the best for Pineau des Charentes, and other producers swear by the juice from the end of the pressing. This vineyard mixes both:

- Jus de Raisin: grape juice bottled during harvest without additives. 🍷
- Vin Blanc Champagnisé: dry white sparkling wine made by the traditional method, from first pressing juice only; still rich, not for keeping. 🍷🍷
- Pineau des Charentes Blanc: white *vin de liqueur*, warm and earthy, mid-range style. 🍷🍷
- Pineau des Charentes Rosé: pink *vin de liqueur*, icing sugar sweetness.
- Cognac-Foussignac: brandy available in three styles, youngest to oldest:

  a   *** (Vintage Roots, 🍷🍷)
  b   VSOP (Vintage Roots, Organic Wine Company, 🍷🍷🍷)
  c   Napoleon, distinctive, heady (Vintage Roots, Organic Wine Company, 🍷🍷).

Roland Seguin

Le Pouzac, Villars les Bois, 17700 Brizambourg
Tel:+33 546 94 94 46
Fax:+33 546 94 53 30

The vines here have been certified organic since 1988 and produce simple but effective wines. Monsieur Seguin's star item is his Crème de Cassis au Cognac:

- Crème de Cassis au Cognac: made from crushed, organic blackcurrant berries (20 per cent) soaked in Cognac (42 per cent) to which organic cane sugar (38 per cent) has been added. Refrigerate once opened and consume rapidly. 🍷🍷🍷
- Vin de Pays Charentais Blanc, le Vieux Souchot: dry white blend of Colombard and Ugni Blanc, good value. 🍷🍷

- Vin de Pays Charentais Rosé, le Vieux Souchot: dry pink, Cabernet Franc and Cabernet Sauvignon-based, drink within two years. ♙
- Vin de Pays Charentais Rouge, le Vieux Souchot: dry red made from Merlot and Cabernet, appealing with bramble fruit and crumbly texture. ♙
- Vin de Pays Charentais, Merlot, le Vieux Souchot: dry red, made with the magic Merlot grape that gives high yields and high sugars here. ♙♙
- Pineau des Charentes Blanc AC: white *vin de liqueur*, made from Colombard and Ugni Blanc; a little confected, needs strong blue cheese to go with it. ♙♙♙
- Pineau des Charentes Rosé AC: pink *vin de liqueur*; less refined than Brard Blanchard's above. ♙♙♙
- Cognac: brandy available in two styles, youngest to oldest:

a   *** ♙
b   VSOP ♙♙.

Jura and Franche-Comté

The Jura is the most important vineyard region of the historic region of Franche-Comté in the extreme east of France, between Burgundy and Switzerland. The Jura vineyards occupy the steep ground of the foothills of the Jura mountain range, which rise eventually into the Alps. As a result the climate is more Alpine than in Burgundy to the west. This poses problems for Jura winegrowers, as late spring frosts cling hard to the ground here. To prevent the crop from being lost each year, the Jura growers must train their vines high off the ground to keep the delicate buds from freezing. However, the cool climate affords slow ripening of the grapes in autumn, some years into early November and even December. Grape varieties with special qualities are needed to hang on the vine this long (see below), and they produce unique wines which are austere and faintly smokey. If it is true that most wines go with food, then Jura wines positively need some kind of accompanying dish to offset this austerity.

The certified organic vineyards here represent about 0.1 per cent of the current Jura total of 1,340 hectares.

JURA STYLE CHECK

Jura wines are consumed locally with the local speciality – coq au vin – a Bresse chicken cooked in the local wines. The wines come in a range of styles:

- Sparkling wines: can be either white or pink and are made by the traditional method (*methode traditionelle, see page 72*). Can be dry (brut) or off-dry (demi-sec).
- White wines: bone dry, and made increasingly from Chardonnay and Pinot Blanc.
- Pink wines: these are bone dry, age well and result when the pale red Poulsard grape is left to ferment on the skins for a couple of days.

- Red wine: still red Jura wines are crisp and dark pink rather than fully red. They contain Poulsard, Trousseau and Pinot Noir. Open the better examples a half day before serving.
- Vin de Paille: 'straw wine', a sweet, white or dried grape wine, made from grapes left to dry inside on straw mats after harvest to concentrate the sugar.
- Vin Jaune, dry white or 'yellow wine' made from the local, yellow skinned Savagnin grape and left to age in barrel for over six years. The barrels are never topped up in order to allow a head-space to form under evaporation. A scum (*voile*) of naturally occurring yeast forms on the exposed surface of the wine (as in real Sherry). By the second winter after picking the film has become a crust preventing the wine turning to vinegar (by oxidation). However, part of the alcohol in the wine does oxidize into ethyl alcohol (acetaldehyde, i.e., the constituent of mothballs), producing a yellow or deep golden-brown colour – hence 'yellow wine'. In bottle it has considerable ageing potential, if sealed with a good cork. The locals recommend pulling this a day before serving the wine.
- Macvin du Jura: a sweet fortified wine formerly known as 'maquevin' or 'marc-vin' but, in fact, a type of mistella (like Pineau des Charentes) because the fortifying spirit is added to grape juice rather than to the wine.
- Fine: brandy made from distilling wine, either red or white.

Clos des Grives
39570 Chillé
Tel:+33 384 47 23 78
Fax:+33 384 47 29 27
Overall Price Rating: ❙

Claude Charbonnier's Clos des Grives has been certified organic since 1968, longer than any other Jura vineyard. He produces sparkling white and pink wines, Chardonnay and Vin Jaune.

Pierre Overnoy

Rue du Ploussard, Pupillin, 39600 Arbois
Tel:+33 384 66 14 60
Fax:+33 384 66 14 60
Overall Price Rating: 🍷🍷

This domaine is owned by Pierre Overnoy and Emmanuel Houillon. They were awaiting organic certification from the 1998 vintage as this book went to press. The wines ferment with natural yeast and are bottled unfiltered. During ageing they receive little or no sulphur. As such they should be stored between 6–8°C in winter and 12–14°C in summer. Styles made include dry whites and Vin Jaune, while the Macvin du Jura is in the planning stage.

Christian and Colette Perrard

Au Biou, 10 L'Ethole, route de Villeneuve d'Arval, 39600 Arbois
Tel:+33 384 66 16 63
Overall Price Rating: 🍷🍷

This domaine has been certified organic since 1995. Styles made include white and pink sparkling wines in both dry and off-dry forms, Arbois Blanc, Arbois Rouge, fortified Macvin du Jura, Fine du Jura and grape juice (red and white).

Michel Terrier

GAEC Terrier, La Lieme, 39750 Pannessières
Tel:+33 384 47 23 93
Overall Price Rating: 🍷

Michel Terrier makes a single dry white wine (Côtes de Jura Blanc) from a small vineyard certified organic since 1969. He will retire when his current stock is exhausted, and is uncertain as to future of the property.

Gérard Villet

16, route de Pupillin, 39600 Arbois
Tel:+33 384 37 40 98
Fax:+33 384 37 40 98

Visits: open every day (except during school holidays when by appointment only)

Overall Price Rating: ♨

Gérard Villet is the cousin of Claude Charbonnier (*see Clos des Grives, above*). The vineyard comprises three hectares of Chardonnay, Poulsard and Savagnin and has been certified organic since 1994. The wines ferment in old wooden casks and enamel vats. Villet produces sparkling white and pink wines (both dry), Arbois Blanc, Arbois Rouge, Chardonnay, Vin de Paille (1985 vintage worth finding), Macvin du Jura and Fine du Jura.

Louis Pasteur

The town of Arbois is home to three of the four organic growers featured above. It is also the place where the great French scientist Louis Pasteur (1822–95) was brought up. Pasteur kept a small vineyard north of the town and used its wine for experiments. His research into the cause of wine, namely an alcoholic fermentation, has made him the equivalent of wine's Darwin. However it took another 100 years for man to discover that wine often undergoes two fermentation events. Knowledge of this secondary fermentation – the *malolactic* fermentation – has given man the power to control the stability of wine in bottle over longer periods.

Pasteur's attempts at rendering wine and other alcoholic beverages stable revolved around heating (hence the term 'pasteurization'). The beneficial effect of pasteurizing wine, as with milk, is to protect the wine from bacterial attack (necessary for cheap wines on bulk bottling lines). Winemakers who use pasteurization claim to require lower levels of the anti-bacterial preservative sulphur dioxide, which also acts as an antiseptic. Pasteurization can also be used to influence a wine's style, by giving a bulk cheap red wine more colour. The grapes are heated to 80°C, so that the red colour cells in the grape skins explode. However heating the grapes like this denatures them, and thus minimizes their nutritional benefit as wine (naturally occurring colour compounds in red wine have been linked to reductions in cancers). See also Chateau de Beaucastel in the Rhone for another view on pasteurization.

FRANCHE-COMTÉ

The vineyards in Franche-Comté lying outside the Jura have their own regional designation of 'country wines' (*vin de pays*). There is one organic producer of note using this designation.

EARL des Coteaux d'Hugier

70150 Hugier
Tel:+33 384 31 56 40
Fax:+33 384 31 56 40
Visits: Saturday mornings, otherwise by appointment; school groups welcome during summer
Overall Price Rating: ♙

This is an emerging certified organic domaine with a bright future. The owners, Serge and Laurence Ballot, planted four hectares of Chardonnay and Auxerrois for white wines, as well as Pinot Noir and Gamay for reds, in 1993. The vines are trained to a lyre system to double the amount of leaves each vine produces. As the number of grapes stays the same ripeness is increased, because more of the sun's energy is put to work by the vine. The trick is to ensure the extra leaves do not block the grapes from the sun, and this seems to be being achieved here.

- VdP Franche-Comté, Blanc: bone dry white, 1998 shows crisp appley taste, a refreshing and flavoursome blend of 65 per cent Chardonnay and 35 per cent Auxerrois. Shows what intensity and clarity of fruit is possible in such a marginal climate.
- VdP Franche-Comté, Rosé: bone dry pink made of Pinot Noir and Gamay; bodied, rapier freshness and medium full fruit, the antithesis of holiday pink wines from Provence.
- VdP Franche-Comté, Rouge: dry red made from Pinot Noir, moderate pale-ruby colour, lively aroma of winter fruits.

USEFUL ADDRESS
INTERBIO Franche-Comté
Chambre Régionale d'Agriculture
Valparc, Espace Valentin Est, 25048 Besançon
Tel:+33 381 54 71 71
Fax:+33 381 54 71 54

This organic association for Franche-Comté (covering the departments of the Doubs, Haut-Sâone, Jura and Territoire de Belfort) produces a guide *L'Agriculture Bio en Franche-Comté* – a list of producers and stockists of local organic products, including wines.

Loire

The Loire is France's longest river. It traverses the middle of the country, beginning in the mountainous centre of France and ending on the Atlantic coast in southern Brittany. On its journey it passes some of France's most famous Renaissance châteaux. These were built by France's 'absolute' monarchs from the end of the 15th century, as hunting lodges and as places to entertain. No regal banquet is complete without wine, so the châteaux were adorned with vineyards.

The Loire spans such a huge distance that it is impossible to make generalizations about the wine styles produced, suffice it to say the region's wines are characterized by their elegance rather than blockbuster power – making Loire the sort of wine you might drink while enjoying the sun in the garden of a French Renaissance château rather than one to keep you warm by the fire on a winter night. Loire wines, whether white or red, dry or sweet, still or sparkling, are mainly varietal wines – made from single grape varieties rather than blends.

The main white grape varieties are Chenin Blanc, a chameleon of a grape happy to make bone dry whites (Savennières), sweet whites (Vouvray moelleux) or sparklers (Crémant de Loire), and Sauvignon Blanc, which is usually made dry (Sancerre, Sauvignon de Touraine). The white Muscadet (or 'Melon de Bourgogne') grape is found only in Nantais for the famous wine of that name. Loire red wines are based on the Cabernet Franc variety (Saumur Champigny, Chinon, St Nicolas de Bourgueil). It ripens up to 10 days earlier than its famous relation the Cabernet Sauvignon of Bordeaux – a fact which makes it ideal in the Loire's more northerly climate. It provides wines of rich colour and fruit, most refreshing if served slightly below room temperature. The other Loire red grape is the Gamay Noir à Jus Blanc (the Beaujolais grape). As the Loire makes its way towards the Atlantic it traverses four vineyard sub-regions – Central Vineyards, Touraine, Anjou-Saumur and Nantais – each of which is dealt with separately below. A fifth sub-region, Fiéfs Vendéens, is immediately to the south of Nantais.

CENTRAL VINEYARDS

The Central Vineyards enjoy (or endure) the most extreme, continental climate of any of the Loire vineyards. Burgundy is less than 100 km to the east and spring frost is a perennial threat. (Note that 'central' here refers to the centre of France rather than to the centre of the Loire.)

Sancerre AC

Sancerre is one of France's classic dry white wines. It is made with Sauvignon Blanc and shows crisp, pungent peach and currant fruit. The rapid expansion of the Sancerre vineyards from 1,000 hectares in 1980 to double that 15 years later has not been matched by expertise in the cellar, so like buying a classic car it is always wise to look under the bonnet before parting with your money.

Cotat Frères

Chavignol, 18300 Sancerre
Stockists: Seckford Wines; Wine Society; Raeburn; Gelston Castle; Justerini & Brooks
Overall Price Rating: 🍶🍶

This Sancerre domaine is owned by Paul Cotat and his brother Francis and is managed by Paul's son François. There are 4.5 hectares of vines, between 20–60 years, old on the steepest slopes of the Sancerre region. The three main plots are called Les Monts Damnés, La Grande Côte and the Cul de Beaujeu (*un cul* being a rump or backside). The Cotats are the latest in Sancerre to begin picking their grapes each harvest, and all the grapes are gathered by hand. The vines are farmed by hand and to organic methods, but without being certified. The grapes are pressed in a wooden press dating from 1900, and the wines are aged in wooden oval-shaped casks. Here the wines can breathe without becoming woody. (Supermarket Sancerre is aged in stainless steel and this may account for its unremittingly metallic taste.) The wines are racked off the sediment twice, in accordance with the passage of the moon in January and March, and are bottled without fining or filtration.

The style of dry Sauvignon Blanc the Cotats make is a million miles from that produced by the star names in New Zealand's Marlborough region (like the non-organic Cloudy Bay, *see page 377*). The reason this is one of the few Sauvignon Blancs to be able to develop in bottle over several years is because the vines grow on their favourite chalky soil and are picked ripe. (European Sauvignon tends to fall over in the bottle when aged for more than 3–5 years, and most examples from the New World are lucky to get past their first anniversary without turning oily.) As the Cotats pick all of the grapes at full maturity their Sauvignon smells as Loire Sauvignon should – of fennel rather than cat's pee or gooseberry bushes! Even eminent wine critics are baffled sometimes as to why Sauvignon Blanc is considered one of the world's nine classic grape varieties. The wines of this domaine provide the perfect riposte.

Christian and Nicole Dauny

Champtin, 18300 Crezancy en Sancerre
Tel:+33 248 79 05 75
Fax:+33 248 79 02 54
Stockists: Vintage Roots; Organic Wine Company; Vinceremos
Overall Price Rating: ♦

This domaine has been certified organic since 1964. A white Sancerre of middling quality is made from eight hectares of Sauvignon Blanc, to be drunk with 2–3 years of the vintage and suitable for vegans. In addition the Dauny's have three hectares of Pinot Noir for Sancerre Rosé and Sancerre Rouge. (Before the enforced adoption of grafting vines onto American roostocks in the 19th century, Sancerre was made predominantly in a red wine style. However white grape varieties proved easier to graft onto the phylloxera-tolerant American stocks, hence we now think of Sancerre as a white first and foremost.)

Coteaux du Giennois AC

This AC covers both banks of the Loire north of Pouilly-Fumé and was known as Cotes de Gien VDQS until 1995. This far from the river Loire the main threat to the vines is spring frost, so they are trained slightly higher than usual off the ground to protect them (this also occurs in the Jura, *see page 86*).

Alain Paulat
Villemoison, 58200 Saint-Père
Tel:+33 386 26 75 57
Overall Price Rating: ♠

The choice of grape variety planted at this certified organic domaine reflects the proximity of Burgundy to the east. Pinot Noir and Gamay Noir à Jus Blanc are used for reds, with a little Chardonnay joining the Loire staples Chenin Blanc and Sauvignon Blanc for dry whites.

TOURAINE

Touraine extends from Blois in the east to Saumur in the west where the Loire takes its most northerly loop. Accordingly the ripening of the grapes is late. However because Touraine is further from the Atlantic than Nantais, levels of rainfall are moderate to low. This means that white wine growers can leave the grapes to hang on the vine into late autumn for late picked or 'noble rot' wines. Touraine reds are made predominantly from Cabernet Franc.

Bourgueil, St Nicolas de Bourgueil and Chinon ACs

Bourgueil and St Nicolas de Bourgueil occupy a plateau on the north bank of the Loire, which catches the sun and is skirted by the rain skimming up the valley from the west. Cabernet Franc grown here acquires a powerful scent of lead pencils, especially on the limier soils. Across the river in Chinon the Cabernet Franc is all charm, smelling of forget-me-nots and violets, on the sandier soils found here.

Catherine and Pierre Breton
Les Galichets, 8 rue du Peu Muleau, 37140 Restigné
Tel:+33 247 97 30 41
Fax:+33 247 97 46 49
Overall Price Rating: ♠♠♠

This domaine became certified organic in 1991 and Demeter-certified biodynamic in 1996. There are 13 hectares, all of which are given to Cabernet Franc. Its Loire synonym is 'Breton', the same as this domaine's owners.

Domaine de la Garrelière

37120 Razines

Tel:+33 247 95 62 84

Fax:+33 247 95 67 17

Stockist: Vinceremos

Overall Price Rating: ♦

This domaine belonged to France's most celebrated bureaucrat, Cardinal Richelieu, in the 17th century. His efficiency as a tax generator and tax collector struck fear into every Frenchman's heart – and the amount of paperwork he produced whilst working has the same effect on modern-day historians. In 1985 the domaine was taken over by its current owner, François Plouzeau. Since then a gradual conversion from organic methods to biodynamic ones has been effected. All the wines are suitable for vegans. They carry the Touraine AC and include: dry white Touraine Sauvignon Blanc; dry white Touraine Chenin Blanc; dry pink Touraine Rosé (made with Cabernet Franc); dry red Touraine Rouge (made with Gamay); and dry red Touraine Rouge (made with Cabernet Franc).

Domaine Georget

La Brosse-Touvois, 37140 Bourgueil

Tel:+33 247 97 83 29

Fax:+33 247 97 49 41

Stockists: contact Organic Wine Company for further details

Overall Price Rating: ♦♦

Christian and Magalie Georget converted their seven-hectare vineyard to certified organic methods in 1980. The only grape is Cabernet Franc now that the small amount of Gamay Noir à Jus Blanc has been grubbed out. Dry red Bourgueil AC and St Nicolas de Bourgueil AC are made in a firm style that rewards keeping.

Guion

Le Pontarin, 37140 Benais

Tel:+33 247 97 30 75

Fax:+33 247 97 83 17

Stockists: contact Organic Wine Company for further details

Stéphane Guion's Cabernet Franc-only vineyard has been certified organic since 1965. Dry pink Bourgueil Rosé AC is made by bleeding juice from the red wine vats early in the fermentation (this is called *rosé de saignée*). These vats contain Bourgueil Rouge AC (🍾) and, when made from the oldest vines, a Bourgueil Rouge AC Prestige, Vieilles Vignes (🍾🍾🍾).

Michel Thibault
L'Echelle, 37140 Bourgueil
Tel:+33 247 97 83 46
Fax:+33 247 97 93 11
Overall Price Rating: 🍾

Michel Thibault's four hectares of Cabernet Franc (95 per cent) and Cabernet Sauvignon (5 per cent) have been certified organic since 1974. Wines made include: dry pink sparkling Touraine Brut Rosé AC, Méthode Traditionelle; dry pink still Bourgueil Rosé AC; and dry red Bourgueil Rouge AC.

Touraine-Mesland AC
The commune of Mesland has its own appellation and comprises a sand and gravel plateau on the right, north bank of the Loire.

Clos du Château Gaillard
41150 Mesland
Tel:+33 264 70 27 14
Fax:+33 254 70 22 56

This ambitious domaine has been Demeter-certified biodynamic since 1992. Owner Vincent Girault draws from 17 hectares of Cabernet Franc and Gamay on sandy soil, and 13 hectares of Sauvignon Blanc and Chenin Blanc grown on flinty clay. Girault produces a sound range and one which seems to be improving. The percentage of the vineyards picked by machine is falling, with a corresponding rise in that picked by hand.

- Crémant de Loire, Les Doucinières: sparkling wine made by the traditional method in both dry white and dry pink styles; better than simple and frothy although exactly that! ♦♦
- Touraine Blanc (Sauvignon) AC: dry white, shows a modern chalk and gooseberry style. ♦
- Touraine Mesland Blanc AC: off-dry white made from Chenin Blanc; shows clean sweetness mixed with earth; good. ♦
- Touraine Mesland Rosé/Gris AC: dry pink, made from Gamay Noir à Jus Blancs; shows soft, easy non-aggressive fruit; machine picked. ♦
- Touraine Mesland Rouge AC: dry red, in 1997 made from 60 per cent Gamay, 25 per cent Malbec ('Cot') and 15 per cent Cabernet Franc ('Breton'); shows appealing cool mint and berry. ♦♦
- Touraine Mesland Rouge AC, Vieilles Vignes: dry red made from 'old vine' selection but no indication of average age given. In 1997 made from hand picked Gamay 55 per cent, with 30 per cent Cot and 15 per cent Cabernet Franc; matures four months in oak; good integration of grape tannins and wood tannins, which means what flavour is present can leave a positive impression in the mouth. ♦♦♦

Vouvray AC

The Chenin Blanc grapes grown for the white wines of Vouvray can be left on the vine so long that they are the last to be picked in France.

Domaine Huet

Le Haut Lieu, 37210 Vouvray
Tel:+33 247 52 78 87
Fax:+33 247 52 66 51
Stockists: widely available from Reid Wines; Bibendum; Seckford; Raeburn; Farr; Gauntleys of Nottingham; Howells of Bristol; Roberson; Vinceremos

Noel Pinguet, who converted this domaine to Demeter-certified biodynamic methods, arrived here in the 1970s when he married the proprietor's daughter. Protected species of flowers and other plants now flourish chez Huet. Copper sulphate and sulphur treatments here have been reduced by five-sixths since conversion to biodynamic methods from 1987, and are now seen to be among the lowest for such a northerly

French vineyard (around 3kg/ha per annum for copper sulphate, compared with an authorized level of 18kg/ha). These vineyards have belonged to the Huet family since 1928, and cover 35 hectares (out of a total 1,800 allowed for Vouvray). The wines ferment with natural yeast in stainless steel, small oak barrels or large oak tuns. Low levels of sulphur dioxide preservative ('sulphites') are used. All wines are suitable for vegetarians and vegans.

- Vouvray Pétillant: sparkling white made by the traditional method in both Brut and the sweeter Sec forms; 2.5 atmospheres of pressure; sets the other wines off well. ♣♣

- Vouvray Mousseux Brut NV: dry sparkling white made by the traditional method, ages three years on the yeast before it is disgorged; shows honeyed warm grass; a full-bodied example of sparkling Chenin, fine *mousse*. ♣♣

- Vouvray Le Clos du Bourg Sec: dry white, from a six-hectare vineyard enclosed by walls made of limestone fragments ploughed up from under the clay topsoil. ♣♣

- Vouvray Le Clos du Bourg Demi-Sec: medium dry white; shows why to describe dry Vouvray as smelling of 'wet wool' (as most wine students, in the UK at least, are taught) is spurious for this smells of fruit, not fibre. ♣♣♣

- Vouvray Le Clos du Bourg Moelleux: sweet white; forceful but crisp sweetness, clear fruit. ♣♣♣

- Vouvray Le Clos du Bourg Moelleux, 1ère Trie: sweet white made entirely from grapes affected by 'noble rot', will retain its freshness for decades (due to the presence of limestone soils that act like a sponge in the way they hydrate the vine). ♣♣♣

- Vouvray Le Haut Lieu Sec: dry white Chenin Blanc from an exposed site where clay in the topsoil keeps the grapes fresh. ♣♣

- Vouvray Le Haut Lieu Demi-Sec: medium sweet white; an angular sweetness which is best set off by something savoury. ♣♣

- Vouvray Le Haut Lieu Moelleux: sweet white, made from berries containing thick juice but dry pips, so it is one of the harder selections of grapes to press. ♣♣♣

- Vouvray Le Haut Lieu Moelleux, 1ère Trie: sweet white, dense. ♙
- Vouvray Le Mont Sec: dry white, made from a hill site with an ideal, southerly aspect and soil which contains flints (locally called *perruche*) and gravels that reflect light onto the Chenin Blanc vines. ♙
- Vouvray Le Mont Demi-Sec: medium dry white, with arresting body. ♙
- Vouvray Le Mont Moelleux: medium sweet white, shows a sweet apricot structure. ♙
- Vouvray Le Mont Moelleux, 1ère Trie: sweet white, shows intense clear honey and blossom. ♙
- Vouvray Moelleux, Cuvée Constance: sweet white, shows a unique taste of white berries at its core (latest vintage 1997). ♙

Domaine de la Saboterie
37210 Rochecourbon
Tel:+33 247 52 59 46
Fax:+33 247 52 82 54
Overall Price Rating: ♙

This domaine produces honourable still and sparkling Vouvray from 3.5 hectares of Chenin Blanc. It has been certified organic since 1994 and belongs to Christian Chaussard.

Domaine des Maisons Brulées
Vignerons de Thesse la Romaine
Tel:+33 254 32 78 78
Fax:+33 254 32 76 76
Stockists: Majestic; Vintage Roots

This domaine expects to have Demeter-certified biodynamic status from the 1999 vintage.

- Gamay de Touraine: dry red, a clean, light bubblegum fruit, picnic quaffer; less serious style of Gamay Noir à Jus Blanc compared to the Beaujolais wines of Gérard Belaïd for example (*see Burgundy, page 68*), but a good contrast nonetheless. ♙

- Touraine Sauvignon AC: dry white, crisp and simple Sauvigon which compares favourably to the more expensive version made by the Daunys in Sancerre (see above), suitable for vegetarians. 🍶

ANJOU-SAUMUR

The Anjou-Saumur region is protected from the worst of the Atlantic weather by the forests of the Vendée (*see Fiéfs Vendéens, below*). This general observation about the climate must be tempered by the fact that the region is a collection of river valleys running off the Loire, each of which enjoys its own private or 'meso' climate. In each, the ripening of the grapes and the style of wine produced will differ: dry whites are made in the valley of the Serrant (*see Clos de la Coulée de Serrant*), while sweet wines are made in the Layon Valley (*see Domaine de la Sansonnière*). Chenin Blanc and Sauvignon Blanc are planted for whites, with Cabernet Franc for red.

Coteaux du Layon AC

The Layon is a tributary of the Loire running through a steep sided valley near Rochefort-sur-Loire. Humidity builds up here in late autumn, enabling sweet 'noble rot' wines to be made from Chenin Blanc vines situated on the slopes (*coteaux*) overlooking the river.

Domaine du Château Gaillard

Château Gaillard, Ruette du Moulin, La Salle, 49260 Montreuil-Bellay
Tel:+33 241 52 31 11
Overall Price Rating: 🍶

This Demeter-certified biodynamic domaine belongs to Mathieu and Sylvanie Bouchet. Mathieu Bouchet's sister is Véronique Cochran of Château Falfas in Bourg AC, Bordeaux (*see page 24*). The wines made here are not quite of the same standard as at Falfas however. They include dry red Cabernet d'Anjou and white wines under the Saumur AC. The Vin de Table which is made here is just the type of budget wine prestigious London restaurants might consider using for cooking with.

Gérard Leroux

Bourg, 49700 Les Vergers-sur-Layon
Tel:+33 241 59 17 59
Fax:+33 241 59 18 76
Stockists: Yapp; Organic Wine Company

This domaine comprises 9.25 hectares. It has been certified organic since 1964 and is still traditionally run by its owner. The style of wine made relies on subtlety rather than blockbuster power which is the sign of a benchmark Loire domaine. Wines made include:

- Saumur Brut: dry sparkling wine made by the traditional method in white and pink forms, suitable for vegans. The white is toasty while the pink shows strawberry fruit (Organic Wine Company, 🍾).
- Anjou Villages Blanc AC: dry white made from Chenin Blanc, rich buttery nose, crisper palate, ideal on its own. 🍾🍾
- Rosé d'Anjou: dry pink made from Cabernet Franc and Grolleau; marzipan style of Loire pink, ideal with company and a dry biscuit. 🍾
- Coteaux du Layon AC: sweet white made from late picked Chenin Blanc; texture similar to apple crumble – one of the few dessert dishes to which this wine might be well matched (otherwise try cheese or fresh fruit like pears). 🍾🍾

SCEA Lorent Bureau/Domaine de l'Echalier

24 Grande Rue, 49750 Rablay sur Layon
Tel:+33 241 78 32 82
Fax:+33 241 78 64 38
Overall Price Rating: 🍾🍾

This organic domaine has been certified since 1996 and may be one to watch. There are 13.6 hectares producing 30 per cent white wines and 70 per cent red and pink under the Anjou and Coteaux du Layon ACs.

Nouteau-Cerisier Père et Fils

Le Verger, 49380 Faye d'Anjou

Tel:+33 241 54 31 40

Overall Price Rating: 👤

This certified organic domaine is planted with Chenin Blanc and Cabernet Franc. Owner Joseph Nouteau-Cerisier produces dry white Anjou Blanc AC, sweet white Coteaux du Layon AC, dry pink Rosé d'Anjou AC and dry red Cabernet d'Anjou AC.

Domaine de la Sansonnière

49380 Thouarcé

Tel:+33 241 54 08 08

Fax:+33 241 54 08 08

Stockist: Yapp

This domaine produces wheat and apples as well as vines. It is Demeter-certified biodynamic and was created by its owner, Mark Angeli, in 1990. Already Angeli has marked himself out as a white wine maker to watch, with some intense late picked, sweet white wines, such as the Bonnezeaux listed below. Angeli also make very creditable reds from Cabernet Franc under the Anjou Rouge AC (👤).

- Domaine de la Sansonnière, Cuvée Mathilde, Bonnezeaux AC: sweet white made from Chenin Blanc affected by noble rot. Shows concentration and balance despite a great level of sweetness, which are signs of well grown grapes. The noble rot element adds a touch of nutmeg to the ripe quince flavour of over-ripe Chenin in the aftertaste (1994 vintage, 👤👤👤).

Saumur-Champigny AC

This red wine appellation south of the Loire and just east of Saumur was known for white wine in the 19th century, but then became fashionable for reds amongst Parisian café society during the 1980s.

Domaine des Frogères

11 bis route de Champigny, 49580 Chacé

Tel:+33 241 52 95 25

Stockists: Vintage Roots; Vinceremos

Overall Price Rating: ♦

This certified organic domaine covers nine hectares and is owned by Michel Joseph. The soil in Chacé is called *tuffeau* – a form of hard limestone upon which the Cabernet Franc grape resides. *Tuffeau* soaks up what limited rainfall there is in Anjou-Saumur (500mm average) and then releases it slowly to the vines during the season like a sponge. This allows the Cabernet Franc to ripen steadily, without which it is unlikely to produce a wine of flavour (violets and blackberries) and colour (cornflower blue).

- Saumur Champigny AC: dry red made with Cabernet Franc; shows bright crimson colour, deep fruit, clean berry flavours; very positive almost chunky fruit, refreshing style, suitable for vegans, one to follow.

Savennières AC

Savennières lies on the north bank of the Loire across south-east facing slopes covered in blue volcanic debris. Here the Chenin Blanc is made in a bone dry style, and can taste severe to the uninitiated.

Clos de la Coulée de Serrant

Château de la Roche aux Moines, 49170 Savennières

Tel:+33 241 72 22 32

Fax:+33 241 72 28 68

Stockists: Yapp; Wine Society; Bibendum; Anthony Byrne

Overall Price Rating: ♦♦♦

For many wine lovers this domaine is synonymous with the development of biodynamics in the modern era. It dates from the 12th century and was purchased by the Joly family in 1959. Biodynamic practices were adopted from 1980 when Nicholas Joly, one of the most vocal proponents of the biodynamic method, took over the running of the domaine. Joly spends as much time at conferences on biodynamics held all over the world as he does in the vineyards, (a fact not missed by some of the more vituperative French wine critics who question Joly's motives and the quality of his wine).

The vineyard of Le Clos de la Coulée de Serrant covers seven hectares and has its own appellation separate from the rest of Savennières (making it what the French call a *monopole*). The wine produced from it is dry and made from Chenin Blanc. It matures in 600-litre oak casks, is racked by gravity (rather than by pump), is unfined (so suitable for vegans) but it is filtered. It is served by its owner at room temperature. Joly also owns other Chenin Blanc vines in the main part of the Savennières AC and from them produces Becherelle and Clos de la Bergerie.

● Le Clos de la Coulée de Serrant, Savennières AC: dry white which shows an intense, lean style of Chenin Blanc, dominated by mineral scents and nut kernels.

NANTAIS

Nantais is most westerly part of the Loire and produces very crisp, white wines from the Muscadet ('Melon de Bourgogne') and Gros Plant grapes. The region takes its name from Nantes, which is Brittany's capital city.

Muscadet AC

The salty tang of the ocean seems to manifest itself in Muscadet, the full-bodied but bone dry white produced within a stone's throw of the Atlantic. Muscadet loses some of its sharpness and acquires a dough-like smell when allowed to age on the fine lees (dead yeast) left after fermentation (*sur lies*). As the yeast cells decompose and split open they release elements into the wine which give it some colour and much-needed thickness.

Domaine de l'Ecu/Guy Bossard

La Bretonnière, 44430 Le Landreau
Tel:+33 240 06 40 91
Fax:+33 240 06 46 79
Stockists: widely available from Organic Wine Company; Vintage Roots; Vinceremos; and others (UK); Chartrand Imports (USA)

Guy Bossard is another of those who converted to certified organic methods for health reasons after his father became very ill from agro-chemicals. He now produces one of the best ranges in the Muscadet region, organic or otherwise, from 30 hectares. The vines are hand picked, and have been certified since 1975. Shire horses are used to plough the oldest plots.

- Vin Mousseux, Cuvée Ludwig Hahn, Méthode Traditionelle: dry white sparkling wine made by the traditional method from 85 per cent Muscadet and 15 per cent Gros Plant. Very dry but full bodied example of a Loire sparkler, and less yeasty than Champagne, stands up well to vegetable pie, suitable for vegans (Organic Wine Company, 👤).
- Vin de Pays des Marches de Bretagne, Cépage Cabernet: dry red made from Cabernet Franc, light picnic style, drink immediately, suitable for vegans (👤👤). Now relabelled under the Vin de Pays du Jardin de la France designation.
- Gros Plant du Pays Nantais VDQS, Sur Lies, Guy Bossard: dry white, made from Gros Plant, aged on the fine lees, shows yeasty character, only 10.5 per cent alcohol; suits oily food. 👤
- Guy Bossard Muscadet de Sèvre et Maine sur Lie AC,: dry white, crisp assertive style of Muscadet with plenty of concentration, body and fruit; suitable for vegans (Safeway, 👤).
- Hermine d'Or, Guy Bossard, Muscadet de Sèvre et Maine sur Lie AC: dry white, as above but ages in casks made of Vosges oak, gaining flavour but losing the rasping primary fruit character typical to Muscadet. This is a very fine example of a Muscadet built to last. Drink from 2–5 years, longer in the best vintages. 👤👤👤

Domaine de la Parentière
44330 Vallet
Tel:+33 240 36 25 71
Fax:+33 240 36 36 34
Stockists: Vinceremos; Vintage Roots; Organic Wine Company

This certified organic domaine is run by Michel Menager and is a source of everyday, value-for-money wines.

- Blanc de Blancs, Sélection Menager: dry white sparkling wine made by the traditional method from Gros Plant and Muscadet varieties; now discontinued and the grapes used for the two still wines below.
- Sélection Menager, Gros Plant: dry white, to drink immediately, neutral, suitable for vegans. ♦
- Domaine de la Parentière, Muscadet de Sevre et Maine sur lie AC: dry white, easy style, suitable for vegans. ♦

Fiéfs Vendéens

The woods of the Vendée give their name to this small ocean-influenced zone south of Nantes. The Vendée acts on the climate of the Loire like the forests of the Landes do on Bordeaux. It soaks up humidity from the Atlantic and helps regulate the temperature for steadier ripening. Therefore look for delicacy rather than power.

Domaine Saint Nicholas

11 rue des Vallées, 85470 Brem sur Mer
Tel:+33 251 33 13 04/+33 251 90 55 74
Fax:+33 251 33 18 42
Email: cncp@caves.particulières.com
Stockist: Vintage Roots

This family domaine obtained biodynamic Demeter certification in 1998 for 34 hectares of vineyard and is due certification for another 32 hectares in 2000. The first swathe of vineyards seemed to take some time to get attuned to the new biodynamics as the debut year, 1993, was a tough one for mildew. The wines made so far are polished, drinkable upon purchase and offer good value. They are labelled as 'Tradition' (♦) or the slightly more expensive 'Prestige' (♦♦), and come in dry white, dry pink and red forms. Brem refers to the name of one of the Vendée's leading wine villages. Examples include:

- Fiéfs Vendéens (VDQS) Brem, Blanc: dry white, shows clean, creamy apple; blend of Chenin Blanc and Groslot Gris.
- Fiéfs Vendéens (VDQS) Brem, Tradition Rosé: dry pink, blend of Pinot Noir, Gamay Noir à Jus Blancs and Groslot Gris; shows attractive

ripples of strawberry and vanilla, round. Also made in 100 per cent Pinot Noir form.
- Fiéfs Vendéens (VDQS) Brem, Tradition Rouge: dry red, blend of Pinot Noir (80 per cent) and Cabernet Franc (20 per cent); shows mint, cherries and fat summer fruit.

Domaine Biau'Céan
3 rue de l'Océan, 85220 Landevielle
Tel:+33 251 22 95 10
Fax:+33 251 22 95 10

This domaine is due full biodynamic Demeter certification from 1999 for 25 hectares under owners Claudie Richard and Bernard Pineau.

The Midi

The Midi is the vast area that hugs the Mediterranean all the way between the Pyrenees in the west and Provence to the east. The Midi gets its name from the fact that the midday sun is higher here than anywhere else in France. The region is divided into two unequal parts, the smaller Roussillon on the Pyreneen side, and the Languedoc on the Provence side. There are 340,000 hectares of vineyards, of which 1,400 hectares were certified organic in 1998 with a further 900 hectares due to come on stream in 1999. This makes the Midi Europe's biggest organic-wine producing region in terms of hectarage. A Mediterranean climate and drying winds minimize the risk of vine fungal diseases and have encouraged over 40 growers to convert to organic methods. The vast majority of wines made here are honest everyday affairs, and the general rule is you get what you pay for.

In the 1950s the Midi was colonized by ex-patriate French fleeing the Algerian Civil War. They brought with them a rather mixed bag of grape varieties, such as Carignan, Alicante Bouschet, Aramon and others. These grapes are generally very disease resistant, produce high yields and are thus ideal for organic viticulture. However, because they make what are deemed 'bland' wines (and in rather too much quantity) the French government, via the EU, has subsidised the replanting of vineyards with 'improver' grape varieties from Burgundy, the Rhône and Bordeaux (like Chardonnay, Cabernet Sauvignon, Merlot and Syrah for example). These are less disease resistant than the Algerian imports and so are more reliant on agro-chemicals, despite the Midi's favourable climate. This means that the growers cited below who have taken the organic option do not have it as easy as some might think. By implication this means that the 'Midi-is-sunny-so-they-can't-use-too-many-chemicals-there' attitude taken by some retailers, who attempt to generate sales of wines made from non-certified organic grapes, is a red herring. For an example of exactly why this is so, see the reason given by Domaine Bassac's owner when he converted to organic methods.

Look out for the wines sold under Vin de Pays ('country wine') designations. The Vin de Pays designation was set up by the French government in 1973 to cater for production from the new improver varieties. It allowed growers the chance to experiment with the new varieties to see which vineyard sites they were best suited to. The designation offers a 'halfway house' between bulk table wine and the more established appellation or AC wines like Corbières, for example. The Midi's Vin de Pays generally offer good value for money and the occasional gem of a wine.

LANGUEDOC

This covers the departments of the Aude, Gard and l'Hérault and has its own regional Vin de Pays destination of Vin de Pays d'Oc. In addition, each department here has its own departmental Vin de Pays designation.

Blanquette de Limoux AC

Blanquette de Limoux is an appley-tasting sparkling white wine from the small town of Limoux high in the eastern Pyrennean foothills, first made in 1531 and thus pre-dating the efforts of Dom Pérignon in Champagne (*see page 71*). It comes in three styles: Blanquette de Limoux, Blanquette de Limoux Méthode Ancestrale (a similar production method to Clairette de Die) and Crémant de Limoux. Clairette is bottled as a still, dry wine under the Limoux AC.

Domaine la Batteuse

11190 Antugnac
Tel:+33 468 74 21 02
Fax:+33 468 74 19 90
Newsletter: first edition (written in French) January 1999
Tasting Room: caveau opened in June 1998 for visitors; open daily
Stockists: Vinceremos; Organic Wine Company; Vintage Roots

This domaine was founded by Bernard Delmas in 1978 and comprises 22 hectares of certified organic Mauzac, Chenin Blanc, Chardonnay and Pinot Noir. Still white wines are made under the Vin de Pays de l'Aude AC from Chardonnay and Mauzac (Vinceremos, 🍸).

- Crémant de Limoux Tradition AC: dry sparkling wine made by the traditional method from Mauzac (70 per cent) and Chardonnay and Chenin Blanc (30 per cent combined); tastes clean and ripe like a Cox apple, delicious and fresh; drinkable upon purchase. ▮
- Blanquette de Limoux AC: dry sparkling wine made by the traditional method from Mauzac (70 per cent or more) and Chardonnay; as above if slightly fuller in body, with a fine yeasty character present in the aroma (Organic Wine Company, ▮▮).
- Blanquette de Limoux Tradition (Ancestrale) AC: sparkling wine made here from Mauzac (80 per cent) and Chardonnay (20 per cent). Shows a creamy aroma, yeasty character and elegant fruit to taste. Less fizzy than the Crémant de Limoux, but deeper and more characterful. Less than 7 per cent alcohol, perfect with scrambled eggs for breakfast (available in half bottles) ▮▮ .
- Blanquette de Limoux Tradition (Ancestrale), Cuvée Speciale, AC: special bottling of the above wine for the Millennium but has enough to age until 2005 at least; young, no great weight, should be good, out in September 1999. ▮▮▮

Domaine de Mayrac
11190 Couiza
Tel:+33 468 74 04 84
Fax:+33 468 74 20 01

This certified organic domaine comprises 22 hectares and belongs to Gino Buoro. Chardonnay, Chenin Blanc and Mauzac (whites) and Syrah, Cabernet, Merlot and Pinot Noir (reds) are planted. From these a range of average quality white, pink and red wines (all dry) are made under Vin de Pays designations (▮▮). The sparkling Blanquette de Limoux AC appears neither as good to taste nor as good value as that from the domaine above. The best wine here is the Limoux AC (▮▮▮).

Cabardès AC

This north-eastern Languedoc sub-region marks the transition from Bordeaux influenced South West France to the Midi. The Bordeaux varieties are fleshed out with Grenache, Syrah and Cinsaut and a declining proportion of Carignan in the Cabardès red wine.

Château/Domaine de Brau

11620 Villemoustaussou
Tel:+33 468 72 31 92
Fax:+33 468 25 91 17
Stockist: Vintage Roots

This domaine dates from 1982 under its current owners Wenny Tari and her husband Gabriel. There are 17 hectares of certified organic vines with a further 11 hectares in conversion (due full organic status from the 2001 vintage). The cellar dates from 1877. Grape juice and a sweet fortified aperitif ('Esprit et le Suc', ♦) are made, in addition to the following wines:

- Vin de Pays de l'Aude: made in dry white, dry pink and dry red forms, all suitable for vegans and all worth trying (♦♦). An oak fermented Vin de Pays de l'Aude Chardonnay is also made, which shows attractive peachy flavour and good use of oak (♦♦♦).
- Cabardès AC Rouge: dry red, non-oak aged, a blend of Merlot, Cabernet Sauvignon and Grenache; shows clean light fruit; balanced; suitable for vegans. ♦
- Cabardès AC Rouge, Cuvée Exquise: dry red, oak aged version of the red wine immediately above; combines Bordeaux freshness with Midi warmth; elegant, excellent value, suitable for vegans. ♦♦

Corbières AC

The Corbières region begins just south of the medieval city of Carcassonne, a world heritage site. It is bounded to the east by the Mediterranean and to the north and west by the river Aude and the Minervois. It covers 14,000 hectares. The Corbières region became very fashionable from the late 1980s when cash-rich château owners from Bordeaux began buying up as much vineyard here as they could find. Few of them came with any organic intentions though, which means that the certified organic domaines listed below and owned and run by locals. Dry red and pink wines are made from Grenache, Carignan and Cinsault with Mourvèdre and the minor Terret Noir and Picpoul Noir. Dry whites are made from Bourboulenc, Maccabeo, Grenache Blanc, with Clairette, Muscat, Picpoul, Terret, Marsanne, Roussanne and Rolle (Vermentino).

Sweet fortified wines (*vin doux naturel*) are also made (see Château Pech-Latt), but they seem to be more popular with the French than the British, which is our loss.

Domaine de la Bouletière

11220 St Laurent de la Cabrerisse
Tel:+33 468 27 88 99
Fax:+33 468 27 88 90
Stockists: Oddbins; Vinceremos; Organic Wine Company
Price Rating: 🍾 for the Domaine de la Bouletière range; 🍾🍾 for the Château de Caraguilhes range

This domaine dates from 1515 when it formed part of the Cistercian abbey of Fontfroide. In 1960 its owner, Lionel Faivre, decided to château bottle, one of the first in Corbières to do this rather than taking the grapes to the local cooperative. The domaine covers 135 hectares of vines and has been certified organic since 1966. The Vin de Pays wines are picked by machine, while the Corbières are picked by hand. Prices are high but the quality is sound. Check with your stockist which wines are suitable for vegetarians and which for vegans (egg white is the only animal-based fining agent used here).

- VdP des Côteaux de Cabrerisse Blanc, Domaine de la Bouletière: dry white blend of Grenache Blanc (70 per cent), and Bourboulenc (30 per cent); clean, very appealing fresh Southern French white (Vinceremos).
- VdP des Côteaux de Cabrerisse Rosé, Domaine de la Bouletière: dry pink made from Carignan and Cinsault; gives you an idea of what to expect from the domaine's Corbières Rosé below (Vinceremos).
- VdP des Côteaux de Cabrerisse Rouge, Domaine de la Bouletière: dry red, Grenache dominated; shows light, creamy fruit (Vinceremos, Oddbins).
- Château de Caraguilhes, Cuvée Classique, Corbières AC Blanc: dry white made from Grenache Blanc and Bourboulenc; shows green lime fruit, appealing weight and texture, more expensive than the equivalent made by Pech-Latt (below) but worth the extra.

- Château de Caraguilhes, Cuvée Prestige, Corbières AC Blanc: dry white, made from hand picked, old vine Grenache Blanc (60 per cent), Marsanne (25 per cent) and Bourboulenc/Malvoisie (15 per cent), partially fermented in French oak. In 1998 shows pinpoint balance between wood and fruit. An example of why the critics now take dry white Corbières so seriously.
- Château de Caraguilhes, Cuvée Classique, Corbières AC Rosé: dry pink, probably the best wine in the Caraguilhes range and one of the most delicious in Corbières, made to be drunk with food ('a structured pink' says the owner). Made from Syrah (35 per cent) and Grenache (65 per cent), and cool fermented to retain the grape aromas (Organic Wine Company).
- Château de Caraguilhes, Cuvée Classique, Corbières AC Rouge: dry red, shows smooth, easy texture, made from Carignan (30 per cent), Grenache (30 per cent), Syrah (30 per cent) and Mourvèdre (10 per cent).
- Château de Caraguilhes, Cuvée Prestige, Corbières AC Rouge: dry red, shows more serious fruit than the wine immediately above, made from old Carignan (40 per cent), Grenache and Syrah; matures in new French oak, shows refined, aromatic herb mixed with pruneaux and cassis.

Château Coulon
11200 Cruscades
Tel:+33 468 27 10 80
Fax:+33 468 27 38 19
Overall Price Rating: ♦

This well-established domaine comprises over 100 hectares, all of which will be fully certified organic by 2000. Two dry white wines are made under regional Vin de Pays designations from Viognier and Sauvignon Blanc, as well as Corbières.

- Corbières AC: dry red made from Carignan, Grenache, Syrah, Mourvèdre and Cinsault; clean, average example offering value for money.

Château Pech-Latt

11220 Lagrasse
Tel:+33 468 58 11 40
Fax:+33 468 58 11 41
Stockists: Waitrose; Organic Wine Company; Vintage Roots

This Corbières domaine comprises 115 hectares of certified organic vines and belongs to Jacques André. A large range of well-made wines offering value for money is produced.

- Château Pech-Latt, Tradition, Corbières Blanc AC: dry white made from Marsanne and Maccabeo; hand picked, suitable for vegans, shows clean full-bodied citrus fruit (Organic Wine Company, 🍷).
- Château Pech-Latt, Tradition, Corbières Rosé AC: dry pink, clean if somewhat flat. 🍷
- Château Pech-Latt, Tradition, Corbières AC: dry red, made in 1997 from Carignan (50 per cent), and Grenache and Mourvèdre which showed clean tannin; appetizing rather than complex, but an approachable style of Corbières (Waitrose, Organic Wine Company, 🍷). In 1998 it was made with more Carignan (80 per cent) and is more concentrated and tannic as a result (this adds rather than detracts to its appeal for this author, although Carignan is frowned upon generally as a grape lacking grace and fruit).
- Château Pech-Latt, Selection Vieilles Vignes, Corbières AC: dry red 'old vine selection' (no average age for vines given) which ages in oak. Representative example of an oak-aged red Corbières with more than enough finesse (Vintage Roots, 🍷🍷).
- Grenache *vin doux naturel*, Les Desmoiselles: fortified sweet red made from partially fermented Grenache which is stunned with grape spirit to kill the yeast and stop the fermentation (*muté sur grains*); a big wine in terms of tannin, sweetness and alcohol but has the concentration to retain its balance. Irresistible (to drink or poured over iced-cream). 🍷🍷
- Grenache vin doux naturel, Les Pièces Nobles: fortified sweet red made like the wine immediately above. 'Les Pièces Nobles' refers to what are the estate's oldest plots of vines. The 1991 vintage was aged

in large oak casks (*foudres*) for seven years before bottling. Shows a brilliant ruby colour and fine, sweet fruit. ♦♦♦

Cellier de Ségur

11220 Ribauté
Tel:+33 468 43 16 23
Fax:+33 468 43 16 23
Overall Price Rating: ♦

This cooperative produces a dry red Corbières from hand picked, certified organic grapes which are bought in. In France the wine is labelled as 'La Bellevie' and shows attractive strawberry bubblegum fruit.

Costières de Nîmes AC

This AC is located between Nîmes, famous for its bull fighting, and Arles and was once known as the Costières du Gard. There are 12,000 hectares on gentle, pebble strewn, south-facing slopes overlooking the Camargue.

Domaine de Cabanis

Mas Madagascar, Vauvert, 30640 Beauvoisin
Tel:+33 466 88 78 33
Fax:+33 466 88 41 73
Stockist: Vinceremos

This domaine covers 17 hectares and has been certified organic since 1984. Owner Jean-Paul Cabanis also has 13 hectares of fruit trees and grazing land for animals to provide manure. The red wines show a rich earth character – some people might called it barnyardy – which marks this domaine out. The white and pink wines are suitable for vegans, and the red wines are suitable for vegetarians (egg white fining is used).

- Vin de Pays du Gard, Mas Madagascar: made in three styles. The dry white is made from Clairette; the dry pink from Grenache and the red from a blend of Grenache, Carignan, Mourvèdre and Syrah. Another red Vin de Pays du Gard is made under the 'Domaine Cabanis' label and displays good balance between thyme-scented fruit and tannin; for drinking within 1–3 years of the vintage. ♦

- Costières de Nîmes AC: dry red, shows a really earthy nose – an indication of old Carignan vines and ripe Grenache. ♙

Minervois AC

Minervois describes itself as a 'land of contrasts'. The region covers nearly 5,000 hectares in over 60 villages in a block directly north of Carcassonne and Narbonne. Styles include tangy dry whites to mouthfilling pinks and lush reds. The latter are similar to Corbières (which lies immediately to the south), but with thicker texture and heavier aroma.

Vignobles Cathares SC, Château Maris
34210 La Livinière
Overall Price Rating: ♙♙

This enterprise belongs to Robert Eden who has been described as 'British and pro-biodynamics'. Unfortunately he seems to have fallen foul of EU law which stipulates that the entire holding from a single proprietor must be organic in order for it to be certified. Eden owns two vineyards (Combebelle and Château Maris) which are managed organically but which are not certified, and he also buys in certified biodynamic grapes for a range called 'Comté Cathare'. Eden's problem is that his status as a merchant grape buyer of certified biodynamic grapes clashes with his status as a non-certified organic grape grower and winemaker, because all the wines are fermented in the same winery. (Contact Vintage Roots for developments on Eden's attempts to convince the authorities to change their minds.) In the meantime one of his wines is labelled as 'biodynamic' in inverted commas (like the 'biodynamic but not certified' wine made at Topolos in California, *see page 328*). The commune of La Livinière where Eden's winery is based lies at the heart of the new Minervois sub-appellation called Minervois-La Livinière, which dates from 1999.

Château Roubia

Rue des Androunes, 11200 Roubia
Tel:+33 468 91 23 38
Fax:+33 468 91 10 87
Stockist: Vintage Roots
Overall Price Rating: ♦

This certified organic domaine comprises 18 hectares of Carignan, Syrah, Grenache, Mourvèdre and Merlot for pink and red wines; and Vermentino, Maccabeo and Roussanne for whites. The wines are fermented and aged in stainless steel and seem to suffer from a lack of air (they taste 'reduced' or eggy).

- VdP de l'Aude: produced in white, pink and red styles (all dry); cheap, but a little pinched.
- Château Roubia, Minervois Rouge AC: dry red, some plum fruit but lacks confidence; suitable for vegetarians.

Domaine Saint Julien

11700 Azille
Tel:+33 468 91 16 57
Fax:+33 468 91 16 57
Stockist: contact Vintage Roots for further details
Overall Price Rating: ♦♦

This biodynamic domaine comprises 5.6 hectares of Carignan, Syrah, Grenache and Mourvèdre for pink and red wines and Terret, Maccabeo, Roussanne and Marsanne for whites. Owners Stefanie Minder and Ernest Aeschlimann produce a highly individual range of wines which are something of an acquired taste. The commune of Azille is the only one in the Aude department to be included in the new Minervois sub-appellation (Minervois-La Livinière) – the rest are in the Hérault (see Comté Cathares, above).

St Chinian AC

The St Chinian region covers 2,100 hectares of vineyards on the foothills of the Cévennes between Minervois and Faugères. Red wines are produced from Grenache, Syrah, Carignan, Cinsaut and Mourvèdre mixed with Cabernet Sauvignon. They can offer excellent value.

Château Bousquette

34460 Cessenon sur Orb
Tel:+33 467 89 65 38
Fax:+33 467 89 57 58
Stockists: Vinceremos; Organic Wine Company; Chartrand Imports (USA)
Overall Price Rating: ♙

Château Bousquette lies in the heart of the St Chinian AC, 30 miles from the Mediterranean and 10 miles north west of Beziers. There are 21.5 hectares of certified organic vines with a further 1.5 hectares in conversion (due full certification in 2001). In 1970 Château Bousquette's former owner retired as a Professor of Medicine at the University of Toulouse and resolved to improve the state of the vineyards. His interest in holistic medicine led to the adoption of certified organic methods. The domaine has since been sold to a Swiss couple, Eric and Isabelle Perret. They have improved the winemaking, and the red wines are smoother as a result. Fizzy grape juice ('Pétillant de Raisin') is also sold, at 3 per cent alcohol, which is suitable for vegans.

- St Chinian Rosé AC: dry pink, meaty and full, serve with charcuterie.
- St Chinian Rouge AC: dry red, in 1996 dominated by the scent of Cabernet Sauvignon (berry fruit on the nose). In 1997 it was lighter, easier, softer and more typical of southern France, showing a leather aroma and warmer tasting tannin. Serve with hot meats or stews.

Domaine des Soulié

Carriera de la Teuliera, 34360 Assignan
Tel:+33 467 89 65 38
Fax:+33 467 89 57 58

Stockist: Vinceremos
Overall Price Rating: 🍷🍷

This domaine belongs to the Soulié family and comprises 27 hectares of certified organic vineyard. The grape varieties are Syrah, Grenache, Carignan, Cinsault, Merlot and Malbec for dry pink and dry red wines, and Marsanne, Roussanne and Sauvignon Blanc for dry whites. Wines are sold under the Vin de Pays d'Oc designation, as well as St Chinian Rosé and St Chinian Rouge.

Coteaux du Languedoc

The best Languedoc villages or 'crus' (literally 'growths') are allowed their own sub-appellations.

Picpoul de Pinet, Coteaux du Languedoc AC

Picpoul de Pinet comes from low lying ground near Mèze on the Bassin de Thau. Pinet is one of the two communes entitled to the AC – the other being Castelnau de Guers. The Picpoul grape from which the wine is made is nicknamed 'lip-stinger' and produces a green-gold, lemon flavoured crisp white wine. This stands out because most of the wines from this part of the Languedoc are reds. These red wines sell as Vins de Pays or under the Coteaux du Languedoc AC.

Domaine de la Grangette

34120 Castelnau de Guers
Tel:+33 467 98 13 56
Fax:+33 467 90 79 36
Stockists: Organic Wine Company; Vintage Roots

This domaine is now run by the third generation of the Mur family and comprises 50 hectares of certified organic vineyards. The grapes are picked by machine and the wines are fermented in a modern style; tropical for the whites and soft fruit rather than tannin for the reds.

● Sauvignon VdP d'Oc: dry white, made from 100 per cent Sauvignon Blanc; aromatic elements (gooseberry, cassis) retained by slow, cool fermentation; good value. 🍷

- Carignan Blanche, VdP des Cotes de Thau: dry white made from white Carignan which is rare (the red Carignan Noir is the one the authorities want to see expunged from the Midi); smells of flowers and aniseed, full bodied, worth finding. ♦
- Tradition, VdP d'Oc: dry red, blend of Carignan Noir, Grenache, Cinsault and Syrah; smells of thyme and cherry; clean, balanced; drink within 1–3 years. ♦♦
- Picpoul de Pinet, Coteaux du Languedoc AC: dry white, broad and weighty, mixes vanilla and pear drop, lush style, a more refined contrast to the example from the domaine below. ♦♦♦

Domaine de Petit Roubié

34850 Pinet
Tel:+33 467 77 09 28
Fax:+33 467 77 76 26
Stockists: Organic Wine Company; Vinceremos

This certified organic domaine belongs to Floriane Azan and her husband Olivier. Monsieur Azan is very much the entrepreneur, with seemingly as many mobile phones as he has vines. There are four main parcels of vines, covering 32 hectares, 24 hectares (both fully certified), 43.1 hectares and 14.7 hectares (in conversion, due 1999 and 2000 respectively). A huge range of white, pink and red wines are produced (all dry) under the following designations: Vin de Pays de Côtes de Thau, Domaine de Petit Roubié (♦); Vin de Pays du Gard, Domaine Olivier (♦); Vin de Pays de l'Hérault, Domaine de Petit Roubié, Châtelaine Stéphanie (♦♦). They are characterized by light, but appealing fruit. Dry white and red wines are available in 10-litre wine boxes, and are good value. Picpoul de Pinet is made under the Château Petit Roubié designation (♦♦), and is tight and appley, and not quite as refined as the example from the domaine above.

Pic Saint Loup, Coteaux du Languedoc AC

Pic St Loup comprises 1,000 hectares of vines amongst scrub and forest on a *pic* or peak north of Montpellier. Daytime temperatures are hot but the nights are cool, and as a result the red wines which are produced show ripeness and cut.

Domaine Beau-Thorey

Chemin Neuf, 30260 Corconne
Tel:+33 466 77 13 11
Fax:+33 466 77 12 06
Email: beau.corconne@wanadoo.fr
Overall Price Rating: 🍶🍶

This domaine comprises 3.5 hectares of Syrah, Grenache, Cinsault and Carignan and has been certified organic since 1996. Another 0.5 hectares are due for full certification in 1999. Owner Christophe Beau produces two dry red wines:

- Coteaux du Languedoc Rouge AC, la Parra: dry red, in 1995 showed clean, brutal tannin making it a good selection for the barbecue. Serve in carafe.
- Pic St Loup, Vignoble Beau-Thorey: dry red, in 1997 was chunky and aromatic with a powerful rather than inhibiting structure. The Pic St Loup AC excludes grapes from vines which are less than six years old; and yields must be no more than 6,600 bottles per hectare (8,000 are allowed for the general Coteaux du Languedoc AC).

Other Languedoc Producers

Domaine de L'Isle des Sables

L'Isle des Sables, Fourques, 13200 Arles
Tel:+33 490 96 38 25
Accomodation: gîte for six people
Stockists: Organic Wine Company; Vintage Roots
Overall Price Rating: 🍶

This domaine has been certified organic since 1969 and is owned by the Albaric family. There are 12 hectares of Grenache, Syrah, Alicante Bouschet and Cabernet Sauvignon located on sandy soil on an island at the mouth of the Rhône. This is where the Languedoc region meets Provence, and is part of the Camargue, famous for its beaches and horses. Dry pink and red wines are made under the Vin de Pays du Gard designation. They age in huge Russian oak vats that date back to the Tsars. The winemaking has settled down here recently after some ups and downs. The wines are suitable for vegans and show very open fruit; drinkable upon purchase. The reds are best when lightly chilled (the sandy soil gives the tannins a roundness which keep the wines from tasting 'mean' when just out of the refrigerator).

Domaine Anthéa

Chemin de Maurel, 11110 Sallèles d'Aude
Tel:+33 468 33 31 59
Fax:+33 468 33 31 59
Stockists: contact Vinceremos for further details
Overall Price Rating: ◊

This domaine lies on the eastern edge of the Minervois AC and comprises 5.5 hectares of certified organic Merlot and Cabernet Sauvignon. From these, owners Serge and Josette Ziggiotti produce two Vin de Pays d'Oc varietal red wines, suitable for vegetarians.

Domaine du Mas Barjac

30360 Monteils
Tel:+33 466 83 52 52
Fax:+33 466 83 59 60
Stockist: Vinceremos
Overall Price Rating: ◊◊

This certified organic domaine comprises 35 hectares of Carignan, Alicante, Cinsault, Grenache, Syrah, Merlot and Cabernet Sauvignon and produces wines (mainly Vin de Pays) of fairly average quality. Some of the grapes are sold to Domaine de Clairac/Jacques Frélin (*see page 126*).

Domaine Bassac

92 rue de la Condamine, 34480 Puissalicon
Tel:+33 467 36 05 37
Fax:+33 467 36 63 27
Stockist: Vintage Roots

This domaine was converted to organic methods in 1991 when the owners, the Delhon family, discovered the vines were becoming resistant to mildew. Helped and encouraged by their German importers the whole of the vineyard was converted and is now certified organic. There are 64 hectares on two sites about five miles apart (9km) near Béziers. White, pink and red wines are marketed under three Vin de Pays designations: Vin de Pays de l'Hérault for the basic range ('Les Pradelles', ♦), Vin de Pays des Côtes de Murviel (♦) and Vin de Pays des Côtes de Thongue ('Domaine Bassac', ♦). The pick are:

- VdP de l'Hérault Rouge, les Pradelles: dry red made from Tempranillo, Grenache, Carignan and Cabernet Sauvignon; tastes of cherries and bubblegum.
- VdP des Côtes de Murviel, Cabernet Sauvignon, Domaine Bassac: dry red, very firm style of tannin but positive fruit, excellent dinner quaffer.
- VdP des Côtes de Thongue, Sauvignon (Blanc), Domaine Bassac: dry white, thick Southern-French style of Sauvignon but retains its elegance, suitable for vegetarians.
- VdP des Côtes de Thongue, Syrah, Domaine Bassac: dry red, stinky raspberry smell typical of Southern-French Syrah; a little little uneven but give it time to settle in the glass.
- VdP des Côtes de Thongue, Muscat Moelleux, Domaine Bassac: medium-dry white, picked early morning for freshness, full grapey flavour, no bitterness so well pressed and not over-fined (with bentonite), the most complete wine in the range. Drink upon purchase.
- VdP des Côtes de Thongue, Cuvée Jacques Delhon, Domaine Bassac: dry red, special bottling made in 1995 from Cabernet Sauvignon (from a one-hectare parcel called Le Plateau) and Syrah (from a one-hectare parcel called Pepet). The grapes were fermented together and once racked off the skins, the wine spent 18 months in American oak.

Shows clear fruit, even texture, but drink before 2003; suitable for vegans. 🍾🍾🍾

Domaine Bourguet
Montimas, 34500 Béziers
Tel:+33 467 35 20 71
Fax:+33 467 76 26 28
Overall Price Rating: 🍾

This 10.5-hectare domaine was converted to certified organic methods from 1987 when it was taken over by the fourth generation of the Bourguet family to farm here. The wines are now made by a member of the fifth generation, André Bourguet. He seems keen to develop his own wine style, notably for thick reds which are sold as Vin de Pays de l'Hérault, and fortified grape juice or *mistelles*. The latter are labelled 'Cartagène' and are made from 80 per cent grape juice (Grenache and Syrah) and 20 per cent grape spirit. The result has a deep tawny colour, an inviting aroma of prune and chocolate and a warming taste of red berries (contains 16 per cent alcohol). The name Cartagène comes either from Carthage or from the local way of describing the blend: 'Quart d'Alcool, trois quarts vin' ('one quarter spirit, three quarters wine').

Domaine de Buzarens
34820 Assas
Tel:+33 467 59 62 89
Fax:+33 467 59 62 89

This certified organic domaine comprises 25 hectares of Grenache Noir, Syrah, Merlot, Carignan, Cabernet Sauvignon and Alicante Bouschet for pink and red wines, and Sauvignon Blanc for whites. Owner M. Brice Hartmann markets the wines under Vin de Pays designations.

Jacques Frélin Vignobles/Domaine de Clairac

34370 Cazouls les Beziers
Tel:+33 467 90 55 62
Fax:+33 467 90 66 07
Email: vins-frelin@terre-net.fr
Stockists: Vinceremos; Chartrand Imports (USA)

This merchant house produces around 70 wines from certified organic grapes that it purchases from growers located mainly in the Midi, the Rhône and Provence (such as Domaine du Mas Barjac, below). It has been described as probably the single most important organic wine supplier in France because of the sheer volume of wines it releases. Some of the wines are bottled and labelled by Frélin under supermarket or chain-store lables (BOBs or buyer's own brand).

The finest wine in the range bears a Northern Rhône appellation rather than one from the Midi, and is an inky, solid dry red – Crozes-Hermitage (stocked by Majestic, ♨). Other wines in the range offer value rather than excitement, but they deserve more than being hidden in a brown paper bag if they become your 'bring a bottle' contribution to a party. They include:

- VdP de l'Aude, Sauvignon Blanc, Jacques Frélin: dry white, over-ripe modern-style example of the Sauvignon Blanc variety; clean, but drink within nine months. ▲
- Marsanne, Jacques Frélin: dry white, undergoes ageing in acacia wood barrels which lends the Marsanne extra dimension; 1998 vintage suitable for vegetarians. ▲
- VdP de l'Hérault, Domaine de Savignac: dry red, suitable for vegetarians in 1997 and 1998. ▲
- VdP de l'Hérault Syrah, Domaine de Clairac: dry red, suitable for vegetarians. ▲
- VdP de l'Hérault, Domaine de Clairac Joubio Blanc: dry white blend of the Midi varieties Ugni Blanc and Clairette, suitable for vegans in 1998. ▲
- VdP de l'Hérault, Domaine de Clairac Joubio Rosé: dry pink, clean, ephemeral. ▲

- VdP de l'Hérault, Domaine de Clairac Joubio Rouge: dry red blend of Syrah, Grenache, Cinsault and Carignan in 1997 and 1998, suitable for vegetarians. ▲
- VdP d'Oc, Cabernet Sauvignon Rosé, Domaine de Clairac: dry pink, with more structure and flavour than the Joubio pink above. ▲
- VdP d'Oc, Cabernet Sauvignon, Domaine de Clairac: dry red, firm example of southern French Cabernet, suitable for vegetarians in 1997 and 1998. ▲
- VdP d'Oc, Merlot, Domaine de Picheral: dry red, shows sweet jammy fruit; a crowd pleaser and suitable for vegetarians. ▲
- Cabardès AC, Jacques Frélin: dry red blend of southern French and Bordeaux varieties, non-oak aged. ▲
- Côtes du Rhône AC, Jacques Frélin: dry red made from 100 per cent Syrah in 1997 and 1998; the junior, more immediately approachable relation to the Crozes-Hermitage mentioned above. ▲

Domaine Costeplan
30260 Cannes et Clairan
Tel:+33 466 77 85 02
Fax:+33 466 77 85 47
Stockist: Vintage Roots

This certified organic domaine belongs to Vincent and Françoise Coste. There are 32 hectares. Wines made include:

- VdP d'Oc, Vermentino: dry white, tropical fruit, clean modern style, slightly dusty. ▲
- VdP du Gard, Chardonnay: dry white, slight woodiness, tastes of oak chips; suitable for vegans. ▲▲
- VdP du Gard, Rouge, Cuvée Speciale: dry red, smells of burnt rubber (Carignan and Merlot grown in a warm climate), cleaner to taste, suitable for vegans. ▲

Domaine du Farlet
34140 Mèze
Tel:+33 467 43 50 05
Fax:+33 467 43 54 60
Stockists: Vintage Roots; Vinceremos
Overall Price Rating: ☖

This certified organic Languedoc domaine is owned by André and Jacques Duplan. There are 14 hectares of Merlot and Cabernet Sauvignon for red wines and Sauvignon Blanc, Chardonnay and Viognier for dry whites. The vines are relatively young because the oldest plots were ripped out to make way for a golf course. The wines are sold under the Vin de Pays des Collines de la Maure designation. The reds are lean but the whites, especially the Viognier, show more substance.

Domaine la Fon de Lacan
34230 St Pargoire
Tel:+33 467 96 75 58
Fax:+33 467 96 75 58

This domaine is due full organic certification in 1999. Owner and winemaker Alain Malric works with 24 hectares of Syrah, Mourvèdre, Grenache, Merlot, Cabernet Sauvignon, Carignan and Cinsault.

- VdP d'Oc, Mas Tessier: dry red; in 1997 a blend of Merlot (70 per cent) and Cabernet Sauvignon (30 per cent); shows thick fruit made in modern style (soft tannins, even texture). In 1998 the blend was reversed – Merlot 30 per cent and Cabernet Sauvignon 70 per cent – and showed more freshness and less puppy fat. Both are satisfying though. ☖
- Coteaux du Languedoc AC, Domaine La Fon de Lacan: dry red, in 1997 a blend comprising Syrah 50 per cent, Mourvèdre 30 per cent and 20 per cent Grenache; shows serious, elegant, ripe fruit, tidy all the way through, so a domaine to watch. ☖

Domaine Lou Pas d'Estrech

SARL le Sauzet, 30760 St-Christol-de-Rodières
Tel:+33 466 82 13 72
Fax:+33 466 82 19 94
Stockist: Vintage Roots
Overall Price Rating: ▮

This certified organic domaine is run by Christian Coste and Ezda Pedler and is located near Avignon. Three wines are made under the Vin de Pays des Coteaux de Cèze designations: dry white from Marsanne, Clairette and Bourboulenc; dry pink from Grenache Noir and Syrah; and dry red from Syrah with a little Cabernet. They offer good quality and value. In addition wine vinegar, which is prepared in oak vats, is made in white and red (i.e., *nature*) forms, as well as flavoured versions scented with raspberry, tarragon and shallot.

Domaine Mas de Janiny

21, place de la Pradette, 34230 Bauzille de la Sylve
Tel:+33 46757 96 70
Fax:+33 467 57 96 77
Overall Price Rating: ▮

This certified organic domaine is run by Thierry Julien, his brother Pascal and Pascal's wife Monique. There are 46 hectares of vines, and the size of the vineyard perhaps reflects the variability of the range. Of the varietals labelled as Vin de Pays d'Oc the Syrah seems to offer the most depth. The Merlot is rather out of balance (more alcohol than flavour) and the Sauvignon Blanc rather neutral (for a better one try Domaine de la Grangette, above).

Château du Parc

34120 Pezenas
Tel:+33 467 98 01 59
Fax:+33 467 98 01 59
Stockist: Organic Wine Company
Overall Price Rating: ▮

This certified organic domaine produces a respectable range of varietal wines under the Vin de Pays de l'Hérault designation. There are 27 hectares of Merlot, Syrah, Grenache Rouge, Cinsault, Mourvèdre, Cabernet Franc and Cabernet Sauvignon for reds, and Marsanne, Chardonnay and Viognier for dry whites. The Merlot holdings comprise two parcels, one of which is within a walled *clos* dating back to the 17th century. This is labelled as Domaine du Parc. The other label used is Domaine du Caillan. Both show plum and leaf flavours typical of this variety. The Chardonnay is a little light, so look for the Vin de Pays de l'Hérault Viognier because of its ripe apricot texture. All suitable for vegetarians.

ROUSSILLON

The Roussillon region occupies the department of Pyrenées-Orientales, between the Pyrenees and the Mediterranean. This part of the Midi began converting from bulk to quality wine production from the 1970s, earlier than Languedoc with which it is usually grouped. However it is now lagging behind as far as organic growing is concerned. The recent but ongoing conversion to organic methods of Domaine Cazes, one of Roussillon's most written about merchant domaines, may spur others here to do the same. For the moment however there is only one certified organic producer to note.

Clos/Domaine Saint Martin

20 avenue Lamartine, 66340 Bompas
Tel:+33 468 63 26 09
Fax:+33 468 63 14 04
Stockists: contact Vinceremos for details

This domaine belongs to the Coronat family and has been certified organic since 1991. There are 25 hectares of vines between Mount Canigou and the Mediterranean. A range of wines are made under the local Vin de Pays designations of Vin de Pays des Pyrenées-Orientales and Vin de Pays Catalanes ( ) (Roussillon was part of Spanish Mallora (Majorca) until 1642, hence the Catalan influence). Dry whites are made from Maccabeo and Vermentino, with Grenache, Syrah, Carignan, Merlot and Cabernet Sauvignon for reds. The dry whites are suitable for vegans. In addition, fortified sweet Muscat wines (*vin doux naturel*) are made under the Muscat de Rivesaltes AC (👣). The Muscat de Rivesaltes *vin doux naturel* is the only one in France to combine the two major Muscat sub-varieties: Muscat d'Alexandrie and the more aromatic Muscat Blanc à Petits Grains. The Coronat's example is representative of the general standard for this style.

USEFUL ADDRESS
Association Interprofessionnel des Vins Biologiques de Languedoc-Roussillon (AIVB-LR)
Mas de Saporta, 34970 Lattes
Tel:+33 467 92 25 02
Fax:+33 467 06 55 75
Email:aivblr@wanadoo.fr

This is the organic producer association for Languedoc-Roussillon.

Provence and Corsica

Potted histories of most French vineyard regions begin by saying that the Romans planted the first vineyards rather than the Greeks – think of Bordeaux and Burgundy for a start. Why did the Romans plant vineyards? To keep their soldiers from being thirsty – not for the wine the vines produced necessarily, but because the wine could be used to sterilize the water: harmful bacteria cannot survive in alcohol. A soldier with an upset stomach from drinking foul water is not going to help win many battles.

Provence, however, is unique in France: its vineyards were planted by the Greeks – from the 6th century BC when they colonized Provence's Mediterranean coastline and the island of Corsica. Today, Provence is best known to wine drinkers for its pink or rosé wines, sold sometimes in bottles designed to resemble Greek 'amphorae'. These pink wines generally taste best when drunk in a Provence restaurant on the Côte d'Azur while on holiday than they do after being shipped out of the region to your local wine merchant. If you want to drink these, or Provence's white or red wines, at home, try them with ratatouille, the region's most authentic and easily prepared dish. This combination of vegetables mixed with olive oil and wine is the basis of the 'Mediterranean Diet' that the health experts are so keen to promote.

Provence's landscape, covered with lavender fields, wild herbs and olive groves, rivals Tuscany as the most desired location for those wishing to buy or establish a 'lifestyle' organic vineyard. The only disadvantage in selecting Provence is the price of land, for conversion to organic methods is as easy here as anywhere in France. This is because the climate is the most Mediterranean in France – lots of sun during the growing season and enough rain during winter to keep the vine's metabolism in balance. Prevailing winds are warm and persistent enough to blow away moisture when this threatens the vine with fungal diseases. Also, the sunlight reflects brightly off the Mediterranean to help ripen grapes above ground, while below ground the region's (generally limestone) subsoils offer every opportunity for deep rooting. These help keep the vine strong enough to produce healthy grapes consistently. The attractions for the would-be organic grower are obvious. Currently organic vineyards account for nearly 4 per cent of the planted area (in 1998 1,100 hectares of 28,000 hectares). In 1999 another 400 hectares of organic vineyards in reconversion were due for full certification.

Côtes de Provence AC

This is the most important Provence regional designation in terms of size (18,000 hectares), and the one most likely to provide dry pink Provence or Provence rosé.

Mas de Gourgonnier

13890 Mouriès
Tel:+33 490 47 50 45
Fax:+33 490 47 51 36
Stockist: Organic Wine Company

Mas de Gourgonnier lies east of Arles in the Alpilles and has been certified organic since 1977. The owners here, the Cartiers, take manure for the vines from their own sheep which graze the Camargue (one brother looks after the sheep, the other makes the wine).

- Côtes de Provence Blanc AC, Mas de Gourgonnier: dry white made from vines planted in the mid-1980s, so now considered mature. This wine contains Ugni Blanc for freshness and Grenache Blanc for body. Drink within a year. For a more structured Grenache Blanc see Albet i Noya in Penedes, Spain (*page 273*). ⅄
- Côtes de Provence Rosé AC, Mas de Gourgonnier: dry pink made from free run juice which runs out of the vat when the grapes for the red wines (below) are put in it after picking. There is little tannin, so drink within 18 months. ⅄
- Côtes de Provence Rouge AC, Mas de Gourgonnier, Cuvée Tradition: dry red, blend of Cinsault, Grenache, Syrah and Cabernet Sauvignon; sturdy but not brutal. ⅄

- Côtes de Provence Rouge AC, Mas de Gourgonnier, Cuvée Réserve: dry red, blend of Grenache, Cabernet Sauvignon and Syrah; more instensity and purpose than the 'tradition', especially good in 1990, 1991 and 1995. ♦♦♦

Other products available include:

- cold pressed first pressing extra virgin olive oil: aromatic and savoury, highly regarded (Organic Wine Company, ♦♦♦).
- Nectar d'Abricot: thick, soup-like apricot juice, suitable for vegans (Organic Wine Company, ♦♦).
- almonds. ♦♦♦

Domaine du Jas d'Esclans
83920 La Motte
Stockists: Vintage Roots; Vinceremos

This Côtes de Provence domaine belongs to René Lorgues. He provides a value for money range for early drinking from certified organic vines.

- Domaine du Jas d'Esclans, Côtes de Provence Blanc AC: dry white, in 1997 a blend of Clairette, Sémillon, Ugni Blanc and Vermentino; good balance, needs chilling quite cool; suitable for vegans (Vinceremos, ♦).
- Domaine du Jas d'Esclans, Côtes de Provence Rosé AC: dry pink; find the most recent vintage to be sure of the fruit; suitable for vegans (Vintage Roots, ♦).
- Domaine du Jas d'Esclans, Côtes de Provence Rouge AC: dry red, ages in old oak vats as opposed to new barrels, making the fruit ready as soon as the wine is bottled, so ask whoever you buy this from when this was (Vintage Roots, Vinceremos, ♦).

Domaine de Landue
83210 Sollies-Pont
Tel:+33 494 28 94 87
Overall Price Rating: ♦♦

This certified organic domaine belongs to Georges Arnaud. A simple tasting range of wines are made under the Côtes de Provence AC.

Domaine de Pierrascas

883 RN97 (Route Nationale), 83130 La Garde
Tel:+33 494 08 25 30
Overall Price Rating: 🍶

This domaine belongs to Christian Berthoux and Anne de Bouard and has been certified organic since 1984. There are six hectares of Grenache, Mourvèdre, Syrah, Carignan and Cinsault for dry red and dry pink wines, and Rolle and Ugni Blanc for dry whites. All the wines are made under the Côtes de Provence AC, with the red the pick of them.

Domaine Richeaume

13114 Puyloubier
Tel:+33 442 66 31 27
Fax:+33 442 66 30 59
Stockists: Vinceremos; Yapp

This sculpture-dotted wine estate lies at the foot of Mont St Victoire and is owned by Henning Hoesch, a former Professor of Philosophy at Harvard. The vineyard covers 25 hectares and has had certified organic status since 1975. A variety of other crops are grown including wheat and olive oil. Nitrogen fixing grasses (*fourrage*) grown between the vine rows are grazed by the domaine's sheep. (For more information about cover crops, see Appendix 2.)

- VdP des Bouches du Rhône, Sauvignon Blanc: dry white, fermented in barrel, aged on the fine fermentation lees for six months; woody example of what lavish winemaking can do to a vin de pays wine. 🍶🍶
- Domaine Richeaume, Blanc (de Blancs), Côtes de Provence Blanc AC: dry white made from Clairette and Vermentino (or Rolle); clean citrus aroma with more southern richness apparent on the palate. 🍶🍶
- Domaine Richeaume, Côtes de Provence Rosé AC: dry pink, a blend of Grenache, Syrah and Cinsault; clean and accessible. 🍶🍶
- Domaine Richeaume, Cabernet Sauvignon, Côtes de Provence Rouge AC: dry red, first made in 1978, now made in the strapping image of California; suitable for vegetarians. 🍶🍶🍶

- Domaine Richeaume, Syrah, Côtes de Provence Rouge AC: dry red, opaque colour, silky-style fruit, too clean for organic Syrah for me (needs a bit of stink for the Syrah's raspberry fruit to be able to let loose); suitable for vegetarians (Vinceremos, Yapp, Tesco, 🍾🍾🍾).
- Domaine Richeaume, Cuvée Columelle Côtes de Provence AC: dry red, in 1995 a blend of Syrah, Cabernet Sauvignon and Merlot; again opaque colour, thick fruit, no rough edges so easier to pin down real flavour beneath sexy winemaking; suitable for vegetarians (Vinceremos, Yapp, Tesco, 🍾🍾🍾).
- Domaine Richeaume, Cuvée Tradition Côtes de Provence AC: dry red, in 1995 a blend of Cabernet Sauvignon, Grenache and Cabernet; indistinguishable from the wine above, suitable for vegetarians. 🍾🍾🍾

Domaine Saint André de Figuière

83250 La Londe des Maures
Tel:+33 494 66 92 10
Fax:+33 494 35 04 46
Internet: www.figuiere-provence.com

This domaine now belongs to Alain Combard, a Burgundian who used to make wine in Chablis. The vineyard was first certified organic in 1979 under the previous owners. In 1998 there were 10 hectares with full certification and another eight hectares in the process of conversion.

- Grande Cuvée Dauphine, Côtes de Provence Blanc AC: dry white, made in 1997 from 50 per cent Rolle, 25 per cent Ugni Blanc, 25 per cent Semillon; shows clean, clear light style of slightly herby fruit more typical of dry pink or Provence rosé. 🍾
- Grande Cuvée Vieilles Vignes, Côtes de Provence Rouge AC: dry red, made in 1997 from 70 per cent Mourvèdre and 30 per cent Vieux Carignan; rather lightweight for these grape varieties. 🍾🍾

Coteaux d'Aix en Provence Les Baux AC

Les Baux is the most prestigious enclave of the Coteaux d'Aix en Provence, and includes the hilltop towns of les Baux and St Rémy. They are sheltered from the worst excesses of the Mistral by the Alpilles hills.

Domaine Hauvette

Chemin du Trou des Boefs, Haute Galine, 13210 St Rémy de Provence
Tel:+33 490 92 03 90
Fax:+33 490 92 08 91
Overall Price Rating: 🍶

This domaine takes its name from its owner, Dominique Hauvette, a former ski instructor. The vineyard covers six hectares and has been certified organic since 1990.

- Domaine Hauvette, Coteaux d'Aix en Provence Blanc AC: dry white, made from the Clairette grape variety, supplemented by Ugni Blanc and Rolle; aged in oak to produce a fat style.
- Domaine Hauvette, Les Baux de Provence Rosé AC: dry pink, shows a range of flavours and good balance.
- Domaine Hauvette, Les Baux de Provence Rouge AC: dry red, made from Grenache, Syrah and Cabernet Sauvignon; shows firm fruit early on but fills out well over 5 years.

Château Romanin

13210 St Remy de Provence
Tel:+33 490 92 45 87
Fax:+33 490 92 24 36
Stockist: Vintage Roots

This vineyard is said to occupy a former Druid site from where the Earth Mother was venerated. In 1990 it became Demeter-certified biodynamic, and now comprises over 50 hectares. There are two halves with the most recent planted from 1989, and the other dating from the 1960s. The grapes are picked by hand.

- Château Romanin, Coteaux d'Aix en Provence Les Baux Blanc AC (unoaked): dry white, in 1997 contained Rolle only; tropical clean modern style. 🍶
- Château Romanin, Coteaux d'Aix en Provence Les Baux Blanc AC (oaked): dry white, in 1997 a blend of Rolle (fermented in barrel) and

Ugni Blanc (fermented in stainless steel tanks), a two-tier approach which works well for the wood adds to rather than detracts from the wine. ♂♂

- Château Romanin, Coteaux d'Aix en Provence Les Baux Rosé AC: dry pink, in 1997 a blend of Counoise, Grenache, Syrah, Cabernet Sauvignon and Cinsault (all red grapes), well made example of this vintage. ♂
- Château Romanin, Coteaux d'Aix en Provence Les Baux Rouge AC: dry red, in 1996 a blend of Grenache, Syrah, Mourvèdre and Cabernet Sauvignon; soft, chewy, easy style of fruit, forgoes structure for easy appeal; suitable for vegans. ♂♂♂
- Vin Cuit: sweet dark white, a dessert wine made from heated juice that is then fermented in glass jars (*bonbonnes*). ♂♂♂

Domaine des Terres Blanches
13210 St Rémy de Provence
Tel:+33 490 95 91 66
Fax:+33 490 95 99 04
Stockists: Vintage Roots; Organic Wine Company; Vinceremos; Chartrand Imports (USA)

This domaine was first certified organic in 1968 and is one of France's benchmark organic domaines. There are over 30 hectares of vines, fertilised by mixing horse manure with straw and ground-up brushwood. Seaweed and plant essences are also applied. The vines are hand picked and the wines offer excellent value.

- Domaine des Terres Blanches, Coteaux d'Aix en Provence Blancs de Blancs AC: dry white, similar to Gourgonnier's (*see page 133*), but fresher and richer. In 1998 a blend of Ugni Blanc and Rolle with smaller percentages of Grenache Blanc and Sauvignon Blanc; suitable for vegetarians (Organic Wine Company, ♂).
- Domaine des Terres Blanches, Coteaux d'Aix en Provence Rosé AC: dry pink, more elegant than Mas de Gourgonnier, but not necessarily any more flavoured. In 1998 a blend of Grenache and Mourvèdre with smaller percentages of Syrah and Counoise; fresh, excellent. ♂

- Domaine des Terres Blanches, Coteaux d'Aix en Provence Rouge AC: dry red, somewhat more Bordeaux in style than Provence, the Cabernet Sauvignon element coming though in the blend, which also contains Syrah and Mourvèdre; light, not for keeping. ♪
- Domaine des Terres Blanches, Cuvée Aurélia, Coteaux d'Aix en Provence Rouge AC: dry red, more consistent and more tannic than the regular red bottling directly above, sees more oak too; suitable for vegans (Vintage Roots, ♪♪♪).

Domaine de Trévallon
13150 St-Etienne-du-Grès
Stockist: Yapp

This domaine practises organic methods but has never been certified organic. The current owner, the ruddy faced Eloi Durrbach, apprenticed at Château Vignelaure (see below) when this vineyard was being farmed organically by its previous owner. The Trévallon vineyard was in ruins in 1974 when Durrbach inherited it, so he replanted it using cuttings taken from the Vignelaure vineyard (and some of the cuttings there came from the Rhône – varieties like Syrah for example). Insects are discouraged by preparations derived from the lavender which surrounds the vineyard, and manure is provided by flocks of sheep.

- Domaine de Trévallon, Vin de Pays Blanc: dry white made from Marsanne and Roussanne, two grapes associated with the northern Rhône; here they produce a broad, generous white with a refreshing quality – and a powerful alcoholic punch. ♪♪♪
- Domaine de Trévallon, Coteaux d'Aix en Provence (Les Baux) Rouge AC: dry red, made from Syrah and Cabernet Sauvignon. First made in 1977, seems to improve with each new vintage as the vines age and can be one of the most complex but understated red wines in Provence. Look for the fine 1982 vintage, the richer 1983, the elegant 1985 and 1994, and the 1995 (labelled as a Vin de Pays Rouge on the orders of the French authorities, who said that the wine did not taste 'typical' enough to bear the Coteaux d'Aix en Provence (Les Baux) Rouge AC – even though this wine is a ringer for the region in general and this domaine in particular). ♪♪♪

Domaine de la Vallongue

BP 4, 13810 Eygalières
Tel:+33 490 95 91 70
Fax:+33 490 95 97 76
Overall Price Rating: ▟

This certified organic domaine covers 38 hectares and is owned by Philippe-Paul Cavalier and Caroline de Clerck. The vines are picked by machine. Wines made include a dry white released as Coteaux d'Aix en Provence Blanc AC, and dry pink and dry red wines made under Les Baux de Provence AC. The wines are dependable, show clean, occasionally complex fruit and are not excessively priced.

Bandol AC

The Bandol region covers just over 1,000 hectares in a chain of hills behind the Mediterranean port of the same name. The main red grape is the Mourvèdre, which gives incredibly thick, bilberry and leather scented wines that repay keeping for a decade at least. The dry white and pink wines made here are improving with every vintage.

Château Sainte-Anne

83330 Ste-Anne d'Evenos
Tel:+33 494 90 35 40
Fax:+33 494 90 34 20
Accommodation: gîtes; bed and breakfast

This is the first Bandol estate to be certified as organic (in 1994). There are 15 hectares of vines, owned by François Dutheil de la Rochère, his wife Françoise and their daughter Marie. All three Bandol styles are made (dry white, pink and red) but in a generally much lighter and accessible style than the Bandol norm.

- Bandol Blanc AC: dry white, in 1995 a blend of 50 per cent Ugni Blanc and 50 per cent Clairette; made in a cool fermented style; shows acacia, vanilla; good balance and length. ▟
- Bandol Rosé AC: dry pink, shows tidy fresh fruit. ▟

- Bandol Rouge AC: dry red, in 1996 showed round plum fruit, and burnt earth, needs years to cool down for sipping (until 2004). ♙
- Vin de Collection, Bandol Rouge AC: dry red, in 1995 made from 98 per cent Mourvèdre, the variety which reaches its apogee on the Bandol slopes; mixes bootleather and violets. 'You either like it or you don't', say they who make it. ♙

Coteaux d'Aix en Provence AC

The part of the Provence vineyard which links Marseilles with Mont St Victoire. There is one producer of historical note.

Château Vignelaure

route des Jouques, 83560 Rians

This estate seems to have disappeared from the list of paid-up certified organic vineyards from 1995 when it was purchased by an English company belonging to globetrotting flying winemakers. The vineyard was planted from the mid-1960s by an organic-minded emigré of Bordeaux. Cabernet Sauvignon and Syrah were given the firmest slopes and Grenache looser, lower lying ground. Until 1995 the one red wine produced here by Château Vignelaure showed a rich mahogany colour (it aged in big Hungarian oak oval shaped casks perversely), a scent of the *garrigue* and ripe tannins with a dry aftertaste.

Côtes de Lubéron AC

The slopes of the Montagne du Lubéron still provide dry white, pink and red wines which are rich but fresh. The producer listed below is arguably the finest in an appellation.

Château de la Canorgue

route du Pont Julien, 84480 Bonnieux
Tel:+33 490 75 81 01
Fax:+33 490 75 82 98
Visitors: except Sundays and public holidays; winter by appointment
Stockists: Vintage Roots; Yapp

This certified organic domaine produced its first vintage under current owners Jean-Pierre Margan and his wife Martine in 1978. The first vintage ever here was under the Romans, who had tracked underground water sources here. There are 34 hectares across 88 small plots, so the current owners must have a lot of fun when it comes to blending. All the wines are hand picked (made easier by pruning the vines to grow horizontally along cordons rather than vertically from canes as is the current fashion in Provence).

- VdP de Vaucluse, Chardonnay: dry white, positive feel all the way through, good example of style and substance combining. ♙
- VdP de Vaucluse, Viognier: dry white, made from vines planted in 1992 but already shows bright apricot fruit, finely woven to the alcohol (13.5 per cent). ♙♙
- Château la Canorgue, Côtes de Lubéron Blanc AC: dry white, a blend in 1997 of Clairette, Bourboulenc and Chardonnay, and in 1998 of Clairette, Marsanne and Roussanne. Shows thick, exotic fruit with a green lime at its core; easy wine to enjoy; suitable for vegans. ♙♙
- Château la Canorgue, Côtes de Lubéron Rosé AC: dry pink blend, in 1997 of Cinsault and Grenache; pale to look at, deeper to greet (John Armit, ♙♙).
- Château la Canorgue, Côtes de Lubéron Rouge AC: blend of Grenache, Mourvèdre, Syrah, Merlot and Cabernet Sauvignon which sees new oak but where the fruit shines (because the tannins within the fruit are refined, and capture the oak, rather than submit to it). Very happy with its wood. ♙♙

Other Provence Domaines

Domaine des Alysses
Bas-Deffens, 83670 Ponteves
Tel:+33 494 77 10 36
Overall Price Rating: ♙

This certified organic domaine belongs to Jean-Marc Etienne and lies in the Coteaux Varois AC. The region lies at relatively high altitude, and is sheltered from the warming influence of the Mediterranean, so dry white and dry pink rather then dry red wine styles are favoured. All three styles are made here under the Coteaux Varois AC, with the pink the pick of the bunch.

Domaine l'Attilon
13104 Mas-Thibert
Tel:+33 490 98 70 04
Fax:+33 490 98 72 30
Overall Price Rating: ❧

This large certified organic domaine covers nearly 80 hectares and is owned by Renaud de Roux. Merlot, Cabernet Sauvignon, Caladoc (an old but disease-resistant Provençal variety), Grenache and Cinsault are planted for red, with Chardonnay, Carignan, Alicante and Sauvignon Blanc for whites. Dry red, pink and white wines are made but showed only moderate varietal character in the middle 1990s.

CORSICA

Corsica is France's equivalent of Sicily – a hot Mediterranean island well-suited to organic wine production. The island is considered to be part of Provence in wine books. Corsica, however, considers Provence its junior, and with some historical justification – vineyards were widespread here under the Greeks at least six centuries before they were introduced on a large scale to what is now mainland Provence by the Romans.

François Francisci
BP 148 Rue Gl. Graziani, Clos P. Rossa, 20230 Ile Rousse
Tel:+33 495 60 00 33

This certified organic domaine could be the most dynamic of the three cited here if the owner's plans for better winemaking facilities reach fruition.

Domaine de Granajolo

20144 Ste Lucie de Porto-Vecchio (Corse du Sud)

Tel:+33 495 71 40 34

Fax:+33 495 71 57 36

Email: MBOU699633@aol.com

Overall Price Rating: 🍷🍷

Domaine de Granajolo is one of the sunniest vineyards in France. Certified organic since 1987 it covers 25 hectares on Corsica's southern Mediterranean coastline. The grape pickers have to complete each day's work before midday and the full heat of the sun at harvest. The wines are made in a local cooperative (the Marana) but standards there appear rudimentary.

- Vin de Corse Blanc AC: dry, full, crisp, slightly resinous white, made from Vermentino Corse, Corsica's most widely planted white wine variety (called 'Malvoisie' on the French mainland).
- Vin de Corse Rosé AC: dry pink, full-bodied, made from Barbarossa (or 'Barbaroux'), which almost died out here in the 19th century.
- Vin de Corse Rouge AC: dry red, made from three dark-skinned varieties, Grenache, Nieluccio and Sciacarello. Grenache arrived on Corsica after the Algerian Civil War of the 1950s. Nieluccio is thought to be the same as the Sangiovese of Chianti (*see Italy*). The last, Sciacarello, is probably one of a number of wine producing vines which are indigenous to the island. Its thick skins resist fungal attack but take a long time to ripen, even in Corsica's abundant sun.

Domaine Martini

Eccica Suarella, 20217 Cauro

Overall Price Rating: 🍷

This certified organic domaine lies in the Coteaux d'Ajaccio AC, the vineyard region surrounding Corsica's capital city (and Napoleon's birthplace). The domaine is a source of light red wines, made (it appears) for local consumption.

The Rhône Valley

The Rhône Valley runs north–south and follows the course of the Rhône River. It links southern Burgundy with the Mediterranean and is divided into two halves. The narrow northern half is famous for its thick, smoky reds made from the Syrah grape. Mediterranean heat is drawn up from the more open southern part of the area with the result that northern Rhône Syrah ripens to high alcohol and tannin (colour) levels. The wines can be so brutal that white grapes such as Viognier, Marsanne and Roussanne are sometimes added to the vats to make the Syrah less aggressive (see Domaine Saint-Apollinaire). When the white grapes are pressed and fermented on their own, the white wines which result can be amongst the most exotic and powerful in France. The terrain is so steep and unforgiving that many of the finest vineyard sites were abandoned until recently. A surge of interest in the northern Rhône wines has made these vineyards profitable again, and has tempted growers to replant.

In the southern Rhône, where the Mediterranean influence is even more pronounced, the Syrah variety is joined by other red varieties such as Grenache, Mourvèdre and Cinsault. The best wine villages here lie further back from the Rhône river than the villages in the northern Rhône, and have their own appellations, such as Gigondas and Vacqueyras, and Châteauneuf du Pape. The arid soils and the dry heat mean yields of grapes can be half of what they are in wetter regions like Bordeaux or Champagne for example. Prices are creeping up for these village names, due to renewed interest from the Far East and the United States, so generic wines labelled as Côtes du Rhône or Côtes du Rhône Villages can offer the best bargains. The white wines from the Southern Rhône are often overshadowed by the reds; however they too can offer immense flavours for modest prices. Villages not entitled to their own appellation are listed under 'Other Rhône – Côtes du Rhône and Côtes du Rhône Villages'.

Growing grapes organically in the Rhône is relatively straight-forward if the vines are kept stress-free – in other words if they are encouraged to produce a reasonable rather than excessive crop in the heat. Otherwise they suffer heat stress, and become more susceptible to attacks from pests and disease. The heat plays its part at harvest too – if grapes are brought into the winery at too warm a temperature a 'wild' fermentation might result, spoiling the wine. This is especially true of industrial sized wineries which use huge tanks which must be chilled artificially. As the EU has no winemaking standard some of the refrigeration or chilling equipment used is environmentally questionable. Look for wines from smaller producers who can use old-fashioned methods to chill tanks or barrels because they hold smaller and more manageable quantities of wine – like stirring the juice to mix hot spots at the top of the tank which are already fermenting with cooler, unfermented juice from the bottom. This simple technique provides a longer fermentation too – and more natural richness in your bottle of Rhône.

NORTHERN RHÔNE

Hermitage AC

Hermitage has been described as producing the manliest red wine in France. It is made from Syrah grown on the steep hill of Hermitage which overlooks the town of Tain l'Hermitage. It is so steep that much spraying is now done by helicopter. There are just 130 hectares of vines, and over 30 of them are owned or managed by the merchant house of M. Chapoutier.

M. Chapoutier

18 avenue Docteur P. Durand, BP 38, 26600 Tain L'Hermitage
Tel:+33 475 08 28 65
Fax:+33 475 08 81 70

The merchant house of M. Chapoutier was founded in 1808. The firm is run by the seventh generation of Chapoutiers – brothers Michel (who looks after the vineyards) and Marc (who looks after everything else). In 1990 they took over from their father Max and are credited with instituting biodynamic methods on the 160 hectares of vineyards which the company owns in various appellations in the northern and southern parts of the Rhône Valley. None of these vineyards were registered with Demeter or any other recognized certification body in 1999. The 'biodynamic' grapes they produce are blended with other grapes bought in from a further 101 hectares of conventionally farmed vines under contract to the Chapoutiers both in the Rhône and in Provence.

Even though their vineyards are not certified biodynamic, and even though biodynamic growers say it takes seven years for the full benefits to be felt, the Chapoutiers are keen to promote their biodynamic credentials. In 1994 this caused what became known as the 'Rumpus in the Rhône'. In 1993 there were catastrophic floods in the Rhône, causing disruption and loss of life. Nevertheless, Michel Chapoutier wrote to the world's leading wine critic, Robert Parker Jnr, outlining how the adoption of biodynamic principles here had saved the Chapoutier grapes – the inference being that Chapoutiers' non-biodynamic neighbours had struggled during this Rhône vintage. This was disputed by the (then) 15 other Hermitage producers. They wrote to Mr Parker to say that the Chapoutiers had sprayed two-thirds of their Hermitage vineyards (presumably against the powdery mildew that was rife), and declared yields to the authorities which differed to those they had described to Parker.

Domaine Combier
Pont de l'Isère, 26600 Tain l'Hermitage
Stockist: Vintage Roots

This certified organic domaine produces one red wine from the commune next to Hermitage (and its junior relation), Crozes-Hermitage.

● Crozes-Hermitage AC: dry red made from Syrah; in 1995 and 1996 showed lovely thick Rhône flavours of pepper and raspberry, but in 1997 was sappier and less balanced, suitable for vegans.

SOUTHERN RHÔNE

Châteauneuf du Pape AC
At over 19,000 hectares in the Rhône this is the region's largest appellation. It is known for thunderous red wines that can leave a painful memory in your head long after the weekend is over. The region is famed for the large stones (*galets*) which cover some of the more famous vineyards. They hinder mechanization (which must be a good thing), help retain

moisture in the soil by shading it from the sun, and absorb and reflect heat onto the grapes making them super ripe. The list of permitted grape varieties for red Châteauneuf is the longest in France at 13, although a handful of these grapes are white. They also produce a small amount of dry white Châteauneuf du Pape.

Domaine Jacqueline André

17, rue Mendès France, 84350 Courthézon
Tel:+33 490 70 81 14/+33 490 70 73 25
Fax:+33 490 70 75 73
Stockists: Vinceremos; Vintage Roots; Chartrand Imports (USA)
Overall Price Rating: 🏭

This biodynamic Châteauneuf du Pape domaine comprises 18 hectares and has been certified by Demeter since 1990. It was certified organic for the 10 years previous to that. Both styles of Châteauneuf are made, but pick your vintage.

- Châteauneuf du Pape Blanc AC: dry white, hefty blend of Picpoul, Bourboulenc, Roussanne, Grenache Blanc and Clairette, suitable for vegans.
- Châteauneuf du Pape Rouge AC: dry red, blend of Grenache, Syrah, Mourvèdre, Cinsault, Muscardin and Counoise, suitable for vegans.

Château de Beaucastel

84350 Courthézon
Tel:+33 490 70 41 00
Fax:+33 490 70 41 19

This is part of a merchant house rather than solely a 'château' in the conventional sense, with a vineyard out front and a winery out back. Grapes are bought in by brothers François and Jean-Pierre Perrin who run the domaine. They say that since 1988 they have instituted a form of organic production on their own vineyards, but whatever form of organic methods this takes it is not certified by an accredited third party. Instead the brothers' green credentials are based on composting the pressed grapes and manure from their own sheep, as well as driving dung-powered cars. All this sounds pretty environmentally helpful.

However, the red wines made here under the Châteauneuf du Pape AC – Château de Beaucastel and its second wine Coudelet – are flash pasteurized (like milk) to 80°C. The only difference being that the price of a pinta here is a lot more expensive than the one delivered by your milkman. At auction Château de Beaucastel and Coudelet can achieve some of the highest prices paid for Châteauneuf du Pape. The Perrins say that the heating process improves the extraction of colour in the red. However, one should not need to extract colour like this, especially in Châteauneuf, because this appellation should (by law) produce the ripest grapes in France (enough for a minimum alcohol rate of 12.5 per cent – the highest in France according to the authorities). Pasteurization is discouraged by organic regulators in British Columbia where the weather is a darn sight colder than it is in the Rhône, because it denatures flavour in the wine (making it smell rubbery) and uses energy.

Even more extraordinary is that the Perrins bang on about how they are one of the few producers to use all of the 13 grape varieties permitted in Châteauneuf. Pasteurization means all the grape varieties end up tasting the same! If God had meant fermentation to reach 80°C then he would have given us yeasts capable of fermenting at that high temperature. Some critics defend the Perrins' approach to pasteurization saying that it protects the wine from spoilage (by destroying 'oxidases' which make the wine turn vinegary), which means less sulphur dioxide preservative (sulfites) need be used. But any Châteauneuf du Pape worth drinking contains at least 14 per cent alcohol (and sometimes up to 16 per cent). Alcohol is the most natural preservative of all for wine – not pasteurization.

Gigondas AC

Gigondas is a heavy, Grenache-dominated red wine that must come in its own crested bottled. Other elements of the Gigondas blend include Syrah and Mourvedre (15 per cent combined minimum), and Cinsault and Clairette (5 per cent maximum). The Romans named the town 'joy'. The modern motto the Gigondas' winemakers give to their reds is 'the perfume of the earth', which is true up to a point, because generally Gigondas is one of the more consistent French appellations. However don't get too carried away because the earth here has been bulldozed to allow mechanization of the flatter vineyards that account for well over 50 per cent of this 1,200 hectare AC. There are 80 main producers here, of which two make wines from certified organic grapes. One of these, Domaine Eric Saurel, is listed in Vacqueyras (*page 151*).

Clos du Joncuas

84190 Gigondas
Tel:+33 490 65 86 86
Fax:+33 490 65 83 68
Email: closjoncuas@caves-particulières.com
Internet: www.caves-particulières.com/membres/clos-du-joncuas
Stockist: Vinceremos
Overall Price Rating: ♦♦

This organic domaine consists of 28 hectares and belongs to Fernand and Dany Chastan. The varieties planted include Grenache, Mourvedre, Cinsault and Syrah for pink and red wine, and Clairette, Roussanne and Marsanne for white.

- Domaine La Garancière, Côtes du Rhône-Villages Séguret Blanc de Blancs AC: dry white, full, natural tasting even though filtered (to remove lactic bacteria to stop them eating the acid, without which the wine would be too flabby). 'Séguret' is a medieval hilltop village neigh-bouring Gigondas.

- Domaine La Garancière, Côtes du Rhône-Villages Séguret Rouge AC: dry red, shows appealing earth in 1996; a marker Côtes du Rhône. The balance of the fruit shows a steady fermentation.

- Clos du Joncuas, Gigondas Rosé AC: dry pink, made with Cinsault and Grenache, raspberry fruit, big style, subtle impact.

- Clos du Joncuas, Gigondas Rouge AC: dry red, shows as elegant per-fume, and raspberry fruit which opens naturally, bottled unfined and unfiltered (thus suitable for vegans).

- La Font de Papier, Vacqueyras AC: dry red, lighter weight than the wine above which signifies typicity – the vital quality for an organic wine to define itself.

Vacqueyras AC

Vacqueyras is one of the Côtes du Rhône communes allowed its own appellation for red wine. It tastes thick and jammy, and resembles Gigondas. It must contain over 50 per cent Grenache, and can be stunning for its warmth of fruit. The vineyards cover 1,450 hectares between the foot of the Dentelles de Montmirail and the valley of the Ouvèze. There are 200 wine families, of which one is converting to biodynamics. See also the organic Vacqueyras made by Clos du Joncuas in Gigondas, above.

Domaine le Clos de Caveau

84190 Vacqueyras
Tel:+33 490 65 85 33
Fax:+33 490 65 83 17
Stockists: Vinceremos, Vintage Roots

This certified organic domaine belongs to members of three families: Dugas, Bungener, and Guimerteau. There are 12 hectares of Grenache, Syrah, Cinsault and Mourvedre producing Côtes de Rhône Rouge AC (🍷) and Vacqueyras AC (🍷). The wines are suitable for vegans and are well worth finding for their easy, uncomplicated tannin.

Domaine Eric Saurel

Le Devés, 84260 Sarrians
Tel:+33 490 65 38 28/+33 490 65 40 34
Fax:+33 490 65 38 28
Email: Eric.saurel@wanadoo.fr
Stockists: Tesco; Vinceremos

This domaine belongs to Eric and Christine Saurel who began converting it officially to biodynamic methods in 1997. They will have full Demeter biodynamic certification from the 1999 vintage. The Saurels ceased using weed-killers in 1987 and abandoned pesticides in 1990. The vines cover 54 hectares of Grenache, Syrah, Mourvedre, Cinsault and Carignan – all dark-skinned varieties, including several parcels dating from the 1920s and 1930s. The grapes are picked by machine and are taken to a local cooperative, the Cave les Vins du Troubadour, where they ferment in temperature-controlled stainless steel vats (other non-organic wines are also made at this cooperative). The wines are yeasted and they age in cement.

- Vacqueyras AC, 'Montirius': dry red made from 24 hectares of Grenache, Syrah, Mourvèdre which showed clean, easy fruit in 1998. ♙

- Vacqueyras AC, 'Clos Montirius': dry red, made from eight hectares of Grenache and Syrah, protected from the Mistral wind by woodland. A tame but diverting Vacqueyras (Vinceremos, ♙♙)

- Gigondas AC, 'Montirius': dry red made from 16 hectares of Grenache and Mourvèdre. In 1998 showed moderate light garnet colour, clean, elegant fruit and fresh acidity (6,000 bottles). The vines are in two blocks at slightly different spot heights, with one on limestone (where the acidity comes from, to keep the wine in the Rhône heat) and the other on pebble, so it needs a bit more colour to be convincing. ♙

Clairette de Die AC

The valley of the river Drôme lies between the mountains of the Vercors and Provence. Today there are 1,250 hectares of vineyards, and the two grape varieties allowed are Muscat à Petits Grains and Clairette. Dry still white wines are made from the Clairette under the Clairette or Coteaux de Die ACs. The real treasures here though are the sparkling wines. They come in two forms, dry (Brut) or medium dry (Demi-Sec):

- Clairette de Die Brut: dry white sparkling wine made by the traditional method from Clairette and which contains 12 per cent alcohol. Labelled as 'Crémant de Die' by Domaine Achard-Vincent.
- Clairette de Die Tradition Demi-Sec: medium dry sparkling wine made using the *méthode rurale* or *méthode Diose*. The wine is blended from at least 80 per cent Muscat à Petits Grains, with Clairette making up the balance. It contains 7.5 per cent alcohol. The *méthode Diose* involves placing the wine, semi-fermented, into sealed bottles. The fermentation continues and the sparkle is retained because the bottle is sealed. After Christmas the bottles are emptied into a large tank, and the wine is rebottled under pressure, but with a filtration to remove the

yeasts which make the wine appear cloudy. The idea is to produce a clean wine with some alcohol and some sugar but not too much of each. Note that unlike in Champagne no sugar is added at the end as a 'dosage' or bottling sweetener.

Domaine Achard-Vincent

Le Village, 26150 Saint-Croix
Tel:+33 475 21 20 73
Fax:+33 475 21 20 88
Stockists: Organic Wine Company; Vinceremos; Vintage Roots; Yapp

This domaine has been certified organic since 1982 and is arguably the finest in this appellation. It belongs to Jean-Pierre and Claudie Achard. They make their own compost and use the 'cover and stir' method for green manures, i.e., they sow cover crops between the rows in autumn, and plough (stir) them in to the ground in spring, together with the prunings which are cut from the vine over winter. It keeps the vineyard tidy and the vines seem to like it too. See also Silver Thread Vineyard (*page 337*) for this method.

- Clos du Vignon, Coteaux de Die AC Blanc Sec: dry still white wine made from the Clairette, aged on the fine fermentation lees in tank (rather than barrel); shows clean, snappy fruit. 🍾
- Crémant de Die AC Brut: dry white sparkling wine made by the traditional method from 100 per cent Clairette. Only the first or 'free-run' juice is used at pressing. Spends nine months on the yeast caused by the secondary in-bottle fermentation before disgorging. Sound quality, half the price of 'real' Champagne, every bit as good in terms of finesse, if lighter in weight. 🍾🍾
- Clairette de Die AC, Gabrielle de Richaud (blue bottle): dry white sparkling wine made by the traditional method from 100 per cent Clairette. Spends 36 months on the yeast caused by the secondary in-bottle fermentation before disgorging, which gives it richer texture than the wine above, but keeps it clean and stylish. 🍾🍾🍾
- Clairette de Die Tradition AC: medium-sweet sparkling wine made by the *Méthode diose ancestrale* and contains Muscat à Petit Grains with

20 per cent Clairette. Shows exotic, grapey fruit that is delicious mid-morning and won't knock you over — only 7–8 per cent alcohol. This is the kind of sparkling wine everybody should try — so much more joy in this than dull old unripe Champagne. ▮

Cave Cooperative de Clairette de Die
avenue de la Clairette, 26150 Die
Tel:+33 475 22 30 00
Fax:+33 475 22 21 06
Overall Price Rating: ▮

This cooperative accounts for three-quarters of the wine produced in the appellation. It is supplied with certified organically grown grapes from nearly 16 hectares, with four hectares in conversion to full certification from 2000. Two sparkling wines are made, a Crémant de Die and a Clairette de Die, Ancestrale, which are sold to supermarkets in France under the 'Jadissanne' and 'Calpella' labels. They are earthy and dull, and lack the cleanliness and vibrancy of the Achard-Vincent range above. A still white wine made from Chardonnay and Aligoté is released under the Chatillon-en-Dios AC, a sub-region of the Die AC, and displays the same characteristics as the sparkling wines.

Côtes du Ventoux AC
The Côtes de Ventoux occupies the southern slopes of the Mont Ventoux on the eastern side of the Rhône Valley. Refreshing red wines are made from Cinsault, Carignan, Grenache, Syrah and Mourvèdre with dry whites from Bourboulenc and Clairette.

Domaine Patrick Pélisson
Les Bartagnons, 84220 Goults
Tel:+33 490 72 23 91
Stockist: Vintage Roots

This Demeter-certified biodynamic domaine comprises 6.52 hectares of vines, melons, tomatoes and garlic. The Côtes de Ventoux is often viewed as a source of light, simple reds but the example made here has real substance.

- Côtes du Ventoux Rouge AC: dry red, blend of Cinsault, Carignan, Grenache, Syrah and Mourvèdre; shows clear, ripe, balanced, damson fruit; delicious and suitable for vegans. ♙

Domaine Terres de Solence
Chemin de la Lègue, 84380 Mazan
Tel:+33 490 60 55 31
Fax:+33 490 60 55 34
Email: solence@club-internet.fr

This Côtes de Ventoux domaine is located near Carpentras, between Gordes and Avignon and its vineyard has been certified organic since 1997. There are 10 hectares and all the vines are picked by hand. The fermentation vats are located in a 13th-century priory, but the origins of the domaine are recent. Owners Jean-Luc and Anne-Marie Isnard only began acquiring their vines since 1992 with the help of three old men – their fathers and an old family friend. They are honoured in the Cuvée des Trois Pères. All the wines are suitable for vegans.

- Cuvée du Prieuré (Saint-Donat), Côtes du Ventoux Rouge AC: dry red, named after the *prieuré* (priory), the oldest building in Mazan. In 1997 a blend of 80 per cent Grenache, 10 per cent Mourvedre and 10 per cent Counoise (an old Châteauneuf variety); a little green, light, lacks a little fruit (12.5 per cent alcohol). ♙
- Cuvée des Trois Pères, Côtes du Ventoux Rouge AC: dry red, made from vines with a higher average age than those in the Cuvée du Prieuré and, accordingly, shows more extract (thickness to its fruit) and alcohol (13.5 per cent). In 1997 a blend of 70 per cent Grenache, 20 per cent Carignan and 10 per cent Syrah. ♙♙♙
- Cuvée du Bois des Amants, Côtes du Ventoux Rosé AC: dry pink, made with Grenache and Syrah; named after a tree which witnessed 'tender moments' somewhere on the domaine... ♙

OTHER RHÔNE – CÔTES DU RHÔNE AND CÔTES DU RHÔNE VILLAGES

Cave l'Arbre aux Soleils
84110 Faucon
Tel:+33 490 46 49 14
Fax:+33 490 46 49 11
Stockist: Organic Wine Company

This small cooperative lies at the foot of Mont Ventoux and is run by a group of organically minded growers headed by Pierre Joly (no relation of *biodynamiste extraordinaire*, Nicolas in Savennières in the Loire). The growers farm 25 hectares of vines and describe themselves as 'Les Paysans Bio de Haute Provence' ('the peasant organic wine growers of the Haute-Provence department'). The vines, all dark-skinned, include Grenache, Syrah and Cinsault, and have been certified organic since 1985. Two red wines are made, as well as honey, herbs, cereals, truffles, fresh fruits and a mean (but expensive) tapenade from local olives. The cooperative also produces grape juice, apricot juice and tomato juice (all organic). Some of the juices are imported by the Organic Wine Company and you can dilute them with water (still or sparkling) to make them go further. 🍷

- Cuvée Racines, Côtes du Rhône Rouge AC: dry red, firm tannic style even though the stems and the pips are removed from the grapes as they are crushed before vatting; needs a barbecued steak, but suitable for vegetarians. 🍷
- Côtes du Rhône Villages Rouge AC: dry red, a touch more elegant than the wine above, suitable for vegetarians. 🍷

Domaine des Cèdres
30200 St Nazaire
Tel:+33 466 89 99 31 (office)/+33 466 89 66 09
Fax:+33 466 89 10 58
Stockist: Chartrand Imports (USA)
Overall Price Rating: 🍷

This organic domaine belongs to the Pons family who make a range of wines from vines in three communes entitled to the Côtes de Rhône AC, and one commune in the Côtes du Ventoux (see above). The style appears to be generally on the light side. Wines made include a dry white sparkling wine made by the traditional method, and Côtes du Rhône in red, pink and white forms (all dry, and still) under the Domaine St Clair, Les Rainettes, Les Romarins and Vignoble Pons labels.

Vignoble de la Jasse
84150 Violès
Tel:+33 490 70 93 47
Stockist: Vinceremos

This domaine has been certified organic since 1972 and under Daniel Combe produces a light, crisp Côtes du Rhône.

- Côtes du Rhône Rouge AC: dry red, made from Grenache, Mourvedre and Cinsault; suitable for vegans. 👭

Louis Mousset
Château des Fines Roches, 84230 Châteauneuf du Pape
Tel:+33 490 83 70 30
Fax:+33 490 83 74 79
Stockists: Booths; Waitrose

This organic domaine produces a range of Rhône wines, including:

- Biovinum, Côtes du Rhône Rouge AC: dry red, approachable style of Rhône. 👤

Domaine de la Roche Buissière, GAEC Les Fleurs de Mai
Le Village, 84110 Faucon
Tel:+33 490 46 46 90/+33 490 46 51 94
Fax:+33 490 46 49 11

This organic Côtes du Rhône domaine was founded by three growers who used to take all of their grapes to the local cooperative (Cave de la

Vigneronne – see below). They are Jacques Llop, Pierre Joly and Joly's son Antoine. In 1998 they kept some of their grapes back for the first time to make wines under their own label. On the evidence of their first vintage their wines show more refinement than those of the cooperative for only modestly higher prices.

- Côtes du Rhône Rouge AC: dry red, first vintage in 1998, a blend of 60 per cent Grenache and 40 per cent Syrah; shows clean, soft red fruit for early drinking. 🌢

Domaine Saint-Apollinaire
Puyméras, 84110 Vaison-La-Romaine
Tel:+33 490 46 41 09
Fax:+33 490 46 44 16
Visits: daily 1000–1200 and 1400–1800 hours
Stockists: Vintage Roots; Organic Wine Company

This domaine belongs to the Daumas family and has been certified organic since 1967. It is the only one in the Rhône with its own certified organic trademark, called Dynorga which stands for 'dynamic and organic'. This reflects the fact that Domaine Saint-Apollinaire manages its vines according to both biodynamic and organic methods. In addition, the 'Dynorga' trademark signifies wines made with no added liquid sulphur dioxide preservative ('sulfites'). (This resembles the Californian system whereby a wine can be called organic only if it is made from organic grapes and without preservatives.) Thus Dynorga goes further than the European standard for wines made from organically or biodynamically grown grapes, where additions of sulphur dioxide are allowed because the EU has no winemaking standard for organic vineyards.

The grapes are hand picked and hand sorted. Even though the Daumas family own plots of vines in prestigious appellations like Hermitage and Condrieu for red and white wine respectively, in the northern Rhône they label their wines under the generic Côtes du Rhône appellations. This is a domaine that does things its own way and does them well as a result. It is a shame there are so few others like it.

- Blanc de Blancs (tirés sur lies fines): dry still white, a blend of Grenache Blanc, Ugni Blanc and Clairette grown on a north–north-east facing site to retain freshness (south facing would be too hot). Some of the vines were planted in the 1940s and 1960s. Shows deep ripe flavours without being heavy. The term *tirés sur lies fines* means the wine was bottled off its fine lees (like Muscadet sur Lie in Nantais, Loire), which minimizes the need for sulphur dioxide preservative. 👙 (when compared to Côtes du Rhône Blanc AC – this wine's nearest equivalent).
- Rosé: dry pink blend of Grenache and Cinsault, expressive fruit, more than a match for most Tavel Rosé, the most celebrated pink wine of the Rhône, which tends to fade early and turn orange. 👙
- Viognier, L'Exceptionnel: dry white, made from Viognier grown at Condrieu in the northern Rhône, planted in 1973 and 1978. Undergoes slow fermentation in large wooden casks; shows very complex layers of tropical fruit; suitable for vegans. 👙 (when compared to Côtes du Rhône Blanc), 👙 (when compared to Condrieu).
- Cuvée d'Apolline, Côtes du Rhône Rouge AC: dry red blend of Grenache, Cinsault and Syrah which ages in small wooden casks and larger oak vats for 12–18 months. Suitable for vegans in 1994 and 1995 when unfined and slightly cloudy. An example of red wines the Romans (who first planted these vineyards) would have drunk and at what seems a very reasonable modern day price. 👙
- Cuvée Prestige, Syrah, Côtes du Rhône Rouge AC: dry red blend of Syrah (grown in Hermitage) and 5 per cent Grenache, or, in 1995, Syrah alone. Shows rich dark chocolate and raspberry fruit; may throw sediment. 👙
- La Quintessence: dry red blend of Grenache, Syrah and Viognier (white grape) which ages in new oak casks. Perhaps the addition of Viognier makes this wine the most floral of the domaine's red wines – most Rhône reds smell of leather rather than flowers. 👙 (when compared to Côtes du Rhône, this wine's nearest equivalent).

Domaine de la Grande Bellane

Earl Gaia, Saint-Mercellin, 84600 Valréas
Tel:+33 490 35 15 05
Fax:+33 490 35 63 82
Stockists: Co-op; Tesco; Sainsbury; Victoria Wine/First Quench; Vinceremos
Overall Price Rating: 👭

Jean Couston's domaine has been certified organic since 1973. There are 40 hectares of Syrah (80 per cent) and Grenache (20 per cent). Dry reds are produced under the following designations: Côtes du Rhône Rouge AC and Côtes du Rhône Villages Rouge AC. With such a large domaine the options for blending are many. The best bottlings here are concentrated, jammy reds that offer pleasurable drinking. Lesser bottlings appear rather less convincing, so taste before you buy.

Michel Delacroix

Route de la Gare
30390 Theziers
Tel:+33 466 57 57 18
Fax:+33 466 57 28 63
Stockist: contact Organic Wine Company for further details

This 14-hectare domaine has been certified organic since 1973. Dry pink and dry red wines are produced under the Vin de Pays du Gard designation (👤), and dry white and dry red wines are produced under the Côtes du Rhône AC (👭). The dry white Côtes du Rhône Blanc AC is a full bodied, crisp white that, with 2–3 years' bottle age, develops even fuller flavour, softer acidity and a honeyed quality. The pink and red wines made here show less clear-tasting fruit.

Domaine des Treilles

26770 Montbrison sur Lez
Tel:+33 475 53 51 69/+33 682 74 64 10
Fax:+33 475 53 68 01
Overall Price Rating: 👤

This organic domaine belongs to Patrice Mery and comprises 26 hectares of Grenache, Syrah, Carignan and Cinsault for reds, and Viognier, Marsanne, Roussanne and Clairette for whites. The wines produced include:

- Côtes du Rhône Blanc AC: dry white, powerful blend of 60 per cent Viognier and 40 per cent Roussanne in 1998, tasting of boiled sweets.
- Côtes du Rhône Rouge AC: dry red, ripe, satisfying but early drinking blend in 1998 of 60 per cent Syrah and 40 per cent Grenache.

Cave de la Vigneronne
Villedieu-Buisson, 84110 Villedieu
Tel:+33 490 28 92 37
Fax:+33 490 28 93 00
Stockists: Vinceremos; Organic Wine Company

This cooperative is run by a group of organically minded growers who draw grapes from 40 hectares of certified organic vines. Three of the cooperative growers here are involved in the new domaine La Roche Buissière in Faucon (see above).

- Côtes du Rhône Rouge AC: dry red, light, stylish; a good reference Côtes du Rhône with earthy Rhône flavours (Vinceremos, 🍷).
- Côtes du Rhône Villages Rouge AC: dry red, similar to the wine above only with a little more depth. 🍷

OTHER DRINKS FROM THE RHONE

Domaine de la Grande Grange
26730 La Baume d'Hostun
Stockists: Vintage Roots
Overall Price Rating: 🍷

This domaine lies in the Drôme department near Grenoble. Owners François and Denise Clot produce two sweet aperitif wines which are similar to Pineau des Charentes, except that they are flavoured with cherries and nuts respectively. In each case the base grape juice originates from Domaine St Apollinaire (see above).

- Cérise Ratafia, Aperitif Natural à Base de Vin: made from grape juice flavoured with organic cherries and grape brandy (rather than neutral spirit – see Pineau des Charentes); 23 per cent alcohol, suitable for vegans.
- Vinoix, Aperitif Natural à Base de Vin: made from grape juice flavoured with organic walnuts and grape spirit; 23 per cent alcohol, suitable for vegans.

Savoy

Savoy lies at the foothills of the Alps on the French-Swiss border. The cool temperatures the region's vineyards experience in autumn mean white, rather than red wines dominate production. Successful winemaking here is all about picking as ripe as you can, when you can. The best Savoy wines exhibit biting freshness, and this makes them the perfect match for the region's thick, creamy fondue (*la fondue Savoyarde*).

Michel Grisard

73250 Fréterive
Tel:+33 479 28 62 10
Fax:+33 479 28 61 74
Stockist: Georges Barbier

Michel Grisard stopped working with his father and three brothers in 1983 and struck out on his own 'for a challenge'. The family vineyards were divided, and Grisard's portion became the only one to be certified organic. He changed the way he pruned the vines to allow more permanent wood to be left after pruning – this helps the vine become more resistant to the cold of the Savoyard winter. From 1995 he began converting to biodynamics, but without Demeter certification. Biodynamic treatments used here include nettle and the biodynamic composts (*see Appendix 3 for more details*).

- Roussette, Roussette de Savoie AC: dry white, made from Roussette Grisard planted in 1985, a full-bodied variety which Grisard ferments like a Chardonnay – barrel fermented, matured on the fine fermentation lees and bottled within eight months. ♦♦♦
- Cuvée Tradition, Mondeuse, Vin de Savoie AC: dry red, made every year; juicy plum fruit. ♦♦♦

- Cuvée de Marquis, Mondeuse, Vin de Savoie AC: dry red, as above but ages in cask, during which time the fruit takes on a matt finish which here works rather well. ♙♙
- Cuvée Prestige, Mondeuse, Vin de Savoie AC: dry red; made only in exceptional years, i.e., 1989, 1990, 1992, 1995 and 1997. ♙♙♙

Château Marignan

Château de la Tour Marignan, 74140 Sciez
Tel:+33 450 72 70 30
Fax:+33 450 72 36 02
Overall Price Rating: ♙♙

This domaine has been certified organic since 1993. It is owned by Bernard Canelli-Suchet and comprises five hectares of Pinot Noir and Chasselas on the southern shores of Lake Geneva. The Chasselas is sold as Cru Marignan, a bone-dry white with a natural spritz (*perlant*), which is aged in large oak casks to soften it.

South West France

The vineyards of South West France are located in the vast area between the Bordeaux region, the Pyrenees mountains and the vineyards of the Midi. With the exception of major cities like Toulouse the area is sparsely populated, and the vine is only one of a number of agricultural crops grown. The terrain varies from the flat land of the Dordogne plain around Bergerac to the rocky ravines around Cahors in the Valley of the Lot. The influence on the South West of the more famous neighbouring wine regions is strong, so producers here have a potentially huge range of grape varieties and wine styles to choose from. Grape varieties associated with Bordeaux's temperate maritime climate are planted alongside grapes associated with the Mediterranean heat of the Midi and northern Spain. This means that unless you are a natural-born risk taker, you need to know what you are looking for as far as wine buying goes. This is especially important if you intend visiting producers direct, because some of them are in fairly remote locations. The many English wine lovers who have second homes in this part of France will tell you that when visiting producers here something good always turns up in the end, and when it does you won't forget where you found it.

Bergerac AC

Bergerac lies at the heart of the Périgord directly east of the Bordeaux region. It is in fact a continuation of the Côtes de Castillon. Bergerac produces the same styles of red and dry white wines as Bordeaux and from the same grape varieties. There are also oddities like Mérille, a red grape locally is known as Périgord. Producers in the sweet white wine appellations of Monbazillac and Montravel are also entitled to the Bergerac AC (see separate entries for these regions below).

Château Haut Pontet

24230 Véines
Tel:+33 553 27 55 63

This certified organic domaine comprises 18 hectares and is owned by Jean-Paul Gérome. Dry white, dry pink and dry red wines are made under the Bergerac AC (🍾), as well as sweet whites under the Montravel and Haut Montravel ACs (🍾).

Château Larchère

24240 Pomport
Tel:+33 553 58 25 84

This certified organic domaine belongs to Thierry Baudry and comprises 22 hectares. Dry white wines are made under the Bergerac Blanc Sec AC, as well as a sweet Monbazillac (see below). The red grape varieties here include a higher than average proportion of Cabernet Franc. In Bergerac most growers seem to concentrate on Merlot because it yields well and ripens earlier than Cabernet Franc. However the Cabernet Franc provides the wine with more perfume, if lighter body, than Merlot.

- Bergerac Rosé: dry pink wine with a peppery aroma, shows the value of Cabernet Franc in pink winemaking (a little bit of tannin, just enough colour, and a refreshing texture). 🍾
- Bergerac Rouge: dry red, shows notable perfume, if moderate structure. Made with a small amount of the local Périgord variety of grape. 🍾
- Monbazillac AC: sweet white, made from a vineyard planted with Sémillon (85 per cent), Sauvignon Blanc (10 per cent) and Muscadelle (5 per cent), although this wine is dominated by Sémillon entirely. 🍾

Cru des Valades

24560 Issigeac
Tel:+33 553 58 72 85
Overall Price Rating: 🍾

This domaine comprises 18 hectares and is owned by Jean Guiraud. It has been certified organic since 1970 and produces red wines only, under the Bergerac AC.

Cahors AC

Cahors is the name of the 'black wine' from the steep valley of the winding river Lot. It is made with the Malbec grape which plays a minor role in Bordeaux (see Bourg AC; here it can also be called Auxerrois or Cot). Up to 30 per cent of the wine can come from Merlot for softness and body, and Tannat for backbone and spice. Cahors was used in the Middle Ages to beef up the red wines of Bordeaux ready for the sea journey in barrel to markets in England and the Netherlands. Allow a day for the wines to breathe otherwise they appear 'dumb' – thick, flat and low on flavour when they should be rich, varied and distinctive. If, however, you're reading this and your dinner party guests are due to arrive in half an hour, pour the wine into a clean glass container, then back into the bottle, then back into the decanter/pitcher for serving. This allows air into the wine, making it more expressive. (A pitcher with a wide rim is better than a narrow necked decanter for Cahors – think of this wine being drawn from barrels below decks and being swigged without ceremony by sailors taking it under sail to the Low Countries.)

Domaine de Antenet
46700 Puy l'Evéque
Tel:+33 565 21 32 31
Fax:+33 565 36 41 89
Overall Price Rating: ▲

This certified organic domaine comprises seven hectares of Malbec (80 per cent) and Merlot (20 per cent) in the west of the Cahors AC. Here the vineyards are located close to the river Lot on low lying, heavy clay soils that produce brutal red wine. Owner Philippe Bessières uses a special fermenting vat (like a cement mixer, known as a rotary fermenter) to turn the juice as it ferments on the skins in an effort to obtain more colour than tannin at the end of fermentation. Two red wines are produced, a vin de table and a Cahors, as well as grape juice.

Domaine des Savarines

46090 Trespoux-Rassiels
Tel:+33 565 22 33 67

This biodynamic domaine lies in the east of the Cahors region, on the limestone hills (*causses*) above the town of Cahors and its magnificent medieval bridge over the Lot. You can spend hours looking for the correct ridge upon which the domaine is sited. The first vines were planted in 1970 by a small, wiry lady from the north of France called Danièle Biesbrouck. She gave up a career teaching in a riding school to live in what was then a ruin, a small stone house on a barren hillside covered in limestone scree. The vineyard now covers two hectares and is worked entirely by hand. Vines take years to root successfully in this soil and the struggle to maintain them almost proved too much for Biesbrouck. She admits that the arrival in 1989 of her partner Jean-Marie Borde proved critical in ensuring the survival of the domaine. Now there is even a small biodynamically maintained plot of fruit and oak trees. One wine is made, from hand picked grapes, and it is the most natural expression of the Malbec grape in this AC. It is suitable for vegans.

● Domaine des Savarines, Cahors AC: dry red, shows deep crimson rather than opaque colour but remains bright right to the rim of the glass. Its aroma is expressive of nuts, dried fruit and upland scrub. The tannins are appetizing and fresh, too good to dilute with any red Bordeaux. This wine shows the elegance that limestone soils can bring to the Malbec, a variety that can lose its balance on clay. ▲▲▲

Château Vent d'Autun

Moustans-Haut, 46800 Saint Matre
Tel:+33 565 31 96 75
Fax:+33 565 31 91 78

This biodynamic domaine takes its name from the warm sirocco which blows in autumn to concentrate and sweeten the grapes. The domaine is owned by Anne Godin and consists of fruit trees (plums) as well as vines. There are 6.5 hectares on both clay and limestone soils. The small amount of white wine made here is hand picked, but the reds are harvested by machine.

- Vigne Blanche: off-dry white, made from hand picked Mauzac, barrel fermented, bottled unfiltered but containing some unfermented (residual) sugar; shows thick, interesting fruit but lacks real clarity. 🍾🍾🍾
- Cahors AC: dry red, in 1997 a blend of 75 per cent Malbec (planted 1987) and 25 per cent Merlot (planted 1991); shows an amenable style of Cahors, a result of young vines running free. 🍾🍾🍾

Vin de Pays des Coteaux de Quercy

This vin de pays can be used by producers in Cahors for 'second string' labels, but also covers communes such as Montpezat de Quercy, which lie just outside the Cahors appellation.

Domaine de Lafage

82270 Montpezat de Quercy
Tel:+33 563 02 06 91/+33 563 02 07 09
Fax:+33 563 02 04 55
Stockist: Vintage Roots

This Demeter-certified biodynamic domaine is owned by Bernard Bouyssou, and consists of fruit trees (plums) and arable land, as well as vines. Bouyssou is an example of a highly animated French winemaker who makes understated wines, riper and thus more enjoyable than most of the wines made in the Cahors AC.

- VdP des Coteaux de Quercy (Rouge), Domaine de Lafage: dry red, made from Malbec, Merlot, Cabernet Franc and Tannat; shows very clean fruit, distinct and inviting for a red of only light to medium body. Tasted on several occasions in a variety of locations and always offers something new. 🍾🍾🍾

Gaillac AC

Gaillac was the first inland vineyard planted by the Romans after they began colonizing what is now France, and is the heart of the South West. Its collection of grape varieties and wine styles reflects both its location and its history. The southern part of the Gaillac region is known as Côtes de Tarn.

Domaine de la Tronque
81140 Castelnau de Montmirail
Tel:+33 563 33 18 87
Fax:+33 563 33 22 18

This certified organic domaine comprises seven hectares and is owned by Claude Leduc. Two red wines are made under the Gaillac Rouge AC from Cabernet Sauvignon (from Bordeaux), Duras (a local variety), Braucol (otherwise known as Fer, another local variety) and Syrah (from the Rhône). The difference between the two is that one is aged in tank (👤) while the other is aged in oak barrels (labelled *fût de chêne*, 👥). A white sparkling Gaillac is made using the same method as Blanquette de Limoux Ancéstrale (except the Blanquette grape here is known as Mauzac). This leaves a slightly cloudy wine, with full body and a slightly sweet taste (👥).

Domaine des Vignals
81150 Cestayrols
Tel:+33 463 55 41 53
Fax:+33 463 53 28 18
Overall Price Rating: 🍷

The owner here, Werner Schwarz, produces a range of dry white, dry pink, sweet white and dry red wines from certified organic vines. They include Côtes de Tarn Blanc Sec AC, Côtes de Tarn Blanc Doux AC, Côtes de Tarn Rosé AC, Côtes de Tarn Rouge AC and Gaillac Rouge AC.

Other certified organic domaines in the Gaillac region include:

Domaine de la Catalauze Lintin
81140 Cahuzac sur Verre
Tel:+33 563 56 07 97

Martine Lecomte
81600 Gaillac
Tel:+33 563 57 43 96

Unfortunately no further details are available on these domaines at present.

Jurançon

Jurançon is centred on the French town of Pau and overlooks the Pyrenees mountains. The vines are trained high off the ground (*en hautains*) to prevent frost damage. White wines predominate and are made in dry (Jurançon Sec AC), medium dry (Jurançon AC) and sweet (Jurançon Moelleux AC) versions. They are picked into November and display full body, exotic flavour and biting freshness.

Domaine de Souch

Laroin, 64110 Jurançon
Tel:+33 59 06 27 22
Fax:+33 59 06 51 55
Stockist: Richards Walford

This Jurançon domaine is adopting biodynamic practices with a view to full Demeter certification under its owners Yvonne and Jean René Hegoburu. Some of the vines occupy steep terraces, which are inconvenient to work but which are well-exposed to the sun. This is critical in late autumn if the grapes are to sweeten on the vine by becoming dehydrated (*passerilé*). The grapes here, all for white wines, include the Jurançon staples of Petit Manseng (70 per cent), Gros Manseng (20 per cent) and Courbu (10 per cent). The winery dates from 1807. The style of wine made here is clean and complex, gaining in intensity as the vineyard ages – much of it having been replanted in the late 1980s. This explains why the best recent vintage is 1994.

Monbazillac AC

Monbazillac produce sweet white wines in the image of Sauternes AC in Bordeaux, except here, since 1993, the grapes cannot be picked by machine. The region lies south west of Bergerac, and has one sub-region called Saussignac (listed separately, below). Monbazillac's dry white and red wines sell under the Bergerac AC.

Château le Barradis

24240 Monbazillac

Tel:+33 553 58 30 01

Fax:+33 553 58 26 13

Stockists: Vintage Roots; Organic Wine Company; Vinceremos

Overall Price Rating: ▮

This domaine belongs to Serge and Christiane Labasse-Gazzini's family and has been certified organic since 1968. The wines are somewhat inconsistent. They include sparkling wines in both dry white and dry red forms, as well as Bergerac Blanc Sec AC and Bergerac Rouge AC. Their best wine is:

● Château le Barradis, Monbazillac AC: sweet white made from late picked Sémillon (60 per cent), Sauvignon Blanc and Muscadelle; suitable for vegans.

Domaine de Cailloux

24240 Pomport

Tel:+33 553 27 86 26

Fax:+33 553 27 86 27

Overall Price Rating: ▮▮

This certified organic domaine comprises 24 hectares. Owner Dominique Jourdas makes dry Bergerac Blanc Sec and sweet white Monbazillac, but no red wine. Jourdas has resisted the temptation to switch to red varieties like the bulk of his Bergerac peers, who are keen to exploit those new wine drinkers who have appeared in the wake of 'red wine is good for you' press coverage. A similar domaine follows.

Domaine Grande Maison

24240 Monbazillac

Tel:+33 553 58 26 17

Fax:+33 553 24 97 36

Overall Price Rating: ▮▮

This domaine converted to certified organic methods under its owner Thierry Despres in 1990. Of 18 hectares, only one is given to red varieties (Merlot and the two Cabernets). These are used for a Côtes de Bergerac Rouge and a Bergerac Rosé. The bulk of the vineyard provides dry white Bergerac Blanc Sec and sweet white Monbazillac from Sémillon, Sauvignon Blanc and Muscadelle.

Château Theulet Marsalet et Gendre Marsalet

Château Grand Conseil, Le Marsalet, 24240 Monbazillac
Tel:+33 553 57 94 36
Fax:+33 553 61 34 81
Stockists: contact Organic Wine Company for details
Overall Price Rating: ▮

This domaine has been certified organic since 1969 and belongs to René Monbouche. There are 28 hectares, 17 for white and 11 for red. Dry wines are produced under the Bergerac ACs (red, white and pink), but the star wine here is the sweet white Monbazillac.

● Sélection de Grains Nobiles, Monbazillac AC: sweet white made predominantly from late picked Sémillon (the term *sélection de grains nobiles* is a play on the Alsace term *sélection de grains nobles*) with little evidence of the fruit being blasted with lots of new oak. The 1994 was moderately priced too. ▮▮

Montravel AC

Montravel is a designation for sweet white wines from within the Bergerac AC like Monbazillac, above. However unlike Monbazillac the sweet white Montravel wines display little 'noble rot' character. This is because the Montravel region lacks the necessary humidity for the rot to form and survive on the grape skins in late autum. The region's dry white and red wines can show succulent fruit and sell under the Bergerac AC.

Château Laroque

Laroque, 24230 St Antoine de Breuilh
Tel:+33 553 24 81 43
Fax:+33 553 24 13 08
Stockists: contact Organic Wine Company for details

This domaine gained biodynamic certification from Demeter in 1993. Its owners, Jacques and Elisabeth Faurichon de la Bardonnie, had farmed it organically for some years prior to that.

- Bergerac Rouge AC: dry red, made from a vineyard planted with Merlot (60 per cent), Cabernet Sauvignon (20 per cent), Cabernet Franc (15 per cent) and Malbec (Cot) (5 per cent). ♙
- Haut Montravel Sec AC: dry white, made predominantly from Sauvignon Blanc with Muscadelle and Sémillon. ▮
- Haut Montravel Blanc Moelleux AC: sweet white, marmalade-style fruit which keeps well for two or three days in the fridge once opened. ♙

Other products:
- Pétillant de Raisin (sparkling grape juice). ▮

Saussignac AC

This small sweet-white-wine producing sub-region of Monbazillac (see above) was first planted with vineyards by monks in the 13th century.

Château Richard

La Croix Blanche, 24240 Monestier
Tel:+33 553 58 49 13
Fax:+33 553 61 17 28
Visits: by appointment
Stockist: Vinceremos

Château Richard's owner, Richard Doughty, describes himself as a Welshman of Anglo-French parentage. He trained originally as a geologist before arriving at Château Richard in 1988. Since then his vineyard has been certified organic, and comprises 13 hectares on rolling slopes.

Just as the wheels were turning in the right direction for Château Richard, disaster struck when a severe spring frost wiped out the 1991 crop. Doughty still seems unsure as to how Château Richard survived this period (in the same vague way Danièle Biesbrouck, the owner of Domaine des Savarines (above), recalls her desperation in Cahors before 1989.) Triumph often comes out of adversity, so it can be a coincidence that these two individuals produce the most original 'bio' wines in South West France. Doughty lets the wines ferment with natural (rather than added) yeast and at their own pace. The sweet whites finish fermenting at Easter sometimes, or even later. Such slow natural fermentation is possible only with perfect grapes.

- Domaine de Richard, Bergerac Sec AC: dry white, mainly Sauvignon Blanc with Sémillon, suitable for vegans. Same style as Entre Deux Mers AC whites in Bordeaux but has much more flavour and is thus better value. ♟
- Château Richard Cuvée Non-Filtrée, Bergerac Sec AC: dry white, made from Sémillon which ages on its fermentation lees in cask (which protects it) and is bottled unfined and unfiltered (thus slightly cloudy). A reviving, tasty style of wine which exudes fruit; suitable for vegans. ♟♟
- Château Richard, Bergerac AC: dry red, Bordeaux-style blend of Merlot, Cabernet Franc and Cabernet Sauvignon. The aroma is ripe and berry scented, and the wine tannins dress rather then destroy one's gums. This wine shows Doughty can make red wine too (by having ripe grapes to pick), suitable for vegetarians. ♟
- Château Richard, Côtes de Bergerac AC: dry red, thicker than the above, shows the reassuring presence of old vines dating to 1933 and the use of oak ageing; suitable for vegans. ♟♟
- Château Richard, 'Tradition' Saussignac AC: sweet white, late picked, made in the image of Sauternes where Doughty studied the late picked, sweet white wine style, but shows fresher, cleaner, more even and more integrated 'noble rot' flavours (50 cl bottles, ♟♟).
- Château Richard, 'Tradition' Coup de Coeur Saussignac AC: sweet white, late picked, as above except made only in years of a natural abundance of 'noble rot' berries, like 1990. All the elements in this

wine co-habit rather than clash: sweetness, acidity, alcohol, noble rot flavours, grape flavours and new oak. Certainly on a par with the finest sweet wines the Loire or Alsace have to offer, too. 🍾🍾🍾

Austria

Austria's growing number of dynamic, quality oriented organic vineyards form part of the biggest organic farming movement in Europe – one in ten Austrian farms is organic. The Austrian government actively subsidizes organic farming and wine grapes attract some of the highest rates – three times more than if the ground was left to pasture for example. As in Switzerland (*see page 283*), minimal input, organic methods are well suited here because Austria's growing season is long and dry and vineyards tend to be small and eclectic (i.e., not geared for mass production and monocultural). Three-quarters of the wine produced is white and made in a full-bodied, dry style, but the current fashion is for red wines, made with Austrian grape varieties as well as imported ones (like Cabernet and Merlot from Bordeaux).

It is tempting to think that part of the impetus for Austria's organic vineyards resulted from the bad press the country received after the so-called 'anti-freeze scandal'. Diethylene glycol, an additive used in anti-freeze (not anti-freeze itself), was found in bulk sweet white wines in 1985. The truth is that Austria already had a core of organic growers before 1985, and this has been augmented by a new generation of producers who understand that quality begins in the vineyard rather than in the winery. The selection of producers below is a small one, but nevertheless includes some outstanding individual growers. They are ensuring that Austria is without question the country to watch as far as organic wine is concerned.

CERTIFICATION STANDARDS BODY

Austria's organic vineyards are certified by independent control agencies that must be approved by the governor of each of the federal provinces (*bundesland*). One of the biggest agencies is 'Ernte – für das Leben' – 'Harvest for Life'. Certified organic vineyards are found in three of

Austria's provinces: 30 hectares in Styria; 204 hectares in Burgenland and 380 hectares in Niederösterreich. The total organic vineyard is just over 600 hectares, or about 1.2 per cent of the country's total of 58,000 hectares. Of 181 certified producers, 180 are controlled according to rules laid down by Ernte, which is the largest organic association in Europe, with over 11,300 members in total (out of over 20,000 organic farmers in Austria). Of the wine producers, 55 sell their wine direct rather than in bulk.

All Ernte members are certified by the government-approved AustriaBioGarantie, but operate to standards that are stricter than the European minimum for wines made from organically grown grapes. During control visits members are inspected for their compliance to these higher Ernte rules. If successfully approved Ernte members can use the 'Bio Ernte' logo. This consists of the four elements: water (symbolized by the rain), earth (by a meadow), fire (by the sun) and air (by a cloud).

Ernte can be contacted at:

Ernte – für das Leben

Europlatz 4, 4020 Linz, Austria

Tel:+43 732 654 884

Fax:+43 732 654 884

Internet: country.co.at/country

Ernte Standards

If an organic vineyard is a member of one of the country's associations for organic farming, Austrian law stipulates that the standards for this association must be higher than the EU minimum. For Ernte members these tougher rules begin with the management of the soil. Growers must maintain vegetation (cover crops) between the vines to prevent erosion for 10 months of the year. They may only plough the cover crops into the ground at specified times during the spring, to prevent the nitrogen that the cover crops bring to the soil being washed into the water table and contributing to nitrate pollution. This ploughing must coincide with the moment the vines begin to need to draw nutrients from the soil, when their buds break and the shoots begin to grow.

There are also strict rules about what kind of materials may be used to clean the winery, with simple hot water and soda preferred. Remember it takes two litres of cleaning water to make a litre of wine and if this water is full of cleaning materials it can contribute to groundwater contamination. Another benefit is that populations of natural yeast are more likely to survive in wineries cleaned just with water than with chemical-based cleaning materials. (See Weingut Steindl for a winery fermenting its wines with natural yeast present on the grapes at picking, and Weingut Diwald for wines made with a variety of purchased strains.) Along the same lines is the rule encouraging growers to work with natural materials like oak vats instead of plastic ones (these are tolerated if already in the winery, but once certified, growers are forbidden to buy other tanks made of plastic). For packaging, plastic capsules must be avoided. Paper neck slips (banderoles) are preferred. The producer must also accept empty bottles returned by clients. The Ernte rules provide a model for future changes to EU legislation on wine growing and for rules on winemaking, should they ever be formulated.

Other Key Ernte Controls

- Production methods which require high inputs of energy and raw material are to be avoided.
- Organic waste must be returned to the vineyards.
- Waste water must not be polluting.
- Cold water, warm water, steam and mechanical methods are preferred for cleaning the winery, although soda, soap and wine acid can be used.
- Temperature control (heating or cooling) of the tanks during fermentation is allowed; pasteurization is not.
- Eggs used during the fining of reds must be organic.
- The synthetic fining PVPP and potassium ferrocyanide (used for the removal of iron and copper) are forbidden, in contrast to the KIP scheme (see below) which requires only that the winery be modified to meet its standards, but not the winemaking itself.
- Rulebreakers are expelled for life (they may, however, join certification bodies elsewhere in Austria or Europe).

THE KIP SCHEME

This is an EU-sponsored, low-input, sustainable scheme that became available to organic minded wine producers once Austria joined the European Union in 1996. It provides the grower with a small subsidy. However it should not be confused with full organic status because KIP allows growers to use one systemic spray treatment per season. Estates who work to this scheme include Mayer am Pfarrplatz in Vienna (UK stockist: Vintage Roots), Umathum in Neusiedlersee (UK stockist: T&W) and Willi Bründlmeyer (UK stockist: Richards Walford) in Wachau. The difficulty here is that readers must first check with the producer or the winery as to what systemic treatments have been employed. These treatments must be noted by the producer in writing. Readers have no need to do this with wines made by growers certified by Ernte – für das Leben.

BIODYNAMICS IN AUSTRIA

Austria's organic history is punctuated by the life of its countryman Rudolf Steiner, who formulated biodynamic methods of agriculture in the 1920s. One of the criteria for an Austrian farm certified as biodynamic by Demeter is that animals be part of the agricultural system. This furthers the notion of sustainable, self-sufficient farming beneficial to both man and the environment and is a rule unique to Austria. There were 1,000 farms certified biodynamic in Austria in 1998, but none were vineyards bottling wine of export quality.

AUSTRIAN ORGANIC LABELS

Products certified as organic carry the red Austria BioGarantie (ABG) certification seal to denote they conform to EU standards. Note that this seal is coloured black on wines made by members of Ernte to denote their stricter standards.

The term for an organic farming product in Austria is *aus biologischer Landwirtschaft*. This phrase may be used to denote wine made by organic vineyards. Austrian words for organic include: *biologisch* (biological), *organisch-biologisch* (organic-biologic) or *biologisch-dynamisch* (biodynamic) – or even *ökologisch* (ecological).

Members of associations like Ernte can also carry the Ernte logo.

Each controlled vineyard must feature the control number of the corresponding control agency. Wine producers subsidised by government for their organic vineyards are inspected by the AMA – the Austrian Ministry of Agriculture – to make sure they maintain their rights to their subsidy.

AUSTRIAN LABEL TERMS

As in Germany, Austria bases its quality wine law on the sugar content (specific gravity) of the grape juice or must at harvest (in contrast to France, Spain and Italy, for example, where the origin of the grapes, i.e., which vineyard/village they came from, is the thing that matters). All the sugar present in the wines with the following label terms will have come from the grapes (not from sugar added during chaptalization):

- *Kabinett*: denotes a dry wine (11–12.7 per cent alcohol). Austrian vineyards are warmer than Germany's and this produces extra ripeness or grape sugar and thus the potential for higher natural degrees of alcohol. The extra ripeness means most Austrian white wines do not need to have unfermented grape sugar present in the wine, as in Germany, to soften high levels of acidity. (Funnily enough, the Germans seem to like the drier styles – Germany is Austria's biggest export market for wine.)
- *Spätlese*: later picked and thus more full bodied Kabinett wine (12–14 per cent alcohol). Can be made dry or sweet, but is usually dry (like Kabinett, above). All the grapes used must be mentioned on the label.
- *Auslese*: picked from riper grapes than Spätlese, and thus sweeter. All the grapes used must be mentioned on the label. The grapes may be affected by 'noble rot'.
- *Beerenauslese*: picked from grapes affected by 'noble rot'; the style has an intense sweetness, and is full bodied and tastes thick ('with lots of extract').
- *Trockenbeerenauslese*: later picked and thus sweeter than Beerenauslese.
- *Eiswein*: 'icewine' must be made from grapes frozen on the vine (but they may be picked by machine, even if certified organic).

Note

All of the wines featured below are 'Quality Wines', so no sugar can be added to them (chaptalization) to boost the alcohol. However, when the producers release wines from the lower 'Table Wine' category they can chaptalize. Under Ernte rules the sugar used must be organic

AUSTRIA'S PROVINCES

Austria is a federal republic comprised of nine autonomous regions (*Bundesländer*). As the western part of the country is mountainous vineyards centre on the four eastern provinces. Three of these are profiled (the fourth, Vienna, encompasses Austria's capital city).

LOWER AUSTRIA OR 'NIEDERÖSTERREICH'

Lower Austria covers the western part of the country and over half Austria's vineyards. Sub-regions with organic vineyards include the following.

Donauland

Donauland forms a ridge of open farmland set several miles back from the north side of the Danube ('Donau'), west of the capital Vienna. Donauland's organic growers produce invigorating light- to medium-bodied, dry white and sparkling wines and light, scented reds. The locals drink them with charcuterie and semi-soft cheese.

Weingut Johann and Paula Diwald

3471 Grossriedenthal 35
Tel:+43 2279 7225
Overall Price Rating: 👥

Johann Diwald was the first grower in Donauland to convert his vineyards to organic methods, having first learnt to farm grain. The vineyards are planted on the wide spaced, high trained Austrian system called high culture (*hochkultur*) which gives agreeable, light wines. (This *hochkultur* system has had mixed results in Entre Deux Mers, Bordeaux.) The Diwald style is for clean, approachable wines made using cultured yeast and cool fermentation. They are bottled using bleach-free and silicon-free corks, and are suitable for vegans and vegetarians.

- Chardonnay: dry white, shows creamy, peach and melon fruit when made in a non-oak aged and Spätlese style; in 1997 a barrel fermented version (*Barrique*) was made.
- Frühroter Veltliner: dry white, with an exotic aroma, the influence perhaps of this variety's auburn-skins; needs drinking young (within 12 months); made from a vineyard called Diebsnest ('thieves nest'). This variety is also made in Kabinett, Spätlese, and Spätlese oak fermented (*Barrique*) styles, all of which are dry but increasingly oily and intense.

- Grüner Veltliner: dry white, shows restrained citrus fruit when made as a Kabinett; more expansive when made as a Spätlese and sourced from a vineyard called Reith.
- Riesling: dry white, shows controlled, linear stone fruit when made in a Kabinett style (11.2 per cent alcohol) from a vineyard called Holzern ('forest'); the style of Riesling which Austria excels at.
- Weissburgunder: dry white, made in Kabinett and Spätlese styles, fuller feel than the Riesling (above), balanced all the way through.
- Zweigelt: dry red made from Blauer Zweigelt which shows pale colour, like the skin of a sloe which needs rubbing for the colour to be revealed. The 1997 fermented three days on skins, was run off and pressed, and then aged a short time in large oak tuns.
- Zweigelt/Cabernet Sauvignon: dry red which gains richer tones from ageing in new (one-third) and two-year old barrels (two-thirds). Shows how dramatically a base wine (Zweigelt) can change its tone even with just a small percentage of Cabernet Sauvignon added (20 per cent).

Weingut Neudeggerhof

Neudegg 14, 3471 Grossriedenthal
Tel:+43 2279 7247
Visitors: tasting room located in an old stable (with doors dating from 1812)
Overall Price Rating: 🍶

Weingut Neudeggerhof is owned by the Mehofers who originate from Italy's Südtirol. Their vineyards began successful conversion to certified organic methods in the early 1980s. The red wines age in casks made from wood grown in forests belonging to the Mehofers. This woodland is protected from Austria's powerful hunting fraternity which, having exhausted the Danube foothills, is currently suffering from a lack of things to shoot. The village of Neudegg in which the winery lies has remained largely monocultural since it was first planted with vines in the 12th century, unlike most of the villages in this part of Donauland which grow arable crops as well as the vine. The following wines are made:

- Sekt: sparkling wine made by the traditional method in a bone dry (*trocken*) or off-dry (*halbtrocken*) form; suitable for vegetarians and

vegans, light- to medium-bodied, bracing fizz with an attractive pine
needle taste.

- Chardonnay: dry white, retains its balance here despite being made in
  a very full-bodied style.
- Gelber Muskateller: white wine made from 'Yellow Muscat' in both dry
  (*trocken*) and icewine (*eiswein*) style. This Muscat is grapier flavoured
  than those made in Alsace (which are more mineral like).
- Grüner Veltliner: dry white, clean; oily when made in a dry Kabinett
  style, resinous when a full Spätlese; suitable for vegetarians and
  vegans.
- Müller-Thurgau: dry white, simple, earthy and full when made in a
  Kabinett style, suitable for vegetarians and vegans.
- Riesling: white wine, warmer than many German versions of this grape,
  most effective here when made as a Spätlese rather than as a Kabinett.
- Roter Veltliner: white made in a range of styles including Eiswein from
  Frühroter Veltiner, an earlier ripening cousin of Grüner Veltliner. It
  shows lime blossom and honey but fades quickly in the bottle (the
  locals drink it within a year of harvest).
- Welschriesling Eiswein: sweet white made from frozen bunches of this
  unfashionable grape; single cream texture which keeps the sweetness
  fresh; suitable for vegetarians and vegans.
- Blauburgunder/Merlot Barrique: dry light red tasting of new oak.
- Blauer Portugieser: dry red, light cherry, can be served chilled.
- Zweigelt/Cabinet Sauvignon: dry red blend in the image of Diwald's
  above.

Weinhof Anna Paradeiser

St. Urbanstrasse 22, 3481 Fels am Wagram

Tel:+43 2738 2249

Overall Price Rating: 🍶

A severe frost here at the beginning of 1985 caused the vines to set no
fruit with which to produce a crop. There was no need of chemical spray
treatments for at least a year, and from that moment it was decided to
convert the vineyards to organic methods (see Corsini Vineyard La
Cantina in Victoria, Australia (*page 370*), for a different approach to
frost and sprays). Since converting the owners say they can see more

clearly where the differences in the potential quality of each grape variety they have planted lies. This allows better use to be made of the grapes at picking — not letting the better ones get mixed up with the more ordinary. The overall result is a very engaging range of wines:

- Sekt: dry white sparkling wine made by the traditional method; shows crystal clear, ripe, piercing fruit with a unique green moss flavour and a fine sparkle. (In style it equates to 'Extra Brut' in Champagne but without the heavy yeasty character and much riper tasting.) The 1996 vintage was made with Welschriesling; drink within six years.
- Frühroter Veltliner: fruity white, soft (low acid), summer wine, slight Muscat aroma, this wine is always bottled early and sold out by May by the Paradeiser family who run the domaine.
- Grüner Veltliner Kabinett: dry white, apply, ripe, needs time to soften; a really good example of how this grape appears to taste thin but ends up bowling you over.
- Blauburger: thick red made from two plots of vines planted in 1978 (so the vines are now mature). The 1992 vintage has a bold scarlet colour, and smells of thick cassis, cherry and vanilla — like a Chilean red wine but with much more natural freshness, so the fruit slips down over the tongue rather than getting stuck to one's gums.
- Blauer Portugieser: light red, aged in large oak tuns, shows clean fruit and inviting tannin.
- Cabernet Sauvignon: dry red; 1998 vintage shows this is still in the experimental stage.
- Junger Satz ('young vineyard'): dry red, tastes like Australian Cabernet/Shiraz; made from eight experimental vineyard plots, unusual style of fruit, syrupy for a red, so a good idea perhaps to share between a group.

Wachau

This is Austria's westernmost wine region. The mainly white wine vineyards tower about the Danube on steep terraces first cut for vines and other crops by the Romans. They produce the most powerful dry white wines in Austria. They need decanting otherwise all the flavours they accumulate on the Wachau's well-sunned slopes remain locked within.

Geyerhof

Oberfucha 1, 3511 Furth bei Göttweig
Tel:+43 2739 2259
Fax:+43 2739 22594
Overall Price Rating: 👬

The Geyerhof vineyards have doubled in size since 1985 when current owners Josef Maier and his wife Ilse took over. The Maiers were influenced in their decision to seek organic certification by their importers in Germany. Dry white wines are made from Chardonnay, Grüner Veltliner, Riesling and Weissburgunder. The reds see some new oak barrels and include Cabernet Sauvignon, Merlot, Blauburger and Zweigelt – the last from a vineyard site (*ried*) called Richtern. All the wines are suitable for vegetarians and vegans. They are clean but ephemeral, reflecting the youth of the vines.

Nikolaihof Wachau

Nikolaigasse 77, 3512 Mautern
Tel:+43 2732 82901
Fax:+43 2732 76440
Events: culinary events organised by Frau Christine Saahs
Stockists: Wine Society; Raeburn; Bibendum; Gelston Castle
Overall Price Rating: 👬👬

Nikolaihof has both Roman and 12th century-monastic origins and is the oldest winery in Austria. Current owners, the Saahs family, entered their vineyards in Ernte's organic certification programme in the early 1990s, but are adopting biodynamic methods. There are 18 hectares, including three main vineyard sites (*riede*) which are worked by hand:

- Im Weingebirge, which contains Riesling (60 per cent) and Grüner Veltliner (40 per cent).
- Vom Stein, which comprises a core of 50-year-old Riesling vines.
- Steiner Hund, the 'stone dog', so named either because its steep nature makes it a dog to work, or because a dog was all the vineyard was worth during the wanton destruction caused to these parts in the Thirty Years War (1618–1648).

All three vineyard sites are exposed to the elements, and the grapes dehydrate slightly when ripening, which concentrates them. A proportion of these dried, golden grapes are kept apart and added selectively to the rest of the crop at pressing. Their effect is to add richness to the wines. Once fermented, these mature in 2,000 variously shaped and sized oak casks. Bottling takes place according to the biodynamic principle of selecting days when fruit influences are felt to be most strong, so that this element is captured at the optimum moment. The label designations below denote an extra degree of natural ripeness in the grapes:

- Steinfeder: the lightest style for wines up to 11 per cent alcohol; refers to a light grass (*Stipa pennata*) which grows on the steepest Wachau sites.
- Federspiel: for wines up to 12 per cent alcohol; refers to the practice of calling in the bird while hawking, a Wachau tradition.
- Smaragd, for wines up to 14 per cent alcohol; refers to the emerald colour of a local lizard (the Idex) which thrives on the warm slopes of the Wachau; older vintages were labelled as Honifogl ('honeybringer') instead of smaragd.

Dry white wines are made from the following grape varieties.
- Chardonnay, Smaragd: dry (but not bone dry) white, labelled as 'Feinburgunder'; rich, resembles peaches stewing in a warm pan.
- Grüner Veltliner, Im Weingebirge, Trocken, Federspiel: shows bright straw colour, dry acacia and mineral, with structured fruit (75 cl and 1.5 litres available).
- Grüner Veltliner, Im Weingebirge, Trocken, Smaragd: allows itself a slice of exotica (pineapple); in the great 1986 labelled as 'honifogl'.
- Riesling, Im Weingebirge, Trocken: rich dry Riesling with incredible body.
- Riesling, Im Weingebirge, Spätlese: as immediately above but wearing more layers.
- Riesling Steiner Hund, Spätlese Trocken: dry Riesling, a 'difficult child' says Frau Saahs, which shows the character of the mineral-rich, primary rock soils it grows upon only after 20 years of ageing.
- Riesling Vom Stein, Trocken, Federspiel: authoritative, firm Riesling, showing the presence of older vines.

- Riesling Vom Stein, Trocken, Smaragd: Riesling you can play with for hours.

BURGENLAND

Austria's hottest vineyards are found on the flat, sandy soils of Burgenland. Over-ripe styles of white wine are made, as well as deep coloured, velvety reds. Sub-regions with organic vineyards include:

Neusiedlersee and Neusiedlersee-Hügelland

Neusiedlersee and Neusiedlersee-Hügelland immediately to the west form a series of lakes (*sees*) in a landscape which is flat all the way eastwards to southern Hungary and Romania. During summer hot air currents warm the water in the lakes, which then attracts enough rare species of marshland birds (heron, buzzard, stork) for the area to be designated a national nature reserve. The warm autumns also allow some of Austria's ripest red wines to be produced, as well as comparatively large quantities of sweet 'noble rot' white wines made from late picked, shrivelled grapes. They stand up well to food cooked with rich sauces.

Rudolf Beilschmidt

Weinberggasse 1, 7071 Rust
Tel:+43 2685 326
Overall Price Rating: ▮▮

The vineyards of Rudolf and Elizabeth Beilschmidt have been certified organic since 1980. A number of wines are produced from them, including whites from Chardonnay, Welschriesling, Weissburgunder, and Müller-Thurgau, and reds from Blaufrankisch. Average quality only, but worth visiting if you find yourself in the area, if only to hear the Beilschmidts explain their techniques for composting.

Weingut Paul Leitner

Quellengasse 4 & 35, 7122 Gols
Tel:+43 2173 2405
Overall Price Rating: ▮

This family estate makes a simple, frothy traditional method sparkling wine (Sekt) which can be mixed with the organic grape juice produced on the property to make a style of 'buck's fizz'. Winemaker Paul Leitner is best known for his brandy, which is distilled on the property both from wine grapes and fruits of the forest.

Weingut Günter Schönberger
Am Markt 41, 8323 St Marein (office)
Tel:+43 3119 2842
Fax:+43 3119 28422
Email: weingut.schoenberger@ccf.at
Overall Price Rating: 𝖬𝖬

This estate was founded in 1991 by a former rock saxophonist called Günter Schönberger. Organic vineyard practices are supplemented with bio-dynamic preparations, and the wines are suitable for vegetarians and vegans.

- Chardonnay: dry white, made partially from 40-year-old vines; fermented in barrel but stands up well to the wood.
- Weissburgunder: dry white showing clean flavours (made with Pinot Blanc).
- Welschriesling: white wine made in dry white, sweet white (Beerenauslese) and very sweet white (Trockenbeerenauslese) styles. All show round and harmonious flavours.
- Herbstcuvée ('harvest blend'): dry white, slightly frumpish thus shows character. The 1996 vintage smells of vanilla and exotic fruits and is blended from 5 per cent Chardonnay, 10 per cent Neuburger and 85 per cent Pinot Blanc.
- Blaufrankisch: red grape variety that Schönberger makes into two styles of wine. The first is a dry red tasting of clean, bitter chocolate aged in older oak. The second style is a sweet red made from grapes left to shrivel on the vine until the onset of winter. The resultant juice ferments partially on the skins to pick up colour and tannin and then as wine in cask. It ends up with a sunset colour with a few years of bottle age and displays considerable brambly sweetness.

Weingut Familie Steindl

Haupstrasse 42, 7083 Purbach

Tel:+43 2683 5595

Overall Price Rating: ♟♟

When Johann Steindl converted to organic methods in the 1980s his neighbours thought he was mad. His wines now rank among the most original of those produced in Austria for their beautiful simplicity. Steindl is a modest, bony man of about 50 with a collection of modestly sited vines, but the grapes produced are exceptionally healthy and balanced. Steindl lets nature takes its course by allowing natural grass to grow between the rows, so there are 30 species of crops present on the vineyard floor rather than just the ubiquitous three commercial cover crops sown elsewhere for green manure. The wine fermentation is allowed to occur naturally too, so the yeast leaves behind alcohol and flavour rather than alcohol alone, as is the case with yeast in packet form. Steindl ages his wines in Hungarian chestnut tuns of 50 years, rather than in swanky new French barrels with a shelf life of three years. His wines ferment with natural yeast. They reek of a type of sustainable, life-enhancing practice alien even to many certified organic growers elsewhere in Europe let alone conventional ones, and so it is ironic that Johann Steindl has no immediate family heir.

- Chardonnay: dry white, far more effective than modern Chablis in combining natural mineral taste and green fruit in a wine with an 11.5 per cent alcohol level.
- Gewurztraminer: exudes butter and rose petal here, shows the skill of pressing the grapes slowly enough to avoid bitterness from the pips without oxidizing the juice. Equivalent to Grand Cru Alsace but from far less auspiciously sited vines.
- Grüner Veltliner: dry white, fresh, peppery and bold; benchmark example of Austria's most overlooked but most widely planted variety.
- Müller-Thurgau: dry white showing straw colour and honey texture.
- Weissburgunder: dry white; weight in middle, fine almond taste at end.
- Welschriesling: white grape made in a range of styles including Kabinett Trocken – which is as fresh as a strong, dry breeze.
- Rosé Zweigelt: dry pink wine, very positive rather than insipid pink with a pure cherry taste.

- Cuvée Blaufrankisch: dry red, sweet ripe black fruit and well defined dry tannin.
- Blaufrankisch/Cabernet Sauvignon: dry red blend in which Cabernet Sauvignon's youthful berry aromas and mature cedar tastes dominate.
- Zweigelt: dry red, sweet texture, shows delicious fruit balanced by ripe dry tannin; destemmed and fermented as loose berries in open vats. This and others of the red wines are fermented on such a small scale that some of the tanks are placed on top of the manure pile to keep the fermentation yeast warm during winter. A blind tasting would never reveal this.

STYRIA

Styria ('Steiermark') forms Austria's densely wooded border with Slovenia and contains the highest vineyards in Austria.

Land- und Forstwirtschaftlichen Fachschüle Silberberg

Kogelberg 16, 8430 Leibnitz
Tel:+43 3452 82339
Fax:+43 3452 82339
Overall Price Rating: ♦

This wine training college undertakes the basic education of teenage students in its three independently run vineyards, the smallest of which is certified organic by Ernte. The students, who mostly come from mixed family farms, are taught how to allow more sunlight and air onto the grapes by plucking leaves. The decision as to which leaf to pluck depends on its size. The biggest, oldest leaves throw too much shade and allow the grape bunches least light. Leaf plucking and tougher selection at picking mean costs on this organic vineyard are 50 per cent higher than in the school's two non-organic vineyards. The organic vineyard lies on the border with Slovenia and covers two hectares out of 3,500 in Styria. It produces:

- Blauer Zweigelt: dry red, crisp but chewable, drinkable on its own (see Hungary too for this grape).
- Riesling-Sylvaner: medium-dry white for early drinking, made from Müller-Thurgau.

- Schilcher: dry pink wine, mouth-wateringly crisp, made from the Wildbacher or 'wild dark skinned grape', Styria's most noted wine style.

Friends of the Earth **Organic Wine Guide**

England

Visitors to England are surprised to find that the country has over 400 vineyards, let alone three which are certified organic by the Soil Association (see below). Their presence amounts to just over 1 per cent of English vineyard area (900 hectares), a similar percentage to English organic agriculture in general.

ORGANIC CERTIFICATION BODY

The Soil Association Cert Ltd is the body responsible for certifying the three English wine producers listed below. The Soil Association's emergence after the Second World War was greatly influenced by the experiences of colonial families which were witnesses for 40 years to food shortages in India caused by unnatural farming methods. The Soil Association is a registered charity and both Avalon and Sedlescombe vineyards take advantage of the fact that Soil Association status entitles them to unpaid help from 'wwoofers' – 'Willing Workers on Organic Farms' (sometimes called 'Working Weekends on Organic Farms'). The WWOF network exists in around 50 countries. The 'willing workers' in question are usually students or future organic farmers keen to learn such things as compost making or vine pruning. Other 'wwoofers' may simply be agricultural tourists keen to work between three and six hours a day in return for board and lodging on a farm or vineyard for example. The minimum stay is two nights.

The Soil Association can be contacted at:

The Soil Association Cert Ltd

Bristol House, 40–50 Victoria Street, Bristol, Avon BS1 6DF

Tel:+44 117 929 0661/+44 117 914 2400

Fax:+44 117 925 2504

Email: info@soilassociation.org

Publications: *Living Earth* (consumers); *New Farmer & Grower* (trade)

Events: Highgrove Organic Workshops, which have featured Fetzer
Vineyards-Brown Forman Corporation (see Bonterra, California, page 300)

Avalon Vineyard

The Drove, East Pennard, Shepton Mallet, Somerset BA4 6UA

Tel:+44 1749 860 393

Visitors: farm shop open all year

Overall Price Rating: 🍶

Avalon Vineyard and its fruit farm lie in the hills near Glastonbury, the
home since antiquity of Arthurian legends and (since the 1970s) of an
annual international rock music festival. Avalon has practised organic
methods since the mid-1980s and has been certified organic since 1993.
The grapes are picked by hand, and the wines produced are dry to medium
dry and white. They display fairly rich golden colours and develop their
nuances of apple core flavour only over time or after decanting. A mail
order case costs the price of 10 75 cl bottles (instead of 12), plus delivery
charge in the UK (mainland). In addition, organic fruit wines are made
from apples, white gooseberries, red gooseberries, strawberries and tay-
berries, and a traditional cider is produced too. It comes in both still and
sparkling forms and is styled to be thick and low in acidity. Avalon's owner, Dr Hugh Tripp, uses a traditional wooden West Country cider press for
this and for the wine grapes. Layers of organic straw are added periodically with the grapes, to help juice from the more gelatinous or slimy
grape varieties to drain more easily.

Chudleigh Vineyard

Farmborough, Chudleigh, Newton Abbot, Devon TQ13 0DR

Overall Price Rating: 🍶

Chudleigh Vineyard's certified organic status ended after the 1998 vintage when it was sold to new owners, who will dismantle the vineyard permanently. Up until then Chudleigh produced a range of clean, crisp and relatively dry white wines. Their more neutral style tempted first-time drinkers of English wine who had been put off by those many English wines that tried, not always successfully, to resemble German Liebfraumilch, which is often flowery and sickly sweet. The wines were made from named single grape varieties.

- Seyval Blanc: off-dry white; some say this hybrid is the definitive variety for the cool English climate, others say simply that it works well.
- Schonburger: off-dry white, made from a crossing well-suited to south west England, and here provides a grey coloured, chalky tasting wine for drinking within 2–3 years.
- Madelaine Angevine: off-dry white, lighter texture than the Schonburger above; made from a grape similar to but not the same as a French table variety of the same name.
- Kerner: off-dry white, made from a German crossing planted often in southern England in the 1970s on unsuitable sites, but here shows an attractive soft yellow fruit and brazil nut.

Sedlescombe

Cripps Corner, Robertsbridge, East Sussex TN32 5SA
Tel:+44 158 083 0715
Fax:+44 158 083 0122
Email: RCook91137@aol.com
Internet: www.tor.co.uk/sedlescombe
Visitors: farm shop and vineyard (located on the B2244 road)
Stockist: Vinceremos

Sedlescombe Vineyard has practised organic methods since its inception in 1979 and became fully certified organic in 1995. Sedlescombe's founders, Roy and Irma Cook, met when Roy went to Germany to learn about cool climate grape growing and winemaking. Annual average temperatures in Southern England are at the limit for the growing of quality wine (10°C, similar to Champagne), yet the Cooks' initial collection of

2,000 cuttings has flourished, turning an experimental plot in a private Sussex garden into a remarkable vineyard.

Everything is done in the vineyard to keep the vines in balance. This mainly consists of working constantly to re-position those vine shoots which bear grapes so that they get air, light and sun and are not stuck behind shoots bearing nothing but leaves. The grapes are picked by hand, in stages, for maximum ripeness. This leaves wines of intense clear flavours. Once in the cellar they are crushed and pressed without pumps or augurs (screws) to cut down on fining agents and filtration, even though there are no pollution taxes in Southern England for such activities (unlike in Germany and Switzerland). All the wines are suitable for vegetarians. They include:

- Vineyard Dry White: a round, light bodied blend of Bacchus and Reichensteiner, 10 per cent alcohol. 🍶
- Sedlescombe Late Harvest White: medium dry white with medium body, 10.5 per cent alcohol. 🍶
- Sedlescombe Reserve: medium sweet white showing rich fruit despite only 8.5 per cent alcohol. Signifies grapes picked for ripeness of flavour rather than ripeness of numbers (i.e., level of sugar and thus potential alcohol). 🍶
- Sedlescombe Dry Red: contains mainly Pinot Noir from vineyards in the grounds of Bodiam Castle, certified organic and rented by Sedlescome; part barrel-aged, 10.5 per cent alcohol, pale cedar colour, balanced ripe red fruit and appealing tannins; an English red wine with purpose. 🍶
- Sedlescombe Brut: sparkling white wine made by the traditional method, 12 per cent alcohol. Sussex's chalk Downs are similar to Champagne, and warm quickly during the growing season, enabling the vine to grow powerful but restrained wines. 🍶
- Sedlescombe Millennium Rosé Brut: pink sparkling wine made by the traditional method. The base wine was drawn from the 1996 vintage and only 500 bottles were made. Probably among the most complex sparkling wines yet made in England. 🍶

Other drinks pressed and bottled at Sedlescombe include:

- Country Apple and Pear Juices: suitable for vegans. 🍾
- Apple Wine (8 per cent alcohol): suitable for vegans. 🍾
- Medium Dry Extra Strong Cider (minimum 8 per cent alcohol). 🍾

Contact the winery for details of a mail order list.

Germany

Organic German wine growers must have nerves of steel, for they have to wait longer than any other European wine growers before the last grapes are ripe enough to be picked. They are the masters of picking the vineyard in stages: returning to the same plot time after time to gather only those bunches which are ripe. The Germans liken this system to milking a cow: what comes out can be used for milk, butter, yoghurt or cheese, depending on what you take and when. The Germans grade their grapes for quality too: first picked are called *kabinet*, then *spätlese* (late picked), *auslese* (late picked with some berries affected by noble rot), *beerenauslese* and *trockenbeerenauslese* (all the berries affected by noble rot) and *eiswein* (grapes picked so late they were frozen on the vine). So, unlike in France, it is the sugar content of the grapes – rather than the origin or appellation – which counts.

Most German wine is white, and made from Riesling, Silvaner, Müller-Thurgau, Pinot Gris, Pinot Blanc and Gewurztraminer. Reds are made from Pinot Noir ('Spätburgunder'), Portugieser and Dornfelder. Two-thirds of all German wine is sold by the grower direct from the winery (*weingut*) while the rest is snapped up by Germany's powerful merchants. This leaves very little for export. In the UK, where consumers seem unprepared to pay the £6 or so for single vineyard, single estate German wine, the number of listings given to German wines made from organically grown grapes is pitiful. Hence the producer profiles which follow are very general and geared more to those prepared to visit German producers direct. However, a list of German wine merchants is included in Appendix 1.

The organic vineyard movement in Germany is strong, well-organized and largely geared to the home market. It has grown out of a general 'green'

German movement dominated in the modern era by concerns over high levels of nitrates in drinking water in wine-producing areas caused by chemical fertilisers. Regional standards for organic production were established in 1984, and in 1985 a national federation for organic wine production was formed, called AGÖL (address: AGÖL, Baumschulenweg 11, 64295 Darmstadt). In 1998 over 1 per cent of the total German vineyard area of 100,000 hectares was certified organic or biodynamic. The key seems to be good information exchange between regional organic groups belonging to the various grower associations. In addition, specialist organic consultants working for the grower associations provide back-up on technical matters.

ORGANIC GROWER ASSOCIATIONS

Bundesverband Okologischer Weinbau e.V (BOW)
Zuckerberg 19, D-55276 Oppenheim
Tel:+49 61 33 16 40
Fax:+49 61 33 16 09

This is the largest association of certified organic wine growers in Germany, with nearly 250 members farming 1,000 hectares. Its registered logo is 'ECOVIN'.

Bioland Bundesverband
Kaiserstrasse 18, D-55116 Mainz
Tel:+49 61 31 23 97 90
Fax:+49 61 31 23 97 92 7
Email: info@bioland.de

Bioland (founded in 1971) hosts an annual organic food, wine and clothes fair (called 'Biofach'). The catalogue and list of producers are available on-line by entering 'bio-fach' on a search-engine.

Naturland – Verband für naturgemäßen Landbau e.V.

Kleinhaderner Weg 1
D-82166 Gräfelfing
Tel: +49 89 80 82 0
Fax: +49 89 80 82 90
Email: naturland@naturland.de
Internet:www.naturland.de

The third largest certification body in Germany for wine is Naturland. It has 17 members with 250 hectares in 1998. Naturland was the first certifying organization for organic agriculture to pass successfully the independent IFOAM Accreditation Programme in the beginning of 1997. It operates world wide and is especially active in fair trade and organic tea and coffee.

One other organic association specific to the former East Germany, Gäa, is listed under the German regions. Germany's 20 biodynamic producers can be contacted through:

Demeter Bund EV

Baumschulenweg 11, 64295 Darmstadt
Tel:+49 61 55 84 69 0/+49 61 55 84 69 51
Fax:+49 61 55 84 69 11
Email: demeterbd@aol.com
Internet: demeter.de/demeter.net

THE GERMAN WINE REGIONS

There are 13 of these. Notes follow on nine (all except the Mittelrhein and Hessische Bergstrasse), with the two former East German regions covered at the end.

The Ahr

Even though Germany is a predominantly white wine country and the Ahr one of its most northerly regions, the highest priced wines here are reds. The vineyards occupy a steep river valley above the Ahr river near Bonn, the capital of the former West Germany. The vineyards catch the sun and are protected from the north, so red grapes have enough warmth to ripen.

Weingut Christoph Bäcker

Waagstrasse 16a, 53508 Mayschoss

Tel:+49 26 43 75 17

Overall Price Rating: 🏰

This domaine has spectacular surroundings at the foot of the ruins of the oldest fortress on the Ahr, which dates from the 11th century. The vines have been certified organic since 1990, and overlook the Ahr's largest loop. The main grape varieties here include Pinot Noir (Spätburgunder) for red, and Riesling and Gewurztraminer for white. Local dishes include game from the local Apfel mountains amd trout from the Ahr.

Baden

Baden is Germany's largest and warmest wine region, and covers the south west of the country, a 250-mile long area south of Franken to Lake Constance. It has everything Burgundy has except on a much bigger, more spread-out scale – red wines made from Pinot Noir (Spätburgunder) and dry whites made from Chardonnay. Over 95 per cent of the wines produced here are sold locally, with most made by cooperatives (like Badischer Winzerkeller, below). However, grower/winemakers are becoming increasingly well represented, and are geared up for those prepared to visit the region in person.

Badischer Winzerkeller eG

Zum Kaiserstuhl 16, 79206 Breisach

Tel:+49 76 67 90 02 21

Fax:+49 76 67 90 02 32

Stockist: Lauriston Wines Ltd

Overall Price Rating: 🏰

This cooperative wine cellar is one of the biggest in Germany. It acts as the centre for a group of 50 other Baden cooperatives located as far south as the Bodensee and as far north as Heidelberg. Its most famous product is Baden Dry, a non-organic blend of Müller-Thurgau, Muskat, Pinot Gris (Ruländer), Gewurztraminer and others. Since 1996 certified organic grapes from some of its contributor producers have been fermented and bottled separately. From these two dry white wines are made from Müller-Thurgau and and Pinot Gris (Ruländer), as well as a light red from Pinot Noir (Spätburgunder).

Weingut Markus Burgin
Dorfstrasse 33, 79592 Fischingen
Tel:+49 76 28 98 79
Fax:+49 76 28 98 79
Overall Price Rating: 🍷

This organic domaine lies in southern Baden, in the Markgräflerland, between Freiburg and Basel on the Swiss border. The speciality is the white Chasselas variety (here called Gutedel or Markgräfler), which is said to acquire a bready, walnut character.

Weingut Matthias Höfflin
Schambachholf, 79268 Bötzingen
Tel:+49 76 63 14 74
Overall Price Rating: 🍷

This organic domaine is located in the Kaiserstuhl, the stump of an extinct volcano between the Black Forest and the Vosges Mountains (see Alsace, *page 1*). Grapes varieties include Müller-Thurgau, Pinot Blanc (Weissburgunder), Pinot Gris (Grauburgunder), Silvaner and Scheurebe for whites, and Pinot Noir (Spätburgunder) for reds. See also Weingut und Hausbrennerei Trautwein (below) for another Baden domaine on the Kaiserstuhl, as well as Cooper Mountain in Oregon (*page 345*) that, as here, produces Pinot Noir from the stump of an extinct volcano.

Weingut Bernard Huber
Heimbacher Weg 19, 79364 Malterdingen
Tel:+49 76 44 12 00
Fax:+49 76 44 82 22

Bernard Huber works nearly 14 hectares of organic vines on the rural foothills of the Black Forest. Not yet 50 years old, Huber has developed both as a grower and as a winemaker throughout the 1990s. His sparkling wines ('Sekt', 👯) are full-bodied, serious examples akin to those of the Aube (see Fleury in Champagne, *page 78*). A vintage dated pink sparkling wine made from Pinot Noir (Spätburgunder) shows subtle cherry blossom (👯). Huber's most unusual wine is Malterer 'Weinkomposition', a white wine blend of Pinot Blanc (Weissburgunder) and a peach-like white variety called Freisamer, which tastes of sweet, over-ripe apricots (👯). (The wine label was copied from a tapestry in Freiberg where the Malterer family once boasted a mayor whose son died in battle with him.) Wines made from other varieties are labelled:

- Chardonnay: white, super balance and weight for this variety, which here weighs in at 14 per cent alcohol. 👯
- Grauer Burgunder (Pinot Gris): white, mealy, full and fresh. 👯
- Muskateller: white, blend of two Muscat sub-varieties, thick but focused. 👯
- Riesling: white, clean, racy, soft with an explosive finish, dry or sweet. 👯
- Spätburgunder (Pinot Noir): dry red, mixes wild strawberries and red cherries. 👯
- Weissburgunder (Pinot Blanc): white, broad and nutty without being oily. 👯

Weingut Kirchberghof
Gert Hügle, 79341 Kensingen-Bombach
Tel:+49 76 44 12 61
Overall Price Rating: 👯

Gert Hügle's domaine has been organic since 1986. It lies in the Ortenau sub-region between Baden-Baden and south of Offenburg on steeply sloping ground, well suited to both dry and sweet wines. Grape varieties include Pinot Noir (Spätburgunder) for reds and sparkling wines, with Pinot Blanc (Weissburgunder), Pinot Gris (Grauburgunder), Müller-Thurgau, Kerner and Gewurztraminer for dry, acacia honey whites.

Weingut Gerd Koepfer

Koepfer Grunern, Dorfstrasse 22, 79219 Staufen-Grunern

Tel:+49 76 33 52 88

Stockists: contact Organic Wine Company for further details

Overall Price Rating: ♙

This organic domaine was founded in 1756 and lies in the Markgräflerland. Current owner Gerd Koepfer produces a fat but bone-dry style of Müller-Thurgau from a single vineyard (*einzellage*) called Grunerner Altenberg. The local wine festival – the Markgräfler Weinfest – takes place at the beginning of April in Staufen in the town's ruined castle.

Weingut & Hausbrennerei Trautwein

Riegeler Staße 2, 79353 Bahlingen

Tel:+49 76 63 26 50

Fax:+49 76 63 26 50

Overall Price Rating: ♙

This organic domaine lies directly to the north of Weingut Matthias Höfflin on the Kaiserstuhl and belongs to Elfried and Hans-Peter Trautwein.

Weingut Josef Wörner

Vollmersbach 5, 77770 Durbach

Tel:+49 78 14 12 52

Overall Price Rating: ♙

This biodynamic producer is another located in Baden's Ortenau sub-region (see above). The town of Durbach is one of the best-known villages here, and the planting centre of Riesling (called Klingelberger locally), Traminer (Clevner) and Pinot Noir (Spätburgunder).

Weingut Wilhelm Zähringer GmbH

Hauptstrasse 42, 79423 Heitersheim

Tel:+49 76 34 10 25

Fax:+49 76 34 10 27

Email: weingut.zaehringer@t-online.de

Overall Price Rating: ♙

This organic domaine lies in the chalky Tuniberg region directly to the south of Kaiserstuhl. The varieties planted include Pinot Noir (Spätburgunder), Chasselas (Gutedel), Müller-Thurgau, Pinot Gris (Grauburgunder), Pinot Blanc (Weissburgunder) and Gewurztraminer. Look for direct, clean, intense aromas and flavours from winemaker Wolfgang Zähringer.

Franken

The Franken region is centred on the historic town of Wurzburg and was Germany's most easterly wine region until reunification. The region's wines are unpopular with wine merchants because they are sold in wide bottles that take up too much space on the shelf. The Franken bottle was modelled on the shape of a scrotum (that of a billy goat rather than a human!) and is known as a *bocksbeutel*. The wines within them are usually white, often dry and high in alcohol, up to 14 per cent. The most common variety seen on labels is the Silvaner, which produces fat, earthy wines in total contrast to the more floral Rieslings of the Mosel. Franken Silvaner complements simple rather than strongly flavoured foods, such as asparagus, fish with butter or Hollandaise sauce or smoked fish.

Note: wines sold in *bocksbeutels* are usually packed in 15 bottle cases (not the more usual 12).

Weingut Bausewein
Breite Gasse 1, 97346 Iphofen
Tel:+49 93 23 52 10
Fax:+49 93 23 67 64
Overall Price Rating: ❚

This organic domaine is situated in one of Franken's key towns. The names of some of the local vineyards owe their origins to the Prince Bishops to whom they belonged during the days of the Holy Roman Empire.

Weingut Erwin Christ
Weinbergstraße 6, 97334 Nordheim
Tel:+49 93 81 28 80
Overall Price Rating: ❚❚❚

This domaine has been certified organic since 1964 and is still one of the most traditionally run. It is located in the Maindreieck or 'Main Triangle', so called because of the shape the river Main takes here. The Maindreieck's limestone-rich soils provide 70 per cent of all the wine produced in Franken. The whites are elegant but full, and are well-suited to the region's asparagus.

Weingut Helmut Christ
Volkacher Straße 6, 97334 Nordheim
Tel:+49 93 81 28 06
Stockists: contact Organic Wine Company for further details
Overall Price Rating: ⚑

This domaine has been certified organic since 1974. The single vineyard sites (*einzellagen*) here have names which hardly trip off the tongue: Dettelbacher Berg Rondell and Wipfelder Zehntgraf for example. However, your mouth will find the taste of the white wines made from them much more amenable. Look for Kerner and Müller-Thurgau made in a grapey, positive style.

Weingut Furstlich Castell'sches Domanenampt
Schlossplatz 5, 97355 Castell
Tel:+49 93 25 60 16 1
Fax:+49 93 25 60 18 5
Stockist: Barrat Proctor
Overall Price Rating: ⚑⚑

This domaine began converting to organic methods in 1988 and became fully certified in 1992. The best wines made here are whites from Silvaner, Müller-Thurgau and Bacchus. They are clean, and lighter in tone than the Franken norm, but this adds to rather than detracts from their appeal.

Weingut Roland Hemberger
Aussledlehof 3, Rödelsee
Tel:+49 93 23 43 5
Fax:+49 93 23 50 72
Overall Price Rating: ♒♒♒

This organic domaine lies in the Steigerwald sub-region of Franken. The terrain here differs from the rest of the region, being more upland in character which accounts for the extra intensity achieved by the Silvaner grapes grown here. They attract a premium as a result. See also Gerhard Roth and Manfred Schwab, below.

Weingut Gerhard Roth
Büttnergasse 11, 97355 Wiesenbronn
Tel:+49 93 26 37 3
Fax:+49 93 25 12 40
Overall Price Rating: ♒♒

This organic domaine lies in the Steigerwald sub-region of Franken. See also Roland Hemberger and Manfred Schwab.

Weinbau Fred Ruppert
Rüdenstrasse 42, 97357 Prichstenstadt-Kirch
Tel:+49 93 83 74 85
Overall Price Rating: ♒

This organic domaine is situated in the northern part of the Maindreieck (see also Weingut Erwin Christ and Weingut Helmut Christ).

Weinbau Manfred Schwab
Ludwigstrasse 7a, 97346 Iphofen
Tel:+49 93 23 59 86
Overall Price Rating: ♒

This organic domaine lies in the Steigerwald sub-region of Franken. See also Roland Hemberger and Gerhard Roth.

Mosel

The Mosel is a source of refreshing white wines which you can drink half a bottle of at a time because the level of alcohol is so low, only from 6 per cent alcohol. The king grape here is the Riesling, and nowhere else in the world is it more nervy. It grows on steep, slatey slopes above the snake-like Mosel river. The Riesling produces searingly crisp whites, so unfermented grape sugar is allowed to remain in the wines to make them more appealing.

Weingut Franz Brohl

Zum Rosenberg 2, 56862 Pünderich/Mosel
Tel:+49 65 42 21 48
Overall Price Rating: ▲

This domaine has been organic since 1982. The most famous vineyard site in Pünderich is the Nonnengarten, which produces soft, fruity Riesling.

Weingut Alfred Cuy

Zandstraße 82, 56856 Zell-Merl
Tel:+49 65 42 22 51 8
Overall Price Rating: ▲

This domaine has been organic since 1987. The best time to visit is during the local wine festival in the last weekend in June.

Weingut Steffens-Keß

Moselstraße 63, 56861 Reil
Tel:+49 65 42 12 46
Stockists: contact Organic Wine Company
Overall Price Rating: ▲▲

This domaine belongs to Harald Steffens and Marita Keß-Steffens. It has been organic since 1982 and produces light wines, capable of gulpable fruitiness in good vintages.

Weingut Rudolf Trossen

Bahnhofstrasse 7, 54539 Kinheim-Kindel

Tel:+49 65 32 27 14

Fax:+49 65 32 15 94

Overall Price Rating: ♨♨♨

This domaine became organic in 1978 but now has Demeter biodynamic certification. The village of Kinheim lies on the edge of the central part of the Mosel – the MittelMosel – where the region's most renowned domaines are sited. Trossen is a determined character keen to emulate those more well-known domaines in the MittelMosel which are content to live off their reputations – and the coachloads of visitors they draw each year.

Weingut Karl Weber

Hauptstraße 3, 56332 Lehmen

Tel:+49 26 07 40 42

Overall Price Rating: ♨

This domaine has been organic since 1987 under the management of Uwe Weber. Lehmen is in the 'lower Mosel', the part of the river closest to Cologne where the Mosel reaches the Rhine. It produces the ripest style of Mosel.

Nahe

The Nahe is one of the larger tributaries of the Rhine. Its vineyards produce accessible but fine-tuned white wines from a range of grape varieties including Riesling, Müller-Thurgau, Silvaner, Kerner and Scheurebe. The climate is dry because the forests of the Hunnsrück mountains trap moisture coming in from the west. The soils are full of sandstones and minerals which glisten in the heat, adding intensity to the grapes while they ripen.

Weingut Klost Krost

Weingut Hof Selene, 55288 Waldlaubersheim

Tel:+49 67 32 37 60

Fax:+49 67 32 37 60

Overall Price Rating: ♨

This biodynamic domaine is situated at the point where the Hunnsrück flatten into the Rhine valley. Until the 1930s most Nahe wine was sold as 'Rhine' but the Nahe has now established its own identity for white wines, which are honeyed without being cloying.

Prinz Zu Salm-Dalberg'sches Weingut

Schloß Wallhausen, 55595 Wallhausen
Tel:+49 67 06 28 9 (Weingut)
Fax:+49 67 06 60 17
Overall Price Rating: 🍾🍾🍾

This estate dates from 1200, and claims to be the oldest in Germany owned uninterrupted by the same family, the zu Salm-Salm. The vines cover 20 acres in the villages of Dalberg, Roxheim, Sommerloch and Wallhausen and have been organic since 1990. The wines display typical Nahe fruit and elegance, and are fermented and matured individually in old oak casks.

Weingut im Zwölbereich

Schützenstraße 14, 55450 Langenlonsheim
Tel:+49 67 04 92 00
Fax:+49 67 04 92 04 0
Overall Price Rating: 🍾🍾

This domaine has been organic since 1987 and covers eight individual vineyards (*einzellagen*) in the lower Nahe. Riesling, Müller-Thurgau, Silvaner and small amounts of Kerner are planted. From 1996 the domaine has had full biodynamic status (Demeter certified). Red white and sparkling whites are made in a fat but invigorating style.

Pfalz

The vineyards of the Pfalz (Palatinate) represent the northerly continuation of Alsace in France. They lie on the foothills of the Vosges mountains, here called the Haardt. Until recently the Pfalz was considered Germany's least dynamic wine region, because production was dominated by cooperatives (they still control two-thirds of the harvest). However a new wave of growers has emerged in the 1990s, keen to bottle wine from their own grapes. Organic and conventional growers alike are experimenting with dry wines, and wine-making techniques imported from the New World. The wines they produce are exuberant and full, occasionally slightly spicy. Look out for the reds made from Pinot Noir (Spätburgunder) and Dornfelder, as well as whites from Pinot Blanc, Pinot Gris and Gewurztraminer.

Weingut Fritz Croissant

Dalbergstrasse 1, 67482 Venningen
Tel:+49 63 23 15 38
Fax:+49 63 23 81 51 9
Internet: www.ims-kirrweiler.com/croissant/index/htm
Overall Price Rating: 𝘸𝘸𝘸

This is the estate to watch in the Pfalz, organic or otherwise, at the moment. Owner Fritz Croissant is also the owner of Vignano (in Tuscany, *see page 253*). Here he produces a thick, blackberry-scented red made from Dornfelder from vines grown near the border with Alsace. The flower-bedecked wine villages in this area are amongst the most rural in Germany and lie along the Südliche Weinstrasse or 'wine street'.

Weingut Rudolf Eymann

Ludwigstraße 35, 67161 Gönnheim
Tel:+49 63 22 28 08
Overall Price Rating: 𝘸

This domaine has been certified organic since 1983 and lies in the northern half of the Pfalz. The style here is naturally leaner than it is to the south around Deidesheim, Forst and Wachenheim.

Weingut Heiner Sauer

Haupstraße 44, 6741 Böchingen
Tel:+49 63 41 61 17 5
Fax:+49 63 41 64 38 0
Overall Price Rating: 𝘸

This is another southern Pfalz domaine, certified organic since 1986. Grapes grown are fairly indicative of the selection common to the Pfalz: Müller-Thurgau, Riesling, Kerner, Portugieser, Heroldrebe, Pinot Noir, Pinot Blanc, St Laurent, Silvaner, Grauburgunder, and Huxelrèbe. Some of these are planted for style (the Pinots) while others are there purely for yield (Portugieser, Heroldrebe).

Weingut Georg Siben Erben
Weinstrasse 21, 67146 Deidesheim
Tel:+49 63 26 21 4
Overall Price Rating: 🍷🍷🍷

This organic domaine is well known for its rich style of Riesling. It enjoys some of the best sites, sometimes terraced, on the slopes around Deidesheim. This area represents the Mittelhaardt where the foothills of the Haardt mountains are most protected by the woods to the rear. Summers are warm and long, and as a result the inherently lean Riesling displays more roundness than in any other German wine region.

Rheingau

The Rheingau vineyards occupy the most prestigious single strip of vineyard above the Rhine river, but the region is in a state of flux. The most famous vineyard sites are owned by the German State which has shown itself to be a lacklustre performer when it comes to wine quality and an absentee from the lists of certified organic producers. Those domaines which are organic are helped by a generally south-facing aspect, without which the late ripening Riesling variety would struggle. Dry Rieslings can be made here, but most are bottled with some sweetness since the arrival of modern filtration methods in the 1960. Filtration kills any chance of re-fermentation once the wine is in bottle by removing the yeast, along with hefty doses of sulphur dioxide preservative to make sure. The Rheingauers could return to a less sulphury and unfiltered wine if all the sugar in the juice was allowed to ferment out naturally. It was this drier wine style that made Rheingau so popular in 19th-century England, a contrast to the situation today.

Weingut Jakob Hamm

Hauptstrasse 60, 65375 Oestrich
Tel:+49 67 23 24 32
Fax:+49 67 23 87 66 6
Overall Price Rating: 🏰

This domaine has been organic since 1980 and lies in the central part of the Rheingau. Its vineyards (*einzellagen*) in Winkel include the Jesuitengarten, which touches the Rhine and two others which overlook it: Hasensprung ('hare leap') and Johannisberg ('berg' meaning hill). All are famous for honeyed Riesling, with Johannisberg the first to produce this in a sweet style in Germany. Legend has it that the picking of the vines was delayed one year when the Bishop, who owned them, forgot to send his messenger in time with the order to pick. When the messenger did get there, the grapes were shrivelled with 'noble rot', which sweetened them considerably. Today wines made from similarly late picked grapes are given the 'Auslese' (late picked) designation under German wine law. The local festival celebrates the flowering rather than the picking of the vines, and takes place in Oestrich during the third weekend in June (the *Weinblatenfest*).

Weingut Hirt-Albrecht

Schwalbacher Strasse 15, 65340 Eltville
Tel:+49 61 23 25 79/+49 61 23 54 71
Overall Price Rating: 🏰

This domaine has been certified organic since 1985 and is run by Michael Albrecht. The vineyards are located in the central Rheingau on broad rather than steep ground, east of the town of Eltville. This was the first town in the Rheingau to receive town rights (1332). This domaine lies in the shadow of Kloster Eberbach, the monastic vineyard now owned by the German State which is one of Germany's most revered. Spirits are high during the *Sektfest* or Festival of Sparkling Wines which takes place on the first weekend in July – so bring waterproofs as well as the suncream!

Weingut Graf von Kanitz
Rheinstraße 49, 65391 Lorch
Tel:+49 67 26 34 6
Fax:+49 67 26 21 78
Overall Price Rating: 🍷🍷🍷

The ancient family property has been run organically since 1968 and certified organic since 1990. Its vineyards cover 42 acres on the downstream and most northerly rump of the Rhine, where the Riesling grape is at its most nervy. The Graf von Kanitz family is one of Germany's most aristocratic. Its wine restaurant (*weinstube*) is located in the oldest Renaissance building in this part of the Rheingau.

Weingut Schloß Reinhartshausen
65346 Erbach
Tel:+49 61 23 67 63 33
Fax:+49 61 23 42 22
Overall Price Rating: 🍷🍷🍷

This property in the central Rheingau is one of the few to own vines on one of the Rhine's narrow islands, the name of which is Mariannenaue. Only Pinot Blanc (Weissburgunder) is planted, but the vines sell under two vineyard names: Erbacher-Rheinhell and Hattenheimer-Rheingarten. They are certified organic, and the wine produced is bottled with a crimson label. Schloss Reinhartshausen was once a Cistercian monastery but now it houses a luxury hotel and restaurant. More down to earth fare is available at the Strawberry and Wine Festival (*Erdbeerfest*) held in Erbach during the third weekend in June.

Rheinhessen

Rheinhessen is the largest of Germany's 13 wine regions, and occupies the left bank of the Rhine between Worms and Mainz. It is known above all for Liebfraumilch, which accounts for one in four bottles of its production. The main grape varieties for this sometimes sickly sweet white wine are Müller-Thurgau, Silvaner and Riesling. They grow on generally low lying ground away from the Rhine in vineyards constructed to suit the needs of a handful of powerful merchants. More high-brow white wines come from vineyards overlooking the Rhine from the Rheinterrasse ('Rhine front'). This is a series of cliffs rising between 100 and 150 metres above the west bank of the Rhine south of Mainz. The two main grapes are Riesling and Silvaner.

Weingut Dr Brüder Becker
Mainzer Straße 11, 6501 Ludwigshöhe
Tel:+49 62 49 84 30/+49 62 49 12 36
Overall Price Rating: 👖

This domaine has been certified organic since 1980. It is situated at the point where the Rheinterrasse descends onto lower lying, and thus more frost-prone ground. The wines are made in a very clean, up-front style, but anodyne rather than characterful.

Weingut Brühler Hof
Talgartenstraße 12, 55546 Volxheim
Tel:+49 67 03 60 6
Overall Price Rating: 👖

This domaine has been certified organic since 1985 and is run by Hans-Peter Müller. It lies directly east of Bad Kreuznach.

Weingut Heyl zu Herrnsheim
Mathildenhof, Langasse 3, 55283 Nierstein
Tel:+49 61 33 51 20
Fax:+49 61 33 58 92 1
Overall Price Rating: 👖👖👖

This domaine lies in the lee of the Rheinterrasse and has been certified organic since 1978. Run by Peter and Isa von Weymarn it is planted with Riesling, Silvaner, Pinot Blanc, Müller-Thurgau and Pinot Noir (Spätburgunder). The von Weymarns are the exclusive owners of the steep Brudersburg vineyard in Nierstein which covers 1.3 hectares. It is one of the finest in Germany and the only steep south-facing vineyard next to the Rhine between Nackenheim and Worms. The grapes gain extra ripeness from the sunlight reflected off the water, and can be fermented to dryness in the traditional Rheingau style. The wine label is famous for its blue monk (*not* to be confused with a blue nun made so famous by a brand of Liebfraumilch).

Weingut Klaus Knobloch
Saurechgässchen 7, 55234 Ober-Flörsheim
Tel:+49 67 35 34 4
Stockist: Vintage Roots

This domaine has been organic since 1988. Sparkling wines, still whites and reds are made. Grape varieties include Riesling, Müller-Thurgau, Silvaner, Pinot Gris (Grauburgunder), Kerner, Bacchus, Ortega, Scheurebe and Faberebe for white, and Pinot Noir (Spätburgunder), Dornfelder and Portugieser for red.

- Hessen Brut Rosé, Frizz Eco Vin: dry sparkling wine, salmon pink colour, soft, easy, drink-upon-purchase fruit. ▮
- Heroldrebe Weissherbst Auslese: medium sweet pink wine made from Heroldrebe, thick taste of ripe, red peach, only 9.5 per cent alcohol. ▮
- Riesling Kabinet Trocken: dry white, smells of warm grass, suitable for vegans, 10.5 per cent. ▮▮

Weingut Burghof Hans-Walter Korn
An der Burgkirche 12, 55218 Ingelheim
Tel:+49 61 32 40 74 1
Overall Price Rating: ▮▮

This domaine is situated directly opposite Oestrich in the Rheingau (see Weingut Jakob Hamm, above). The owners apply biodynamic treatments to the vines. They overlook the remains of a Roman aqueduct on soils suited to red wines produced from Pinot Noir (Spätburgunder).

Weingut Sander

In Den Weingärten 11, 67582 Mettenheim
Tel:+49 62 42 15 83
Fax:+49 62 42 65 89
Overall Price Rating: 🍶

This family domaine has been certified organic since 1954 and is regarded as one of the pioneers of German organic wine. Styles produced include sparkling wines (*sekt*), white wine, plus brandy. Mettenheim lies just north of Worms in the extreme south eastern part of the Rheinhessen. From here it is a short train journey to Mainz. The Rhine is on your right hand side and the Rheinhessen's most famous sweep of vineyards, the Rheinterrasse, on your left.

Weingut Helmut Sander

Wormser Strasse 63/64, 55239 Gau-Odernheim
Tel:+49 67 33 37 2
Overall Price Rating: 🍶

This biodynamic domaine lies well away from the Rhine in an area known for mixed farming. The local wine festival takes place on the last weekend in May and is dedicated to St Urban.

Weingut Wittmann

Mainzer Strasse 19, 67593 Westhofen
Tel:+49 62 44 70 42/+49 62 44 90 50 36
Fax:+49 62 44 55 78
Overall Price Rating: 🍶

Günter Wittmann's domaine has been certified organic since 1990. The local festival to celebrate the flowering of the vine takes place 14 days after Whitsun.

Weinkellerei St Ursula GmbH

Mainzer Strasse 186, 55411 Bingen am Main

Tel:+49 67 21 70 22 8

Fax:+49 67 21 70 26 6 (exports)

Overall Price Rating: ▮

This merchant cooperative is owned by Nestlé and produces a range of wines made from certified organic grapes. The export wines are designed to taste quite neutral and are packaged to look like French wines – so as not to scare off wine drinkers with bad memories of drinking sugary Liebfraumilch (see also Chudleigh Vineyard, England, *page 194*).

Württemberg

Most of the wine Württemberg produces comes from cooperatives and is drunk by locals. The region follows the river Neckar between the Black Forest and the Swabian Alps. Crisp, simple reds are made from Trollinger and neutral, slightly coarse whites are made from two crossings, Müller-Thurgau and Kerner (see StaatsWeingut Weinsberg, below).

Weingut Ernst-Friedrich Haller

Im Brunnengarten 7, 73630 Remshalden

Tel:+49 71 61 73 63 7

Fax:+49 71 81 73 63 7

Overall Price Rating: ▮

This biodynamic domaine lies directly east of Stuttgart in the valley of the river Rems, a tributary of the Neckar.

Schloßgut Hohenbeilsten Weingut Hartmann Dippon

Schloßstrasse 40, 71717 Beilstein

Tel:+49 70 62 93 71 10-0

Fax:+49 70 62 93 71 1-22

Overall Price Rating: ▮▮

This Württemberg domaine started conversion to organic methods in 1988 and became fully certified organic in 1992. There are 13 hectares of Trollinger, Lemberger, Samtrot, Pinot Meunier (Schwarzriesling), Pinot Noir

(Spätburgunder) and a crossing called Regent for red wines, as well as Riesling, Kerner, Silvaner and Pinot Blanc (Weissburgunder) for whites. The majority of wines are made in a dry style, with white, pink, red and sparkling wines made. Solid quality throughout the range, with the reds especially good.

StaatsWeingut Weinsberg

Traubenplatz 5, 74189 Weinsberg
Tel:+49 71 34 50 46 7
Fax:+49 71 34 50 46 76 8

This state-owned Viticultural, Horticultural and Oenological (wine) school was founded in 1868. There are 40 hectares of vines under certified organic management. Weinsberg is perhaps best known for Kerner, a white grape crossing which was bred here in 1969. Kerner was developed for its resistance to fungal rot, both to the kind that rots the grape skin (grey rot) and the one that rots the grape stem (stem rot). Stem rot causes bunches to fall to the ground, and the grower is left without a crop. Although a white variety, Kerner has mixed parentage – Trollinger (a black grape) and Riesling (a white one). Kerner's rot resistance comes at a price. The vine grows a lot of unnecessary shoots which the students here keep down by removing excess buds in spring (see also the Silberberg wine school in Styria, Austria, *page 191*). (Kerner was named after Justinus Kerner, a doctor and poet who wrote Romantic poetry as well as some famous 19th-century drinking songs.)

THE FORMER EAST GERMANY

Two of Germany's 13 wine producing regions are found in the former East Germany. They are Saachsen and Saale-Unstrut. There are two certified organic growers with a total of five hectares of vineyard. Details can be obtained from Gäa eV, the main organic association, founded in 1989:

Gäa eV

Vereinigung Ökologischer Landbau
Plauenscher Ring 40, 01187 Dresden
Tel:+49 35 14 01 23 89

FURTHER READING

Ökologischer Weinbau, by Hoffman-Kopfer-Werner, is the German standard text for organic winegrowing. An English version is planned. Contact Uwe Hoffman at IFOAM (Fax:+49 67 22 50 76 8) for further details.

Greece

Greece's potential for organic wine production is enormous. The country has a dry, Mediterranean climate generally unfavourable to vine fungal diseases and the majority of Greek vineyards are on hill slopes. These provide optimum exposure to the sun and mean manual or animal labour rather than machines are often first choice in the vineyards. Greece's most famous wine, Retsina, is familiar to the 10 million tourists who flock here annually, but there are no Retsinas yet commercially available that conform to EU organic standards. (Retsina theoretically relies on pine tree resin. There are no standards for organic forestry management in the EU.)

The Greek term for organic is *biologik*.

One domaine certified as conforming to EU standards is found in the region of Mantinia in mountainous southern Greece.

Domaine Spiropoulos
32 Poltechniou Str, Iraklion Attica, 14122 Greece
Tel:+75 1 284 5962
Fax:+75 1 282 0207
Stockists: Vinceremos; Vintage Roots
Overall Price Rating: 🍾

The Spiropoulos family, who own this domaine, became involved in wine in 1876. They replanted the vines here in 1973 and there are now over 120 hectares. Organic certification to EU standards began in 1994 and was completed in 1996. The Spiropoulos family changed the pruning of the vines from spurs to canes in 1973, which augmented the potential for mechanization here.

Spur-pruned vines need no supporting wires if all of the fruiting shoots are spread out on one of three short spurs growing off the vine trunk. This means the leaves and bunches can droop down to the ground around the vine trunk, which has the advantage of shading the topsoil from the heat of the sun to retain moisture. It is sometimes called the bush system. Vines pruned to the other system of long canes produce shoots which grow upwards and away from the ground. They need supporting with horizontal wires. This system is called cane pruning because all the fruiting shoots grow off a single long cane that is left at pruning. This one cane has to carry the weight of all of the grapes produced by the vine. If the shoots are not supported between wires the cane will snap off once the grapes form and become heavy. Cane-pruned vines with upward growth can be sprayed from the side by a tractor, and picked by machine quite easily. Spur-pruned bush vines, on the other hand, lend themselves less well to mechanization. They cannot be picked by machine and are much harder to spray with a tractor because the vine's shoots cover the ground and get in the way of the tyres.

Domaine Spiropoulos built a new winery here in 1990, replacing the original one dating from the 19th century. The wines are made in a modern style, using cool temperature fermentation and imported French yeasts. Their use here tends to obscure the highly original flavours that the indigeneous Greek grape varieties planted here are capable of. These include the white Moshofilero, which produces a fresh, dry, aromatic and slightly spicey wine. When the grape skins are left to soak with the juice they add enough colour for a pink wine to be produced. Nevertheless the wines made here are clean and balanced in a light to medium style, and are thus ideal for the international export market, which all Greek wine producers are desperate to tap into. A sparkling wine called Panos, not listed here, is also made.

- Orino, AO Mantinia VQPRD: dry white made from Moshofilero, 11 per cent alcohol; shows peach, melon and basil but could easily match the best dry whites in France with a bit more ambition; suitable for vegans.
- Meliastos, Peleponnese Country Wine: dry pink made from Moshofilero.
- Porfyros, Peleponnese Country Wine: dry red, tastes very similar to Merlot-dominated red Bordeaux AC wines made in Entre Deux Mers (*page 38*), albeit with much more convincing ripeness; suitable for vegetarians (Vinceremos).

For details of several other Greek wine estates which are converting to organic methods, contact Vintage Roots. These domaines should provide some useful competition for the domaine above once they come on stream from 2001. Look out for a 100 per cent varietal Cabernet Sauvignon made by an Australian winemaker.

Italy

Italy vies with France as the world's largest wine producer. The variety of organic wines available from here is impressive, even perhaps bewildering, but they probably account for less than 1 per cent of total plantings (official figures are hard to come by and difficult to reconcile with what is going on on the ground). Producers can draw from 1,000 grape varieties – more than in any other European country. When combined with French and other European imports some fascinating blends result. However getting producers to show the necessary paperwork in order to prove their vineyards are certified organic can be problematic. Check with your wine merchant before committing yourself to a purchase.

The buzz phrase amongst Italy's organic wine growers is *Agrituristica* or agri-tourism: using a vineyard as a holiday destination or base. The idea seems most popular in Tuscany (Chianti country) and Umbria in central Italy. The choice of accommodation and prices vary. Those looking for the quietest retreat should avoid vineyards which can cater for several families at a time, while those looking for social interaction should avoid the 'one bedroom over a private courtyard' style vineyard (*azienda vitivinicola* or *azienda agricola*).

Some Italian vineyards discussed below still practise promiscuous culture. This means more than one crop is grown on the same piece of land. For vineyards this works by allowing the vines to grow up fruit trees rather than wooden posts, with the ground below farmed for vegetables for example. This style of agriculture was deemed too inefficient in the 1960s when a vineyard revolution swept Italy. Vineyards were converted to monoculture and high yielding vine clones were planted. As the move back to organic methods gathers pace, expect more promiscuously managed vineyards to emerge from Italy.

WINE LABELLING

The Italian term for organic is *biológico* – the same as in Portugal. On labels look for the term: *Agricoltura Biologica Controllo.*

The following certification/producer bodies are the ones to check with in the first instance about who has been certified organic for what and for when.

Associazione Italiana Agricultura Biologica (AIAB)

Via Strada Maggiore 45, 40125 Bologna
Tel:+39 51 272 986
Fax:+39 51 232 011
Email: aiab@aiab.it

Bioagricoop SCRL

Via Fucini 10, 40033 Caselecchio di Reno (BO)
Tel:+39 51 613 0512
Fax:+39 51 613 0224
Email: bioagric@iperbole.bologna.it

Ecocert Italia

Via delle Provincre 60, 90217 Catania
Tel:+39 95 442 746

Abruzzi

The Abruzzi is a mountainous region on the Adriatic coast. The main grapes are Sangiovese and the slightly later ripening Montepulciano for reds, and Trebbiano for dry whites. Producers are experimenting with new forms of vine training to capture all the heat of the sun without sacrificing freshness of flavour in the grapes. This stops the reds from tasting of prunes when they should taste of plum. The success of the new training systems is encouraging the planting of imported French grape varieties like Chardonnay. However, even with the new training systems success is far from guaranteed. Chardonnay ripens so quickly in the final few days that it can lose its balance (too much alcohol, not enough flavour).

Azienda Agriverde S.R.L.

Via Monte Maiella n.118, 66020 Caldari-Ortona

Tel:+39 85 903 2101

Fax:+39 85 903 1089

Email: info@agriverde.it

Internet: www.agriverde.it

Stockists: contact Organic Wine Company for details

Overall Price Rating: 🍾

This certified organic estate has been in the hands of the Di Carlo family since the early 1800s. There are 50 hectares in all, with 12 hectares under vine. In addition to their own land, a further 25 hectares are leased from other members of the family. The present owner, Giannicola Di Carlo, markets a wide range of organic products. These include wine, olive oil, tomato products, pastas and gourmet food products in jars – artichoke hearts, aubergines, zucchini and peppers, all in olive oil, and an olive paste (called *tapenade* in France). The wines produced evolve quickly in the bottle, and show subtle if diffuse flavours. They include dry whites made from Trebbiano and Chardonnay. Reds are made under the Montepulciano d'Abruzzo DOC, labelled as 'Riseis'. The dry pink version of this red wine is allowed the Cerasuolo DOC. During 1999 a new winery was under construction, so expect the wines to become more overtly international in flavour: tropical whites and cherry squash reds.

Az. Ag. Pepe

Via Chiesi 10, 64010 Torano Nuovo (TE)

Tel:+39 861 856 493

Email: pepe@advcom.it

Stockists: contact Organic Wine Company for details

Overall Price Rating: 🍾🍾🍾

This certified organic vineyard is run very traditionally by the Pepe family who have been here for four generations. The latest generation is represented by Sofia, Daniela and Stefania Pepe, who are looking to introduce more modern methods of winemaking. These include temperature control of the tanks during fermentation of the wines and new French oak barrels for the wines as they mature. The grapes are hand picked. The dry white

wine made from the Trebbiano d'Abruzzo is still pressed by foot. The dry
red Montepulciano d'Abruzzo is destemmed by hand to allow just the
whole grapes to enter the fermentation vat. This protects the natural yeast
on the grape skins so the wines can ferment without the addition of a
yeast culture. The wines are bottled by hand, without filtration. Their price
is high, but the wines appear to have the depth of flavour to match this.

- Trebbiano d'Abruzzo: dry white, full for a Trebbiano, intense and rich
  like white southern Rhone.
- Montepulciano d'Abruzzo DOC: dry red, thick colour, extracted style
  overlaid with oak; fruity rather than tannic; signals the arrival of the
  new generation of Pepes.

Donatello Jasci
Via Colli, 5, 66054 Vasto (CH)
Tel:+39 873 368 329
Fax:+39 873 368 329
Overall Price Rating: 🍶

This certified organic producer releases wines from the Montepulciano
grape in the two main local forms: dry pink Cerasuolo DOC for immediate
drinking, and dry red Montepulciano which sees some oak. A dry white is
made from Trebbiano d'Abruzzo DOC too.

Apulia

This Italian region contains nearly twice as many vines as Bordeaux and
produces more wine annually than all bar six of the world's largest wine
producing countries. The Greeks called Apulia Oenotria or land of the
vine. It is mainly flat, fertile and agricultural, and artichokes and tomatoes mix with the vines.

Il Noce di Ugo Arno

Contrada Marroco SN, 74024 Manduria (Taranto)
Tel:+39 099 973 4943
Fax:+39 099 973 4943
Overall Price Rating: 🍾

This certified organic domaine makes two red wines from the soft-skinned Primitivo grape. These are Vino di Tavola Rosso, Minnu Nueu and Primitivo di Manduria DOC. Even though both wines contain over 14 per cent alcohol, they retain their balance and a surprising degree of freshness. Some think the Primitivo to be the forefather of California Zinfandel (see H Coturri & Sons in California (*page 324*) for a Zinfandel producer).

Nuova Murgia

Via T Grossi 29, 70022 Altamura
Tel:+39 803 114 245
Fax:+39 803 114 245
Tel:+39 805 181 125 (office)
Fax:+39 805 481 020 (office)
Stockist: Organic Wine Company

This certified organic domaine comprises 10.5 hectares and is run by two brothers, Franco and Andrea di Benedetto. Franco went off travelling while Andrea studied agronomy at university. Together they converted the domaine to organic methods. Fertiliser is provided by sheep manure from over 100 hectares of pasture attached to the domaine. The wines are made in naturally cool limestone cellars which reduce the need for high levels of sulphur dioxide preservatives.

- Vin de Table Blanco, Erbaceo: dry white, made from Malvasia Blanca, Chardonnay, Trebbiano Giallo and Moscato Giallo. A full, floral white which ages well over 3–5 years and sometimes beyond. 🍾🍾
- Vin de Table Rosso, Selvato: dry red, made from Aglianico with lesser amounts of Sangiovese and the two Cabernet varieties. Shows deep aromas of forest nuts and wild cherry. 🍾🍾🍾

Emilia-Romagna

Emilia-Romagna in east central Italy is flat and fertile and home to wine's equivalent of fizzy cola – Lambrusco, made from the grape variety of that name (there are 60 sub-varieties of Lambrusco). This is usually sweet, lightly fizzy and not too high in either alcohol or flavour. Other wines made here tend to be neutral tasting – with the best still red wines showing light damson fruit and the best still whites peachy richness.

Maria Bortolotti

Via Risorgimento 327, 40069 Zola Predosa (BO)
Tel:+39 051 756 763
Fax:+39 051 757 064
Overall Price Rating: 🍾

This family owned domaine lying near the city of Bologna comprises six hectares and has been certified organic since 1991. Local grape varieties such as Albana and Pignoletto mix with imports such as Riesling and Cabernet Sauvignon. The wines are sold under the Colli Bolognesi DOC and can be red or white, but always dry.

Coltiva Scarl (Gruppo)

Via Polonia 85, 41100 Modena (MO)
Tel:+39 059 413 411
Fax:+39 059 346 084

This is one of the largest cooperatives in Italy. It produces a dry red Lambrusco di Modena IGT Secco, Fratello Sole, from a six-hectare vineyard, certified organic since 1988, and planted with Lambrusco di Sorbara, Lambrusco Salamino and Montuni del Reno. The wine is ruby red in colour and fermented dry – which is unusual. It is sealed with a cork too, rather than with a plastic stopper or crown cap (🍾). Other wines made here from organic grapes include a semi-dry sparkling white labelled Bianco di Castelfranco Emilia IGT Frizzante (🍾) and a still dry red Sangiovese di Romagna IGT (🍾).

La Corte d'Aibo (Cooperative Agricola)

Via Marzatore 15, 40050 Monteveglio (BO)

Tel:+39 051 832 583

Fax:+39 051 830 937

Overall Price Rating: 🍷🍷

This cooperative works to a much smaller scale than the one cited above and produces finer wines as a result. They include two red wines from 15 hectares of vineyards certified organic since 1990. The first is a still dry red Cabernet Sauvignon (labelled Colli Bolognesi Cabernet Sauvignon Le Borre DOC), and the second is a dry sparkling ('frizzante') red labelled Colli Bolognesi Barbera Cucherla DOC.

Graziano

Strada degli Ossi 30, Castelvetro di Modena

Tel:+39 59 799 162

Overall Price Rating: 🍷

This organic domaine belongs to Vittorio Graziano and lies on hills above the fertile plain of the Po Valley. A red Lambrusco is produced.

- Lambrusco Grasparossa di Castelvetro: sweet sparkling red, made from a sub-variety of the Lambrusco grape; gulpable.

For another, unrelated Italian called Graziano, see Domaine St Gregory in Mendocino, California (*page 307*).

Mustiola S.R.L.

Via Ravennate 801, 47023 Cesena FO

Tel:+39 547 632 020

Fax:+39 547 639 126

This certified organic producer makes an organic Extra Virgin Olive Oil from hand picked olives which are ground over stone (granite). Wines produced include:

- Sangiovese di Romagna DOC: dry red made from Sangiovese (the main Chianti grape), light fruit, warm but ephemeral.
- Vino Bianco, Mustiola: dry white made from Trebbiano; drink no later than the summer following the vintage on the label.

Fattoria degli Orsi
41040 Baggiovara (MO), Stradello degli Orsi 105
Tel:+39 059 511 076
Fax:+39 059 511 076
Overall Price Rating: ♙

This certified organic domaine is owned by the Lorenzo family. A range of semi and fully sparkling wines are made, such as the sweet red Lambrusco Grasparossa DOC and dry sparkling Pinot Nero (Pinot Noir). Balsamic vinegar is also made.

Quattracque di Fabio Morbin
Via Monticino 1, 40050 Dozza (BO)
Tel:+39 542 673 333
Overall Price Rating: ♙♙

This domaine is a mixed farm consisting of three hectares of vines and nearly five hectares of cereals. It has been certified biodynamic since 1990. Production is tiny, just 2,000 bottles of dry red from the Sangiovese, and 3,500 bottles of dry white from Albana and Trebbbiano. The wines are sold with the Italian 'Country Wine' designation or 'IGT' – Indicazione Geographica Tipica – the equivalent of French Vin de Pays.

Friuli Venezia Giulia

Friuli in north eastern Italy is credited with spearheading the modern white-wine making revolution in Europe. It developed its own ideas on temperature control, cultured yeast and stainless steel tanks rather than pinching them from the New World. Friuli's white wines can show great subtlety – the aromas are present but not so overt as to be 'in your face', while the red wines are marked by intense but elegant tannin and moderate levels of alcohol.

Mont'albano di Braidot Mauro

Via San Roco 23, 33010 Colloredo di Monte Albano
Tel: +39 452 889 003
Fax: +39 452 889 003
Overall Price Rating: ♦

This 12-hectare domaine belongs to Mauro Braidot and has been certified organic since 1987. The wines are made under the Fruili Grave DOC
from Pinot Grigio (Pinot Gris in Alsace) and Tocai Friuliano for dry
whites and Merlot, Cabernet Franc and Cabernet Sauvignon for reds.
These three red Bordeaux varieties are well suited here – the soils drain
quickly to keep the roots dry enough for the grapes to ripen and concentrate. Another red variety which benefits from the warm soils here is the
late ripening Refosco (Mondeuse Noir). It shows a beetroot colour and a
sometimes fierce bite.

Latium

Latium comprises the soft hills which surround Rome, and is famous for
its Frascati, a dry white wine destined for near immediate consumption.

Az. Ag. 'Tre Palme'

Strada Muti 73, loc Landi, 00045 Genzano di Roma (RM)
Tel:+39 039 370 286
Fax:+39 039 370 286
Overall Price Rating: ♦

This domaine is run by Ernesto Lercher and has been certified organic
since 1979. Nearly half the three-hectare property is given to vines, with
the rest used for olives and berry fruits for jam production. Two wines are
made: a dry white from Malvasia and Trebbiano, which sells under the
Colli Lanuvini Bianco DOC and which tastes similar to Frascati; and a dry
red Vino di Tavola called 'Renana', which is aged in large oak casks.

Liguria

Liguria forms the moon shaped strip along Italy's north western Mediterranean coast. The vineyards are picturesque, being steep and over-looking the sea, but are expensive to work and therefore Ligurian wine is relatively highly priced.

Az. Ag. Sommariva

Via Patrioti 80, 17031 Albenga (SV)
Tel:+39 182 559 222
Fax:+39 182 541 143
Overall Price Rating: 👑👑👑

This domaine has been certified organic since 1976 and is nearly five hectares in area, although less than two of these are under vine. Wines produced include dry white Pigato DOC from a variety of that name, and a citrus-like dry white – Riviera Ligure de Ponente Vermentino DOC from the Vermentino, known as Rolle in Provence, further east along the Mediterranean coast (others link it to the Favorita of Piemonte to the north west – see below). A cherry scented dry red from the Rossese grape is labelled Riviera Ligure di Ponente Rossese DOC.

Marches

The Marches centre on the town of Ancona. Soils here are richer in lime-stone than in Emilia-Romagna to the north, so the wines are lighter in texture but generally more elegant.

Campo Societa'Coop Arl

Via Sterpeti 30, 61030 Montefelcino (PE)
Tel:+39 721 725 400
Fax:+39 721 725 133
Overall Price Rating: 👑 (wines only)

This cooperative boasts organic pasta, tomatoes and Italy's first organic vinegar, as well as three wines: Astore, a dry red; Pennellato, a dry pink and Talento, a dry white. One of Italy's most celebrated modern winemakers, Dino Nardi, was a director here, and began developing this cooperative's wines from organic grapes in the 1980s.

Aurora

Contrada Ciafone 98, zona S. Carro, 63035 Offida (AP)

Tel:+39 736 810 007

Fax:+39 736 810 007

Overall Price Rating: 🍶 (wines only)

This mixed farm and vineyard has been certified organic since it was founded in 1980 by a German group. There are 30 hectares of vines in the first range of hills 10kms from the Adriatic coast. As well as wine, products include shelled barley, which can be used to make coffee (moka machine, espresso or infusion); apricots (for jam and juice); extra virgin olive oil; olives; plus hard wheat, spelt, millet, and some varieties of pulses. The wines include:

● Falerio dei Colli Ascolani Bianco DOC, Aurora: dry white made from Trebbiano and two local varieties, Passarina and Pecorino. The label shows a view of the farm with the mythical cart of Aurora. The Pecorino grape has been largely abandoned in the Marches due to its low yield.

● Rosso Piceno DOC, Aurora: dry red made from the Sangiovese and Montepulciano grapes. The label shows the Offida carnival scene (named *bavurd*).

Castoldi Santino

Via San Maria 74, 69913 Corinaldo (AN)

Tel:+39 717 975 102

Fax:+39 717 975 102

This domaine has been certified organic since 1979 and comprises just under one hectare of Montepulciano and Sangiovese (both red grapes). A light red is produced under the Rosso Piceno DOC, but is mostly sold off in bulk (at half the price of the same wine when bottled on site).

Terre Cortesi Moncaro SCRL
Via Piandole 7, 60036 Montecarrato
Tel:+39 073 189 245
Fax:+39 073 189 237
Overall Price Rating:

This cooperative producer releases a range of wines made from certified organic grapes including a dry white Verdicchio dei Castelli di Jesi DOCG, sold in a Bordeaux-style bottle. The Verdicchio grape has been grown around Ancona since the 14th century. Its name translates as 'yellowish-green skin' and in taste it mixes citrus-like freshness with full peachy fruit. Ideal with nearly all fish dishes.

Piemonte/Piedmont

Piedmont in north-western Italy has been a battleground in recent years. Those who made the region renowned for brutal red wines have been overthrown. A younger generation has wrested the winemaking rules from its predecessors, changing Barolo DOCG and Barbaresco DOCG, the region's two main red wines, from being sour to petal fresh. Both are made with the late ripening, complex but often prickly Nebbiolo grape. The Dolcetto is an earlier ripening and more accessible tasting red grape (its name means 'little sweet one'), and produces lush, mouthfilling dry reds for drinking between 1–4 years old. The main white grape here, Moscato, makes frothy sweet, grapey sparkling wines labelled as Moscato d'Asti or Asti Spumante. Dry whites are made with Cortese, and sell for ambitious prices as Gavi DOCG.

Az. Ag. Antico Borgo del Rondino
Via dei Fiori 13, 12050 Trezzo Tinella (CN)
Tel:+39 173 630 313
Fax:+39 173 630 313
Cellar Door Sales: yes

This domaine has been certified organic since 1978, and covers 17 hectares, but only three of these are under vine. Wines made include dry red Dolcetto d'Alba DOC, dry red Barbera d'Alba DOC, dry white

Favorita delle Langhe (see also Liguria, above) and a sweet, late picked Moscato Passito. Wines are sold at the cellar door only.

Pierre Berutti

La Spinona, 12050 Barbaresco
Stockists: contact Organic Wine Company for further details
Overall Price Rating: 🍶🍶

This domaine just outside the town of Barbaresco belongs to Pietro Berutti and his wife Romana. The Beruttis were the only producers of Barbaresco to make wine from certified organic grapes until they pulled out of the certification programme in 1996. The wines were selling so well in the US that the fee for organic certification was deemed a needless expense by Pietro Berutti.

- Chardonnay delle Langhe, Vin de Table: dry white, very refined fruit with a touch of oak.
- Barbera: dry red, spends 6–7 months in oak, chewy style.
- Dolcetto: dry red, light, early appeal, sourced from a vineyard called La Ghiga.
- Nebbiolo: dry red, from younger vines than the Barbaresco below; less intense (undergoes a shorter fermentation as a result, so as not to over-extract).
- Barbaresco DOCG, La Spinona: dry red made from Nebbiolo grown in a five-hectare vineyard called L'Albina in the hills on the right bank of the Tanaro river. Each lot of picked grapes is pressed and aged separately in oak casks.

Bianchi

Via Roma 37, 28070 Sizzano (NO)
Tel:+39 321 810 004
Fax:+39 321 820 382
Email:e.bianchi@bianchibiowine.it
Stockists: contact Organic Wine Company for details
Overall Price Rating: 🍶🍶🍶

This domaine has been certified organic since 1984. The property is situated in the Novarese hills in north-east Piedmont at the foot of Monte Rosa. It was founded in 1785 by the first Guiseppe Bianchi, with a vineyard at that time of 1.75 hectares. At the end of the 19th century, in the hands of grandson Pietro, more and better land was bought from Count Tornielli, taking it to five hectares. Thanks to the ambassadorial efforts of Count Camillo Benso di Cavour, a committed customer, word of the wines spread to France, and thus an export business began. Since World War II, the property has expanded to its present size of 40 hectares and is now in the hands of the sixth generation of Bianchis. Nebbiolo, Bonarda and Barbera are planted for reds, with Vespolina and Erbaluce for whites. The vines enjoy good south-facing exposure. The vines appear better balanced since the adoption of organic methods which have regulated the soil. Chemical weed-killers were eliminated and replaced by clippings from grass grown between the vines. The wines are made in a clear, sophisticated style.

- Erbaluce Colline Novaresi Bianco DOC: dry white, made from Erbaluce planted in a three-hectare vineyard called Colle Priosa on the San Giacomo hill in Sizzano. The vines were planted in 1992, so the wine is made for early drinking. The 1998 vintage showed little nose, but had crisp fresh fruit on the palate, moderate acidity, quite a full body with a moderate finish.

- Barbera Colline Novaresi DOC: dry red, made from a one-hectare Barbera vineyard in Sizzano village called Colle Giannini, planted in 1992. The 1997 vintage was a deepish crimson colour, with full waxy fruit on the nose. Very soft, full of fruit, for drinking over the next two years.

- Spanna Nebbiolo Colline Novaresi DOC: dry red made from Nebbiolo (Spanna) from Valle San Guiseppe and Colle Fiorito vineyards in Sizzano village, planted in 1978, comprising 2.5 hectares in total. Similar deep crimson to the Barbera, a little lighter in style but as elegant, with sweeter fruit, and a little less structure.

- Sizzano DOC: dry, blend of three varieties, first made in 1994 from five hectares across three sites in Sizzano called Archiusa, Val San Giacomo, and Val Fre. Two-thirds of the vines date from 1978 and the rest from 1988. The wine is a blend of Nebbiolo (60 per cent), Vespolina (25 per cent) and Bonarda (15 per cent). It ages for two years in Slovenian oak, and a minimum 10 months in bottle. Shows firm, briary fruit, the sort of wine to keep you from nodding off in front of a warm fire.

- Vigneto Valfre Colline Novarese DOC: dry red made from Nebbiolo (70 per cent) and Barbera (30 per cent) grown in a one-hectare vineyard called Val Fre in Sizzano planted in 1975. Spends 12 months in French barrels.

- Ghemme DOC: dry red, made from vines planted across 4.8 hectares on two hills called Bataggiole and Sanclemente in Ghemme village; 40 per cent were planted in 1979 while the rest were planted in 1997, and will come into production in 2000. A blend of Nebbiolo (80 per cent), Vespolina (10 per cent) and Bonarda (10 per cent), which ages two years in Slovenian oak. Tastes of clean, bitter violets.

- Ghemme DOC Colle Baraggiole: dry red, made from 100 per cent Nebbiolo grown on Bataggiole hill (see above) and which spends a year in large oak vats and then 10 months in small oak barrels. Shows brown brick colour, and a sandy, understated taste.

- Gattinara DOCG: dry red, made from a 1.8 hectare Valferana hill vineyard in Gattinara village, planted 60 per cent in 1975, 40 per cent 1992 with 100 per cent Nebbiolo. Ages two years in Slovenian oak. Drink within five years to capture this wine's crimson colour and ripe fruit.

- Gattinara Vigneto Valferana: same vineyard as the above, but higher up the hill; grapes are selected twice, once in the vineyard, and again in the winery, with 18 months in oak vats and six months in small barrels. Very firm but not over structured; one to take your time over, superb Nebbiolo perfume.

- Passito di Uva Erbaluce 'Autunno degli Artisti': sweet white, made from late harvested (i.e., the end of October) Erbaluce grapes which are then dried on straw mats. They are pressed in December, with slow barrel fermentation. Classic dried grape wine, with a deep gold colour and a lovely aroma of peaches and figs, complex and concentrated. This grape is being rediscovered. Also made here in a sparkling and grappa form.

Cascina degli Ulivi

Strada della Mazzola 12, 15067 Novi Ligure
Tel:+39 143 744 598
Fax:+39 143 744 598
Overall Price Rating: 👖👖👖

This domaine converted to certified organic methods in 1980 and to biodynamics in 1985. It is run by Stefano Bellotti and his wife Zita. Stefano's family arrived here in the 1930s. There are six hectares of Cortese, Trebbiano and Malvasia for whites, plus Dolcetto, Moscato Rosso and Barbera for reds. The grapes are hand picked into small baskets and the wines are fermented and aged in wood (oak vats for reds, small barrels for whites).

- Barbera delle Piemonte DOC, Moumbè: dry red, shows bramble fruit, very clear and precise. Also made as a special bottling called La Venta Quemada.
- Dolcetto delle Monferrato DOC, Nibio: dry red made from a small berried (i.e., concentrated) sub-variety of Dolcetto. Very positive style all the way through, punchy colour, mouthwateringly ripe and fresh.
- Gavi DOC: dry white, made from Cortese, shows a clear nut aroma, unusual oxidized style in which the fruit is retained.
- Gavi DOC, Monte Marino: dry white, made from Cortese grown on south-west facing limestone slopes, which account for the wine's piercing aroma of fern and flower. This is a benchmark example of this ultra fashionable grape variety.
- Gavi DOC, Filagnotti di Tassarolo: dry white, made from Cortese which ferments in Slovenian casks made of acacia wood (rather than oak which would be too heavy). Tassarolo is the name of the hills the estate is located in.

Az. Ag. Casetta Agostino

Via Belvedere 5, 12050 Treiso D'Alba (CN)
Tel:+39 173 638 310/+39 173 630 223
Overall Price Rating: 👖

This domaine has been certified organic since 1991. Although it lies in the heart of the red wine Barbaresco DOCG zone, the only wine produced here is dry red Dolcetto d'Alba DOC. The Dolcetto can be picked much earlier than the Nebbiolo variety used in Barbaresco, and the Dolcetto vats finish fermentation here sometimes even before the first Nebbiolo is picked.

Erbaluna

Borgata Pozzo 43, 12064 La Morra
Tel:+39 173 508 00
Fax:+39 173 509 336
Stockist: Vinceremos
Overall Price Rating: 🍾🍾🍾

This family domaine has been certified organic since 1985. It lies in the hills south east of La Morra, in the heart of the Barolo area. It is run by Severino Oberto and his brother Andrea. There are 6.89 hectares of Nebbiolo, Barbera, Dolcetto and Grignolino for red wines, which here are made in 'fruit driven' style. The wines are not suitable for vegetarians.

- Barbera d'Alba DOC, La Bettola: dry red from a single vineyard.
- Barbera d'Alba DOC, La Rosina: dry red, made from south-facing Barbera vines; shows heavy colour, unusually thick texture and heaps of new oak.
- Barolo DOCG: dry red made with Nebbiolo. The 1994 vintage faded quickly but the 1995 showed better flavour and softish tannins (Nebiolo is a raspingly tannic grape).
- Barolo DOCG, Vigna Rocche: dry red made with Nebbiolo from a vineyard first mentioned in 1477 as Rochectare. The wine shows big structure and tar-like flavours.
- Dolcetto d'Alba DOC: dry red made with two vineyard designations, Le Liste and Le Ghiaie. Both show stylish deep cherry fruit and solid rather than aggressive tannin.

Foja d'Or
Via Belvedere 5, Treiso (CN)
Tel:+39 173 638 310
Overall Price Rating: 🍶🍶🍶

This certified organic domaine lies eight kilometres from Alba in an area known for its white truffles. Owner Agostino Casetta produces a dry white Chardonnay delle Langhe DOC, a dry red Dolcetto d'Aba DOC and a sparkling sweet white Moscato d'Asti DOCG.

Aldo Marenco & Figlio
Fraz., Pamparalo-Pironi 25, 12063 Dogliani (CN)
Tel:+39 173 721 090
Overall Price Rating: 🍶🍶

This organic domaine is a source of single vineyard red wines made from Dolcetto and Barbera. Wines made include: Dolcetto delle Langhe DOC; Dolcetto di Dogliani DOC, Vigna Pirun; Dolcetto di Dogliani DOC, Vigna Ouria; Dolcetto di Dogliani DOC, Vigna Brice; Barbera delle Piemonte DOC, Vigna Pirona; and Barbera delle Piemonte DOC, Vigne Pirona (Barrique).

Nuova Cappelletta
Ca'Cappellatta 9, 15049 Vignale Mon
Tel:+39 142 923 13
Fax:+39 142 923 550
Stockist: Vintage Roots
Overall Price Rating: 🍶🍶

This domaine is owned by Adele Fracchia. It was converted to certified organic methods in the 1980s and to biodynamics in the 1990s. Grape varieties include Grignolino for light reds and Cortese for laurel-scented dry whites. The domaine also makes:

- Barbera del Monferrato DOC: dry red, crisp and briary, suitable for vegans.
- Chardonnay delle Piemonte DOC: dry white, non-oak aged which means the fruit can express itself; good value Northern Italian Chardonnay, suitable for vegans.

Rovero

Fraz. San Marzanotto – Loc Valdonata, 14100 Asti
Tel:+39 141 592 460
Fax:+39 141 598 287
Overall Price Rating: 🍷🍷🍷

This organic domaine comprises 15 hectares of vines as well as one hectare of fruit trees and four hectares of cereals. It is run by Claudio Rovero, his brothers Michelino and Franco and sister Rosanna. The style of wine produced is typical of contemporary Piedmont: a mix of traditional flavours with imported ones in the form of oak from small French barrels. This gives a range in which there is something for everyone. Red wines are made from Grignolino (which is native to the province of Asti) and Brachetto, as well as from imports such as Pinot Noir and Cabernet Sauvignon. Red wines from Barbera are made under three vineyard names: Gustin, Rouvè and Vigna del Mandorlo. Dry whites are made from Sauvignon Blanc (one of which is barrel fermented) and Riesling, the latter being (for this author) the pick of the range. Marc and grappa are also made using the traditional 'bain-marie' method (i.e., indirect heat on the still rather than direct heat during distillation).

Mario Torelli

Regione San Grato, 142, 14051 Bubbio
Tel:+39 014 483 380
Fax:+39 014 483 380

This certified organic vineyard comprises six hectares in the Cascina Milana high in the Langhe hills. Owners Mario and Gianfranco Torelli produce an attractive range of wines.

- Chardonnay delle Piemonte DOC, La Milana: dry white, shows an arresting mineral aroma (due in part to a Canadian yeast culture used for alcoholic fermentation). ♠♠
- Chardonnay delle Piemonte DOC, La Milana Barrique: dry white, barrel ('barrique') fermented; very attractive combination of mineral, peach and vanilla. ♠♠♠
- Dolcetto d'Asti DOC, Bricco Rochetto: dry red, aged in wooden vats rather than stainless steel, which allows Dolcetto's bitter cherry fruit to soften. ♠♠
- Moscato d'Asti DOCG, San Grod: sparkling sweet white containing 6 per cent alcohol, made with Moscato Rosso and Malvasia Rosso (for grapey fruit flavours) with a litle Trebbiano (for lift and acid). A simple wine which shows super fruit and balance. ♠♠

Viberti
Via delle Viole, 2-Fraz. Vergne, 12060 Barolo (CN)
Tel:+39 017 356 192
Fax:+39 017 356 192
Stockist: Vintage Roots
Overall Price Rating: ♠♠

This certified organic domaine comprises nine hectares. It was founded in 1896 by Antonio Viberti (or 'Toni d'Giuspin' as he is referred to by his descendants). The wines are made by Giovanni Viberti and his son Gianluca. All the wines are suitable for vegans.

- Barbera d'Alba DOC, Bricco Airoli: dry red, shows simple but effective cherry fruit well served by a touch of oak.
- Barolo DOC: dry red made from Barolo and released as three single vineyard designations, namely Bricco delle Viole, La Volta and San Pietro. Medium weight, for drinking within 3–8 years with rich food.
- Chardonnay delle Langhe DOC: dry white, shows balanced knit, clean pear and pineapple fruit. Also made as a single vineyard wine called Juan Lucas Vineyards.
- Dolcetto d'Alba DOC, Toni d'Giuspin: dry red, flat rather than fruity style of Dolcetto.

Sardinia

The island of Sardinia was ruled for four centuries until 1720 by the Spanish. They have left their mark with grape varieties such as Cannonau (Grenache or Alicante) and Monica, both for red wine. The first wines made here however were influenced by the Phoenicians from as far back as the eighth century BC, using indigenous grapes like Nuragus.

Cantine Meloni Vini SARL

09047 Selargius (CA), Via A.Gallus, 79
Tel:+39 70 852 822
Fax:+39 70 840 311/+39 70 846 583
Email: info@meloni-vini.com
Internet: www.meloni-vini-com

Overall Price Rating: 🍾

This organic domaine is family owned and comprises 250 hectares in four main plots: Su Danieli (100 hectares of Cannonau and Monica on south east facing slopes of sand and pebble at Decimomannu); Azienda di Simbirizzi (20 hectares of Vermentino on low lying sand and limestone fragments at Quartu Sant'Elena); Campu Piratsu (100 hectares of mixed varieties at Senorbi); and Santa Rosa (30 hectares of mixed varieties at Selargius). The wines are labelled under either the Natura or Il Germmoglio labels.

- Cannonau di Sardegna DOC: dry red made from the Grenache variety, shows cedar and pine flavours, not overly alcoholic, drink within 1–4 years.
- Monica di Sardegna DOC: dry red, very soft but appealing style of berry fruit with adequate body to age for up to 18 months, made from the Monica (90 per cent), Bovali and Carignano (French Carignan) varieties.
- Vermentino di Sardegna DOC: dry white, seafood quaffer, shows little aroma but a subtle lime citrus flavour.
- Nuragus DOC: dry white, shows clean nettle and earth tones, understated rather than overt, and for enjoying, not for keeping. Nuragus is named after the stone towers (*nuraghe*) found on the island as look-out posts.

Sicily

The island of Sicily has been producing wine since the eighth century BC when it was colonized by the Greeks. It now produces twice as much wine as Australia, but little of this is organic. Local politics rather than the climate, which is benign, may play a part in this.

Ruggero Vasari
Tel: +44 118 976 1999
Fax: +44 118 976 1998
Stockist: Vintage Roots
Overall Price Rating: 🍷

This organic domaine produces two wines of note:

- Mistral Bianco: dry white, full bodied, soft herby flavours and a warm texture, made predominantly from the local Catarratto variety, and is suitable for vegans.
- Mistral Rosso: dry red, evolves quickly so find the most recent vintage, but capable of highly individual wild fruit flavours, suitable for vegans.

Trentino

Trentino is to Italy what Alsace is to France: a northern vineyard with predominantly hill sloping vines, making full, dry whites and peppery reds. The one difference is that here the foreign influence is Austrian rather than Germanic.

Loacker Schwarhof (Vineyards)
Sankt Justina 3, 39100 Bolzano
Tel:+39 471 365 125
Fax:+39 471 365 313
Email: Vineyards@loacker.net
Internet: www.loacker.net
Stockists: contact Organic Wine Company for details
Overall Price Rating: 🍷🍷

This certified organic domaine lies on the Austrian/Italian border. Owner Reiner Loacker is also proprietor of Tenuta Corte Pavone in Tuscany (*see page 249*). Varietal wines are made from Chardonnay and Sauvignon Blanc (dry whites), as well as from Cabernet Franc and Lagrein. The best wines here are reds made from Schiava under the Santa Maddalena denomination. Schiava is the Trollinger of Germany's Baden region.

Tuscany

Tuscany rivals Provence and California and is one of the most fashionable places to have a vineyard, organic or otherwise. Who wouldn't like to spend hours over lunch nibbling olives and sipping the region's Chianti, Brunello di Montalcino or 'vin santo' wines while staring across olive groves peppered with ancient ruins and picturesque farms? Tuscany has its share of wineries keen to market their products on the back of a lifestyle bandwagon, and organic producers are no exception. The region's main wine, dry red Chianti, is made predominantly from Sangiovese, although small of amounts of virtually any red or white variety seem to season the final blends.

Az. Ag. Bulichella
Localita Bulichella 31, 57028 Suvereto (LI)
Tel:+39 565 829 892
Fax:+39 565 829 553
Overall Price Rating: ♕

This domaine has been certified organic since 1984. There are 10 hectares of red varieties including Sangiovese Grosso, Cabernet Sauvignon and Merlot. Wines produced include Toscanio Val di Cornia DOC, Rubino Val di Cornia DOC and Buli Val di Cornia DOC.

Buondonno
37 Loc. La Piazza, 53011 Castellina in Chianti
Tel:+39 577 749 754
Fax:+39 577 749 754
Stockist: Vintage Roots

This organic domaine was purchased by its current owners, Valeria Sodano and Gabriele Buondonno, in 1989. Both are qualified agronomists. There are 5.5 hectares of vines located between Florence and Sienna. One dry white wine is made under the regional Bianco di Toscana designation. The red wines include:

- Chianti Classic DOC, Buondonno: dry red, shows clean, restrained fresh fruit with a solid core, seems to have some Cabernet Sauvignon as the wine smells of blackcurrants; suitable for vegans, well worth finding (🍷). Also made in a Riserva style (it spends an extra year in oak, 🍷🍷).

Other products:
- Grappa di Vinace di Chianti Classico, 42 per cent alcohol (50cl, 🍷).

Canneta
Località San Lucia 27, 53037 San Gimignano (SI)
Tel:+39 577 941 540

This domaine lies in the hills around the historic town of San Gimignano. It has been certified organic since 1989 and comprises six hectares of Vernaccia di San Gimignano, Sauvignon Blanc, Riesling, Trebbiano and Malvasia del Chianti for whites; and Sangiovese, Aglianico, Canaiolo and Cabernet Sauvignon for reds. The space between the vines is permanently grassed to encourage beneficial fauna and flora into the vineyard. Winemaker Stefano Grandi avoids using sulphur dioxide preservative ('sulfites') by allowing the grape juice to oxidize before fermentation (thus allowing any unstable elements in the juice to be removed during the yeast fermentation, so that they can cause no problems during ageing). This is particularly important for the white wine, Vernaccia di San Gimignano.

- Rosso di Tavola, Fiore Rosso: dry red, a blend of the red varieties listed above; serve chilled for best effect. 🍷
- Vernacchia di San Gimignano DOCG: dry white, full bodied, markedly acid and slightly bitter, yet with a slightly oily texture which adds

intrigue. Known as 'vernage' in medieval London because of its 'varnishy' taste. 🍷

- Vernacchia di San Gimignano DOCG, La Lune e le Torri: dry white, same as above except fermented in French oak; spends six months on the fine fermentation lees (dead yeast) to nourish the wine and to protect it from spoilage. 🍷🍷

Casale

Via San Martino – Casale 47/A, 50052 Certaldo (FI)
Tel:+39 571 669 262
Fax:+39 571 669 262
Stockist: Organic Wine Company
Overall Price Rating: 🍷

This vineyard belongs to Guiseppe Giglioli and his wife Piera M. Rinaldi who amalgamated their vineyards together. The land has been cultivated by the Giglioli family for 230 years – they have account books from 1770 (a similar record to the Labuzans at Château Moulin à Vent in Graves in Bordeaux (*page 19*)). In 1994 the vineyards were converted to organic methods, and in 1998 they obtained biodynamic certification.

- Sangiovese, Rosso dei Collina della Toscana Centrale IGT, Il Casale: dry red, light, fruity, agreeable, twist of bitter chocolate in the aftertaste.
- Trebbiano, Bianco dei Collina della Toscana Centrale IGT, Il Casale: dry white, tastes of bitter citrus.

Other products:

- Olio Extra Virgine d'Oliva: extra virgin olive oil (50 cl or 1 litre bottles).
- Aspretto di Uvaggio Chiantigiovese: vinegar made from Sangiovese and oak aged (250ml smoked glass flasks, with ribbon and wax seal).

Casina di Cornia

Località Cornia 113, 53011 Castellina in Chianti (SI)

Tel:+39 577 743 052

Fax:+39 577 743 052

Email: cornia@chiantinet.it

Internet: www.chiantinet.it/casinadicornia

Stockist: Chartrand Imports (USA)

This Chianti Classico domaine dates from the 12th century. It was converted to organic methods in 1980 when it was purchased by Antoine
Luginbühl, a Swiss German. As well as Chianti (🍴), another red wine is
made from Cabernet Sauvignon called L'Amaranto (🍴).

Concadoro (Fattoria)

53011 Castellina in Chianti (SI)

Tel:+39 577 740 284

Overall Price Rating: 🍴

This Chianti Classico domaine lies in the province of Sienna and belongs
to the Cerasi Brothers. It converted to organic methods in 1989. Wines
made include Chianti Classico DOCG and Chianti Classico Riserva DOCG
(both dry reds) and Vin Santo, Vino da Tavola (a sweet white tasting of bitter quince) made from sun-dried grapes aged for several years in barrel.

Corte Pavone (Tenuta)

Località Casanuova, 53024 Montalcino

Tel:+39 577 848 110

Overall Price Rating: 🍴

This organic domaine is owned by Reiner Loacker (see also Loacker
Schwarhof, *page 245*). There are 90 hectares of vineyard, meadow and
scrub in the hills above Montalcino where days are warm but nights
are cool. Two red wines are made: Brunello di Montalcino DOCG and
Brunello di Montalcino DOCG Riserva. The wines age in Slavonian,
French and Austrian casks.

Ispoli
Via Santa Lucia 2, 50024 Mercatale/Val di Pesa (FI)
Tel:+39 055 821 613

This organic domaine has been certified since 1988. Owner Bernd Mattheis produces a 'Super Tuscan', i.e., a red table wine sold at a high price rather than a red Chianti sold at a moderate one. Innovative Tuscan producers use the table wine designation to counter the stifling appellation rules introduced in 1963. This way the producers can blend fashionable and often French grape varieties, such as Cabernet Sauvignon, with the native Tuscan ones. Here a dry white Chardonnay (🍾🍾) is made, in addition to:

● Vino di Tavola di Toscana, Ispolaia: dry red, made from Sangiovese, Sangioveto, Canaiolo and Cabernet Sauvignon. 🍾🍾🍾

Az. Ag. Marcialla
Via Matteotti 96, 50020 Marcialla-Barberino (FI)
Tel:+39 558 074 157
Fax:+39 558 074 157
Overall Price Rating: 🍾

This certified organic domaine belongs to Giovanni Passaponti. It comprises six hectares of Sangiovese, Canaiolo Nero, Cabernet Sauvignon, Colorino and Merlot for Chianti Classico DOCG dry red wines, and Trebbiano, Malvasia Bianca del Chianti and Sauvignon Blanc for Colli Etruria Centrale Bianco DOC dry whites.

Az. Ag. Massavecchia
Podere Fornace, loc Rocche 11, 58024 Massa Marittima (GR)
Tel:+39 566 915 522
Overall Price Ratings: 🍾🍾🍾

This domaine has been certified organic since 1993 and comprises four hectares of vineyards. Dry red wines are made in a modern, oaked style and include: Vino da Tavola di Toscana La Fonte di Pietrarsa from

Cabernet Sauvignon, and the more alcoholic Vino da Tavola di Toscana Terziere from Alicante. Another Sangiovese-based red is labelled Monteregio di Massa Marittima. Dry whites are made from Vermentino and Sauvignon Blanc.

Da Morazzano
Via Morazzano 5, 56040 Montescudaio (PI)
Tel:+39 (0)650015
Overall Price Rating: ♙♙

This domaine has been certified organic since 1975 and comprises 1.48 hectares of Sangiovese, Canaiolo and Cabernet Franc. Wines made include a dry pink Vino di Tavola di Toscana, Rosato and a Chianti look-alike dry red called Montescudaio DOC.

Il Palagio
San Andrea 9, 53030 Ulignano, San Gimignano
Tel:+39 577 940 404/+39 577 940 521
Fax:+39 577 940 404

This domaine is named after the palace (*il palagio*) built in the Tuscan hilltop town of San Gimignano in 1564 by the local ruler as a summer retreat. There are now six hectares of south-west facing vines, with another eight hectares of agricultural land, woods and vineyards. Its current owner, Silvia Sircana, converted it to organic methods from 1980. Vernaccia di San Gimignano, Sauvignon Blanc, Trebbiano, Riesling and Malvasia del Chianti are planted for whites, with Aglianico, Sangiovese and Cabernet Sauvignon for reds. The wines ferment in stainless steel tanks and include:

● Vernacchia di San Gimignano DOCG: dry white, floral. ♙
● Vernacchia di San Gimignano DOCG, Silvia: dry white, picked later than the above wine so more intense. ♙♙
● Chianti Classico Colli Senesi DOCG: dry red from the largest and arguably least remarkable Chianti sub-zone. A light style blended from

two red grapes and two white ones (Sangiovese, Canaiolo, Trebbiano Toscano and Chianti Malvasia), as is allowed under the DOCG rules. ♦♦
- Il Poggio alle Rocche Bianco IGT: light dry everyday white wine, fresh and pleasing, but unremarkable (Organic Wine Company, ♦♦).

J. Soidler
55050 Massaciùccoli

This organic domaine is owned by Dario Pongiluppi and produces a light dry red Chianti Classico (♦), as well as olive oil (♦♦).

Az. Ag. Terra d'Acoiris
Strada della Maglianella 5, 53042 Chianciano Terme (SI)
Tel:+39 057 860 270
Accommodation: available

This domaine has been Demeter-certified biodynamic since 1987. There are 5.5 hectares of Sangiovese, Canaiolo and the much underrated Mammolo, for dry red wines sold under the Chianti Colli Senesi DOCG and Chianti Colli Senesi Riserva DOCG. Dry white table wines are also made, from Trebbiano and Malvasia.

Tracolle di Broggi Anita
5 Strada in Greve, Badia a Passignano, 50020 Sambuca Val di Pesa (FI)
Tel:+39 558 071 234
Fax:+39 558 071 234/+39 558 071 438/+39 558 071 482

This Chianti Classico domaine has been certified organic since 1985 when the current owners, the Broggi family, arrived. There are just 2.6 hectares of vines in two sites, planted in 1971 and 1983. There are also olive groves, pasture and woodland. The domaine originally belonged to the Abbey (*badia*) of Passignano. A dry pink wine (first made in 1998) and two red wines are made:

- Chianti Classico DOCG: dry red, made from Sangiovese Toscano with a little Malvasia (a white grape); it ferments in stainless steel, and ages 12 months in 225-litre and 550-litre French oak casks. In 1997 it showed thick, ripe fruit, elegant texture, good integration of oak, lots of extract without losing freshness; very good. 🍶🍶

- Chianti Classico DOCG, Marchio Storico: dry red, from one of the two vineyard sites, similar to the above wine; solid in 1996 and outstanding in 1997. Very limited production. 🍶🍶🍶

Other products produced include Extra Virgin Olive Oil, made from 7.4 hectares of olives, although these were severely hit by frost in December 1996 (🍶🍶).

Vignano
Loc. Vignano 47, 50020 Marcialla (FI)
Tel:+39 571 660 041
Fax:+39 571 660 144
Accomodation: yes
Overall Price Rating: 🍶🍶

This domaine lies between Florence and Sienna and has been certified organic since 1986. It belongs to Fritz-Claus Croissant who also makes organic wine in the German Pfalz. Some experimental varieties are planted, along with the Tuscan staples like Sangiovese and Canaiolo. Vignano comprises 27.8 hectares, of which 10 hectares are vineyard. Olive oil, vinegar and grappa are also produced.

- Vino da Tavola Bianco: dry white, made from Trebbiano.
- Vino da Tavola Bianco, Favoloso: dry white, made from Trebbiano using older vines than the above and barrel fermented too.
- Vino da Tavola Rosa: dry pink made from Sangiovese and Canaiolo.
- Vino da Tavola Rosso Nr 3: dry red, light blend of Sangiovese and Malvasia, drink within 2–3 years.
- Chianti, DOCG Rosso Nr 4: dry red, made from Sangiovese, Canaiolo and Trebbiano, drink within 3–4 years. This is a standard Chianti formula but this wine has unusual intensity.
- Vino da Tavola Rosso, Nr 5: dry red made from Sangiovese, aged 15 months in oak. The Sangiovese grape works only as a single varietal if the clone planted in the vineyard is a good one. Modern clones of

Sangiovese planted in Tuscany from the 1960s gave yield rather than flavour, i.e., lots of big juicy berries. The clones here give smaller, darker and tastier berries, and can stand up to oak ageing.

- Vino da Tavola Rosso, Nr 12: dry red made from Sangiovese, spends 22 months in oak.
- Vino da Tavola Rosso, Nr 13: dry red made from Pinot Nero (Spätburgunder or Pinot Noir), spends 12 months in oak; has less body than a Baden or Pflaz Pinot Noir from Germany.
- Vino da Tavola Rosso, Nr 15, Barrique: dry red made from Sangiovese, spends 12 months in barrel.
- Vino da Tavola Rosso, Selection Rosso, Nr 15, Barrique: as above but made from selected bunches of Sangiovese; contains 14.5 per cent alcohol (other red wines here come in at 13 per cent, which already is higher than most Italian wines). Keep 6–8 years.

Vitigliano
62 Case Sparse, 50022 Greve in Chianti (FI)
Tel:+39 055 853 016
Fax:+39 055 853 016
Overall Price Rating: ♙♙

This organic domaine covers 16 hectares in the heart of the Chianti Classico region. Owners Marco Ridomi and Deidre Woode produce two Chianti Classicos, one of which is a Riserva (extra oak aged), as well as a dry pink wine under the Rosato della Toscana Centrale designation. A Vin Santo is also made.

Tenuta San Vito in Fior di Selva
Via San Vito, 32, 50056 Montelupo Fiorentino (FI)
Tel:+39 057 151 411
Fax:+39 057 151 405
Stockists: Vinceremos; Chartrand Imports (USA)

This certified organic domaine is family run and radiates an infectious enthusiasm for everything it does. Traditional winemaking techniques, such as adding overripe (dried) grapes to the red wine vats to spin out the fermentation (called the *governo* method), gives the wines an old style richness. An appealing range of vegetarian-suitable wines includes:

- Bianco Colli dell'Etruria Centrale DOCG, Tenuta San Vito: dry white made from Trebbiano and Malvasia and, since 1997, with Chardonnay and Sauvignon Blanc too. ▎
- Chianti San Vito DOCG: dry red made from Sangiovese and Canaiolo, it spends eight months in oak; juicy fruit (Safeway, ♦♦).
- Chianti Vigna la Reina Tenuta San Vito DOCG: dry red with extra richness from older Sangiovese vines and the *governo* method. ♦♦♦
- Fior di Selva Barrique DOCG: dry red blend of Sangiovese and Cabernet Franc which spends 15 months in oak. ♦♦♦
- Fior di Selva Spumante: dry white sparkling wine made from Verdicchio, Chardonnay, Pinot Blanc and Sauvignon Blanc. ♦♦♦
- Verdiglio, Tenuta San Vito: dry white blend of Trebbiano and Malvasia. ♦♦♦
- Vin Santo, Tenuta San Vito DOCG: sweet white, made in 1989 from Trebbiano and Malvasia picked over-ripe at high sugars to leave over 15 per cent alcohol; balanced sweetness, 50cl bottles. ♦♦♦

The domaine also makes olive oil (♦♦♦).

Thomas Wulf (Podere Lignano)
53026 Pienza (SI)
Tel:+39 578 748 005
Overall Price Rating: ♦♦♦

This domaine has been certified organic since 1988 and is planted with Sangiovese, Canaiolo, Brunello, Trebbiano Toscano and Malvasia. The vineyard manager, John Porcelli, trained with Roy Cook at Sedlescombe Vineyard in England (*see page 195*). Wines made include a Brunello di Montalcino, a red wine made with an especially small berried version of the main Chianti grape, Sangiovese. Firm and blisteringly tannic, Brunello reveals its fruit only after years of bottle ageing and careful decanting (for aeration).

Podere Zollaio
Via Pistoiese 29, 50059 Vinci (FI)
Tel:+39 057 156 439
Fax:+39 057 156 439

This domaine has been certified organic since 1983. Two simple wines are produced from 1.5 hectares of Chardonnay, Malvasia and Trebbiano (for the white) and Sangiovese, Canaiolo, Colorino and Cabernet (for the red).

Useful Tuscan Address
Coordinamento Toscano Produttori Biologici (CTB)
Piazza Dalmazia, 201C, 50141 Firenze
Tel:+39 055 413 173

The umbrella group to which the certified organic producers above belong.

Umbria
Umbria has the reputation in some quarters for being a poor man's Tuscany. However although its choice of wines produced from organically grown grapes is small, Umbria's selection is notable for more reasonable pricing and often more pleasurable flavours.

Colle del Sole
06015 Colle di Pierantonio, Perugia
Tel:+39 075 939 156
Fax:+39 075 939 448
Accomodation: 15th-century farmhouse with swimming pool and tennis court, as well as seminar and conference rooms, and an Umbrian restaurant
Overall Price Rating: 🍷

This organic domaine is located in the Altotiberini hills, which cradle the Tiber as it flows south from the Tuscan border to Perugia. The owners, the Polidori family, produce dry whites from Trebbiano, Malvasia del Chianti, Verdicchio and Chardonnay, and reds from Sangiovese, Merlot and Barbera. Grappa and Grappa Riserva are also made.

Marella

Loc Ferretto, 06061 Castiglione del Lago
Tel:+39 075 954 139/+39 075 954 316
Overall Price Rating: 🍷

This domaine has been certified organic since 1988. It comprises 7.5 hectares of Sangiovese, Gamay, Canaiolo and Cileigiolo for reds, and Trebbiano Toscano, Verdello, Malvasia del Chianti and Grechetto for whites in the province of Perugia. The wines are tasty, balanced and show good body – not something Italian wines are renowned for. The trick here seems to be that the grapes are picked at maximum maturity, and so they give up all their flavour easily during fermentation.

- VdT Blanco: off-dry white blend of 90 per cent Grechetto (for body) and 10 per cent Trebbiano (for freshness); shows lovely honeyed fruit.
- VdT Rosso: dry red, ages four months in wood, has a long taste of cherries and plum.
- Bianco Colli del Trasimeno DOC: dry white, in 1997 made from Malvasia and Trebbiano; a clean, bodied example from the shores of Italy's largest lake, Trasimeno.
- Rosso Colli del Trasimeno DOC: dry red. In 1996 concentrated. In 1997 a blend of Sangiovese and Gamay, which spent 15 months in oak; shows sweet but ripe fruit, supple style, delicious.

Italo di Filippo

Voe Conversino, 160, Cannara 06033 (PG)
Tel:+39 074 272 310
Fax:+39 074 272 310
Email:difilippo@besnet.it
Stockist: Vintage Roots
Overall Price Rating: 🍷

This domaine converted to organic methods in 1996 and produces a very attractive range from 14 hectares of vineyards.

- IGT Umbria Bianco, Villa Conversino: dry white, creamy and fresh.
- IGT Umbria Rosso, Villa Conversino: dry red, made in 1998 from Montepulciano, Barbera, Merlot, Sangiovese and Canaiolo; bottled unfiltered, tastes of soft stone fruits; suitable for vegans, good value.
- IGT Grechetto, Pieve Santa Lucia: dry white made from a much underrated variety; shows good body for such vines planted only in the early 1990s.
- Colli Martani Bianco DOC, Terre di San Nicolo: dry white, made from older vine Grechetto; rich without being heavy, ripe without being too tropical, very good.
- Colli Martani Rosso DOC, Terre di San Nicolo: dry red made from Sangiovese, Merlot and Barbera, aged in barrel; mixes mint and berry fruit with velvet texture.
- Colli Martani Sangiovese DOC, Properzio: dry red made from Sangiovese with 15 per cent Merlot and Barbera, more tannic than the IGT Rosso above so well-suited to food.

Veneto

Veneto is the region which surrounds Venice and which runs north from the Adriatic to the Alps. The wines are characterized by moderate levels of alcohol and crunchy fruit. Veneto's best known wine is Valpolicella, which is sometimes so dilute from over-production so as to resemble pink rather than red wine. The dry white styles are led by Soave.

Bettili/Serenel
Tel: +44 118 976 1999
Fax: +44 118 976 1998
Stockist: Vintage Roots
Overall Price Rating: ◆

This organic brand produces a range of light, clean, refreshing wines for early drinking. They offer good value.

- VdT Verona Bianco, Serenel: dry white, a blend of Garganega and Trebbiano, shows light, green citrus and pear drop fruit.

- VdT Verona Rosso, Serenel: dry red, a blend of Corvina and Molinara grapes, shows light morello cherry fruit; suitable for vegans.
- VdT Verona Frizzante, Bettili: lightly sparkling white wine, perfect to drink while waiting for your pizza; suitable for vegans.
- Soave DOC, Serenel: dry white, similar to the VdT Verona Bianco, suitable for vegans.

Az. Ag. La Capuccina
Via S. Brizio 125, 37030 Costalunga
Tel:+39 456 175 036
Fax:+39 456 175 755
Stockist: Organic Wine Company

This organic domaine produces a single vineyard dry white Soave called La Capuccina with full body (🍾🍾🍾). A sweet Recioto di Soave called Arinzo is also made from Garganega grapes left to dry on racks after picking (50cl bottles, 🍾). A red wine is also made from Cabernet Sauvignon and Cabernet Franc, called Il Madego (🍾). The domaine belongs to brothers Pierantonio and Sisto di Tessari. Pierantonio has a degree in winemaking from Italy's leading wine school at Conegliano, while his brother is a qualified agronomist.

Gino Fasoli
Via Cesare Battisti 41, 37030 Colognola ai Colli
Tel:+39 457 650 741
Fax:+39 457 650 741
Stockists: Vintage Roots; Vinceremos

This Veneto domaine is run by brothers Amadio and Natalino Fasoli. It has been certified organic since 1987. The wines are made at the local cooperative (Cooperative Agricola Otto Marzo, see below).

- Soave Superiore DOC: bone dry white made predominantly from Garganega; light and crisp, shows almond and lemon flavours; good above average example, suitable for vegans (Vintage Roots, 🍾)

- VdT di Colognola ai Colli, Orgno: dry red, made from 100 per cent Merlot; ages in new oak which must account for the price, shows light and rather green fruit. 🍶🍶🍶

Fongaro
Via Motto Piane 10, 37030 Ronca (VR)
Tel:+39 457 460 240
Fax:+39 457 460 240
Stockist: Vintage Roots

This Veneto domaine belongs to Guerriono Fongaro and has been certified organic since 1980. There are seven hectares of white grapes (Chardonnay, Durella, Sauvignon Blanc and Garganega) and the wines are made at the local cooperative (Cooperative Agricola Otto Marzo, see below).

- Lessini Durello Spumante Classico: dry white sparkling wine, made from the native Durello grape and Garganega; frothy, suitable for vegans. 🍶🍶🍶
- Chardonnay del Veneto VdT: dry white, clean but neutral, some carbon dioxide present in the glass, suitable for vegans. 🍶
- Sauvignon Blanc del Veneto VdT: dry white, clean but neutral, some carbon dioxide present in the glass, suitable for vegans. 🍶

Massimo Mutta
Via S. Silvestro 21, 35030 Vo'Euganen
Tel:+39 499 940 867
Fax: +39 499 940 867
Overall Price Rating: 🍶🍶

This certified organic domaine produces a range of light, refreshing and mainly white wines. The lightest wine made here is the Moscato Colli Euganei DOC, which contains 7 per cent alcohol, grapey sweetness and a slight spritz on the palate. Fully sparkling wines are made from the Prosecco variety. The still dry white Pinot Bianco DOC is less bodied than its equivalent in Alsace, and accentuates the fruit rather than spice character this variety possesses.

Otto Marzo (Cooperative Agricola)

Località Ca'Verde, 37020 S. Ambrogio di Valpolicella
Tel:+39 457 730 760
Fax:+39 457 731 888
Stockists: Vintage Roots; Vinceremos

This cooperative is supplied with certified organic grapes by two of the growers cited above: Fasoli and Fongaro. Wines made here include:

- Bardolino Chiaretto DOC: dry pink from the south eastern shores of Lake Garda; cheesy, suitable for vegans. ♦♦
- Bardolino Classico DOC: dry red, ephemeral cherry; suitable for vegans. ♦♦
- Valpolicella Classico DOC: dry red, indistinguishable from the Bardolino above, suitable for vegans. ♦♦
- Amarone di Valpolicella Classico DOC: dry red, mossy, made from grapes aged on metal grills after picking to concentrate them, leaving a full-bodied, bitter cherry wine with 14.5 per cent alcohol; suitable for vegans (Vintage Roots, ♦♦♦)
- Recioto di Valpolicella Classico DOC: off-dry red, made as the Amarone above but from riper grapes. The fermentation sticks with a high (15 per cent) level of alcohol and some grape sugar left unfermented in the wine; tastes warmer and more knit than the Amarone due to the extra sweetness. The Veronese call this style and the Amarone *vini di meditazione* – meditation wines – for sipping at the end of a meal. ♦♦♦

Paladin & Paladin SRL (Bosco del Merlo)

Via Postumia 12, 30020 Annone Veneto, Venezi
Tel:+39 422 768 167
Fax:+39 422 768 590
Email: paladin@paladin.it
Internet: www.paladin.it
Accomodation: country house with guest quarters
Overall Price Rating: ♦♦♦

This certified organic domaine is owned by the Paladin family. A large range of wines is made under the Lison-Pramaggiore DOC, from Chardonnay, Pinot Grigio, Sauvignon Blanc and Tocai Friuliano (dry whites), and from Cabernets Franc and Sauvignon for reds. Seaweed and molasses (from beetroot) are applied to the vines as fertiliser. The wines are fermented in stainless steel tanks using cultured yeast and temperature control. Grappa and balsamic vinegar also made.

Sante Strumendo

Via Castellina 6, 30020 Pradipozzo
Tel:+39 421 704 757
Fax:+39 421 704 757

This organic domaine lies in the province of Venice and produces dry white wines from the Tocai Friuliano grape, and grassy reds from Merlot and Cabernet Franc. The wines are sold under the Lison-Pramaggiore DOC. No details available on certification.

Portugal

Vines account for 25 per cent of agricultural land in Portugal, but only two vineyards in the northern part of the country are currently certified as organic. They produce Port and a Vinho Verde white wine. There are a number of unofficial organic vineyards in Portugal, particularly in the south in the emerging Alentejo region, but the organic grapes end up mixed with non-organic ones in local wine cooperatives. Portugal's 'island wine' of Madeira has one shipper using sustainable methods to heat the stocks for the Madeira effect (called 'maderization').

The EU-approved national certification body for organic agriculture in Portugal is known as Agrobio, and can be contacted at the following address:

Agrobio – Associaçao de Agricultura Biológica
Calçada da Tapada 39 R/C Dto., 1300-545 Lisboa
Tel:+351 1 36 41 354/+351 1 36 23 585
Fax:+351 1 36 23 586

LAFOES (VINHO VERDE)

Lafoes is the finest of the sub-regions producing Vinho Verde, a crisp, bone dry and almost green tasting white wine.

Quinta da Comenda

3660 San Pedro do Sul
Tel:+351 1 96 13 943

Quinta da Comenda has been in existence for over 1,000 years and in 1985 became the first member of Agrobio. The vineyards face south on the slopes of a river valley where near sub-tropical conditions prove some of the most challenging for organic wine grape growing. The grapes are crushed in open stone troughs and then fermented. This traditional form of winemaking reflects the way the grapes are grown, based on a maximum of work by human hands and a minimum of mechanization. This keeps the vines strong enough to resist the constant threat from vine fungal disease.

- Quinta da Comenda, Lafoes VQPRD: white wine, bone dry, made from the Arinto (lemony), Sercial (see Madeira) and Dona Branca varieties (10.5 per cent alcohol); has a salty taste, like the foreheads of the women who work the vines when kissed in greeting. Any form of Vinho Verde style wine like this is ideally consumed in its northern Portuguese home with the local seafood. ᵚᵚ
- 'Ansemil' Beiras Blanco, Regional Wine: dry white wine, lean biting fruit, made from some of the dozens of strains of vine varieties which exist all over the Portuguese mainland, including a white grape identified as Esgana Cao ('the dog strangler') and one called Rabo de Ovelha (11 per cent alcohol). ᵚ
- 'Ansemil' Beiras Rosado, Regional Wine: dry pink, firm, dry taste of rhubarb (11 per cent alcohol). ᵚ

PORT

Production of organic Port totals just a few hundred cases out of over eight million produced and is sufficient to provide for only a token number of boxed sets of organic Port and English Stilton at Christmas. The irony is that this dearth reflects most badly on the English themselves, who still dominate the trade from their Port lodges. These are situated on the quayside of Oporto, the point at which the valley of the river Douro joins the Atlantic.

The Douro Valley

The best way to get to this part of the remote Port region is on the train running from Oporto to Pinhão. This small town takes its name from a key tributary of the Douro above which the vineyards of the following two producers are found.

Casal dos Jordoes

5085 Pinhao
Tel:+351 54 72 470
Stockist: Vintage Roots

The vineyards of Casal dos Jordoes occupy schistous, split terraces and are the only ones currently certified organic in the Port region. They belong to Arlindo da Costa Pinto e de Cruz. Olive trees mingle with the authorized Port grape varieties which are planted – Touriga Nacional (the best), Touriga Francesa (the last to ripen), Tinta Roriz (Rioja's Tempranillo) and Tinta Barroca (an all-rounder).

- Casal dos Jordoes Organic Vintage Character Port, Bottled 1998: fortified sweet red made from hand picked grapes; appetizingly evokes the dry heat of the Douro summer, and hides all trace of the neutral spirit used during its fortification; 20 per cent alcohol. ♦♦

Quinta do Infantado

Rua Pedro Escobar, 140A, 4150 Porto (mailing)
Email: qtainfantado@mail.telepac.pt
Stockists: Vintage Roots; Organic Wine Company; Vinceremos

Quinta do Infantado belonged to a Portuguese king before it was purchased by its current owners, the Roseira family. In 1990 they began an organic trial on a half-hectare plot called 'Barreira'. It contained Touriga Francesca (85 per cent), Tinta Roriz (10 per cent) and Tinta Barroca (5 per cent) grapes planted in 1985. The following year a plot of mainly Touriga Nacional vines covering 1.2 hectares called Serra also joined the trial. Since Portugal's accession to the European Union in 1992 these vines have not been certified organic. However the grapes they produced have been used in the following wine:

- Quinta do Infantado Organic Vintage Character Port, Bottled October 1994 without filtration: fortified sweet red made from hand picked grapes, which shows deep but bright crimson colour, a warm mouthful of sweet tannin, and a long, elegant aftertaste; 19.3 per cent alcohol; 350 cases made; suitable for vegans. ♦♦♦

A Note on Vintage Character Port

Vintage Character Port is fermented and fortified like any other one of the 20 or so Port styles available. This means the grapes are picked, crushed and the pulp and juice fermented together vigorously. After between two and three days the still fermenting, bright purple, still sugary wine is racked off the skins and fortified with clear, neutral grape spirit – in a ratio of four parts wine (6 per cent alcohol) to one part spirit (60 per cent alcohol). The mix is called Port. It gets its 'Vintage Character' by ageing in fat chestnut puncheons (*pipas*) and upright vats (*toneis*) for between 4–5 years. Ordinary Port is bottled once wines from several vineyard sites and more than one vintage are assembled, whereas Vintage Port is made of wine from a single year. The time spent ageing in cask allows a Vintage Character to soften and evolve quickly. The spirit added to the wine during fortification loses its alcoholic, medicinal kick. Thus Vintage Character Port is ready to drink once it is bottled, and so it is a style of little interest to wine speculators. The wine label should carry a bottling date and, ideally, it should be no more than five years old.

MADEIRA

Madeira is exposed to air and heat during its creation to create the 'maderization' effect to which Madeira gives its name. The combination of oxidation and heat causes Madeira to be one of the longest lived of all wines, and even partially full bottles can be left for months on end without spoiling. Carefully stored Madeira is so indestructible that bottles from the early 1800s are still traded as drinkable commodities at auction. These old vintage-dated Madeiras pre-date the era of chemical cultivation, however, some present-day Madeira vineyards are so humid and conducive to downy mildew and botrytis that they receive over 16 chemical treatments during a season – four times as many as a vineyard in Provence for example. As long as the cork has remained free of attack from the spirit in the wine, then the Madeira within has the potential to provide a wine of almost magnetic power.

The best examples show a burnished green colour, and combine the sweetness of stewed apples with the tang of the sea. The variety to look for is the dark Bastardo or 'the difficult one', because it yields so little and tastes so wild. Sercial produces the longest lived, driest wine. Malmsey produces the richest, with Bual and Verdelho somewhere in between. Prices for bottles of these time-lapse treasures remain low compared to prestige Champagne, Bordeaux and Vintage Port, wines which possess a fraction of Madeira's ageing potential.

Artur Barros e Sousa, Lda.

109 Rua dos Ferreiros,

9000 Funchal, Ilha da Madeira, Portugal

Tel:+351 912 0622

Overall Price Rating: ♙

Madeira requires heat to be 'maderized' and before the steam age this was achieved by having the wines moved back and forth across the Equator as ballast on ships. Nowadays heat is often provided at the expense of fossil fuel burning. This shipper is the only one on Madeira to mature the entirety of its production (albeit from non-organic grapes), according to the more environmentally friendly *canteiro* method. A *canteiro* is a rack of casks placed high in the eaves of cellar buildings where the heat of the sun beating on the cellar roof can be felt. The unfermented grape sugar remaining in the young wines after fortification is caramelized by the heat, but more gradually than with artificial heating, and as a result the effect is a greater level of intensity.

Spain

In Spain bureaucracy rather than the weather seems to be the only hindrance to converting vineyards to organic farming methods. The organic control system in Spain is owned by the central government but run by the local political regions rather than privately. The bureaucratic wheels can be painfully slow to turn in Spain, and impetus for change is often provided from abroad, e.g., from Germany. Pre-paid orders from bulk wine buyers in Germany are helping to finance conversion costs for some growers, particularly in the regions of Rioja and Navarra in the north. The boom area for general organic produce seems to be Andalucia in the south of the country, which includes Seville and Cordoba, as well as the Sherry region. A number of new vineyards there should finalize conversion to organic methods between 1999 and 2000. Prices and quality can compare very favourably to wines from the French Midi across the Pyrenees.

The producers below are certified organic by the Regulatory Council for Organic Agriculture (Consejo Regulador de la Agricultura Ecológica or CCPAE) according to EU norms on organic agriculture (normativa sobre agricultura ecológica). Certified wines carry the term 'Agricultura Ecológica' and bear the name of the local certification body.

SPAIN'S WINE REGIONS

Spain's wine regions are signified by the initials DO – meaning Denominacion de Origen (region of origin) – the equivalent of the French Apellation Contrôlé or 'AC' designation.

DO Ampurdan-Costa Brava

These vineyards lie in the soft, quiet hills above the crowded beaches of the Costa Brava.

Mas Estela Soda S.A.

CP 17489 Selva de Mar (Girona)

Tel:+34 972 126 176

Fax:+34 972 126 176

Email: soda@catalonia.net

Overall Price Rating: ▲

This family-owned estate has been certified organic since 1992. It comprises 10 hectares of Macabeu, Xarel-lo, Sauvignon Blanc, Grenache (Garnacha Negra), Tempranillo (Ull de Lebre — which means 'hare's eye' in Spanish), Carignan (Carinyena), Merlot and Syrah. The vines surround the winery on a single broad hill slope. Contact Madame Nuria Dalmau (who speaks English).

- Mas Estela Vinya Selva de Mar, Vino Tinto: dry red. The 1996 was made mainly from Grenache vines as the Syrah planted here in 1994 were too young. The wine sees some oak (large oak tuns rather than small oak barrels as Albet i Noya (*see page 273*) uses), is clean tasting, shows ripe red fruit and is for drinking within a couple of years. The 1997 vintage, which contained 80 per cent Grenache, 20 per cent Syrah, is similar. A full-bodied but not overpowering style of Spanish red which is worth finding.
- Mas Estela Vin Doux Naturel Garnacha: sweet fortified red wine made from Grenache, 15 per cent alcohol; light style, but elegant, aged in large tuns, best drunk from a small tumbler on a hot day when time is not of the essence.
- Mas Estela Vin Doux Naturel Moscatel: sweet fortified white wine made from Muscat de Frontignan, 15 per cent alcohol; appealing thick colour, straw flavour, lovely aftertaste of exotic raisins; more interesting than the Muscat de Rivesaltes made across the Pyrenees by Clos St Martin (*see page 130*).

Cellier Mas Fita

Rda Firal, 23. 8é A, 17600 Figueres (Girona)

Tel:+34 972 502 041

Fax:+34 972 502 041

Overall Price Rating: 🍶

This family-owned estate has been certified organic since 1992. It comprises 17.5 hectares and is planted with a similar range of grape varieties to Mas Soda Estela (above). Current owner, Albert Fita i Alegre, is the fourth generation of his family to manage here. Several labels are used including Torlit, Montepedró and Fita for a range of dry white, pink and red wines of slightly below average quality.

DO Bierzo

Bierzo lies in the province of Léon where coal and cattle rather than wine are the main activities. The region is protected from Atlantic influences by the Cantabrian mountains that extend along Spain's north western coastline.

Perez Carames S.A.

Pena Picon s/n 24500 Villafranca del Bierzo

Tel:+34 987 540 197

Fax:+34 987 540 314

Stockists: contact Organic Wine Company for details

Overall Price Rating: 🍶

This certified organic vineyard comprises 30 hectares in four separate but adjoining vineyards, which combine to make this the largest holding in El Bierzo. The domaine was founded in 1986, and boasts a spacious modern winery with stainless steel tanks, a pneumatic press and French oak casks. Six wines are made from both local grapes with noble varieties. Note that non-organic wine are also produced here. The pick of the organic wines are the dry red Casar de Santa Ines Cabernet Sauvignon and the dry red Consules de Roma Bierzo DO Mencia. This is made like Beaujolais from a whole berry fermentation and shows attractive bubblegum-like fruit (the wine gets its name from the Roman seventh legion of 'leon' stationed in the region during antiquity). The dry white Casar de Santa Ines Chardonnay is a take or leave example of this grape, but the dry pink Casar de Santa Ines Cabernet Sauvignon may be worth investigating.

DO Carinena

There is one producer of note in the emerging sub-region of Carinena. This lies between the Pyrenees and Madrid in the basin of the river Ebro.

Bodegas Tosos Ecologica S.A.

T.9645 Calle Cuevas 2, 50154 Tosos (Zaragoza)
Tel:+34 9 976 147 040
Fax:+34 9 976 147 040
Stockist: Organic Wine Company
Overall Price Rating: ⚱

This certified organic vineyard is located in Tosos, a few kilometers away from where the great painter Francisco de Goya grew up, and where the house in which he was born is still preserved.

- Carinena Blanco DO, Lagrima Virgen: dry white made from Macabeo; shows coppery yellow colour and clean, balanced fresh fruit – words alien to Spanish white wine only a few years ago – and more concentration than the white wines of La Mancha.
- Carinena Rosado DO, Lagrima Virgen: dry pink, generous style, drink in the first summer after the vintage to catch the fruit.
- Carinena Tinto DO, Lagrima Virgen: dry red made from Grenache (Garnacha), Tempranillo and Mazuelo; rich ruby colour, full fruit taste, attractive, positive style of Spanish red, organic or otherwise (don't be deceived by the old hat wine bottle label).

DO Canarias (Canary Islands)

The one certified organic domaine on the Canaries, Vina Peraza (⚱), produces very nondescript wines.

DO La Mancha

La Mancha is Don Quixote country and covers central Spain.

Bodegas Parra Jimenez

c/ Gloieta no.4, 16650 Las Mesas (Cuenca)
Tel:+34 967 155 243
Fax:+34 967 155 243
Stockists: Organic Wine Company; Vintage Roots
Overall Price Rating: ♟

This domaine began a successful conversion to certified organic methods
for its own vines in 1993. In addition certified organic Airén is bought in
from the Cooperative Jesus de Perdon (see below). This is bottled under
the Bodegas Parra Jimenez label. The domaine's own vines produce:

- La Mancha DO, Caballero de Mesasrubias Tinto: dry red, 100 per cent
  Tempranillo (Cencibel), partly oak aged for a few months; vibrant fruit
  on the palate, could take chilling in the summer months; good
  value; suitable for vegans.
- La Mancha DO, Parra Jimenez Tinto Barrica: dry red, 100 per cent
  Tempranillo (Cencibel), oak aged for six months; deeper plum fruit to
  match the oak, satisfying and stylish.

Jesus del Perdon (Cooperative)

Poligono Industrial Ctra. de Alcazat S/N, 13200 Manzanares (Ciudad Real)
Tel:+34 926 610 309
Fax:+34 926 610 516
Stockists: Vinceremos; Vintage Roots; Organic Wine Company
Overall Price Rating: ♟

This cooperative was founded in 1954 by a group of local winegrowers
whose vineyards extend across what was once the bed of the Guadiana river.
The soils are relatively fertile and help to produce wines that need drinking
young. In recent years, a few of the producers have converted to organic
methods, and combine to produce two wines under the Mundo de Yuntero
label.

- DO La Mancha Blanco, Mundo de Yuntero: dry white made from Airén
  which rivals an obscure Russian grape called Rkatsiteli as the most

widely planted variety on the planet. Here it produces a vaguely floral wine for immediate drinking.

- DO La Mancha Tinto, Mundo de Yuntero: dry red made from Tempranillo (Cencibel); shows a warm, inviting style of creamy red fruit.

DO Penedes

Penedes encompasses the area of Northern Spain around Barcelona and has been the scene of much recent vineyard experimentation, with grape varieties imported from Bordeaux (Merlot) and Burgundy (Chardonnay).

Albet i Noya SAT

Can Vendrell de la Codina s/u, 08739 St Paul d'Ordal, Barcelona
Tel:+34 938 994 056
Fax:+34 938 994 056
Email: albetnoya@troc.es
Stockists: Vinceremos; Vintage Roots

This family-owned business claims to be the most senior organic wine producer in Spain, with organic practices dating back to 1980. Now managed by Josep Maria Albet i Noya (merchant), the Albet i Noya vineyard amounts to 26 hectares. In addition to grapes from its own vineyards Albet i Noya buys in from growers farming over a hundred hectares of certified organic vineyards. Some of these vineyards are still in conversion, while other suppliers like Mas Soda Estela (above) have full certification. The winemaking is sharp, and succeeds in providing a clean and consistent product using modern methods – temperature control, French and Spanish yeasts, French and American oak barrels, and so on. This is one of the new wave Spanish producers, much respected by its peers in Spain.

- DO Cava, Can Vendrell NV: dry white, non-vintage sparkling wine made by the traditional method, and blended from three white grapes: Xarel-lo, Parellada and Macabeu. Clean, appealing modern fizz which is both cheaper and more flavoured than the well-known brands of non-organic Cava such as Freixenet Cordon Negro (Vintage Roots, ♨).

- DO Cava, Brut Reserva: same style as above but with a vintage designation. The 1995 vintage shows soft yeasty character; ready to drink now but will age to its tenth birthday if stored cool. Again a very fairly priced sparkler (Vintage Roots, ⚑).

- DO Penedes Rosado, Pinot Noir/Merlot d'Anyada: dry pink with an orange tinge which indicates a warm climate; suitable for vegetarians although an excellent match for Spanish salchichon (salami) (Vintage Roots, ⚑).

- DO Penedes Blanco, Can Vendrell: dry white blend of Xarel-lo and Chardonnay, shows gentle tropical fruit; suitable for vegans (Vintage Roots, ⚑).

- DO Penedes Tinto, Can Vendrell: dry red, made from the early ripening Tempranillo; here fermented initially as whole (i.e., uncrushed) bunches to obtain colour and flavour rather than tannin. The same method is used with the Gamay grape in Beaujolais (in France). This wine is suitable for vegans (Vintage Roots, ⚑).

- Can Vendrell Red Unwooded: dry red, a soft light medium-bodied example of the otherwise tannic Cabernet Sauvignon, Carignan and Grenache from which it is made. ⚑

- DO Penedes, Cabernet Sauvignon, Col.lecció, Albet i Noya: dry red, aged in new oak; for fans of Cabernet and oak because it tastes of blackberry and vanilla; suitable for vegetarians (Vintage Roots, ⚑⚑).

- DO Penedes, Chardonnay, Col.lecció: dry white, partially fermented in new oak, shows ripe fat fruit and a buttery texture; suitable for vegans (Vintage Roots, ⚑⚑).

- DO Penedes, Macabeu, Col.lecció: dry white made with juice from the first pressing only, fermented in barrel, aged on the fine fermentation lees; shows intriguing bitter pineapple; suitable for vegans (Vintage Roots, ⚑⚑⚑).

- DO Penedes, Xarel-lo, d'Anyada: dry white, made from Xarel-lo juice which is allowed to soak on the skins to draw out Xarel-lo's primrose freshness (Vintage Roots, ⚑).

- DO Penedes, Xarel-lo, Col.lecció: oak fermented version of the above wine in which the oak tends to obscure the floral notes of the Xarel-lo (Vintage Roots, ⚑⚑⚑).

- DO Penedes, Tempranillo, d'Anyada: dry red, made from Tempranillo which shows very much like another early ripening variety – Merlot. In other words a wine with generous purple colour, soft red fruit flavours and attractive medium body; suitable for vegetarians (Vintage Roots, 🍾).
- DO Penedes, Tempranillo, Col.lecció: dry red, same as above, aged in oak, only worth the premium if you like vanilla with your red fruits; suitable for vegetarians (Vintage Roots, 🍾🍾🍾).
- DO Penedes, Marti: dry red, a blend in 1995 of Tempranillo, Cabernet Sauvignon, Merlot, Syrah and Petite Syrah; produces a chunky red in a clean, fat, modern style. 🍾🍾🍾
- DO Priorato, Mas Igneus FA-206: dry red, in 1996 and 1997 made from Garnacha, Carignan and Cabernet Sauvignon vines in reconversion. The term 'FA-206' stands for French oak (F), Allier (A – the forest of the wood's origin), 2 for two years, and 6 for six months, or the time this wine spent in oak. This sort of labelling takes some getting used to, but is very useful for consumers who can work out what level of oaking they like in a wine. This one shows thick ruby colour, rich fruit, good use of oak integrated with the fruit, and is suitable for vegans (Vintage Roots, 🍾🍾🍾).

  Priorato produces some of the most alcoholic red wines in Europe (the dry, flaky soils heat up very quickly in the sun and almost end up baking the grapes hanging just above).
- Priorato, White Grenache: dry white made from white Grenache grown in the Priorato region which is thick, heavy, and strong enough to cope with the oak flavours picked up in barrel. The 1995 vintage was labelled 'FA 104' or 'aged in French Allier oak for 1 year and 4 months'. 🍾🍾🍾
- DO Rioja, Urubi: dry red, made from purchased grapes from a single vineyard in the Rioja region. The 1996 was marked as made from vines in reconversion, and shows thick fruit overlaid with charred vanilla from time spent ageing in new American oak casks. Suitable for vegans. This is a red Rioja that won't give you or your wallet a headache (Vintage Roots, 🍾🍾).

DO Rioja/Navarra

Rioja and the adjoining region of Navarra in north central Spain produce red, white and pink wines. The majority of the producers here are in the process of conversion to certified organic methods.

Bodega Biurko Gorri S.A.L.
C/ Las Cruces s/n, Bargota
Tel:+34 948 648 370
Fax:+34 948 648 370
Overall Price Rating: 🍾🍾

This Basque producer releases a red Rioja.

Bodegas Aristu
Vta. de Judas s/n, 31440 Lumbier
Tel:+34 948 398 098
Stockists: contact Organic Wine Company for details.
Overall Price Rating: 🍾🍾🍾

Produces a varietal (100 per cent) oak-aged Grenache (Garnacha).

Vina Ijalba SA
26006 Logrono
Stockists: contact Vintage Roots for details

The 1998 vintage will be produced from certified organic grapes. Wines include: Blanco Seco (a dry white, 100 per cent Viura, 🍾); Rosado (dry pink, 🍾); Tinto (dry red made from Tempranillo in a Beaujolais style, 🍾🍾); Tinto (dry red made from Tempranillo and some Graciano, 🍾🍾); Tinto (dry red made from 100 per cent Graciano, which can produce more structured wines than Tempranillo – this one spends six months in oak, 🍾🍾🍾).

Navarrsotilo

Santa Cruz s/n, 31261 Andosilla
Tel:+34 948 690 523
Fax:+34 948 690 523
Email: nsotillo@arrakis.es
Stockist: Vinceremos

Red Rioja DOC called 'Noemus', made from Tempranillo, Mazuelo and
Garnacha, matured in French oak barrels (👪).

Bodegas Parraldea

31152 Muruzabal
Tel:+34 948 344 146
Overall Price Rating: 👪

Producer with a name similar to one of the white grape varieties used in
sparkling Cava.

DO Utiel Requena

DO Utiel Requena is located in the western hills of the province of
Valencia, some way inland from the Mediterranean coast, on plateaux
made of hot, red sand.

Bodegas Iranzo

Ctra Madrid 24, 46315 Caudette de las Fuentas (Valencia)
Tel:+34 962 319 882
Email: boiranzo@tdv.net
Overall Price Rating: 👪

This domaine is run by the Iranzo Perez-Duque family and covers
43 hectares. So far great emphasis seems to have been placed on the
packaging. Unbleached natural corks are used at bottling, the capsules
are free of base metals, the labels, the cardboard for the boxes and the
glass for the bottles all come from recycled sources. Only red wines are
made, sold under the Iranzo, Perez-Duque and Cañada Honda designations.

- DO Utiel Requena, Tinto, Cañada Honda: dry red, made in 1997 from Cabernet Sauvignon and Tempranillo. Shows over-ripe berry fruit, so appealing if a little out of balance (too much alcohol in the aftertaste which burns the lips when you blow outwards after swallowing the wine); suitable for vegans.

DO Valdepeñas

Valdepeñas lies in the southern part of La Mancha, midway between Madrid and the Mediterranean. It is known for soft, light reds.

Dioisio de Nova Garci

C/Union 82, 13300 Valdepeñas (Ciudad Real)
Tel:+34 926 313 248
Fax:+44 926 322 813

This family producer has been established for 50 years and is located just outside Valdepeñas on the slopes of Sierra de Peral and Sierra del Cristo. Grapes grown include Airén for whites and Tempranillo for red. The vines have been certified organic since 1997. The winemaking mixes traditional earthenware jars (*tinajas*) with temperature controlled stainless steel. The wines age in oak casks, some of which are French.

- White Dionisos: dry white made from Airén, soft and pale with moderate alcohol. 🍾
- Red Dionisos: dry red made from Tempranillo (Cencibel), shows attractive ripe fruit, light toastiness, hint of spice on the nose and a slightly bitter finish. 🍾
- Citeron Rosé: dry pink made from Tempranillo in a fresh cherry style with some oak; named after Citeron, the mountain where Dionysos met the bacchantes. 🍾
- Citeron Tinto: dry red, a step up from the Red Dionisos in terms of colour, fruit and harmony but still fresh so ideal for richer foods. 🍾

Also made is Crianza (oak aged) vinegar – expensive but refined (🍾).

DO Valencia

The producer below is located in the southern part of the province of Valencia. It lies in a valley named corn chamber (Los Alhorines) by the Arabs who occupied much of southern Spain until 1492. Now French grape varieties like Merlot and Cabernet Sauvignon are the staples.

Dominio los Pinos

E 46635 Fontanares-Valencia
Tel:+34 962 222 090
Fax:+34 962 222 086
Email: pinos@jet.es
Stockists: Vinceremos; Vintage Roots
Overall Price Rating: 🍷

This family domaine covers 50 hectares on a chalky clay soil. This needs to be sticky enough to make the most of just 450mm rainfall a year (500 mm is considered the minimum for a vine to grow successfully), and robust enough in winter to protect the vine's shallow roots when temperatures drop to well below freezing. The owners here, the Oleacha family, make a range of solid, unspectacular wines.

- DO Valencia Blanco, Dominio los Pinos: dry white, made from Macabeu and Malvasia which, in 1998, show full bodied, cidery flavours indicating the presence of dried, over-ripe grapes.
- DO Valencia Tinto, Dominio los Pinos: dry red which in 1998 was blended from Cabernet Sauvignon, Cabernet Franc and Merlot. Shows good deep aroma, soft, like a Bordeaux Supérieur AC from southern Entre Deux Mers but without the aggressive tannin in the background; drink this as soon as you buy it; suitable for vegetarians.
- DO Valencia Tinto Crianza, Dominio los Pinos: dry red, in 1996 an oak aged blend of Cabernet Sauvignon and Monastrell, simple but effective combination of vanilla (oak barrels) and cedar (wine breathing in the wood and developing); suitable for vegans and ideal for cold cuts.

ANDALUCIA – SHERRY AND SHERRY STYLE

The south western corner of Spain occupies bright white soil and is called Andalucia ('land of light'). It is home to one organic producer making wines similar to sherry, and to the Sherry region itself. The Arabs brought the secrets of distillation to Andalucia when the region was under Moorish settlement. Distillation of the grape produces the spirit which fortified wines (such as Sherry) contain.

Bodegas Gabriel Gómez
Villaviciosa de Cordoba
Tel:+34 957 478 313
Fax:+34 957 486 449
Stockist: Vinceremos
Overall Price Rating: 🍷

Bodegas Gabriel Gómez was founded in 1870 and for a hundred years sold its grapes and wines to the Sherry houses. Then sherry sales dropped off, the Sherry region shrank, and Bodegas Gabriel Gómez found itself left on the outside. Its location at Villaviciosa in the Cordoba mountain range is much hotter than on the Atlantic coast where sherry comes from. The main grape in both regions is the Palomino Fino but only here does it ripen to a high enough degree (15 per cent alcohol) to require no fortification. (Wine merchants often seem to sneak Bodegas Gabriel Gómez into sections on their lists marked 'sherry' but remember, Sherry is fortified, the two wines made here are not.) The grapes are picked by hand. They are pressed, and the juice fermented like a normal white wine. After fermentation the wines are aged for a year in stone vats (*tinajas*). Then they are racked into casks or butts made of American oak, some of which are older than the cellar workers. The butts are only partially filled, to allow a film of yeast called 'flor' to form on the surface of the wine.

The same thing occurs in Sherry, and also in the Jura in Eastern France for 'vin jaune' (see Jura, *page 87*). In Sherry the oak butts the wines mature in have to be stood on cement rather than wooden racks, otherwise the sea air would rot them. The warehouses of Bodegas Gabriel Gómez are much drier than the ones in Sherry, being further from the Atlantic Ocean, and the butts can be stacked on wooden supports. However the lack of moisture does mean that the flor which forms on the surface of the wine to give it its character is less pronounced in Villaviciosa than it is in Sherry. This is why the wines of Bodegas Gabriel Gómez show the intense crab-apple pungency of Sherry in a minor key. The two wines made by Bodegas Gabriel Gómez are almond in colour, and are bone dry and smell of burnt almonds.

- Sierra Morena, Seco, Vino Pálido.
- Sierra Morena, Seco, Vino Dorado.

Both are suitable for vegans. They are unfiltered and as a result may throw a deposit. They should be stored upright. Serve chilled or at room temperature, refrigerate after opening and consume within 1–7 days for the pálido and up to 14 days for the richer dorado. The pálido is the lighter, and equates to a 'fino'-style sherry. The dorado has rougher edges, but these do add to the depth of texture in the wine, necessary for the fruit to survive the high level of alcohol.

Sherry

Real sherry comes only from Spain, but unfortunately no Spanish sherry is as yet certified organic. This may change if the region's biggest producer looks set to link up with the region's most go-ahead. The big house is located in the main sherry town of Jerez de la Frontera. Its vineyards are extensive and mainly lie between Jerez and the coast marked by the town of Sanlucar de Barrameda, where the region's most go-ahead producer is located. Their vineyards lie next to each other and the two have agreed to 'integrated pest management' systems to reduce their pesticide treatments.

The main problem a potential organic sherry vineyard has to overcome is the tiny red spider mite. This bores into the trunk of the most widely planted sherry vine, the Palomino Fino, and saps it of its energy. Instead of anti-spider pesticides the two sherry growers have begun using sexually confusing pheromone traps left strategically in the vineyard to disrupt the spider's mating cycle. The more go-ahead sherry house would have begun an organic trial on its vines but, because it lies downwind of the big sherry house, the threat of spray drift acted as a disincentive. Although there are no organic sherries the region does have a link with what claims to be the world's first organic malt whisky, Dà Mhìle Millennium Malt.

Dà Mhìle Millennium Malt – Sherry Aged

Dà Mhìle Millennium Malt is a one-off whisky bottling which was distilled by the Springbank Distillery, Campbeltown, Argyllshire, Scotland in 1992 from 10 tons of organic Welsh barley. The stills had to be cleaned of traces of previous distillations from non-organic barley for the UK's organic certification body, the Soil Association, to be satisfied there was no cross-contamination. This avoidance of cross-contamination concerns only the transformation part of the whisky production, namely the distillation. Once made the whisky was matured in Sherry casks to acquire a sherry flavour. These casks, 15 in all, have never contained organic sherry (because none exists). The flavour these casks impart to the whisky is one of the major selling points for this spirit, but this flavouring is non-organic. Thus the old adage about keeping grain and grape apart might have some truth after all (Vinceremos, Vintage Roots, 🍾🍾🍾).

Switzerland

Switzerland has a wealth of organic growers, but little of the wine they produce is exported because, as the sixth largest consumers in the world, the Swiss are primarily importers. What organic Swiss wine does leave the country is invariably bound for Germany. (Either that or it is being served on Swiss Air, the first airline to offer organic in-flight meals.) Prices for Swiss wine are high due to the hilly terrain, the high cost of land and the fact that the vineyards are so small in average size — just 167 hectares between 87 certified organic growers (out of a national total of 15,000 hectares). Most growers belong to BioVin, the main Swiss umbrella organic accreditation body, certified by BioInspecta. Bear in mind that organic growers in Switzerland do not operate according to the EU organic standard established in 1992, but according to their own, stricter codes.

Switzerland's growers have a wealth of local varieties which are found nowhere else in Europe, although at the domaine highlighted below, international grape varieties dominate.

Domaine des Balisiers

12, route de Peney-Dessus, 1242 Peney
Tel:+ 22 753 1958
Fax:+ 22 794 1507
Overall Price Rating: 🍶🍶

This domaine is located in the south-west of the country, in the intensely rural area around the Swiss capital Geneva. It has been BioInspecta-certified organic since 1984, and is run by Gerard Pillon and Jean-Daniel Schlaepfer, who studied winemaking in Bordeaux and at Davis University in California. To counter the cool Swiss climate, and to maximize sun, the lyre system of training the vines is used. This was perfected in Bordeaux and doubles the amount of leaves in the vineyard to increase the health and flavour of the crop without changing the yield.

The lyre system works by dividing the vine's annual upward growth of shoots and leaves into two vertical canopies as opposed to just one. The effect is to create a cup of leaves to the sun, to catch all of its energy. This enables the leaves to dry quicker after rain, minimizing the risk of rot. At ground level, standing at one end of a vine row with one's nose to the first post, the vines exhibit a 'Y' shape like an pitchfork stood on its handle, the two (split) vine leaf canopies representing the forks while the vine trunks represent the handle.

Domaine des Balisiers is one of the largest Swiss organic domaines, with 17.5 hectares of Aligoté, Chardonnay, Chasselas, Pinot Blanc, Pinot Gris, Cabernet Franc, Cabernet Sauvignon, Gamay Noir à Jus Blancs and Pinot Noir.

Tunisia

Tunisia has one wine producer with organic status.

Almory
Route Henna, BP 57, 1124 Jdeida, Tunisia
Tel:+216 290 0105
Fax:+216 290 0105
Overall Price Rating: ▥

The mainly red wines are priced ambitiously for what is moderate quality and concentration of flavour. Olive oil and vegetables are also produced here.

Eastern Europe: Bulgaria

Bulgaria is a reliable source of cheap, cheerful and mainly red wine but up until now little of it has been classified as organic. This situation should change, because Bulgaria's National Wine Institute is drawing up an organic certification programme for vineyards. There are two ways in which this programme can be formulated. The larger, privately owned wineries (like Haskovo, below) seem to want a certification programme mirroring the rules at EU level, which are concerned mainly with what goes on in the vineyard. Smaller individual Bulgarian wine producers (like Bozoukov, below) favour the more flexible, Californian approach, which stipulates as great an emphasis on winemaking standards such as levels of sulphur dioxide preservative ('sulphites').

The two producers below use organic practices but have yet to be certified by an EU inspection body. Both claim to farm only a portion of vineyards managed or owned by them organically and current EU law prescribes an all or nothing approach to the organic certification of vineyards.

One of the legacies of the Communist system in Eastern Europe is that significant areas of the vineyard there could be considered as unofficially organic. This is because often those individual growers who manage the vineyards still lack the funds to purchase synthetic chemical sprays. Cash-rich Western investors and some clever Bulgarians are snapping up both planted vineyards and virgin land and some of these vineyard projects will be organically maintained from day one. One of the new wineries being constructed to handle some of this organic fruit is a US$20 million project that includes a water recycling system to minimize the impact on the local town. However the construction of this new winery at Sliven (partly funded by the EU) in the south of the country might itself be considered an ambiguous advert for recycling. Sliven already has a winery working at less than 20 per cent of capacity. It was constructed during the Communist era but will be mothballed once the new one comes on stream.

Bozoukov

Distributor in the UK: Bozoukov, c/o Balkan Business Ltd, Wolsey Hall, 66 Banbury Road, Oxford OX2 6PR
Tel:+44 186 531 1883
Fax:+44 186 531 0407
Email: bozoukov@ocx.com
Overall Price Rating: ᴝ

This family domaine was nationalized during the Communist take over when Bulgaria became designated 'most favoured wine producer' in the Eastern Bloc. The vines were returned to the Bozoukov family under the acts of restitution passed by the new democratic government since 1990. This well-intentioned process has been a bureaucratic quagmire, and has left one-quarter of the Bulgarian vineyards abandoned and, apparently, un-owned (Communist record keeping as to who owned what is being blamed). The wines produced by Bozoukov come from Iambol and Plovdiv in southern Bulgaria (Thrace). The vineyards for the following wine are described as organically farmed by the producers. Wines for which no organic claim is made originate from the same cellars.

● Cabernet Sauvignon, Karlovo: dry red, shows incredibly pure, blackcurrant fruit and natural texture with ripe tannins and a long complex taste of healthy grapes and a natural fermentation. This wine attracted the attentions of the Bulgarian World Cup football squad for it bought the entire batch of the 1996 vintage before leaving for what became a rather ignominious campaign at the finals of France 98. The footballers bought the entire stock of the follow-on 1997 vintage Cabernet Sauvignon, Karlovo, too!

Haskovo

Tel:+44 171 278 8047
Fax:+44 171 833 3127
Stockists: contact Bulgarian Vintners Company, London
Overall Price Rating: ᴝ

This former cooperative winery takes its name from a sub-region of Southern Bulgaria and is now privately owned. It was founded in 1947 as a direct result of the Communist accession to power, but became one of a group of Bulgarian wineries to develop strong links with the West even before 1980s glasnost. These links involved making internationally acceptable styles of wine for western buyers (supermarkets and wine shop chains) and sometimes contracting 'flying winemakers' from Australia and New Zealand. They arrive each year in time to make sure the grape varieties get picked in the right order and that they are pressed and crushed as hygienically as possible. They return to the Haskovo winery complex a few months after fermentation has finished to supervise bottling (having kept in contact with what's going on in the tanks by fax). Amongst 11 million bottles of wine produced each year at Haskovo, 25,000 bottles are from organically grown but uncertified grapes. The vines – all Merlot – grow in a single plot amongst non-vine crops on a hilly site close to Bulgaria's southern borders with Turkey and Greece.

- Merlot Eco: dry red wine, single varietal (100 per cent Merlot), displays a rich plum colour but tastes somewhat flat due to the extractive style of winemaking favoured here. The winemaking here was more successful in 1996 than 1997. The 1998 vintage was on the light side.

Hungary

In Hungary the certified organic community spans both ends of the production scale. As in Bulgaria, it involves small private wine producers at one end and larger cooperative-style public companies at the other. The difference between the two is that whereas in Bulgaria the best wines tend to be red, in Hungary it is white wines that catch the eye. Some of the purest and most powerful sweet white wines in the world originate from the cellars of an organic, but uncertified, producer making Hungarian Tokay near the country's Ukranian border (Istvan Szepsy, town of Mád). Incredible sweet white wines such as this can usually be produced only in tiny quantities (literally buckets at a time, or *putts*), perhaps one reason why they are suited to organic production.

Bigger volumes of white wine made in a medium sweet, fruity style are becoming easier to produce with the arrival of grape varieties like Bianca. It is disease resistant (no anti-fungal disease sprays needed), early ripening (no-anti-rot sprays needed) and hardy (it survives the central European winter). Bianca has these attributes, and high yields too, because it is a hybrid — as its rather ersatz name suggests. One of the biggest organic projects in Hungary involves a Bianca vineyard in the Markaz region, north of Budapest. The first vintage from certified organic grapes for the UK market is 1999, stocked by Tesco and Safeway under the Hilltop Cellars label ( ). The wine is dry but not bone dry, and slightly aromatic, like Gewurztraminer from Alsace in France, but slightly lighter in body. Certification is by the Italian Biocultura organization. Contact Vinceremos in the UK for further details.

Laszlo Toth

Torokbalint utca 24, 8630 Balatonboglar

Tel: +36 85 35 07 55

Contact: Budapest Wine Society (Bortársaság), 1015 Budapest, Batthyány utca. 59

Tel:+36 12 12 25 69/+36 12 12 02 62

Fax:+36 12 12 25 69

Email: BudapestWineSociety@mail.datanet.hu

Overall Price Rating: ▮

This private grower/winemaker in the emerging wine region of Lake Balaton claims organic status (no details of certification available). A greater number of vineyards managed to remain in private ownership in Hungary than in Bulgaria under the Communists, and this estate is an example.

Szekszárdi Mezogazdasági Kombinát/Liszt Cellars

Rákóczi utca 32, 7100 Szekszárd

Tel/Fax: +36 74 41 01 19

Stockist: Vinceremos

Overall Price Rating: ▮

This cooperative (*kombinát*) producer is located in the town of Szekszárd, after which one of Hungary's wine sub-regions is named. The vines have been certified organic by the Dutch-based Skal, since 1988. The major varieties planted are workhorse grapes like Léankya and Welschriesling (Olasz Riesling) for white wines, and Bibor-Kadarka, Zweigelt and Kekfrankos for reds. Workhorse grapes like these are not helped by erratic winemaking, which inevitably resulted in the early 1990s due to the uncertainty caused by the fall of the Iron Curtain (the workers had a habit of helping themselves to the stocks if they thought they were unlikely to get paid). Everything now seems to be back on track. There are three varieties to note, all producing table wines:

● Léankya: white east central European grape providing attractive, daffodil-scented white wines for early drinking.

- Zweigelt: red variety yielding huge quantities of cherry and chocolate-coloured grapes to produce crisp, medium bodied red wines with a slight aroma of icing sugar. Grown in Austria too (see Donauland, page 182, for example).
- Kekfrankos: red variety which produces wine with dark colour, discernible tannin, rich cranberry/raspberry fruit, like Merlot. Known as Blaufrankisch in Germany, and Lemburger in Austria.

The New World: USA

Rules governing organic production in the United States are set by the National Organic Standards Board (NOSB). In 1998 the NOSB opposed the US Department of Agriculture's attempt to downgrade the standards for organic farming and food processing. The Federal Government had wanted to downgrade the rules to make it easier for big business to enter organics, and involved the acceptance of:

● irradiation
● biotechnology (genetically modified organisms)
● sewage sludge as fertiliser (i.e., human waste as well as animal sources).

The NOSB's arguments against these proposals won the day, with huge backing from the American public. The acceptance of biotechnology would affect vineyards if genetically modified rootstocks, which have already been developed (notably by Champagne house Moet et Chandon), become more widely available. The use of sewage sludge for fertiliser brings with it the risk of contamination from heavy metals contained in human faeces, which is why organic vineyards use fertiliser from animal sources.

Irradiation is not a technique relevant to wine once in the bottle (it is used to prevent food from spoiling). However irradiation technology may play a part in the selection of vine cuttings for replanting to render them virus-free (the organic, 'lo-tech' way of rendering plant material virus-free is by using hot water).

The proposed changes to the existing standard were dropped after public hostility (only the proposed new rules for tobacco regulation in the US in 1995–96 drew more letters of outrage from the public). Had the new standard been adopted American 'organic' produce would have fallen below the standards required for sale in Europe under the

European Union's directive on organics. Wine merchants in the UK were prepared to launch legal suits against US wines claiming organic status under trades descriptions laws. The result of all this is that the organic community in the US is asking itself whether it should develop its own standards (accreditation) and policing (certification) independent of the Federal Government in its guise of the US Department of Agriculture. (If anyone wishes to follow the Federal Government's work on the rules for a national standard for certified organic produce, the National Campaign for Sustainable Agriculture has a useful website, at: www.sustainableagriculture.net.)

Organic wine grapes are California's biggest and fastest growing organic crop. In 1998 they amounted to around 4 per cent of California's total crop of about 135,600 hectares (author's estimate). Organic growers are helped by the fact that all the main threats in the vineyard are controllable with natural methods (e.g., botrytis bunch rot by canopy management and powdery mildew with sulphur). Reliance on copper to treat downy mildew is minimal here thanks to low levels of humidity, in contrast to New Zealand, Oregon, New York State and parts of Australia (Tasmania and Langhorne Creek). Californian winegrowers are also the only ones in the world required to make public at county level which pesticides they use, and pesticide use is diminishing through fears of writs from the vineyard workers who apply them, from neighbouring farms affected by spray drift and from environmental lobbyists. These fears may be why the totals of certified vineyards rose from 81 hectares in 1989 to nearly 2,500 hectares in 1992.

Only one of the big wineries that got into organics then has stayed the course — Fetzer Vineyards-Brown Forman Corporation. Others like Sutter Home and Gallo — which along with Fetzer are among the four biggest wineries in America — jumped out of organics as quickly as they jumped in. In Gallo's case the company jumped out not long after it had become the largest owner of third-party certified organic vineyard in the world when it converted its 1,105 hectare Ripperdam Ranch. The vineyard was fallow but before it was replanted it was fumigated with methyl bromide to disinfect the soil. This made the subsequent conversion to organic methods easier as vines in infested soils are less likely to resist disease and thus survive the three year transition to full organic status. Gallo was perfectly entitled to keep its options open but the fumigation technique does have an environmental cost. Sutter Home's organic status lapsed after they used what they called 'soft' (but unnamed) chemicals.

ORGANIC CERTIFICATION BODIES

The California Certified Organic Farmers (CCOF) organization is a certification body with IFOAM accreditation, the leading organic certification agency in California and the largest state-wide, non-profit making organization of organic growers, processors and handlers in the US.

The CCOF Standards cover 120 pages and mirror those of the National Organic Standards Board. The land must be farmed for three years without the use of synthetic chemicals such as pesticides, fungicides, herbicides, soil fumigants, growth regulators or hormones. There are two inspections prior to certification with annual ones after it. Growers must file an annual plan with the CCOF office in Santa Cruz and maintain detailed records of their activity in the field. A fee must be paid per acre, and the money raised is used for policing the standards.

Fertilisation and pest management agents must originate from 100 per cent naturally occurring substances which break down organically in the vineyard (this does mean bonemeal is allowed). Hence sulphur for powdery mildew must be mined and not chemically produced (as an industrial by-product for example). Pyrethrins may be removed from the list as they are toxic and remain in the soil. In the winery hot water or steam rather than cleaning fluids must be used to sterilise and clean equipment (this is similar to the rule laid down by Ernte – für das Leben in Austria). Only non-synthetic fining agents can be used to clarify the wine (like bentonite). The CCOF legend may appear on the bottle only if the wine has been made without added sulphur dioxide preservatives ('sulfites'). The 'Transitional Seal' was introduced in 1996 and is awarded to those vineyards in transition. To qualify a grower must pass two farm inspections, have at least a one year hiatus from the date of the last prohibited material being applied to the land, and meet all CCOF standards except for the three year land history requirement. Higher prices for transition grapes might encourage more growers away from conventional farming.

CCOF has 650 members, including over 70 vinegrowers, and publishes a statewide newsletter. Its address is:

California Certified Organic Farmers (CCOF)
1115 Mission St, Santa Cruz, CA 95060
Tel:+1 408 423 2263
Fax:+1 408 423 4528

Email: dianeb@ccof.org
Internet: www.ccof.org

Another organic certification body – Organic Certifiers – is not recognized by IFOAM but is licensed by the State of California. Contact Randy Siple, Director of Organic Certifiers, for a list of standards. The one member of Organic Certifiers featured below is Durney Vineyards.

Organic Certifiers
6500 Casitas Pass Road, Ventura, CA 93003
Tel:+1 805 684 6494
Fax:+1 805 684 6494
Email: s.siple@get.net

ORGANIC CERTIFICATION STATUS

Wines Labelled as 'Made From Organically Grown Grapes'

Wines labelled as 'made from organically grown grapes' are subject to the 1990 California Organic Food Act (section 26569.1 i of the California Health and Safety Code) and the California Organic Farming Agreement (COFA). The grapes must be certified by a private group which is registered with the State, such as Demeter (for biodynamics), CCOF (which is also IFOAM accredited), or Organic Certifiers.

Wines Labelled as 'Organic Wines'

For the label to read 'Organic Wine' (a category which does not exist in Europe) there are two main criteria on their content:

- Only wines which are minimum 95 per cent organic by weight (i.e., permitted inorganic substances (excluding salt and water) may comprise no more than 5 per cent of the product by weight) are eligible. By implication they must be made from certified organic grapes.
- Only wines with no added sulphur dioxide preservative ('sulfites') and less than 10ppm of sulphur in total are eligible. Even when no sulphur has been added, the label must state 'Contains Sulfites' if it contains more than 10ppm when the wine is released. (In the EU the 'contains sulfites' legend is not allowed to appear on the bottle.) Thus wines

from Frey Vineyards which are made without recourse to sulphur and have a natural total sulphur level not exceeding 10ppm (see below), can be labelled as organic (or biodynamic too in their case), whereas those from Bonterra Vineyards, which contain the additive sulphur, can be labelled only as made from certified organic grapes.

Wines Labelled as 'Made From Organically Grown Grapes' for the EU

Wines labelled as 'made from organically grown grapes' to be sold in the EU have to be certified according to the EU organic standard. This is why Fetzer's Bonterra wines are labelled as certified by the 'Soil Association (Cert Ltd)' when sold in the UK. The Soil Association is itself certified to UKROFS (United Kingdom Register of Organic Food Standards) approved standards. Demeter's higher standards are recognized directly by the EU in the case of a biodynamic wine from Frey (although the Bureau of Alcohol, Tobacco and Firearms, which controls the production of all wine — not just organic — in the US had some initial trouble apparently accepting Frey's first biodynamic labels, being unaware of what biodynamic farming was).

Wines With a Natural Total Sulphur Level Exceeding 10ppm

In this case the sulphur would have been formed during the fermentation by the yeast as they transform the grape sugar into alcohol. So even though the wine is 'preservative free' and made with organic grapes it can not be labelled as organic. This rule has caused some organic winemakers to revert to fermenting with cultured yeast strains selected to produce lower levels of sulphur by-product than the yeast occurring naturally on the grapeskins. It acts as a disincentive to those trying to promote the natural yeasts found in the vineyard. This is one of the advantages of the EU's lack of winemaking standards for organic wines.

Registered Organic Status

In addition there is a junior category of organic status called Organic Registration. Vineyards are eligible for organic registration once they have been free for at least three years of synthetic fungicides, herbicides and pesticide, sulphur dioxide, soil fumigants (like methyl bromide) and petroleum derivatives. The County Agricultural Commissioner, to maintain Registration, determines periodically that the farm is complying with the tenets of the California Organic Foods Act, but the farm/vineyard is never inspected. Vineyards can still maintain registration and use chemical fertilisers, for example, which are not covered by the rules of entry for registration.

Warning: There are a growing number of Californian producers who are claiming 'organic' status without specifying that their vineyards are only registered organic and not certified organic. If visiting the area, be sure to ask the guide on the 'organic winery tour' to be specific about the winery's organic status – third-party certified; state certified; or just registered?

The big question is why so many wineries in California are jumping on the organic bandwagon? The simple answer is that demand for organic products is soaring in America and nobody with anything to sell wants to be thought of as non-organic. Some wineries are unwilling to pay the necessary fees to get organic registration or organic certification so they play the sustainable trump card instead. Beware!

The list of producers below is representative of the current organic scene in this fast-moving State, rather than exhaustive. They are divided into three main sub-regions: the North Coast, Central Coast, and the Sierra Foothills.

NORTH COAST

This covers the area north of San Francisco, and includes the Napa Valley which, for many, is the heart of the California wine scene. This view may be justified only as far as conventional winemaking goes, for the history of organic vineyards in California begins not in Napa Valley, nor in Sonoma Valley, Napa's immediate (and some would say) potentially superior neighbour. California's first organic vineyards originate nearly 160kms to the north, in Mendocino County. This can justifiably claim to be the world's most organic wine region, such is the concentration of organic and biodynamic growers there. Napa and Sonoma are catching up in the organic stakes, but there is more than a whiff of corporate opportunism in the way some of the bigger wine producers view organic certification. The irony is that Mendocino's – and California's – biggest organic winery (Fetzer) was family owned for 30 years, until it was bought by a publicly quoted Bourbon manufacturer, Brown Forman. Such is California.

Lake County

Lake County in Northern California boasts a longer history of making wine than its immediate neighbour to the west, Mendocino County (see below) but, in contrast to Mendocino, the Lake vineyards did not survive Prohibition. Recent vineyard replantings on high altitude sites, where days are hot and nights are cool, have produced grapes noted for their intensity and freshness.

Bartolucci Vineyards

PO Box 169, Finley, CA 95435
Tel:+1 707 263 0183
Fax:+1 707 263 9265
Email: bvrgrapes@pacific.net

This domaine is run by Ron Bartolucci and comprised 31.5 hectares of CCOF-certified organic vineyard in 1998. Bartolucci converted to organics in 1990 after some persuasion from his largest grape purchaser, Fetzer Vineyards, when it was still family owned. Bartolucci sold Cabernet Sauvignon, Merlot and Chardonnay to the Fetzer family, and now sells his Muscat Canelli and Viognier (both for white wines) to Fetzer Vineyards-Brown Forman Corporation for the Bonterra range (*see page 300*). He makes no wines himself.

Mendocino County

Winegrowing in Mendocino County in northern California dates to the 19th century when vines joined timber (in Redwood Valley which runs north of Ukiah) and fishing (along the Russian River Valley, from Ukiah south to Hopland) as major economic activities. The vineyards survived Prohibition because the local wineries were so isolated from San Francisco. Mendocino vineyards now cover 4,455 hectares. Around 25 per cent of the county's vineyards are certified organic, compared to less than 5 per cent for the rest of the State. Growers here use the least amount of pesticides of any Californian region, as shown in returns on pesticide use submitted to county agricultural commissioners. There is more certified organic vineyard here than there is in the whole of the Southern Hemisphere combined. The high incidence of organic vineyards may be explained by:

- the arrival of well-educated metropolitans open to sustainable farming practices during the 1960s and 1970s. They have been succeeded by a second generation as keen to maintain these practices as they were.
- the climate combines the cold wet winters common and necessary for good vine health in Europe with a warm, dry growing season typical of the New World, which is a perfect combination for ripe, healthy grapes.

Barra Vineyards

9901 East Road, Redwood Valley, CA 95470
Tel:+1 707 485 8606
Fax:+1 707 485 0836

This domaine belongs to Pete Barra, brother of Charlie (*see Redwood Valley Vineyards, page 314*), and his wife Bea. There were 14 hectares of CCOF-certified organic vineyard between 1992 and 1996, with most of the grapes sold to Fetzer Vineyards-Brown Forman Corporation for Bonterra. The Barras have now dropped out of the CCOF programme, and make no wines themselves.

Beckstoffer Vineyards/Mendocino Vineyards

PO Box 218, Talmage, CA 95481
Tel:+1 707 462 6624
Fax:+1 707 462 5145

The owner of this vineyard, Andy Beckstoffer, is the largest vineyard owner in Napa Valley, and is looking to augment his holdings in Sonoma Valley and Mendocino County. The grapes he produces are sold under contract. Some clients want the grapes to be certified organic, which explains why Beckstoffer has had 42.8 hectares of vineyard CCOF-certified organic in 1999, with another 6.5 hectares pending. He sells organic Cabernet Sauvignon and Chardonnay from Mendocino County to Fetzer Vineyards-Brown Forman Corporation for Bonterra.

Bonterra Vineyards

Fetzer Vineyards-Brown Forman Corporation
12625 East Side Road, Hopland, CA 95449

Tel:+1 707 744 1521
Fax:+1 707 744 1844
Internet: www.fetzer.com or www.bonterra.com
Attractions: The Food and Wine Centre, which opened in 1989, includes a tasting room, a visitor centre, and Culinary Pavilion.
Stockists: Organic Wine Company, Vintage Roots, Vinceremos, and widely available in the UK; Young's Market Co. (California, USA), National Distributing Co. (Colorado, USA), Romano Bros (Chicago, USA), Charmer (New York, USA), Glazer's Distributing (Texas, USA)

Bonterra Vineyards is the name given by Fetzer Vineyards-Brown Forman Corporation to a range of wines made from organically grown grapes. This range dates from 1992 when Brown Forman, which is best known for producing the Jack Daniels brand of Bourbon, purchased the Fetzer Vineyards name.

Fetzer Vineyards dates from 1957 when a lumber executive called Bernard Fetzer (1920–1981) bought a Mendocino ranch as a home for himself, his wife Kathleen and their 11 children. The 'Home Ranch' consisted of almost 300 hectares, including a vineyard planted in the mid-19th century. This was ripped out and replaced with Cabernet Sauvignon and Zinfandel, the grapes being sold to home winemakers throughout the US. In 1985 (with the help of Michael Maltus – see Masút, page 313) the Fetzers began the Bonterra ('good earth') organic garden, to remind consumers of the connection that the land has with what they eat and drink. In other words wine is a form of food or 'you are what you drink'. The quality of the vegetables produced in the Bonterra garden led the Fetzer children to convert their vineyards to certified organic methods. In 1992, with Fetzer's wine brands like Sundial Chardonnay and Eagle Peak Merlot among the biggest selling wines in America, the family sold up to the Brown Forman Corporation.

The business took the name of Fetzer Vineyards-Brown Forman Corporation. Brown Forman had wanted to get into wine production after noticing how consumers were skipping their hard liquors like bourbon in favour of wine – Fetzer was a 2.5 million cases brand with an organic message and so proved an ideal acquisition target. Brown-Forman was new to the wine game and so had no experience of vineyards. So it purchased the winery, the brand name and some of the land, but left the

Fetzer family as vineyard proprietors of 608 hectares. The deal was the grapes from these vineyards (collectively known as Kohn – Mrs Fetzer's maiden name) must be sold exclusively to Brown Forman until 2000. Some members of the Fetzer family look sure to drop the organic certification, being unwilling to pay the premium for organic certification if their grapes are destined – as may be the case – to be blended with conventionally farmed grapes, rather than be used for Bonterra.

The majority of the vineyards are certified organic, and the grapes from these are used for the Bonterra range of organic wines. Brown Forman also purchases certified organic grapes from other suppliers (there are 608 hectares under contract from other growers in Mendocino County and elsewhere), as are organic grapes from those vineyards which Brown Forman agreed to purchase outright from the Fetzers (the smallest of these is an experimental vineyard called 'Blue Heron' – see Alvaro Espinoza, Chile, *page 394*). Two of the Fetzers used the proceeds of their business with Brown Forman to purchase additional Mendocino vineyards called Masút (Robert Fetzer) and Ceãgo Vinegarden (James Fetzer), which are run independently of each other and of Brown Forman. With a total production of 2.2 million cases Fetzer Vineyards-Brown Forman Corporation is the biggest commercial winery in California. By 2005 Fetzer hopes all wines sold under its label will be from certified organically grown grapes, although there are no plans to make 'organic wine' (i.e., wines with no added sulphur dioxide preservative, like their neighbours at Frey Vineyards). For the moment the Bonterra range accounts for 1–2 per cent of total production here, but will increase from 90,000 cases in 1998 to over 200,000 cases in 1999. The Bonterra range appears to be made for drinking upon purchase, or for keeping for 2–4 years maximum.

Not all of the organic grapes are used for Bonterra. Some are blended with non-organic grapes for Fetzer branded wines like 'Bel Arbors' and 'Sundial Chardonnay'. In 1998 the grapes from a total of 790 hectares of CCOF-certified organic vineyards, over 12 per cent of the state total, were processed at Fetzer Vineyards-Brown Forman Corporation.

• Chardonnay, Bonterra Vineyards: sourced from Russian River Valley, between Ukiah and Hopland (or 'Sanel Valley'), with lemon and citrus the dominant characteristics. First released in 1992, contained 2–4 per cent Pinot Blanc, barrel fermented in American oak, now fading. The 1993 vintage was similar to 1992. The 1994 was picked riper than the previous vintage and fermented in oak barrels made by Fetzer's own coopers. 1995 was a cooler year, producing a dominant citrus character. 1996 was an 'oddball' hot year, and the wine showed butter rather than citrus. 1997 was a cooler, leaner year showing a pineapple character. 1998 shows depth as the grapes could hang a long time on the vines due to a later than usual vintage. ♦♦

- Viognier, Bonterra Vineyards: dry white, shows peach and honeysuckle, over-oaked in 1994, but 1995 shows more integration. The 1996 got the balance right between the vanilla taste given by fermentation in barrels of French oak with the taste of the fruit. 1997 showed a strong peach character. ♦♦

- Bonterra Red: dry red, blend of 55 per cent Petite Syrah and 45 per cent Zinfandel, existed only until other vineyards from Home Ranch came on stream.

- Cabernet Sauvignon, Bonterra Vineyards: dry red, first made in 1994 with a blend of Cabernet Sauvignon, Syrah and Petite Syrah. 1996 was a warm, almost too warm year, so the Syrah content (10–15 per cent of the final blend) added alcohol and depth to the Cabernet; 1997 was a cooler year with some rain and was reflected in a lighter style, the final blend contained 13–14 per cent Syrah; suitable for vegetarians. ♦♦♦

- Sangiovese, Bonterra Vineyards: dry red, bitter chocolate twist to the fruit, young vines so only moderate intensity. ♦♦♦

- Zinfandel, Bonterra Vineyards: dry red, sourced from Fetzer Vineyard's Blue Heron site from vines planted in 1993; first made in 1996; the 1998 showed rich, classic black pepper Zinfandel; suitable for vegetarians. ♦♦

Other wines in the Bonterra range include Merlot, Muscat and Roussanne.

Butow/Frey Vineyards
7100 East Road, Redwood Valley, CA 95470
Tel:+1 707 485 5038

This domaine consists of 10.8 hectares of Chardonnay, Cabernet Sauvignon and Syrah grapes. The vines have been CCOF-certified organic since 1985. The owners, Luke Frey and Clara Butow, sell the grapes to Luke's family at Frey Vineyards, the owners and managers there.

Ceãgo Vinegarden at McNab Ranch

2002 McNab Ranch Rd, Ukiah, CA 95482
Tel:+1 707 468 0377
Fax:+1 707 468 1314
Email: ceago@inreach.com

Ceãgo Vinegarden is arguably the most innovative vineyard project featured in this book. It dates from 1993 when James Fetzer began transforming what was a run-down vineyard and sheep ranch – McNab – near Hopland. Fetzer was the fourth of Bernard Fetzer's eleven children (see Bonterra, above). He paid for the 219 hectare McNab property with his share of the proceeds from Brown Forman Corporation's purchase of the Fetzer Vineyards brand name in September 1992.

Ceãgo Vinegarden consists of 58 hectares of Petite Syrah and Viognier (planted 1975), Merlot and Chardonnay (planted 1994) and Cabernet Sauvignon (planted 1998) vines. It is called Vinegarden because the whole domaine has been designed to create a vine garden atmosphere, promoting diversity in plant and animal life. It is thus extensive rather than monocultural. The vine plots are located around habitat breaks made up of flowers, shrubs and fruit trees. These foster beneficial predator insects and contain herbs like lavender (for oil and dried flowers), two varieties of olive trees and vegetables. James Fetzer was the driving force behind the original 'Bonterra' organic vegetable garden (see Fetzer Vineyards-Brown Forman Corporation above). Here the vegetables grown between the rows are intrinsic to the concept of a vine garden (they provide food for the staff – locally grown, locally consumed). Fetzer's reasoning seems to be that if wine and food go together on the table, then they should at least get to know each other in the vineyard first.

The vines at Ceãgo are managed backwards. This seems a strange thing to say about such a forward-thinking domaine. What it means is the vines are managed according to how many grapes they are capable of producing rather than how many grapes the owner would like them to produce. This allows nature to set all the subsequent checks and balances which follow. In winter when the vines are pruned the cut shoots are weighed. The weight of the cut prunings ('the pruning weight') will indicate what potential the vine has to produce ripe grapes, i.e., older vines which produce dense shoots can ripen more grapes than younger vines producing thinner, less strong shoots. The pruning weight will determine how many fruiting buds should be left at pruning – i.e., what number of bunches each vine should aim to produce in the coming season. Weighing the pruning wood like this in winter allows James Fetzer to know how much yield each plot of vines will give him in nine months' time, during harvest. He can then determine the exact amount of compost to apply as 'green manures' or cover crops. As a result his vineyard plots are unlikely ever to be over-fertilised.

The cover crops are grazed with sheep that also provide bedding for compost (their waste is mixed with horse manure from a neighbour's barn – a contrast to imported Peruvian bird guano, which is all the rage amongst California's organic winegrowing fraternity). Chickens roam to eat cutworms (see Badger Mountain (*page 347*) for another way of dealing with these). In 1996 Fetzer began converting 10 hectares of the Ceãgo Vinegarden to biodynamic methods as a trial and within three years the whole vineyard had been converted to Demeter-certified biodynamic standards. All the biodynamic compost preparations and the biodynamic sprays are made on site rather than bought in.

Until 1998 there was no winemaking facility at Ceãgo Vinegarden so all the grapes were sold. Most were taken by Fetzer Vineyards-Brown Forman Corporation to be used for its Bonterra range. Of all the grapes used in the wines for Bonterra in the 1998 vintage, those with the highest levels of natural sugar came from Ceãgo Vinegarden. James Fetzer is also selling biodynamic grapes to Greg Graziano for the Monte Volpe (now Fox Creek) range (see Domaine St Gregory, *page 307*). Biodynamic certified lavender and olive oil (🍷🍷🍷) are also released by Ceãgo.

Chance Creek

c/o Bock Vines & Wines, Inc., 310B Locust Street, Santa Cruz, CA 95060
Tel:+1 408 423 3006
Fax:+1 831 423 1026
Email: wines@bockwines.com
Overall Price Rating: 🍷🍷

Chance Creek is part of Bock Wines, a distribution company for organic wines owned by Louis Bock. He came to Mendocino in 1979 having spent six years raising cattle in Santa Cruz. His vineyards cover 5.5 hectares and have been certified organic by CCOF since 1989. He used to sell all his grapes but in 1991 began making wine under his own label. Weeds are controlled with sheep, a practice that may reflect the influence of gardening guru Alan Chadwick whom Bock studied under at the University of Southern California in the late 1960s. Levels of total sulphur dioxide content are low in these wines, helped by high levels of alcohol (which acts as a preservative).

- Chance Creek Sauvignon Blanc, Mendocino AVA: dry white. In 1997 442 cases were made; 1998 was blended from 95 per cent Sauvignon Blanc and 5 per cent Viognier, with an alcohol level of 14.8 per cent (most Sauvignon Blanc in Bordeaux rarely get above 12.5 per cent).
- Chance Creek Sangiovese, Mendocino AVA: dry red. The 1997 contains a percentage of non-Sangiovese grapes; shows liquorice and violets; 220 cases made. The 1998 is 100 per cent varietal, 13.7 per cent alcohol (higher than most Chiantis, which are made predominantly from this grape).
- Chance Creek Viognier, Mendocino AVA: dry white; 1997 110 cases made; 1998 blended from 84 per cent Viognier and 16 per cent Sauvignon Blanc; 15.8 per cent alcohol (stronger than most fino sherry).

Cold Creek Ranch
5010 Highway 20, Ukiah, CA 95482
Tel:+1 707 485 8583

This Mendocino domaine covers 1.8 hectares and has been certified organic by CCOF since 1985. Owner Charles Guntly sells the grapes to Frey Vineyards who make Guntly Vineyard-designated wines from them.

Dennison Vineyards

PO Box 613, Boonville, CA 95415

Tel:+1 707 895 3718

Fax:+1 707 895 3639

Overall Price Rating: 👬

This domaine belongs to brothers Peter and William Dennison and covers 9.7 hectares of mainly Chardonnay grapes. The vines lie in the Anderson Valley AVA, which is Mendocino County's most coastal (and thus coolest) wine region. The vines have been CCOF-certified organic since 1982. The majority of the grapes are sold but most buyers mix Dennison's organic grapes with non-organic ones (an exception was Fetzer Vineyards-Brown Forman Corporation in 1994, which kept the Chardonnay for its Bonterra range). As a result the brothers have decided to keep more of their own grapes back to produce their own range of wines. These are called Octopus Mountain (after a nearby small mountain). Dennison's Octopus Mountain range includes dry white Chardonnay, dry white Sauvignon Blanc, dry red Cabernet Sauvignon and dry red Pinot Noir.

Domaine St Gregory

1170 Bel Arbres Road, Redwood Valley, CA 95470

Tel:+1 707 485 9463

Fax:+1 707 485 9742

Tasting Room/Sales: available at 13251 S. Hwy 101 Suite 3, Hopland, CA 95449

Stockist: Schneider's Liquors (Washington DC)

Domaine St Gregory was established by Greg Graziano and his wife Trudi in 1988. Greg Graziano's father farmed vines in Redwood Valley, although Greg's reputation is as a winemaker first and foremost, rather than for grape growing. He makes his wines in a Mendocino winery above Calpella, owned by Robert Fetzer of Masút (*see page 313*). A range of grapes are bought in, including from certified organic and biodynamic sources. The Domaine St Gregory wines are Burgundian in emphasis (Pinot Noir reds made in small, open-top fermenters), while those under the Monte Volpe label are described as Californian-Italian, and Graziano has the biggest range of wines made from Italian grape varieties in

California. Wines sold under the Fox Creek label are sourced from the bio-dynamic Ceãgo Vinegarden (rated 👥). Graziano's winemaking produces elegant, approachable wines styled very much for the table. He is also a contract winemaker for Yorkville Cellars (*page 316*).

El Rancho Chiquito

1921 Foothill Drive, Redwood Valley, CA 95470
Tel:+1 707 485 5253
Email: rfparker@pacific.net

This Mendocino domaine belongs to Robert and Claudia Parker, and comprises 1.8 hectares of Zinfandel. It has been CCOF-certified organic since 1993 and the grapes are sold to Frey Vineyards (below). No wines are made on site.

Emandal, A Farm On a River

16500 Hearst P.O. Road, Willits, CA 95490
Tel:+1 707 459 5439
Fax:+1 707 459 1808
Email: emandal@pacific.net

The vineyard here comprises 5.2 hectares and has been CCOF-certified organic since 1996. Chardonnay and Gewurztraminer grapes for white wines are sold to Frey Vineyards. There are also 3.2 hectares of CCOF-certified flowers and vegetables on this farm, which covers 405 hectares in total. The farm was purchased at the turn of the century by Emma and Al Burns as a retreat for overstressed city families, particularly wives and children (husbands could visit at weekends). Current owners, Tamara and Clive Adams, run children's camps.

Fowler Ranch

8989 Adobe Creek Road, Kelseyville, CA 95451
Tel:+1 707 279 2375
Fax:+1 707 279 2375

This ranch is a mixed farm, comprising 191.5 hectares of cattle, wine grapes, hay, mushrooms, pears and rangeland. All have been CCOF-certified organic since 1992. The wine grapes are sold, rather than made into wine on site, by owner Charles Fowler.

Frey Vineyards

14000 Tomki Road, Redwood Valley, CA 95470

Tel:+1 707 485 5177/+1 800 760 3739 (toll free)

Fax:+1 707 485 7875

Email: frey@saber.net or E:frey@pacific.net

Tasting: available at Redwood Valley Cellars, 7051 N State St, Redwood Valley, CA 95470

Overall Price Rating: 🍴 (for wines); 🍴🍴 (for herbs)

Frey Vineyards was founded in 1961 by Paul and Marguerite Frey and is considered the father of organic Californian vineyards. The family originates from northern Germany. The Freys were doctors rather than vintners and fell into vineyards and organics by accident. They planted their first vines in 1967 as a means of protecting themselves against a public engineering project that threatened part of the ranch. If the Freys were going to be forced to sell their land, they wanted the best price. The project never materialized but the vines stayed. They were managed with the minimum of expense. They were sprayed little and rarely and so were organic by default. The Frey grapes were sold to other winemakers, who started to win medals making wine from them. Seven of the Freys' children joined their parents in establishing the family's own wine business, and Frey Vineyards was born, with its first commercial release in 1980.

The organic element became official after one of the Freys' sons, Jonathan, studied with English master gardener and organics guru Alan Chadwick (see also Topolos *page 328*, Chance Creek *page 305*). All the Frey vineyards (32.5 hectares in total) are Demeter-certified biodynamic, and all the grapes they buy in are either CCOF-certified organic or Demeter-certified biodynamic. The vines are managed without irrigation. This saves water and prevents the level of humidity rising to high enough levels to foster vine fungal diseases. Manure is taken from a herd of 500 Guernsey cows owned by a neighbour. The main cover crops are clover, vetch, barley, rye and mustard, all of which have now become standard 'green manures' in California. Managing both vines and cover crops without water put the Freys '30 years ahead of their time' said one neighbour. In a recent pan-California test of soil samples, those at Frey were found to be most resistant to phylloxera.

In 1996 the Freys began making and applying their own biodynamic preparations for the vineyard. The vineyards were Demeter-certified immediately. Frey released the first biodynamic wines in the US in 1997, despite an initial battle with the Bureau of Alcohol, Tobacco and Firearms (BATF) which was apparently unaware of what biodynamic wine was (the BATF controls all wine labelling in the US). The winery building itself was rescued from being torn down and most of the equipment within is recycled. No sulphur preservative is used on the wines (the Freys recommend storing white wines at below 10°C, but say the reds can be stored as normal). All are suitable for vegans and vegetarians.

Organic wines are made from Chardonnay, Sauvignon Blanc and Gewurztraminer (all whites) and Merlot, Cabernet Sauvignon Petite Syrah, Pinot Noir, Syrah and Zinfandel (all reds), usually with the vineyard designation marked on the label when the grapes have been purchased from other suppliers (Butow/Frey, Guntly, Uncle Bob's, Upton, Walker, etc.).

The biodynamic wines are:

- Redwood Valley Biodynamic Chardonnay: dry white, in 1996 made from 100 per cent Chardonnay, estate grown; fermented with wild yeast, aged five months in French oak; 950 cases, tastes wild and herby.
- Redwood Valley Biodynamic Cabernet Sauvignon: dry red, in 1997 made from 100 per cent Cabernet Sauvignon, estate grown 31-year-old vines; fermented with wild yeast, aged nine months in French oak; 1750 cases, tastes of berry and pepper, earthy in the fullest sense.
- Redwood Valley Biodynamic Merlot: in 1997 made from 90 per cent Merlot and 10 per cent Cabernet Sauvignon, estate grown; fermented with wild yeast, aged nine months in French oak; 400 cases, bright colour, chewy berries, simple.
- Redwood Valley Biodynamic Zinfandel: dry red, in 1997 made from 100 per cent Zinfandel, estate grown; fermented with wild yeast, aged nine months in French oak; 420 cases, benchmark fruit, seductive core.

Also available are BD Herbs (biodynamic herbs), the US's first range of biodynamic extracts. The plants are started in the greenhouse in farm-made biodynamic compost mix. When the starts are ready they are planted in 200 feet long raised beds between the rows of Frey's biodynamic vines. The herbs are hand-harvested and extracted with certified organic alcohol. Angelica, camomile, motherwort, hyssop, echinacea, valerian, feverfew and other extracts are made.

Hidden Cellars/Headlands

13265 South Highway 101 Hopland, CA 95449
Tel:+1 707 462 0301
Email: hc@hiddencellars.com

Hidden Cellars is a partnership between Dennis Patton and Phil LaRocca (see LaRocca Vineyards, *page 333*) for hand made premium wines, some of which are labelled as organic (Chardonnay, Sauvignon Blanc and Pacini Vineyard Zinfandel). These are price rated 👜👜👜. A new range called Headlands (👜) appeared in 1998. All the grapes are bought in.

Konrad Estate Vineyards

Redwood Valley, California

This domaine was converted to certified organic methods in 1988 and was purchased in 1993 by Admiral Edmond G. Konrad, US Navy (ret'd). He made a number of wines, including dry white Fumé Blanc (Sauvignon Blanc), dry red Zinfandel and a fortified Petite Syrah called Admiral's Quinta. The 1993 vintage of this wine contained 19.3 per cent alcohol, was sold in 500 ml bottles and was made from 29-year-old vines. The wines were marked by their depth of character, but unfortunately Konrad went out of business. The vineyard is now known as Fife 'Redhead' Vineyards, but is not certified organic.

Lakeview Vineyards

PO Box 581, Hopland, CA 95449
Tel:+1 707 744 1279
Fax:+1 707 744 1643

This domaine is owned by Kurt Ashurst and his father (in part), but is run separately from Shadowbrook Farms (see below). There are 92 hectares of land, with 35 hectares of vineyard – CCOF-certified organic since 1992. Syrah, Chardonnay, Cinsault, Roussanne, Marsanne and Viognier are sold to Fetzer Vineyards-Brown Forman Corporation for their Bonterra range. Ashurst was the first to supply Syrah and Viognier grapes for Bonterra, and is the only supplier of Roussanne and Marsanne. His Cabernet Sauvignon and Chardonnay also feature in Bonterra.

Light Vineyards

11535 East Road, Redwood Valley, CA 95470
Tel:+1 707 485 1335

This Mendocino domaine consists of 12 hectares of vineyard, CCOF-certified organic since 1994. Owners Rudolph and Linda Light have planted many different grape varieties, including Cabernet Sauvignon, Gewurztraminer and one of the original clones of Chardonnay (the 'Wente' clone), which gives richer, buttery wines. The grapes are sold to Frey Vineyards, amongst others.

Lolonis Winery, Inc

2901 Road B, Redwood Valley, CA 95470
Tel:+1 707 485 8027
Fax:+1 707 485 5428
Email: lolonis@pacbell.net
Internet: www.lolonis.com

This domaine was established in 1920 by Tryfon and Eugenia Lolonis, Greek immigrants who were 16 and 17 years old respectively at the time. It is currently run by their grandchild, Ulysses F. Lolonis, a former school-teacher. There are 85.8 hectares of vineyards, CCOF-certified organic since 1993, although organic management practices began here in the 1950s. Petite Syrah and Chardonnay grapes from Lolonis have featured in wines made by Fetzer Vineyards-Brown Forman Corporation for Bonterra, and for Fetzer when it was still family owned. The family are developing their own range of wines, and are reckoned to produce some of the best grapes in Mendocino. The wines include: Merlot, Mendocino AVA,

Redwood Valley, Private Reserve; Cabernet Sauvignon, Mendocino AVA, Redwood Valley; Chardonnay, Mendocino AVA, Redwood Valley; and Sauvignon Blanc, Mendocino AVA, Redwood Valley.

Masút

PO Box 309, Calpella, California 95418
Tel:+1 707 485 1293
Fax:+1 707 485 0635

Masút is a Native American term meaning rich (sút) earth (ma). It is the name of a vineyard comprising 65 hectares owned by Robert Fetzer. The principles followed here mirror those of Robert's brother James at Ceãgo Vinegarden. Conversion from CCOF-certified organic status to full Demeter-certified biodynamic status was achieved in 1999. The first bio-dynamic wines under the Masút name are due in 2000 (the chosen winery is called Calpella). Masút's vineyard manager, David Koball, created habitat breaks here from 1994, and is conducting a detailed study on which insects are attracted into the vineyard when a habitat break is planted. Koball acknowledges his debt to garden designer Michael Maltus. Maltus created the original Bonterra biodynamic garden at Fetzer Vineyards when it belonged to the Fetzer family. The Fetzers said they sold out to Brown Forman to 'get back to their roots'. Swapping the 'good earth' of Bonterra for the richer earth of Masút should be Robert Fetzer's way of achieving this.

McFadden Farm

Powerhouse Road, Potter Valley, CA 95469
Tel:+1 707 743 1122
Fax:+1 707 743 1126
Email: mcfadden@pacific.net

This mixed farm comprises 232.5 hectares of cattle, cereals, vines, vegetables and herbs — all of which have been CCOF-certified organic since 1990. Owner Guinness McFadden hails from Brooklyn, and has sold (Johannisberg) Riesling and Gewurztraminer to Fetzer for Bonterra, and produces organic processed, bottled and bulk herbs and herb blends.

Redwood Valley Vineyards

PO Box 196, Redwood Valley, CA 95470

Tel:+1 707 485 8771

Fax:+1 707 485 8771

This domaine belongs to Charlie Barra. His grandfather grew grapes on the Rhône as a labourer. Barra (whose brother is the proprietor of Barra Vineyards, page 300) had over 162 hectares of CCOF-certified organic vineyards, but sold off a portion to spend more time fishing. Of the 60.7 hectares of Pinot Noir, Cabernet Sauvignon, Chardonnay, Sangiovese and Petite Syrah that remain, some are sold to Fetzer Vineyards-Brown Forman for Bonterra, Domaine St Gregory for Monte Volpe, Hidden Cellars/Headlands, and to Frey Vineyards. Others are made into wine by Barra under the Barra of Mendocino label (🍷). Barra's wines are pleasant but light.

Redwood Valley, Juice Company

567 Laughlin Way, Redwood Valley, CA 95470

Tel:+1 707 485 7567

This Mendocino domaine belongs to Randy Dorn, of Randy Dorn Construction, and his wife Sandy, and comprises 0.8 hectares of Carignan and Zinfandel. It has been CCOF-certified organic since 1994 and the grapes are sold to Frey Vineyards, who also manage these vineyards.

Shadowbrook Farm

1320 University Road, Hopland, CA95449

Tel:+1 707 744 1279

Fax:+1 707 744 1643

This domaine belongs to Kurt Ashurst (see Lakeview Vineyards, above). There are 19 hectares of Syrah, Cabernet Sauvignon, Viognier and Pinot Noir, roughly half of which have been certified organic since 1994. Grapes are sold to Fetzer Vineyards-Brown Forman Corporation for the Bonterra range, and to other wineries in Mendocino County and Dry Creek Valley, which mix them with non-organic grapes.

Smitty's Vineyards

300 Pinoleville Drive, Ukiah, CA 95482

Tel:+1 707 462 4029

This Mendocino domaine belongs to Smith Williams and comprises 2.4 hectares of wine grapes and walnuts. It has been CCOF-certified organic since 1992 and the grapes are sold to Frey Vineyards, who are also the managers here. No wines are made on site.

Sozzoni Bros. Vineyards

PO Box 174, Calpella, CA 95418

Tel:+1 707 485 7585

This Mendocino domaine belongs to Edward Graziano (uncle of Domaine St Gregory's Greg Graziano, *see page 307*), and comprises 6.9 hectares. It has been certified organic since 1991 and the grapes are sold to Frey Vineyards, who also manage the vineyards here. No wines are made on site.

Uncle Bob Vineyards

11000 West Road, Redwood Valley, CA 95470

Tel:+1 707 485 7590

This Mendocino domaine belongs to Robert J. Fetzer, uncle of Masút's Robert Fetzer, and comprises 0.8 hectares of organic Pinot Noir. It has been CCOF-certified since 1992 and the grapes are again sold to Frey Vineyards, who act as managers. No wines are made on site.

Upton Vineyards

9800 Laughlin Way, Redwood Valley, CA 95470

Tel:+1707 485 5972

This 10-hectare Mendocino domaine belongs to John and Jan Upton, and grows Sauvignon Blanc, Petite Syrah and other grape varieties. CCOF-certified organic since 1991, the grapes are sold to Frey Vineyards, the managers of the domaine. No wines are made on site.

Walker

2730 Road E, Redwood Valley, CA 95470

Tel:+1 707 485 7803

Email: cwalker@pacific.net

This Mendocino domaine belongs to Charles and Louise Walker and consists of four hectares of Chardonnay. It has been CCOF-certified organic since 1991, with the grapes being sold to Frey Vineyards, who also manage the vineyards. No wines are made on site.

Yorkville Vineyards & Cellars

PO Box 3, 25701 Highway 128 (milemarker 40.4), Yorkville, CA 95494

Tel:+1 707 894 9177

Fax:+1 707 894 2426

Email: yvcellars@pacific.net

Stockists: Winelink International Ltd; Waitrose (UK)

Overall Price Rating: ♙

Yorkville consists of 12 hectares of vines across two named sites – Randle Hill for white wine and Rennie for red. Both have been certified organic by CCOF since they were planted from 1987. Yorkville sold grapes to Fetzer Vineyards until 1994 when it opened its own winemaking facility. Some grapes are still sold to Fetzer (mainly Merlot and Cabernet Sauvignon). Yorkville's owners, Edward and Deborah Wallo, produce single varietal wines from Sauvignon Blanc, Semillon and Chardonnay (all dry whites); and from Cabernet Franc, Merlot and Cabernet Sauvignon (all reds). There is one blended wine:

● Eleanor of Aquitaine: dry white blend of Sémillon and Sauvignon Blanc, named after the French Queen (Aliénor) whose marriage to Henry Plantagenet (the future Henry II of England), united the French and English crowns from 1152. The real result of the marriage was that Eleanor's local wine, Bordeaux, became so popular in England that the vineyards were expanded. This dry white blend is an imitation of wines made in the area of Bordeaux vineyard which benefitted most from Eleanor's marriage – today's Graves AC. The only major difference between this and a Graves AC is that this wine undergoes

100 per cent secondary or malolactic fermentation, whereas Graves AC generally does not. The result here is a very rich, buttery wine.

Napa Valley

The Napa Valley stretches 48kms north from the San Francisco Bay Area towards the town of St Helena. Napa means 'plenty' in the local Native American language, but the Native Americans have been hunted out and 'plenty' here now refers to the 'plenty' of tourists, winebuses and cars which jam the valley every weekend. Napa is America's most famous wine region but this arguably owes as much to its accessibility as to the quality of its wine, much of which is bland, overpriced pap from flat, overly fertile and intensely irrigated sites, unsuited to the white man's vines but ideal, as the Native Americans knew, for grazing.

With several million tourists to entertain, Napa's winemakers are learning how to give the 'organic wine tour', although you would be hard pressed to find a winery here producing wine from 100 per cent own-grown, certified organic grapes. There is plenty on the Napa Valley floor to reflect upon, but not necessarily to enjoy. The most interesting wines tend to come from the mountain sites, where the vines enjoy finer soils and cooler temperatures at critical moments during the day.

Chavez & Leeds Vineyards

1581 St Helena Highway, St Helena, CA 94574
Tel:+1 707 963 2474

This estate belongs to Frank Leeds, vineyard manager of Frog's Leap (see below). It consists of 14 hectares of organic vineyard, CCOF certified since 1992. The grapes include Cabernet Sauvignon, Cabernet Franc, Petite Syrah and Sauvignon Blanc, and are sold to Frog's Leap.

Cypress Ranch

1889 Zinfandel Lane, St Helena, CA 94574
Tel:+1 707 963 1659
Fax:+1 707 963 7968

This comprises 18.2 hectares of organic vineyard, CCOF certified since 1995, spread over 10 ranches, rather than just a single one. The owners sell to about 15 wineries, none of which mention the organic origins of the grapes. These include Cabernet Sauvignon, Zinfandel, Melot and Sangiovese.

Frog's Leap Wine Cellars (Frog Farm)

8815 Conn Creek Road, PO Box 189, Rutherford, CA 94573
Tel:+1 707 963 4704/+1 800 959 4704 (toll free)
Fax:+1 707 963 0242
Events: Frogtoberfest, a tasting of older vintages for customers (invitation only)
Overall Price Rating: 🍷

Frog's Leap Wine Cellars (motto: 'time's fun when you're having flies') lies in the heart of the 'Rutherford Bench' – a strip of land containing some of the more prized Napa Valley vineyards. The phylloxera louse has bitten hard here due to the failure of a supposedly phylloxera-tolerant rootstock. To raise the capital for replanting costs, some of the most famous family names went public from the late 1980s. The owner of Frog's Leap, John Williams, claims organic management has revived a vineyard in Rutherford that he purchased even though it was infested with the phylloxera louse. Conventional practice would have been to plough in the middle of the row only; analyse the leaves to see if there was a lack of potassium; find that there was and then spray the vines with the chemical potassium. Instead Frog's Leap added manure as grape pomace (pressed skins, stalks, pips, sludge from settling of the juice prior to fermentation) for nutrients, gypsum to help the soil texture and sulphate of potash – all of which are approved by CCOF. Irrigation is kept to a minimum. Using these treatments has meant that the vineyard Frog's Leap purchased as dead from its previous owner in the early 1990s has come back to life, and cropped in 1998. This saved burning the vines and treating the phylloxera in the soil with a chemical.

All the vineyards owned by Frog's Leap will be CCOF-certified organic in 1999 (Williams and his wife Julie also own a four-hectare vineyard called Williams Ranch, certified organic since 1992), and certified grapes will continue to be bought in from a handful of other, mainly local growers (such as Chavez & Leeds, above), who are paid a premium for staying organic.

- Chardonnay: dry white. The 1990 vintage was barrel fermented; uneven, cracking up; 1991 carbon dioxide spritz, very youthful, crisp and tight; 1992 barrel fermented in French oak with native yeast, more evolved than 1991, earthy, real, lively; 1993 organic growing, fermented with natural yeast, bottled unfiltered, warm, round and harmonious.
- Sauvignon Blanc: dry white. The 1990 was fermented with native yeast, 10 per cent in barrel and 90 per cent in tank (tank fermented wine was aged in oak); shows stinky vanilla character in keeping with an aromatic grape variety grown in a hot climate and fermented/aged in oak. Not classic, but intriguing. The 1991 vintage was advertised as organically grown, with a mineral nose, clean lemon sherbet, good balance – evolving; 1992 vintage warm, starting to fade; 1995 organically grown, shows stone fruit, natural freshness.
- Zinfandel: dry red; 1989 light, drink up; 1990 hit by the rain; 1991 made from organically farmed grapes, fermented with wild yeast, with a sweet lemon taste, more extract than previous two wines; 1992 fading sherbet; 1993 dusty; 1994 Turkish delight; 1995 sweet and peppery.

Johnston Vineyards

PO Box 658, Napa Valley, CA 94559
Tel:+1 707 942 4956

This comprises 2.5 hectares of vineyards, CCOF-certified since 1992. Owner Charles L. Johnston sells all of his grapes, and so makes no wine.

Niebaum-Coppola Estate

PO Box 208, Rutherford, CA 94573
Tel:+1 707 963 9099
Fax:+1 707 963 9235

This domaine belongs to the film director Francis Ford Coppola and his wife Eleanor, and was created in 1994. Vineyards owned by the couple are certified organic by CCOF and totalled 21.5 hectares in 1998. The most famous plot is the Rubicon, because it lies on the 'Rutherford Bench', although the wine bearing this name comes both from Rubicon and from a separate, Coppola-owned, plot which arguably has more potential than Rubicon itself (🍷🍷🍷). Other wines made from estate (organic) grapes include Cask Cabernet (🍷🍷🍷), Pennino Zinfandel (🍷🍷), Family Cabernet Sauvignon (🍷🍷), Family Zinfandel (🍷🍷), Family Merlot (🍷🍷) and Family Cabernet Franc (🍷🍷). Note that the Family Chardonnay (from the Carneros region) is made with non-estate, non-certified organic grapes.

Primitivo Vineyards

3358 St Helena Highway, St Helena, CA 94574
Tel:+1 707 963 4804
Fax:+1 707 963 8683
Email: D-RT@napanet.net

Primitivo Vineyards is a CCOF certified, non-irrigated vineyard owned by Larry Turley, ex of Frog's Leap. Turley was born on an organic farm and all 15 of the vineyards he owns, rents or works for others are organically farmed, although this is the only one which is CCOF-certified organic. Primitivo is a synonym for the Zinfandel grape variety used in Southern Italy from where it is thought to have originated. This reflects very much an 'Italian is in' mood in California. (See Il Noce di Ugo Arno, Apulia, *page 228*, for Primitivo di Manduria.) The vineyard covers 3.25 hectares and is called the Earthquake Vineyard (it was planted in 1906 – the year San Francisco was devastated by the famous earthquake).

Spottswoode Vineyard

1902 Madrona Ave, St Helena, CA 94574
Tel:+1 707 963 0134
Fax:+1 707 963 2886
Email: spottswde@aol.com
Internet: www.spottswoode.com

Spottswoode Vineyard consists of 17.4 hectares of CCOF-certified organic vineyard, although only one of the two wines made here by owner Mary Novak is from it. This is a dry red Cabernet Sauvignon (🍷🍷🍷). In addition, a dry white wine made from purchased Sauvignon Blanc grapes is produced (🍷🍷) – arguably the better value of the two.

Vigil Vineyards (Winery)

660 Stanton Drive, St Helena, CA 94574
Tel:+1 707 963 5885
Email: vigilwine@aol.com

The owner of this operation, James William Pawlak, produces three ranges of wines, but only those labelled Terra Vine are from certified organic grapes. Terra Vine comes from a vineyard of that name owned by Pawlak in Calistoga, which is one of Napa Valley's warmer areas: hence dry red wine varieties like Zinfandel, Carignan and Refosco are planted. Wines from non-organic sources include Vigil and Bella Vigna.

Viader

1120 Deer Park Road, PO Box 280, Deer Park, CA 94576
Tel:+1 707 963 3816
Fax:+1 707 963 3817
Email: DeliaVia@aol.com
Internet: www.Viader.com
Stockists: Slocum & Sons (Connecticut), Franklin Selections (Maryland); Southern Wine & Spirits (Florida), Grapefields, Inc (Georgia), The Wine Source (Washington, DC), Lauber Imports (New York/New Jersey); Marquis Wine Cellars (Canada); Domaine Direct (UK)

Delia Viader was born in Argentina and graduated in Philosophy before founding Viader in the mid-1980s. The vines cover seven hectares in Deer Park, on Howell Mountain, one of five mountain sites in the Napa Valley renowned for intense red wines made from Cabernet Sauvignon, Cabernet Franc and Merlot. They were CCOF-certified organic from planting in 1987–88. In 1998 certification was withdrawn when Viader used a restricted fertiliser to boost the vines which were flagging on the rocky, low nutrient soil (the vines were planted originally with the aid of dynamite). Delia Viader intends re-submitting to the CCOF programme to undergo the mandatory re-conversion for three years from the 1999 harvest. Without the restricted fertiliser Viader's yields would have been uneconomic from the owner's standpoint. The vine rows here were arranged to follow the slope to allow better exposure to the sun and create the conditions for the dramatic colour and ripeness of Viader's single red wine. It is rare to plant like this in California where the vine rows tend to go across the slope to make mechanized tractor work easier.

● Viader, Deer Park AVA: dry red, first made in 1989 from mainly Cabernet Franc and Cabernet Sauvignon. The Cabernet Franc grapes are picked slightly over-ripe, and partially crushed to allow some whole clusters (to lengthen the fermentation time, which creates the impression of richness in the wine), fermented with a yeast culture, aged two-thirds in new French and one-third in Russian oak and bottled unfiltered. One of the more seductive, complex and balanced Californian attempts at imitating the rarest style of red Bordeaux – one with a dominance of Cabernet Franc (see Touraine in the Loire for 100 per cent Cabernet Franc reds, *page 95*). 🍶

Volker Eisele Vineyard
3080 Lower Chiles Valley Road, St Helena, CA 94574
Tel:+1 707 965 2260
Fax:+1 707 965 9609

The German owner of this hillside vineyard, Volker Eisele, sold his mainly Cabernet Sauvignon grapes to the Fetzer family during the 1980s. At the time he practised organic but non-certified methods. Since 1996 the 10.9 hectare vineyard has been CCOF certified. One wine is made:

● Cabernet Sauvignon, Volker Eisele Vineyard: dry red, usually a blend of Cabernet Sauvignon (90 per cent) and Cabernet Franc (10 per cent), but in 1997 it was 80 per cent Cabernet Sauvignon and 20 per cent Cabernet Franc. The wine shows rich Cabernet fruit in the best Napa mountain tradition. 🍶

Napa Wine Co
7830-40 St Helena Highway, PO Box 434, Oakville, CA 94562
Tel:+1 707 944 2514
Fax:+1 707 944 9749

This winery, established in 1887, produces a range of varietal wines from CCOF-certified grapes under the Napa Wine Co label. Examples include

Pinot Blanc, Sauvignon Blanc and Cabernet Sauvignon. The company also farms an additional 245 hectares of CCOF-certified vineyard, with the Cabernet Sauvignon being sold to Fetzer Vineyards-Brown Forman Corporation for Bonterra wines.

Sonoma County

Commercial winemaking in Northern California began in Sonoma Valley in the 1840s, although Sonoma has only recently begun to be thought of as a possible rival to its junior relation across the Mayacaymus mountains to the east – Napa Valley. A far greater proportion of the vineyard area here is on sloping ground than in Napa, and this gives the wine potentially greater texture and range of flavour. Being closer to the Pacific helps too – the grapes stay cooler for longer, ripen more gradually, and retain their acidity. All of which helps to reduce the potential for winemaking tricks such as adding preservatives like sulphites – wine acid being a great pre-server, at least of wine, if not one's teeth.

Brody (Michael) Vineyards
5895 W Dry Creek Road, Healdsburg, CA 95448
Tel: +1 707 484 3596

This domaine lies in Dry Creek Valley, which runs north of the town of Healdsburg and enjoys relatively high rainfall and relatively warm temperatures – a potentially perfect balance for organic Californian wine-growers. This history of certified organic vineyards in Dry Creek has taken a downturn with the decision in 1998 of Brody (Michael) Vineyards to drop out of the CCOF programme after only three years. The owners, who grew 4.2 hectares of Cabernet Sauvignon, said the fees for certification were not balanced by the weak dollar premium being paid by the wineries they sold their grapes to.

Other vineyards in the Dry Creek area that claim to farm organically but without ever being independently certified include Bellerose Vineyard. This was founded by Charles Richard in the early 1980s, after he gave up his concert career as a classical guitarist, and the vines (Cabernet Sauvignon) were ploughed with two draft horses. One other non-certified 'organic' vineyard was Preston, which was founded in 1975 and which contained Marsanne and Viognier for white wines and Syrah and Barbera for reds.

Coturri Winery (H Coturri & Sons Ltd)

PO Box 396, 6725 Enterprise Road, Glen Ellen, CA 95442

Tel:+1 707 525 9126

Fax:+1 707 542 8039

Sales: mail order. US prices are given for these wines, but check with the winery for which US states can receive UPS shipments from California (laws vary from State to State on the importation of alcohol into different jurisdictions).

Coturri Winery is another organic Californian domaine with roots in the 1960s. In 1963 it became the property of Harry Coturri, a businessman from San Francisco. Coturri had made the family wine with his father and began making wine from fruit grown in surrounding vineyards with the help of his two sons. They now run the business – Phil as vineyard manager and Tony as winemaker. Coturri's own vineyards include Glover Vineyards, Judges Vineyards and Views Land Vineyards. All are farmed organically but not all are registered with CCOF. This is a question of politics rather than of practice (i.e., because CCOF's main role now is inspection rather than, as it used to be, a mechanism for information exchange between growers at local level).

The wines, mainly red, are made in a wooden farm shed with little insulation. For reds the grapes are picked and sorted by hand before crushing into small one ton (or smaller) fermentation vats made of the local redwood oak. The juice ferments on the grape skins with natural yeast. The skins are pressed in a basket press. The wines are bottled without fining agents, filtration or the addition of sulphur dioxide preservative (sulphites). The results are wines so rich in pure tasting fruit that they are unique in the context of this book. The secret of such natural wine, says Tony Coturri, is to keep the scale small and to use good grapes (here that means grapes with good physiology – a ripe colour and firmness to the skins). It means also maturing the wine in barrels which are kept clean and topped up, and relying on the ripe tannins and the alcohol present in the wine to act as a natural preservative. The Coturris advise those who buy their wines on how best to store them with regard to temperature and humidity levels by precise instructions on the label.

Comparable wines from Europe include Chateau Meylet in St Emilion Bordeaux, Domaine Saint-Apollinaire in the Rhône and Domaine Eugène Meyer in Alsace.

- Alberello Sonoma Red, Sonoma Valley AVA: dry red, sourced from a vineyard planted in south-east Sonoma Valley in the 1930s using a head pruned (i.e., low pruned, or *albarello* in Italian) system. The varieties were mixed at planting to leave approximately 40 per cent Zinfandel, 40 per cent Petite Syrah and 20 per cent Alicante, Carignane, Early Burgundy and Barbera. The wine contained nearly 16 per cent alcohol in 1997 (550 cases produced, 🍾🍾).
- Assemblage Millénaire: dry red Bordeaux-style blend in 1996 of Cabernet Sauvignon and Merlot. 🍾🍾🍾
- Cabernet Sauvignon, Sonoma Valley: dry red, in 1996 a 100 per cent varietal wine sourced from Judges Vineyards, Views Land Vineyards and Glover Vineyards (120 cases, 🍾🍾).
- Cabernet Sauvignon, Jessandra Vittoria, Sonoma Valley AVA: dry red. Produced 660 cases in 1996. See below for details of the vineyard. 🍾🍾🍾
- Chardonnay, Views Land Vineyards: dry white, in 1996 fermented in 60 gallon French oak barrels, bottled unfined, 36 cases. 🍾🍾🍾
- Jessandra Vittoria, Santa Vittoria: dry red sourced from a vineyard established in 1979 by Robert Kamen on rocky, volcanic soil at 1500 feet, within walking distance of the Monte Rosa Vineyards of Louis Martini. In 1996 comprised a blend of 90 per cent Cabernet Sauvignon and 10 per cent Sangiovese, bottled unfined and unfiltered in April 1998 (1,000 cases, 🍾🍾🍾). In July 1996 a third of the vines were hit by a fire which raged across the Mayacaymus, necessitating replanting after harvest (these damaged vines were used for a bottling below).
- Jessandra Vittoria, 'Port': fortified red, made in 1996 from vines which were damaged by fire, see above (148 cases, 375ml, 🍾🍾).
- Merlot, Maclise Vineyards, Sonoma Valley: dry red, first made in 1996, sourced from 3.2 hectares planted in 1993 by Gay Maclise (72 cases, 🍾🍾)
- Pinot Noir, Jewell Vineyards, Sonoma Mountain: dry red, sourced from 6.5 hectares of Pinot Noir, planted in the early 1960s on a non-vigorous rootstock (St George), dry farmed and managed organically

by Bob Cannard and owned by Barry and Kate Roach. The 1997 vintage produced 220 cases. 𝄢

- Pinot Noir, Sessions Cuvée: dry red, in 1997 sourced from California Vineyard Hanzel from three blocks numbered 54, 57 and 76 (the numbers refer to the year of planting); named in honour of Bob Sessions, a friend of the Coturris and a renowned winemaker at Hanzel (300 cases, 𝄢𝄢).

- Zinfandel, Chauvet Vineyards, Sonoma Valley AVA: dry red, sourced from a vineyard owned since 1972 by Robert and Blythe Carver, and located two miles south of Glen Ellen on Sonoma Highway 12. It consists of four hectares in equal sections: East Block which was planted in 1936 by the Canuccio family (apparently by using a quarter stick of dynamite in each vine hole), and West Block, planted in 1976 by the Carver family. In 1997 the harvest was early, hot, and fast as the sugars raced up. The acids remained high enough however to give the wine its freshness, bringing alive its sensational thick, pure damson fruit. 1,000 cases made. The label reads: 'Our grandfather "Nono" would call this wine one that goes to your head and not your stomach.' It's true even though the alcohol content is over 16 per cent. 𝄢

- Zinfandel, Chauvet Vineyards East Block: dry red, made in 1997 as a separate bottling from the above (48 cases, 𝄢).

- Zinfandel, Chauvet Vineyards West Block: dry red, made in 1997 as a separate bottling from the above (72 cases, 𝄢).

- Zinfandel: also made with the following designations – Estate Vineyards, Freiberg Vineyards, P Coturri Family Vineyards, Sonoma Mountain and Views Land Vineyards.

Grebennikoff Vineyards

18470 Carriger Road, Sonoma, CA 95476
Tel:+1 707 939 0722

This 1.8 hectare domaine is owned by Nick Greben who is looking to develop his own range of wines. For the moment his wine grapes, CCOF-certified organic since 1996, along with grapes, soft fruit and vegetables, are sold on.

Kenwood Vineyards

9592 Sonoma Highway, PO Box 447, Kenwood, CA 95452

Tel:+1 707 833 5891

Fax:+1 707 833 1146

Email: kenwine@pacbell.net

Kenwood Vineyards will harvest the first grapes from its 46 hectares of CCOF-certified organic vineyards in 1999. These are found in southern Sonoma in Carneros, where Chardonnay performs elegantly, and in northern Sonoma near the Kenwood Winery. Other varieties to look for include Zinfandel, Sauvignon Blanc and Sangiovese. Kenwood gives a percentage of its waste winery water to a local privately owned composting company. This contracts with the county authorities to recycle municipal grass clippings, and the water is used to keep the compost moist.

Lisa's Vineyard

18655 Foss Hill Road, Calistoga, CA 94515

Tel:+1 707 942 1174

Fax:+1 707 942 1174

This domaine is located in Knights Valley AVA, in the hilliest part of northern Sonoma County. Owner Lisa Carr is a research physician, and has 4.5 hectares of vineyard, CCOF-certified organic since 1996. The Cabernet Sauvignon is sold to Fetzer Vineyards-Brown Forman Corporation for Bonterra.

Mark West Estate Vineyard & Winery

1531 Chablis Road, Healdsburg, CA 95448

Tel:+1 707 544 4813 (tasting room)

Fax:+1 707 836 0147

This estate consists of five CCOF-certified vineyards:

- Creekside Vineyard, contains Gewurztraminer, five hectares, planted 1974
- Le Beau Vineyard, contains Chardonnay (Wente clone), 13 hectares, planted 1974

- Ellis Vineyard, contains Pinot Noir, six hectares, planted 1974
- Gold Ridge Vineyards, contains Merlot, one hectare, planted 1991
- Sunrise Vineyard, contains Chardonnay, one hectare, planted 1990.

The owners, Associated Vintage Group, release a range of wines which are labelled as organically grown with origins in Chalk Hill AVA (bottling called Chardonnay Godwin) and Russian River Valley AVA (Sauvignon Blanc). The company also makes wine under contract for other grape suppliers ('custom winemaking'). Check with them for latest details on organic bottlings.

Topolos at Russian River Vineyards

5700 Gravestein Highway, Forestville, CA 95436
Tel:+1 707 887 1575/+1 800-Topolos (toll free)
Fax:+1 707 887 1399
Email: topolos@topolos.com or alibou@ix.netcom.com
Attractions: Russian River Vineyards Restaurant with on-site organic herb and vegetable gardens (reservations, tel: +1 707 887 1562)
Stockist: Bibendum

This vineyard and winery dates from 1963. Its current owners, a group headed by Michel Topolos, released their first vintage in 1978. Vineyards owned by Topolos run to 20 hectares and another 60 hectares are leased. A total of 26 hectares have been CCOF certified since 1990. Topolos uses some biodynamic treatments but has never had Demeter certification for any part of its vineyard. Total production is around 18,000 cases. Wines labelled or marketed as organic include:

- Alicante Bouschet: dry red, first made in 1980 and first labelled as organic in 1992. ⚑⚑⚑
- Chardonnay: dry white described as 'biodynamic but not certified'. For similar labelling see Robert Eden of Château Maris/Comté Cathare in Corbières, Midi, France (*page 117*). ⚑⚑⚑
- Sauvignon Blanc Sonoma Valley: certified organic in 1996 when sourced from a Valley of the Moon vineyard (not known whether owned or leased), 800 cases produced. ⚑⚑⚑

- Zinfandel Rossi Ranch: dry red, certified organic in 1992; in 1994 produced 1,700 cases. 🍾

Wild Hog Vineyard
PO Box 189, Cazadero, CA 95421
Tel:+1 707 847 3687
Email: wildhog@mcn.org

This domaine lies in the Sonoma Coast AVA, eight kilometres from the Pacific. Owners Daniel and Marion Schoenfeld farm 1.6 hectares of Pinot Noir and Zinfandel, CCOF certified organic since 1983. They buy in non-organic Zinfandel from two friends. Two wines are made: Pinot Noir, Wild Hog Vineyard (🍾) and Zinfandel, Wild Hog (🍾).

CENTRAL COAST

This covers the area between San Francisco south to Santa Barbara. The vineyards here proved a magnet for Philosophy graduates from universities in the San Francisco area in the 1960s who were looking for a change of direction. Allow plenty of extra time for vineyard visits, which can turn into mammoth discussions on the role of wine in man's spiritual evolution . . . The intellectual organic idealism found here is a contrast to the practical organic idealism of northern California, which attracted middle-class professionals in the 1960s who wanted to be hands-on farmers. Most of the vineyards cited here are located on hill sites above the Central Valley — a huge, flat, sun-baked hotplate kept cool by a million irrigation drippers. The best vineyards are around the Santa Cruz Mountains and in the Sierra Foothills: the area exploited during the 1849 Gold Rush when vineyards were planted to provide drink for thirsty miners.

Cattarin Vineyards
3545 Neal Road, Paradise, CA 95969
Tel:+1 530 872 3143

This small Sierra Foothills domaine is owned by Gino and Laura Cattarin. They have one hectare of vines, CCOF-certified organic since 1995. They grow and bottle Cabernet Sauvignon for dry red wines for private (i.e., their own) consumption, and the Native American variety Concord, which can be used to make jelly.

Donner Trail Fruit

PO Box 26, Chicago Park, CA 95712
Tel:+1 530 477 5992

This domaine lies on the western slope of the Sierra Foothills, 80kms from Sacramento, 160kms from Reno, off Interstate 80. It comprises 6.4 hectares of farmland which has been CCOF-certified organic since 1994. Owner George C. Bierwagen grows nectarines and peaches mostly, although there are 1.2 hectares of Pinot Noir, Chardonnay and Syrah wine grapes. These are managed by a third party under contract for a range of wines labelled as Nevada County Wine Guild. Contact Tony Norskog (Tel:+1 530 265 3662 for details). Note that part of this ranch comprises non-certified organic orchard.

Durney Vineyards (Heller Estate)

PO Box 999, Carmel, CA 93924 (mailing) or 69 West, Carmel Valley Road, Carmel Valley Village (tasting)
Tel:+1 408 659 6220/+1 800 625 8466 (free phone US)
Fax:+1 408 659 6226
Stockists : contact Durney Vineyards UK, PO Box 3660, London SW1Y 4AF. Tel:+44 171 930 9910; Fax:+44 171 930 6213

Durney Vineyards lies in the Carmel Valley AVA, around the Pacific Coast town of Carmel in Monterey County where Clint Eastwood was once mayor. Durney Vineyards is the oldest estate here, and is located on a hillside site in the Cachagua Valley ('hidden springs'). Formerly a cattle ranch, Durney Vineyards has expanded since it was founded in 1968 by a Los Angeles couple, Bill Durney and his screenwriter wife Dorothy. The estate passed from family ownership and since 1993 it has belonged to a group of European investors led by Gilbert Heller, a London-based banker. The vineyard has been certified by Organic Certifiers since 1999 and covers 48 hectares. The vines are irrigated (Monterey County was the first wine region in the west to depend entirely on irrigation) and are picked by hand. The first organic vintage will be 1999. Previous to this the most intense wines in the range are dry whites made from cooler climate varieties like German Riesling and Loire Chenin Blanc, which on the evidence of these wines appear better adapted to Carmel Valley's blustery conditions than Chardonnay. The red wines are made from Cabernet Sauvignon, Merlot and Pinot Noir. They are unsuitable for vegans and vegetarians because of egg white and gelatin fining.

Fitzpatrick Winery & Lodge/Famines End Farm

7740 Fairplay Road, Somerset, CA 95084
Tel:+1 209 245 3248/+1 800 245 9166
Fax:+1 916 620 6838
Email: brian@fitzpatrickwinery.com or fitzwine@footnet.com
Internet: fitzpatrickwinery.com
Accommodation: B&B (the 'lodge' of the title)
Tasting room: open Fridays through to Monday
Stockists: Chartrand Imports, Rockland (Maine); Boston Wine Co (Massachusetts); Organic Vintages (New York City/New Jersey); Apple a Day (Florida); Natural State Wines, Columbus (Ohio); Hart Distributing (North Carolina); Mountain Peoples (California)
Overall Price Rating: 🍾

Brian and Diana Fitzpatrick became vinegrowers in 1980 when the apples they were raising for hard cider had become uneconomic. This part of the Sierra Foothills had no water subsidy programme so water had to be provided expensively from a well. Wine grapes need less water than apples and soon the wines made from them began winning awards at county fairs. There are now two vineyards. One covers 16 hectares and is CCOF certified. The other covers nearly seven hectares and is not certified.

There are 11 grape varieties in all: Chardonnay and Sauvignon Blanc for white wines; and Cabernet Sauvignon, Grenache, Cinsault, Syrah, Merlot, Nebbiolo and Sangiovese for reds. Most of the grapes fermented here under the Fitzpatrick or Famines End label, however, are bought in. The wines are bottled with untreated corks in recycled glass. Levels of total sulphur dioxide preservative are low (typically below 30 ppm). Brian Fitzpatrick was the founding member of California Certified Organic Farmers and was a unifying voice in the organic wine movement in this State during the battle with the Federal Government in 1998 over the revised production standards for organic growers (*see above, page 292*).

Four Gates Vineyards
503 Happy Valley Road, Santa Cruz, CA 950 65
Tel:+1 831 426 0845

This Santa Cruz Mountains domaine is owned by Bruce Cantz, and has 1.6 hectares of vineyard, CCOF certified since 1995. All of the grapes are sold.

Hallcrest/Organic Wine Works
at Hallcrest Vineyards Inc, 379 Felton Empire Road, Felton, CA 95018
Tel:+1 408 335 4441/+1 800 699 9463 (toll free)
Internet: WebWinery.com/Hallcrest
Stockist: Golden Valley (USA)

Organic Wine Works is located 80kms south of San Francisco amongst forest, meadow and scrub in the Santa Cruz Mountains. It was set up in 1989 by John C. Schumacher as a label for the first certified organic US wines, i.e., made from organic grapes, without the addition of sulphur dioxide preservative (sulphites). Wines containing sulphites are labelled Hallcrest Vineyards or under a more minor second label, St Croix. The wines from all three labels are suitable for vegans. Most of the grapes are bought in from CCOF-certified sources, including Sogomonian Farm (see below), although Organic Wine Works has 0.4 hectares of CCOF-certified vines (plus 1.6 hectares of non-certified vines as well). Schumacher enjoys his reputation for being a rebel in the wine industry. He made his first wine at the age of 13 when his parents went on vacation and left some plums on the tree.

Ponderosa Vineyards

13570 North Ponderosa Way, Nevada City, CA 95959

Tel:+1 530 272 5580

This Sierra Foothills domaine comprises four hectares of organic vineyard, which has been CCOF certified since 1994. Owners Paul and Kelly Manuel have sold their Cabernet Sauvignon to Fetzer Vineyards-Brown Forman Corporation for Bonterra, but now sell to other producers.

LaRocca Vineyards

PO Box 541, Forest Ranch, CA 95942

Tel:+1 530 899 9463/+1 800 808 9463 (toll free)

Fax:+1 530 894 7268

Email: phil@laroccavineyards.com

Internet: laroccavineyards.com

Overall Price Rating: 🍾

LaRocca makes all its wines from its own CCOF-certified grapes. Owner Phil la Rocca has 97 hectares of his own grapes to work with. Some are sold to Fetzer Vineyards-Brown Forman Corporation, Frey Vineyards and Organic Wine Works amongst others. La Rocca was born in the USA to Sicilian parents. His grandmother and his father made wine for the rest of the family, which consumed 18 litres a week. La Rocca farmed apples originally, but the orchards he leased were given over to housing. His vineyards are in two locations. One at Forest Ranch (45 hectares) on high mountain foothills marks the point where the Cascades end and the Sierra Nevada ranges begins. The other, mainly white wine vineyard is lower lying, in Sutter County on the Sutter Bute Mountain Range.

La Rocca was one of the first to promote clover as a cover crop for vineyards on mountainous elevations. The wines are made without sulphur dioxide preservatives (sulphites). Styles made include Cabernet Sauvignon, Lush Zinfandel, White Cabernet Sauvignon, Chardonnay and Vino di Tavola Blanco. La Rocca was President of CCOF in 1998 when the United States Department of Agriculture (USDA) proposed downgrading the US organic standard (see above).

Silver Mountain Vineyards

PO Box 3636, Santa Cruz, CA 95063-3636

Tel:+1 408 353 2278

This Santa Cruz Mountains domaine is owned by Jerold O'Brien, who has 5.4 hectares of vineyard, CCOF certified since 1992.

Soghomonian Farm

8624 S Chestnut, Fresno, CA 93725

Tel:+1 559 834 2772

Fax:+1 559 834 3212

This domaine is owned by Joe Soghomonian, who farms 190 hectares. Juice grapes, wine grapes (French Colombard, Grenache, Carignan), table grapes and raisin grapes are grown, and all are CCOF-certified organic. Soghomonian sells his organic wine grapes to Hallcrest for the Organic Wine Works label.

Wente Bros.

5565 Tesla Road, Livermore, CA 94550

Tel:+1 510 447 3603

Wente is the largest vineyard owner and biggest producer in the Livermore Valley, which forms the foothills of the coastal range east of San Francisco. Wente has an annual output of half a million cases. The company is family owned and has farmed 72.6 hectares of wine grapes and olives according to CCOF norms since 1991. Non-certified grapes are bought in (from Arroyo Seco AVA to provide Pinot Noir and Chardonnay for sparkling wines). Check with the winery for wines labelled as 'made from certified organic grapes' or 'organic wine' if bottled with no added sulphur.

CALIFORNIA: USEFUL ADDRESSES

Californians for Alternatives to Toxics

PO Box 981, Glen Ellen, CA 95442

Tel:+1 707 939 3893

Internet: http://www.mapcruzin.com/cats.

History: founded in 1982 by community groups throughout Northern California to serve as a resource centre for information and action about hazardous chemicals, especially pesticides, and to promote alternatives to their use

Status: a non-profit, 501(c)(3) organization (under California State law)

Funding: by private donations which are tax deductible

Publications: *Time for a Change: Pesticides and Wine Grapes in Sonoma and Napa Counties, California*, 42 pages, $7. This is the first publication to detail pesticide use, farm by farm, for one crop in this state.

New York State

New York State promotes its $40 million a year wine industry with the line 'Uncork New York', decidedly bad advice to heed because most of the wines exported to the UK appear to be unconvincing imitations of Bordeaux and Burgundy, tasting of winemaking rather than of grape. The State's one certified organic producer, Silver Thread Vineyard, provides an exception to this, and is found in the Finger Lakes region.

The Finger Lakes wine region accounts for 85 per cent of New York State's production. It lies in up-state New York around 11 lakes of glacial origin. The four main ones are Keuka, Cayuga, Canandaigua and Seneca. Finger Lakes is home to an influential cooperative group of organic fruit and vegetable farmers that sells produce direct via its own market in Ithaca. This is strategically located to appeal to right-minded students of nearby Cornell University.

NORTH EAST ORGANIC FARMERS ASSOCIATION NEW YORK (NOFA)

NOFA members must use separate equipment for organic and non-organic farming activities. This means that wine growers who also grow another, non-organic crop, such as apples for example, must purchase two sets of spray machinery. Richard Figiel of Silver Thread Vineyard (below) believes that NOFA's policy is prohibitive in areas such as up-state New York, where mixed farming predominates and where wine may be only one of a number of agricultural cash crops grown by a single farmer. The costs of doubling up on farm machinery are excluding several mixed farmers who would like to convert their parcels of vines to organic farming from the NOFA certified programme. The most significant grower for the future appears to be Steven Shaw who has 40 acres of European vines above Lake Keuka in conversion to organic methods under NOFA.

Silver Thread Vineyard

1401 Caywood Road, Caywood, NY 14860

Tel:+1 607 582 6116

Sales: from the cellar door or to local restaurants

Visits: weekends and holidays (by appointment)

Silver Thread Vineyard lies on the east bank of Seneca Lake between the towns of Valois and Caywood. It has been certified organic by the North East Organic Farmers Association (NOFA – see above) since 1992. Silver Thread's owner, Richard Figiel, was born in New York City and worked as a book and magazine editor. He came to Finger Lakes to research an article on its wine, and stayed after purchasing Silver Thread – at the time an abandoned vineyard containing a red-pink skinned American vine called Catawba (in the 18th century it was planted with peach trees). Figiel replanted five acres with Chardonnay, Pinot Noir and Riesling, and total production now amounts to 9,000 litres out of an annual total for New York State of 94.6 million litres (25 million US gallons). The vines overlook the deepest part of Lake Seneca (200 feet below sea level) where the tempering influence of the water is most strong. Without this these European vines would struggle to survive New York State's unforgiving cycle of blistering, humid summers and deep, frozen winters. Even then the vines survive only if their heads are buried under protective earth during winter to protect them from the huge, sudden and fatal changes in temperature.

Figiel places great emphasis on keeping the vines in a sanitary state. This sounds clinical but in this climate a small effort gets a big result and involves nothing more serious than rigorous application of common sense practices. In winter the prunings which fall to the ground are covered quickly with ploughed soil to prevent the spores of fungal diseases (like Black Rot) from becoming established in the dead wood as it rots down. In spring the soil is tilled down, revealing the prunings which can then be chopped. This 'cover and stir' method prevents the fungal disease spores from jumping up onto the vine later and drastically reduces spray treatments. Figiel made his first estate-grown wine (in carbouys) in 1985 and successfully applied for his licence to bottle wine in 1991. His winery is made of local materials, mainly wood, like Hainle's (see British Columbia, *page 354*). All the wines are picked by hand and are bottled with natural, unbleached corks. No refrigeration, chemical additives or processing aids (except sulfites and filtration) are used. These are New York's to uncork:

- 'Medley': an attractive, slightly aromatic, medium dry white blend of Riesling and Chardonnay, proving popular with Silver Thread's clientele. ▮

- Dry Riesling: dry white wine; a unique interpretation of Riesling from the kind of extreme climate this variety loves, made from grapes pressed as whole clusters to maximize finesse and fermented with a Champagne yeast (unfortunately); suitable for vegetarians and vegans. The 1993 vintage matured at six years (i.e., in 1999); the 1994 vintage is fading; the 1997 has discreet and fine fruit, and will be ready between 2000 and 2008. ▮▮

- Semi-sweet Riesling: off-dry white wine with satisfying fruit, equivalent to a late picked German Riesling (or 'spätlese'); suitable for vegetarians and vegans. ▮

- Chardonnay: dry white wine, subtle, refreshing, earthy and balanced; pressed like the Rieslings above and fermented in new and used American oak barrels. Partial or complete malolactic fermentation lowers the level of acidity in the wine naturally; suitable for vegetarians and vegans. The 1995 vintage fermented with wild yeast causing some acetic problems; the 1996 produced an aromatic wine in a cool year; 1997 dispays a lovely integration of rich citrus fruit, earth and fine toasty oak. ▮▮

- Pinot Noir: red wine, first made in 1993 (previous to this the grapes were sold). The 1994 vintage was fermented with French yeast, and smells of Clos Vougeot in Burgundy. The 1995 gets its 'barnyardy' smell from a natural fermentation – has a moderate cherry colour, lovely fruit and tannin in the background; suitable for vegetarians and vegans. The 1996 fermented with wild yeast again and received little (if any) addition of sulphur dioxide – as a result the wine aged quickly. The 1997 matured in American oak barrels. ▮▮▮

Four Chimneys Farm Winery

Road 1, 211 Hall Road, Himrod, NY 14842

Tel:+1 607 243 7502

Four Chimneys Farm Winery is located on Lake Seneca and is run by Walter Petersen as part of a family trust. The vineyard is certified organic by NOFA but the vines planted are hybrids and American varieties, unlike Silver Thread where only varieties from the European species of vine like Pinot Noir and Chardonnay are planted. Four Chimneys winemaker Scott Smith produces a range of bone dry red and white wines, semi-dry wines and grape and fruit wines. The top seller is Coronation, a bone dry sparkling wine made partly from Delaware (🍾).

Swedish Hill Vineyard

4565 Rt. 414, Romulus, NY 14541

Tel:+1 315 549 8326

Fax:+1 315 549 8477

Email: swedishhill@flare.net

Internet: www.fingerlakes.net/swedishhill

Swedish Hill Vineyard is located on another of the Finger Lakes, Cayuga. It purchases certified organic grapes of the American vine species (Deleware variety) for its Swedish Hill sparkling wine (🍾).

Other growers

Other growers producing certified organic grapes for sale to be made by others into (grape) wines, fruit wines or jellies include Ken Farnan at Buzzard Crest Vineyard and Joseph Ottati of Glendale Farm.

Cultivated vineyards in Oregon date from mid-19th century gold rushes that brought thirsty miners north. The influence of foreign settlement is still felt today, as Oregon's modern wine estates are as often as not run by immigrant Californians as native Oregonians. The fervour with which Californians have adopted organic vineyard practices has not yet manifested itself so fiercely here though. Even though the quality of grapes produced by the State's three certified organic growers (Brick House Vineyards, Cattrall Brothers Vineyards and Cooper Mountain) proves such farming methods are economically successful, grapes bearing organic certification are acknowledged rather than revered by the rest of the winemaking community.

Growing grapes using organic or biodynamic methods is much more of a challenge in Oregon than in either neighbouring Washington State or California because the vineyards are exposed to the direct influence of the Pacific Ocean. The ocean air and the warmer winters it brings helps the spores of vine fungal diseases to over-winter in the ground, ready to jump up onto the vine once its foliage starts to grow during summer. The signal for this is usually cloud cover from the ocean that produces the shade and humidity which mildew thrives on.

OREGON CERTIFICATION BODY

Oregon Tilth Inc is the main certification body for organic farmers in the state of Oregon, and is accredited by IFOAM. The standards it sets for vineyards and winemaking are similar to those adopted by California Certified Organic Farmers (CCOF). It was founded in the 1970s by a group of college graduates associated with Marcus Whitman College in Walla Walla in southern Oregon. Initially headed by a landowner called Woody Derryckx, Oregon Tilth worked with farmers supplying natural foods to local health food stores. (Tilth is the word given to the texture of topsoil after it has been ploughed – hence the expression 'to a fine tilth'.) The address is:

Oregon Tilth Inc
1860 Hawthorne NE, Suite 200, Salem, OR 97303
Tel:+1 503 378 0690
Fax:+1 503 378 0809
Email: organic@tilth.org

LEISA – LOW EXTERNAL INPUT SUSTAINABLE AGRICULTURE IN OREGON

Oregon's Low External Input Sustainable Agriculture programmes are run in conjunction with the State Department of Agriculture and work on a points system: points are deducted every time sulphur is sprayed in the vineyard to counter powdery mildew. In the same way, points are gained for the number of species of weeds remaining between the vine rows after herbicides (weed-killers) are applied to encourages more moderate doses. LEISA's adherents say the system helps awareness of organic practices and reduces negativity between organic and non-organic growers. The benefits of LEISA in Oregon are being studied by the Department of Horticulture at the State University of Oregon at Corvalis. (See also the KIP programme in Austria, *page 179.*)

Willamette Valley AVA

The Willamette Valley AVA is home to the only certified organic growers in the state. It comprises two-thirds of the State's total vineyard of 2,200 hectares and rolls for nearly 200 miles directly south of the city of Portland. Climatic conditions in Oregon are among the most suitable in the New World for growing the Pinot Noir variety. As in Burgundy the most complex red wines are produced when the Pinot grapes are able to ripen on the vine late into the season. Here this is possible, whereas in Washington State and California generally the heat generates a degree of over-ripeness in the fruit which causes it to become banal. So synonymous has the Willamette Valley become with American Pinot Noir that the following annual events are organized:

- the Pinot Noir Conference in McMinnville (July)
- the Yamhill County Wine Country Thanksgiving (November).

As regards pronounciation 'it's Willamette, damn it', as one native wine-maker was heard to rhyme.

Amity Vineyards

18150 Amity Vineyards Road SE, Amity, OR 97101
Tel:+1 503 835 2362
Email: amity@macnet.com

This Willamette Valley domaine is owned by Myron Redford and was one of Oregon's pioneering wineries. A wine labelled Eco Wine is produced from certified organic Pinot Noir grapes purchased from Cattrall Brothers Vineyards (see below). The wine is made without the addition of sulpher dioxide (sulfites) (♨).

Archery Summit

18599 NE, Archery Summit Road, Dayton, OR 97115
Tel:+1 503 864 4300
Email: archerysummit@onlinemac.com

This domaine is owned by Gary and Michelle Andrus, co-owners of Pine Ridge in California's Napa Valley (*page 317*). Archery Summit purchased certified organic Pinot Noir grapes grown by Brick House Vineyards (below) from 1993 until 1997, but these were blended with non-organic grapes, in contrast to the approach taken by Cameron and St Innocent (see below).

Brick House Vineyards

18200 Lewis Rogers Lane
Newberg, OR 97132
Sales: wines sold on allocation
Overall Price Rating: ♨

Brick House Vineyards was planted in 1989 and comprises nine hectares of Pinot Noir and Gamay Noir à Jus Blanc, plus a little Chardonnay, on high rolling hills known as Ribbon Ridge. The vines have been certified organic by Oregon Tilth Inc since 1990. Brick House grapes are eagerly bought by other Willamette Valley winemakers each year. Two of these estates, Cameron Winery and St Innocent, keep the purchased Brick House grapes separate from their own to make 'organic' bottlings (see below). Brick House's owner Doug Tunnell keeps the rest. A native to this part of Oregon Tunnell spent most of his working life travelling the world's news hotspots as a reporter for the American television network CBS. Brick House wines sell on allocation and for higher than average prices, helped no doubt by Tunnell's higher than average media profile. However it seems that here the crop, rather than the reputation of the person who grows it, is paramount.

- Chardonnay, Brick House Vineyards: dry white wine that is enriched by being left on fine lees in cask.
- Clos Ladybug, Brick House Vineyards: dry red wine, made from Gamay Noir à Jus Blanc (the Beaujolas grape); shows clear ripe cherry fruit which is ideal for a harvest lunch.
- Pinot Noir, Brick House Vineyards: dry red, fermented in stainless steel, oak aged, the junior partner to the wine below.
- Pinot Noir, Brick House Vineyards, Cuvée du Tonnelier: dry red, made from estate-grown certified organic Pinot Noir grapes. The grapes are put by hand into the tanks with only a gentle crushing, with some stems. Slow fermentation precedes ageing in barrels made of Oregon oak. The effect of the wood ageing is to temper the fierceness of the tannin which Pinot Noir can manifest when grown in the New World in dry-farmed vineyards (i.e., without irrigation as is the case at Brick House). The result is a wine showing generous red and black fruit, thick tannin and a fine perfume.

Cameron Winery
8200 Worden Hill Road, Dundee, OR 97115
Tel:+1 503 538 0336
Fax:+1 503 538 0336
Overall Price Rating: 🍶🍶🍶

Cameron resembles a number of the leading boutique Willamette Valley vineyards and wineries founded during the mid-1980s in that they have

Californian rather than Oregonian roots. This is true of two of Cameron's three founding families for example, the Pauls, the Waynes and the Dochezs. Cameron's current winemaker and one of its co-founders is John Paul. A former marine biologist Paul spent his first 30 years immersed in water and the last 20 involved in wine. Cameron buys in most of its grapes, including certified organic grapes from Brick House Vineyards. These are kept separate for an organic bottling (see below). Cameron's own small vineyard is managed according to a low external chemical input, sustainable programme or LEISA (see above). Such an approach, Cameron's owners believe, 'teaches better vineyard practice and is not so exclusive as organic farming'.

● Cameron Vineyards Brick House Pinot Noir: dry red, made from certified organic Pinot Noir grapes grown by and purchased from Doug Tunnell (see above); the 1996 vintage smells floral, of peonies, and displays elegant fruit and tannin. The wine was bottled without the addition of sulfites. During fermentation the juice is run off the Pinot Noir skins and into barrel before all the sugar is converted to alcohol. A less forceful contrast to the Pinot Noir made at Brick House.

Cattrall Brothers Vineyards
7320 SE Sartore Road, Amity, OR 97101
Tel:+1 503 835 2144
Fax:+1 503 835 1613
Email: juliac@viclink.com

This Willamette Valley domaine comprises 3.2 hectares and was certified organic by Oregon Tilth Inc in 1999. It was first certified organic in the 1980s. It dropped out of the Orgeon Tilth programme in the late 1980s, and again in the 1990s, although the owners here, Bill and Tom Cattrall, maintain organic practices have always been adhered to. The implication is that the financial cost of maintaining certification has at times proved prohibitive. This is understandable because the brothers sell all of their grapes – allowing other winemakers to collect the premium for wine sold as 'made from organically grown grapes'. The two varieties here are Pinot Noir for red and Pinot Gris for white. In 1998 the Pinot Noir was sold to Amity Vineyards, and the Pinot Gris to Château Lorane.

Château Lorane

27415 Suislaw River Road, Lorane, OR 97451

Tel:+1 541 942 5830

This domaine was founded in 1992 by Lindy Kaster. It comprises 12 hectares. In 1998 certified organic Pinot Gris grapes were purchased from Cattrall Brothers Vineyards, but these appear to have been mixed with non-certified organic grapes.

Cooper Mountain Vineyards & Winery

9480 SW Grabhorn Road, Beaverton, OR 97007

Tel:+1 503 649 0027

Tours: by appointment

Cooper Mountain Vineyard lies on an extinct volcano and was a stud farm until 1978 when its current owner, Dr Robert J Gross, planted it as a vineyard. It has been certified organic since 1998 by Oregon Tilth Inc and is also in line to become the State's first Demeter-certified biodynamic vineyard (in 2000). Dr Gross describes biodynamics as 'taking organics and making it real'.

- Cuvée Tradition Brut Méthode Champenoise: dry white sparkling wine made by the traditional method; pneumatic press used to extract the grape juice with the minimum of grape solids; clean, concentrated. ▮▮▮
- Chardonnay: dry full white (▮▮▮), also made in an oak barrel fermented (▮▮▮▮) and aged 'Reserve' style (▮▮▮).
- Pinot Gris: dry full white; nutty, potentially overpowering, made from arguably Oregon's most successful white grape. ▮▮
- Pinot Noir: dry red, the junior version of the wine immediately below. ▮▮▮
- Pinot Noir Reserve: dry red; smells both of the soil (mushrooms) and of the grape variety (sous-bois), aromas which New World wine in general and New World Pinot Noirs in particular find notoriously difficult to manifest. ▮▮▮

St Innocent

1360 Tandem Ave NE, Salem, OR 97303

Tel:+1 503 378 1526

Fax:+1 503 378 1041

Sales: via the winery's own shop – Oregon Wines on Broadway, Morgans Alley, 515 SW Broadway, Portland

Tours: on Memorial Day and Thanksgiving weekends, or by prior appointment

Overall Price Rating: 🍶

St Innocent produces one red wine from certified organic Pinot Noir grown by Brick House Vineyards (see above). St Innocent pays more dollars for organic grapes from Brick House than it does for those from any other grape supplier. The St Innocent winery is located in a lot on a business park in downtown Salem, Oregon's State capital. All of the wines are made from purchased grapes.

- St Innocent Pinot Noir Brick House Vineyards: dry red, made from certified organic Pinot Noir grapes purchased from Doug Tunnell (see above). Bottled without added sulphur dioxide. Offers broad appeal without the power of Brick House or the charm of Cameron Vineyards' Pinot Noir. Suitable for vegans.

Washington State

Washington State is the second biggest wine producer in the United States. Washington State's certification programme is similar to California's CCOF but is overseen by Washington State Department of Agriculture. The State's two certified organic growers lie at different ends of the organic production spectrum, and opposite geographical ends of the state.

Columbia Valley AVA

Washington State relies on the Columbia Valley AVA for 99 per cent of its wine production. The region runs parallel with the Pacific Ocean but is shielded from its moisture by hills. As a result Columbia Valley is cloud-less and would have remained a dustbowl but for the arrival of irrigation in the form of New Deal dam projects in the 1930s. Columbia Valley's great natural advantage as a wine producer is that even though it is blis-teringly hot here during daytime, at night it is positively cold. Unlike in California there are no clouds from the Pacific to trap heat rising off the land at night. This means that Washington grapes ripen and keep their acids, while Californian grapes ripen but don't always keep enough acid and need to have some added. Natural acid wines seem to be the most versatile with our modern love of bright food.

Badger Mountain Vineyard & Powers Winery

1106 S Jurupa Street, Kennewick, WA 99337-1001
Tel:+1 509 627 4986
Fax:+1 509 627 2071
Internet: www.BadgerMtnVineyard.com.
Tasting Room: open daily 1000–1700
Stockists: Liberty Wine Merchants (Canada); Chartrand Imports (USA); Organic Vintages (New York)

Badger Mountain Vineyard is the oldest and largest certified organic vineyard in Washington State. It covers 76 acres in southern Washington, on south facing slopes on the outskirts of the town of Kennewick. Flanked in parts by houses with garages and gardens front and back, Badger Mountain's situation contrasts with most Columbia Valley vineyards further north, which occupy a Mars-like landscape. Badger Mountain was converted to organic management after chemical spray drift from fruit orchards on a neighbouring farm adversely affected the health of the owner's wife in 1989. One change here since is that cutworms (caterpillars) which eat emergent vine buds in spring are removed by physical rather than chemical means – the leaf eaters are blown from the emerging vine shoots by a fan in a converted vineyard sulphur duster dragged between the rows by a tractor (the sulphur is dusted to treat powdery mildew or oidium).

These certified organic grapes are fermented and bottled under the Badger Mountain Vineyard label and make up 40 per cent of the total 25,000-case production here. The Badger Mountain Vineyard organic range is an appealing one geared to the mainstream. Tropical flavours feature in all of the white wines with sometimes a little sweetness. The red wines are marked by soft rich fruits and well-judged tannin. The wines are:

- 'Sevé', Badger Mountain Vineyard, Columbia Valley AVA: white wine, off-dry, light, tropical blend of two-thirds Sémillon, one-third Chenin Blanc, with small amounts of Gewurztraminer and Riesling. ▮
- 'Mountain Blush', Badger Mountain Vineyards, Columbia Valley AVA: pink wine, off-dry, light, blend of Gewurztraminer seasoned with Cabernet Franc. ▮▮
- Johannisberg Riesling, Badger Mountain Vineyards, Columbia Valley AVA: white wine with light sweetness, made from potentially the finest white grape variety in southern Washington. ▮▮
- Johannisberg Riesling No Added Sulfites, Badger Mountain Vineyards, Columbia Valley AVA: white wine with light sweetness. Riesling oxidizes with difficulty, and so is well suited to winemaking without sulfites (sulphur dioxide preservative). ▮▮
- Chardonnay, Badger Mountain Vineyards, Columbia Valley AVA: white wine, dry, lightly oaky, full-bodied and clean. ▮▮

- Chardonnay No Added Sulfites, Badger Mountain Vineyards, Columbia Valley AVA: white wine, dry, lightly oaky, full bodied; first made in 1995; darker in colour than the Chardonnay above, takes longer to open in the glass but has clearer flavour. 🍾
- Cabernet Franc, Badger Mountain Vineyards, Columbia Valley AVA: dry red. Of the eight European grape varieties planted at Badger Mountain, perhaps the most valuable one day will be the 1.2 hectares of Cabernet Franc. This red variety was planted in 1988, but already it has shown its hardiness against cold, surviving the harsh winter of 1996 when more established European varieties (like Sauvignon Blanc) failed. 🍾🍾
- Cabernet/Merlot, Badger Mountain Vineyards, Columbia Valley AVA: dry red, blend of Cabernet Franc and Merlot. 🍾🍾
- Merlot, Badger Mountain Vineyards, Columbia Valley AVA: dry red, made from Washington's most fashionable grape variety in the 1990s. 🍾

The Powers family and their associates also make wines from non-certified organic grapes under the 'Powers Winery' label in the same cellar as the organic grapes for the Badger Mountain Wines.

Washington State AVA

All wine producers in Washington State outside the Columbia Valley have the right to the Washington State AVA.

China Bend Vineyard & Winery

3596 Northport Flatcreek Rd., Kettle Falls, WA 99141
Tel:+1 509 732 6123
Fax:+1 509 732 1401
Internet: www.chinabend.com
Tours: by appointment
Tasting room: open daily

China Bend Vineyard & Winery lies close to the British Columbia border in north-eastern Washington, and is the most northerly vineyard in the US. It covers 2.6 hectares of virgin pasture in pine woodland on Lake

Roosevelt, the reservoir created by the Coulee Dam. China Bend's owner, Bart Alexander, has planted 70 different grape varieties in an effort to find out which ones work best here. They are watered by the irrigation system erected by Alexander in the mid-1980s and are protected from the nearby bears by a deer fence. China Bend comfortably sells its entire 750-case production of hand-made wines each year, mainly to those who come to sail on the lake. The wines express something of the variety of small production, boutique winemaking unique to North America. They are suitable for vegetarians and vegans. From 1995 they have been made without the addition of sulphur dioxide preservative (sulfites).

- Aurora, Washington State AVA: medium sweet white, musk-like, made from a winter hardy hybrid grape variety which is set to replace European varieties like Riesling (from Germany) and Sémillon (from France). These varieties fail to ripen here. ♠♠
- Victory White, Washington State AVA: full white wine made from a blend of Siegerrebe, an early ripening white German crossing, and the hybrid Aurora (see above). ♠♠
- Maréchal Foch, Washington State AVA: thick, meaty red with no particular nuance. Thrives in here in Lake Roosevelt which is prone to bitter winters and desert summers and where no particular nuance is needed. 150 cases made in a Reserve style for the first time in 1997. ♠♠♠

China Bend's success has inspired two others to plant organic vineyards in the vicinity: Stan Sutton of Twin Eagle half a mile away, and Dilbert Young of Crown Creek five miles away. Both are in conversion to organic farming under the State's certified programme.

US BIODYNAMIC BODIES
The Demeter Association, Inc.
Britt Road, Aurora, NY 13026
Tel:+1 315 364 5617
Fax:+1 315 364 5224

The Demeter Association, Inc. is the body responsible for certifying biodynamic vineyards.

The Biodynamic Farming and Gardening Association, Inc. (BDA)

PO Box 29135, San Francisco, CA 94129-0135
Tel:+1 415 561 7797
Fax:+1 415 561 7796

This non-profit making body was founded in 1938 and is open to the public. It supports regional, grassroots membership associations and funds more formal research and training institutions, including the Josephine Porter Institute (below) and the Demeter Association. Its publications include: 'Biodynamics, Farming and Gardening in the 21st Century' – a bi-monthly journal and America's oldest ecological farming and gardening magazine, which contains profiles of biodynamic producers. Also, 'Stella Natura', the American seedling calendar that indicates the right days for planting, ploughing, treating and picking according to planetary and natural cycles. (See Appendix 3 for more information about biodynamic theories and principles.)

Josephine Porter Institute for Applied Biodynamics, Inc.

PO Box 133, Woolwine, VA 24185-0133
Tel:+1 540 930 2463
Fax:+1 540 930 2463

Produces and distributes biodynamic preparations throughout North America.

Canada

Canada has two main wine producing provinces, Ontario on the east coast and British Columbia on the west. Ontario lacks a certified organic vineyard, partly because the growing of wine grapes by organic means is made difficult by the humid conditions. This means Canada's certified organic vineyards and wine producers are found in the central part of the province of British Columbia, in the Okanagan Valley. Only 30 years ago Canada produced sweet, fizzy fruit-flavoured wines with names like Pussycat and Pink Flamingo, to copy what was then in vogue in the United States. Now British Columbia's organic winemakers are among those making Canada's reputation for Chardonnay, Riesling and Pinot Noir wines in a more classic, European style.

Okanagan's dry climate suits organic growing but necessitates irrigation. Run-off from this is causing Lake Okanagan a serious nitrate problem, threatening the local Kamloops trout. Okanagan's accredited organic vineyards have their water quality tested every five years in order to monitor compliance with minimum national guidelines.

ORGANIC AND GENERAL LABEL TERMS

- VQA: stands for Vintners Quality Alliance, similar to the French Appellation Contrôlée.
- COABC: stands for Certified Organic Associations of British Columbia, the national organic certification body for wine production, overseeing organic accreditors like SOOPA (below). Its address is:

COABC
PO Box 9120
Stn Prov Govt. Victoria, BC V8W 9B4
Tel:+1 250 356 6660
Fax:+1 250 356 2949

- SOOPA: stands for Similkameen Okanagan Organic Producers Association, an accreditation body to which the grape producers listed below belong.

OKANAGAN VALLEY, BC

The Okanagan Valley is the northernmost desert viticulture region in the world (with 2,000 hours' annual sunshine). It produces 95 per cent of British Columbia's wine and is nicknamed 'Napa Valley North'. Since 1995 a growing number of organic vineyards have appeared here, on the mountainous foothills overlooking Lake Okanagan.

Hans and Christine Buchler

RR 2, Oliver, BC V0H 1J0
Tel:+1 250 498 2786

The Buchler vineyard covers eight hectares in the mountains above the town of Oliver in south central Okanagan and was established in 1981 by Hans Buchler. His appetite for travel led him to British Columbia from his father-in-law's mixed farm (orchards and vines) near Morges in Switzerland. Buchler does all the farming by hand on his own, leaving his Swiss wife Christine (a nurse) to worry about bears – small brown bears specifically. These damage the vines, and eat the fruit, but most of all could maul her husband. Nevertheless Hans still relies on his wits, rather than the protection of a shot gun and armour plated car, during the short morning walk from log cabin to vineyard.

The vines here have been certified organic by SOOPA/COABC since 1995, but all the grapes are sold by the Buchlers to wineries who blend them with non-organic ones. 'It's a shame to blend them but it doesn't mean the grapes are any less good' they say. Their proof is their own wine, made from a tiny quantity of grapes which are left back each year and then fermented. Only a few cases of these wines are made each year and they are not for commercial sale:

- Chardonnay: dry white, smells of earth, minerals and ripe green fruits, delicious and wholesome – what all white Burgundies could taste like if they tried.

- Maréchal Foch: dry thick red, smells of over-ripe forest fruit, the taste is simple, agreeable, no astringency but lots of extract and a long, satisfying aftertaste. Made from a winter-hardy hybrid (see also China Bend Vineyard and Winery just over the US/Canada border in northern Washington State for other wines made from this same grape).

Hainle Vineyards Estate Winery Ltd

5355 Trepanier Bench Road, RR #2, S27A, C6, Peachland, British Columbia V0H 1X0 (mailing Box 650)

Tel:+1 250 767 2525

Fax:+1 250 767 2543

Email: sandra@hainle.com or tilman@hainle.com

Internet: www.hainle.com (the most informative web-site mentioned in this book by a considerable distance)

Visitors: visitors welcome; the winery has its own restaurant with locally grown produce, mostly organic (food recommendations with these wines courtesy of Hainle chef David Forestell)

Stockists: wines available direct from the winery shop and via mail order anywhere in Canada. For local stockists see Appendix 1.

Overall Price Rating: ♙♙

Hainle Vineyards lies on the west of Lake Okanagan and has been certified organic since 1995. It was founded in the 1970s by a German, Walter Hainle (1915–1995), who was a devotee of fully fermented, dry white wines rather than of the fruity sweet Germanic imitations like Pink Flamingo (see above) then favoured by Canada's modern vineyard pioneers. Walter's German-born son Tilman now runs the domaine with his wife Sandra. The Hainle winery must produce 10,000 gallons (15,000 litres) of wine per annum to meet the conditions of their winery licence. To do this, organic grapes grown in Hainle's own 7.5 hectare vineyard are supplemented by grapes which are purchased from both organic (Harbeck) and non-organic (Holt) growers in the Okanagan. The Hainles are on course for 100 per cent organic sourcing but, in the interim, keep their organic and non-organic grapes separate.

- Bibendum Rosé, VQA: dry pink wine, made from certified organic grapes for first time in 1997 when it contained 100 per cent Merlot (previously Pinot Noir). The juice is run off the skins after three days of fermentation and into stainless steel tanks to leave crisp, delicate fruit (150 cases made).
- Bibendum White, VQA: dry white, full-bodied and full flavoured for what is the junior white wine in the range.
- Hainle Vineyards, Chardonnay, VQA: dry white. The 1996 vintage was lost due to vandalism (someone opened the tap on an outside tank during the night). Try with onion, garlic, smoky and herb flavoured foods.
- Hainle Vineyards, Kerner: dry white, similar to that once made by Chudleigh Vineyard in England, but a shade drier. The Hainle chef recommends this with curry and other Asian flavours.
- Hainle Vineyards, Pinot Blanc, Elizabeth's Vineyard, VQA: dry white, fermented in stainless steel, subdued, crisp nose and a rich taste; the certified organic grapes for this wine are sourced from Elizabeth Harbeck's vineyard in the Okanagan. Try with a green and yellow bean salad.
- Hainle Vineyards, Pinot Gris, VQA: dry white, picks up richness and texture from ageing on the fine yeast lees left after fermentation.
- Hainle Vineyards, Riesling, VQA: dry white which shows the elegance and character befitting older vines (the oldest here date from the early 1970s and were brought from the Geisenheim Institute in Germany – the intellectual if not spiritual home of this grape variety). Hainle's example shows it to be an ideal grape for the Okanagan. Oilier or brinier seafoods (e.g., fresh oysters, smoked salmon) suit this bone dry style of Riesling.
- Hainle Vineyards, Traminer, VQA: dry white, 50 cl bottles (the 1996 vintage produced 1,320 of them). The grapes are crushed and the juice is left on the skins overnight. This softens the wine and gives it flavour and body, although it needs a couple of years' ageing in bottle for this to become apparent. Subtle style of Traminer, similar to what Jura-produced vin jaune tastes like when young (i.e., before going into barrel – see page 87). The Hainle chef recommends this with veggies or grains like yams, sweet potatoes, corn, parsnip, winter squash or carrots.
- Hainle Vineyards, Icewine, VQA: the debut 1973 vintage was the first icewine in Canada (winter weather conditions in Canada's vineyards

mean icewine can be made nine years out of ten). The 1997 vintage was made with 88 per cent Riesling and 12 per cent Traminer grapes picked on 3 January 1998 with the temperature at −12°C for the grapes to be frozen. They were pressed and the juice fermented in small plastic tanks with two yeast cultures for four months (to make sure the fermentation did not stick half way through), leaving the wine with 12.2 per cent alcohol and 100g/l of residual (unfermented) grape sugar. Shows integrated aroma of icing sugar and apricot, real balance on the palate for such sweetness, intensity of flavour apparent all the way through, far more subtle and with more believable sweetness than any of the examples produced by the non-organic competition (375 ml, 235 bottles).

- Hainle Vineyards Merlot: dry red, made from a variety which has shown susceptibility to cold winters just to the south in Washington State where it is being replaced with Cabernet Franc. Try with roast lamb.
- Hainle Vineyards Pinot Noir, Elizabeth's Vineyard: dry red, made with certified organic Pinot Noir for the first time in 1997 (grapes from the same source as the Pinot Blanc, above). The wine ages in 100-gallon sized French oak puncheons as it might in Burgundy to bring out the meatiness hidden in the thickness of the fruit. Try with duck.
- Hainle Vineyards Cuvée Zero: bone dry sparkling wine made by the traditional method, first made in 1991 from Riesling (46 cases), with the follow up in 1993.

Note on Canadian Icewine

Canadian icewine cannot be exported to Europe under current EU law because the level of potential alcohol is deemed too high. In Hainle's case the level of potential alcohol is 12.2 per cent plus 5.5 per cent – 17.5 per cent in total (it takes 17 grams of sugar to make one degree of alcohol, i.e., 5.5 times 17 equals roughly 100g/l residual sugar). Canada's reputation as an icewine producer has suffered recently due to the unscrupulous practice of bulk bottling establishments that favour refrigeration equipment and added sugar to make their 'icewines'.

Summerhill Estate Winery

Unit 1, 14870 Chute Lake Road, Kelowna, BC, V1W 4M3

Tel:+1 250 764 8000

Fax:+1 250 764 2598

Email:info@summerhill.bc.ca

Internet: summerhill@summerhill.bc.ca

Attractions: Mallam House, an early two-storey, hand hewn settlers' log cabin built in 1897 (refurbished in 1998 in a joint-effort between Summerhill and the Kelwona Museum Society). There are also regular tours of the winery, and a restaurant.

Stockists: wines available direct from the winery shop (staff there are fluent in Japanese, Italian, Spanish, French, German, Mandarin, Cantonese and English), and via mail order anywhere in Canada. Wines can also be ordered using the secure ordering system on Summerhill's website. For local stockists, see Appendix 1.

Summerhill Estate Winery is located in Okanagan Mission east of Lake Okanagan and is owned by Stephen R. Cipes, a native of Manhattan. The vineyard covers 20 hectares and has been certified organic since 1995. Non-organic fruit is bought in too. This is the only vineyard in Canada to be sown with ground rock dust as a source of micronutrient for the vines. They appear more balanced and less disease prone than the non-organic neighbours here.

- Cipes Sparkling Brut 'Pyramid Aged': bone dry sparkling white wine made by the traditional method from 100 per cent Riesling; basket pressed (as in Champagne) then aged in the Cipes pyramid (a scale model of the Giza Great pyramid at the winery, aligned with true north and built without ferrous metals in order to capture the atmosphere's negative ions). Shows cream and toast; elegant dryness – a sign of ripe grapes – clear style; subtle and classy.
- Chardonnay: dry white, the 1996 vintage was due for organic certification; made in a Burgundian style which shows very convincing broad, butter, mineral and peach and melon flavours with a hint of oak. Comparable to Derain in St Aubin in Burgundy (*page 64*). Tastes very different in style to the non-organic wines made here, which show more overt citrus characters.

Australia

Australian winemakers took the world by storm in the 1980s with their oaky Chardonnay and peppery Shiraz (Syrah) wines. However they are unlikely to do the same with organic versions of these and other grape varieties, at least for a while. This is because the certified organic vineyard area in Australia amounts to less than 200 hectares, out of a total vineyard area of 60,000 hectares. This relatively small amount is a pity for fans of Australian wine because the country has obvious climatic advantages over Europe for organic production. It's also a pity for Australians themselves, who drink the most wine per head of any English speaking people, at 21 litres per annum. Australia grows and harvests its grapes more economically than California or South Africa, due to the fact that more Australian vineyards are pruned and picked by machine as a percentage of the total than any others in the New World. This minimizes labour costs. It is also cheaper to ship wine from Australia to the UK than it is from Italy. With this in mind the Australians have decided to massively expand their vineyards under a plan called 'Australia 2025'. One planned vineyard, Rosnay, is in the process of obtaining full organic certification.

AUSTRALIAN ORGANIC CERTIFICATION

There are five organic certification bodies in Australia, of which currently two are relevant for vineyards: the National Association for Sustainable Agriculture, Australia Ltd (NASAA), and the Organic Vignerons Association of Australia, Inc. (OVAA). Wines may be labelled as made from grapes 'In Conversion to Organic' for the first three years after conversion, and then as made from 'Organic' grapes after that (a conversion period of two years was allowed until 1994, since when it has been three years).

The governmental body overseeing organic certification agencies is the Australian Quarantine Inspection Service (AQIS). Certification bodies like OVAA and NASAA must be recognized by AQIS in order for their members to sell their wines in the EU under Australia's third country status (AQIS issues the export certificates).

Certifying Bodies

National Association for Sustainable Agriculture, Australia Ltd

PO Box 768, Stirling, SA 5152

Tel:+61 8 8370 8455

Fax:+61 8 8370 8381

Email: nasaa@dove.mtx.net.au

Internet: www.green-pages.com.au or www.earthlink.com.au/nasaa

NASAA was founded to represent producers in all agricultural areas rather than merely vineyards. NASAA has two sets of operating standards – one for production (grape growing) and one for processing (turning the grapes into wine). The NASAA label may not be applied to a processed product unless all stages of production and processing have been carried out under certified conditions. Only two wine producers cited below are NASAA certified for both the vineyard and the winemaking – Penfold's (Southcorp) and Settlers Ridge (Organic Wines). Note however that Settlers Ridge processes only organic grapes in its winery at harvest, whereas Penfold's makes its Clare Valley wines in the presence of non-organic wines in two different winery facilities. NASAA has been accredited by AQIS and by IFOAM since 1994.

Organic Vignerons Association of Australia, Inc.

1 Gawler Street, (PO Box 503), Nuriootpa, SA 5355

Tel:+61 8 8562 2122

Fax:+61 8 8562 3034

Email: boss@dove.net.au

OVAA was founded in 1992 specifically to represent wine grape growers and wine makers. It appears to operate to less stringent standards than NASAA. For example, NASAA allows a maximum level of 30ppm of free or active sulphur dioxide preservative (sulfites) at bottling, whereas producers with OVAA have quoted levels of 40ppm for wines during research for this book. OVAA was accredited by AQIS in 1999, but has not been accredited by IFOAM.

Australian Quarantine Inspection Service

GPO Box 858, Canberra, ACT, 2601
Tel:+61 2 6272 5789
Fax:+61 1 6271 6522
Email: gary.luckman@aqis.gov.au
Internet: www.aqis.gov.au

This Australian government body regulates the organic inspection bodies,
like NASAA and OVAA, that are referred to in the producer profiles.
AQIS ensures through audits that all approved domestic certifying organizations comply with a National Standard for Organic and Bio-dynamic
Produce. This National Standard was formulated using the EU Com-
mission's legislation as a benchmark (i.e., EU Directive 2092/91).

NEW SOUTH WALES

New South Wales produces a quarter of Australia's wine from hot and
humid vineyards on the eastern side of the country.

Hastings Valley

Hastings Valley is home to the world's most famous vineyard consultant,
Dr Richard Smart, who has made 'canopy management' the buzz term for
spray-less vineyard practice in humid, cool climate areas like New Zealand
(where Smart is originally from – *see canopy management details on page
377*). Hastings Valley is also home to Cassegrain Vineyards.

Cassegrain Vineyards

Hastings River Winery,
Fernbank Creek Road,
Port Macquarie, NSW 2444

Cassegrain Vineyards is owned by John Cassegrain, devotee of a vegetable
oil called Codacide. This is used to reduce the rates at which other protective vineyard sprays are applied. The codacide acts as a micro-emulsion on
spray droplets to make them finer and easier to apply to the vines. This
reduces the amount of water lost through spray drift and evaporation by
up to 80 per cent, and the number of visits into the vineyard on the back
of a tractor, thus saving water and reducing compaction of the vineyard

soil. Cassegrain is certified organic by OVAA. The owners claim to farm one plot called Clos Françoise according to biodynamic methods, but Demeter biodynamic certification requires the whole vineyard be converted. This particular plot contains Chambourçin, a red French hybrid, similar to the Maréchal Foch grown in Washington State and Canada.

Mudgee

Mudgee lies 150 miles north west of Sydney in the Great Dividing Range and is a predominantly red wine region. The region's clay soils here and the dry heat it experiences from budbreak until harvest makes for rich, concentrated wines.

Botobolar Vineyard Pty Ltd

Botobolar Lane, PO Box 212, Mudgee, NSW 2850
Tel:+61 2 63 733 840
Fax:+61 2 63 733 789
Email: botobolar@winsoft.net.au
Stockists: Vintage Roots; Organic Wine Company
Overall Price Rating: 👣

Botobolar covers 26.3 hectares of vines and has been certified organic by NASAA since May 1996. The vineyard has been farmed according to organic methods since it was planted in 1971 by its original owners, Gil and Vincie Wahlquist. Botobolar was the flagship organic vineyard in Australia when the Wahlquists sold it in 1994. The new owners, Americans Kevin and Trina Karstrom, continue to dry farm (non-irrigate) and hand pick the vines. These were spaced wide enough by the Wahlquists to allow Suffolk sheep room to graze the weeds. Under the new owners a winemaking style is continuing to evolve. Wines here are labelled 'Preservative Free' when they contain no sulphur dioxide preservative.

- Chardonnay, Mudgee: dry white, seen as a key variety here, and in 1997 rated by Kevin Karstrom as the best wine he has ever made (organic winemakers too are never guilty of talking down the vintage); suitable for vegans.

- Marsanne, Mudgee: dry white made from a Rhône variety capable of Viognieresque complexity, power and exotica. Note how the 'every Aussie vintage is the same' idea does not work here for this variety, which shows marked vintage variation – just compare the alcohol levels in the 1996 (11.5 per cent) and 1997 (13.5 per cent) vintages.
- Cabernet Sauvignon/Merlot: dry red, shows very distinctive eucalyptus character, a classic tasting note for an Australian red with a high Cabernet content (70 per cent plus). Clear fruit and tannins on the palate signal healthy grape skins.
- Shiraz, Mudgee: dry red, fine grained tannins, tighter, leaner, less overtly flavoured than the wine immediately above; suitable for vegans.

Martins Hill Wines

Sydney Road, Mudgee, NSW 2850

Tel:+61 2 6373 1248

Fax:+61 2 6373 1248

Overall Price Rating: 🍷

Martins Hill was established in 1984 by a partnershhip made up of a former engineer, Michael Sweeney, and a high school teacher, Janette Kenworthy. The land had previously been given to grazing. Sweeney regarded Gil Wahlquist of Botobolar Vineyards (above) as something of a mentor, and grazes 80 sheep on the vineyard for weed control. The vines slope quite steeply and cover 2.5 hectares of grapes. The first 1.5 hectares of Pinot Noir and Sauvignon Blanc were planted in 1985. In 1997 and 1998 Cabernet Sauvignon (first release planned for the 2001 vintage) and Shiraz (first release planned for the 2002 vintage) were added. There are also 0.8 hectares of cherries, peaches and plums. Martins Hill has been certified organic by OVAA since 1990. The grapes are made into wine in a local winery, Martins Hill being without its own. So far 300 cases of dry white Sauvignon Blanc have been released from each of the 1996 and 1997 vintages. Another 300 cases of dry red 'Pinot Noir Light Red' were made in 1997, hand picked and aged in new French oak.

Thistle Hill Vineyard

McDonalds Road, Mudgee, NSW 2860
Stockist: Organic Wine Company
Overall Price Rating: ♙♙♙

Thistle Hill Vineyard has been certified organic by NASAA since May 1993. Two wines are made by owners David and Lesley Robertson – a dry Chardonnay, fully oaked, suitable for vegans; and a dry red Cabernet Sauvignon, also suitable for vegans.

Cowra Region

The vineyard below is in the planning stage.

Rosnay Vineyard

Rivers Road, Canowindra, NSW 2804
Tel:+61 2 6344 3215
Fax:+61 2 6344 3229
Email: statham@lisp.com.au

Rosnay belongs to Richard Statham, for 18 years a cattle producer until he 'got fed up grazing cattle in drought conditions and decided to give grapes a try'. Rosnay consists of 65 hectares of potential vineyard. Chardonnay and Shiraz were planted in 1997 (eight hectares), with plantings of Merlot, Cabernet Sauvignon and Sémillon planned for 1999. Organic certification will be via OVAA. Potential investors can buy a block of vineyard and build their own winery on it (or retirement home). Statham will look to his son Sam, 24, who has studied conservation in Europe, for organic inspiration and practical knowledge.

SOUTH AUSTRALIA

South Australia produces 60 per cent of Australia's wine and contains some of the country's most prestigious wine regions, like Adelaide Hills, Clare Valley and Barossa Valley. South Australia's organic vineyards mirror those of California where both idealistic individuals and the broader minds of big business share the organic bounty.

Adelaide Hills

The Adelaide Hills provide an agreeable climate for organic vineyards, with little summer rain and plenty of sea breezes to prevent the scorching of the grapes as they ripen.

David & Adam Wynn Pty Ltd

High Eden Road, Eden Valley, South Australia 5235

This family partnership produces a range of wines from grapes certified organic by OVAA under the Eden Ridge label. Dry white wines are made from Chardonnay and Sauvignon Blanc, and a dry red from Cabernet Sauvignon. They are suitable for vegetarians. Irrigation is used in the vineyards, in contrast to Glenara, below. Other wines made by the Wynn family included the Mountadam range, but from non-certified organic grapes. Both ranges provide appealing, approachable premium wines styled for the international market, but blind tasters could have trouble telling the two apart.

Glenara Wines Pty Ltd

126 Grange Road North, Upper Hermitage, SA 5131
Tel:+61 8 8380 5056
Fax:+61 8 8380 5056
Email: glenara@senet.com.au
Stockists: Cellar Choice, Vintage Roots, Vinceremos (UK); The Grape stores (Brisbane, QLD), Camperdown Cellars stores (Sydney, NSW), Philip Murphy stores (Melbourne, Vic), Vintage Cellars stores (Adelaide, SA)

Glenara has been certified organic by OVAA since 1993 and is run by Leigh and Jan Verrall and their sons Ralph and Bill. Even though the vineyard is at the drier end of the Adelaide Hills organic fertilisers are turned into the soil, not applied via irrigation. In 1994 the vineyard, which covers 12 hectares, was designated a sanctuary by the Department of Environment and Natural Resources.

It was a mixed farm used for woodcutting, orchard fruits, dairying, market garden vegetables and strawberries at the time of its purchase in 1923 by Leigh Verrall's grandfather. The strawberries were first planted in the 1950s. The first vines, Shiraz and Cabernet Sauvignon, were planted in 1971, and the total vine plantings (all varieties) are now 12 hectares.

Glenara sold all its grapes to other winemakers until 1983, when it first used the whole crop for its own wines, although some grapes were still sold to other winemakers up until the early 1990s.

- Bottle Fermented Pinot Noir: sparkling red wine made by the traditional method; grapes sourced from vines planted at Glenara in 1989. More Pinot Noir was planted in 1996, together with another dark-skinned member of the Pinot family common to Champagne, the Pinot Meunier (see Champagne, Yves Ruffin et Fils, *page 81*). This wine is now marketed under the label 'Glenara White Quartz', and has become a sparkling white wine made to the traditional method, containing predominantly Pinot Noir, with the 1996 vintage also containing 10 per cent Chardonnay. The Pinot Meunier is also being used in this wine, from the 1998 vintage onward. 🍾🍾🍾
- Dry Riesling, Adelaide Hills: dry white Riesling is synonymous with this part of Australia; made from mature vines planted at Glenara in 1972; 12 per cent alcohol; suitable for vegans. 🍾🍾🍾
- Sauvignon Blanc: dry white, made from vines planted at Glenara in 1989. 🍾
- Sémillon: dry white, made in 1996 from grapes purchased from Corkscrew Vineyards in Montacute, Adelaide Hills for the first time; these vines were certified organic in 1997 by OVAA. 🍾
- Unwooded Chardonnay: dry white made from vines planted at Glenara in 1984, supplemented since 1996 by grapes from Corkscrew Vineyards. 🍾
- Cabernet Rosé: pink made from Cabernet Franc vines planted at Glenara in 1988. 🍾
- Cabernet Merlot: dry red; made from Merlot vines planted at Glenara in 1987 and Cabernet Sauvignon; the 1993 and 1994 vintages were sold as 'organic in re-conversion'. 🍾🍾🍾
- Pinot Noir Dry Red: dry red, made in 1996 from grapes sourced from Corkscrew Vineyards; Glenara planted more of its own Pinot Noir in 1996 so that the 1998 Pinot Noir (dry red) was made entirely from the Pinot Noir grapes grown at Glenara. 🍾🍾🍾

Wilkie Estate Wines

Lot 1, Heaslip Road, Penfield, SA 5121
Tel:+61 8 8284 7655
Fax:+61 8 8284 7618

Wilkie Estate has been certified organic by OVAA since 1994 and is located 30km north of the city of Adelaide at the point where the Adelaide Plains begin. Its owner, Bernard Wilkie, was nearly 50 by the time he planted his first vines here in 1976. His original choice of grape, Riesling was replaced by red Bordeaux varieties like Merlot and Cabernet Sauvignon, which are more suited to the heavier soils of the Plains. The vines are pruned and picked by hand.

- Wilkie Estate Red: blend of Cabernet Sauvignon, Merlot and Ruby Cabernet, aged in American and French oak barrels. Prior to 1990 these grapes were sold; 1994 was their debut vintage with organic certification; contains low levels of added sulphur dioxide preservative so look for the most recent vintage. ⚎
- Wilkie Estate Verdelho: dry white, non-oak aged, fermented in stainless steel tanks; filtered to reduce the risk of a secondary (malolactic) fermentation which would cause the wine to turn flabby. Prior to 1990 these grapes were sold; 1994 was their debut vintage with organic certification. ⚎

Clare Valley

Clare Valley lies 130km north of Adelaide and is South Australia's most northerly vineyard sub-region. Clare was developed from the late 1970s because the region's relatively cool climate offered a chance to produce more elegant, European wine styles in Australia. Now these are emerging in organic form, thanks to Penfold's.

Penfold's (Southcorp Wines Pty Ltd)

Magill Estate Cellar Door, 78 Penfold Road, Magill, SA 5072
Tel:+61 8 8301 5400
Fax:+61 8 8301 5562

Cellar Door Sales: yes

Stockists: E H Booth & Co; Waitrose; Safeway; Classic Wines & Spirits Ltd; Anthony Byrne Fine Wines; Selfridges; Victoria Wine (First Quench); or contact

Southcorp Wines Europe Ltd, 12 King St, Richmond, Surrey TW9 1ND

Tel:+44 181 334 2000

Fax:+44 181 334 2010 (for up-to-date details of UK stockists)

Penfold's began as a family concern in the 19th century but has developed into Australia's largest wine company by some considerable margin. It crushes 35 per cent of the grapes harvested annually in Australia, a majority of which are purchased from private growers and contractors (the name for the group's activities is Southcorp). Penfold's converted the first portion of its Clare Valley Estate Vineyard to organic methods from early 1991 under the NASAA-certified organic vineyard programme, with a second portion following by January 1997 (leaving a total of 52.7 hectares certified out of 202 hectares in total). The company view of the organic vineyards is that they attract media attention and they provide useful training grounds for future vineyard managers and winemakers – and they give the Penfold's sales team an extra product to sell. These vines are pruned and picked by machine, and the wines are made to vegan requirements.

- Penfold's Clare Estate Organic Chardonnay-Sauvignon Blanc: dry white first made in 1993, and usually made two-thirds Chardonnay and one-third Sauvignon Blanc; partially fermented in French oak butts (20 per cent of the blend in 1993, 70 per cent in 1997). Since 1995 the wine has been suitable for vegans. Clean, light to medium-bodied citrus with no rough edges, well-judged level of oak, in the technically proficient international style for which Australia in general and Penfold's in particular are renowned. ♦♦♦

- Penfold's Clare Estate Organic Cabernet Merlot: dry red, first made in 1993 from Cabernet Sauvignon, Shiraz and Merlot, non-fined so suitable for vegans; level of oak more restrained in this than in Penfold's other conventionally farmed reds (oaking on red wines using toasted American oak casks is Penfold's trademark). ♦♦

- Penfold's Clare Estate Organic Shiraz Cabernet: dry red, first made in 1995 when this and the following vintage were made from 70 per cent

Shiraz and 30 per cent Cabernet Sauvignon. The wine aged nine months in a mix of new and second wine French oak butts and was bottled unfined so it's suitable for vegans. The less successful 1997 vintage was labelled Cabernet Shiraz. 🍶

Langhorne Creek

This is one of the few wine sub-regions in Australia humid enough for copper treatments to be needed on the vines to protect them from downy mildew. This vine fungal disease is the one which both organic and conventional growers have to treat in the same way by using 'Bordeaux Mixture' (see page xiii).

Temple Bruer Wines

RSD 226, Strathalbyn, SA 5255
Tel:+61 8 8537 0203
Fax:+61 8 8537 0131
Email: templebruer@olis.net.au

Temple Bruer Wines comprises 24 hectares of vineyard and is due for full organic certification in 2001. An initial eight-hectare block became fully certified organic by OVAA in 1998 and the remainder began its three-year conversion under OVAA protocols in the same year. Temple Bruer's owner, David Bruer, has reservations about the term 'organic', especially when it means copper sulphate can be used on the vines. This gets washed into the soil and never degrades. One step away from a reliance on copper is to try to make the vineyard as uncomfortable a place for the fungal disease as possible by using more sustainable means. Fungal diseases love vines which grow big, sprawling tendrils because they have been given too much space in which to grow. One solution is to add an extra row of vines between each existing row but it does mean the number of hours needed to farm the same plot increases. The equation works if the consumer decides that the extra premium the wines attract when they are grown the sustainable way is justified by the quality in the bottle. At Temple Bruer these bottles contain (in ascending order of price):

● Shiraz/Malbec: dry red blend of Australia's most popular red grape (the French Syrah) and the Malbec of Cahors, Bordeaux (Côtes de Bourg) and Argentina. 🍷

- Grenache 'Cornucopia': dry red, made from a Mediterranean variety coping with conditions in the Outback. ♙
- Cabernet/Merlot: dry red, Bordeaux-style blend. ♙
- Merlot Reserve: dry red; the 1996 was made from vines in their first year of organic conversion. ♙♙♙
- Cabernet Sauvignon: dry red; the 1998 vintage was the first red wine made at this winery without the addition of sulphur dioxide preservative. The 1998 blends Cabernet Sauvignon (86 per cent) and Petit Verdot (14 per cent), is fined with egg white but is suitable for vegetarians. 1,200 cases made. ♙♙♙
- Botrytis Riesling: modelled on Riesling Spätlese rather than the Auslese style of sweet white wine from southern Germany. (Spätlese is late picked with some 'noble rot' berries, while Auslese is late picked with almost all 'noble rot' berries.) ♙♙♙

STATE OF TASMANIA

Tasmania has lower land costs than on the mainland, but the downside is a cool island climate where hail and attacks from both the mildews are commonplace – no other Australian region is so far from the Equator.

Petcheys Bay Vineyard

Tel:+61 3 6295 1344
Fax:+61 3 6295 1344
Email: PetcheysBayVineyard@tassie.net.au
Internet: tassie.net.au/PetcheysBayVineyard
Overall Price Rating: ♙♙♙ (blueberry fruit wines)

Petcheys Bay Vineyard is located on the Huon River in the southern part of Tasmania. It lies about 25km downstream from Huonville following the Cygnet Coast Road, which departs the Cygnet–Huonville Road at Cradoc. The vineyard takes its name from William Petchey who settled in the district after 1834 (the time of the earliest settlement at Cygnet). This property was settled by Fitzpatrick (the first warden, i.e. mayor, of Cygnet municipality) in 1836. He had 200 ticket of leave men (probationary convicts) cutting wattle for barrel staves. He ran an hotel here and grew hops. While the current owner John Middleton has no plans to run an hotel, it seems some sort of circle has been completed for it was he who, in 1988, planted the farm with blueberries. These were certified organic in 1990. In 1996 a small organic vineyard comprising 2,000 vines was added. Petcheys Bay will produce its first wines in 2000 from Pinot Noir and Chardonnay. Middleton's blueberries are made into fruit wines at a neighbouring winery called Panorama. They are made in both non-fortified (14 per cent) and fortified (18 per cent) styles; a fortified black-currant fruit wine (18 per cent) is made from purchased, certified organic blackcurrants. No preservatives are used on these fruit wines unless stated on the label.

STATE OF VICTORIA

Australian's third most important wine producing state is increasingly known for cool climate wines from Central Victoria made with classic European grapes like Chardonnay and Pinot. The hotter, irrigated vine-yards of North Eastern Victoria mark the border with New South Wales along the Murray River.

Central Victoria

The Central Victoria vineyards were devastated by phylloxera in the 19th century, but today are in the forefront of Australia's new 'cool climate' regions (in contrast to Murray River, below).

Corsini Vineyard La Cantina

RMD 9460, King Valley, Vic 3678
Tel:+61 3 5729 3615
Fax:+61 3 5722 9145
Overall Price Rating: ♦

Corsini Vineyard La Cantina is a family-owned vineyard located in Central Victoria's cool King Valley. The vineyard has been certified organic by NASAA since 1993. It comprises 24 hectares of Cabernet Sauvignon, Chardonnay, Shiraz and Rhine Riesling. However Corsini Vineyard La Cantina had its organic certification withdrawn by NASAA in 1999, and the last grapes that were certified were used in wines bearing the 1998 vintage. A chemical herbicide was sprayed in 1998 to counter the effects of a freak frost. The herbicide burns back buds that have been damaged by frost, encouraging secondary buds on the shoots to break and produce a restricted crop (the spray technique appears to have been pioneered in California). Corsini sells around 90 per cent of its grapes to one of the major wineries in the King Valley area but they make no mention of the (hitherto) organic origins of their wines. Corsini retains a small amount of grapes for the following range of wines. They are made without the addition of sulphur dioxide preservative:

- La Cantina Rhine Riesling: dry white, unfiltered, unfined since 1996 thus suitable for vegetarians and vegans.
- La Cantina Chardonnay: white, unfiltered, unfined since 1996, thus suitable for vegetarians and vegans.
- La Cantina Cabernet Sauvignon: unfiltered, fined with egg white until 1996, since when it has been unfined and thus suitable for vegetarians and vegans.
- La Cantina Shiraz: full dry red, unfiltered, fined with egg white before 1996, but since then unfined and thus suitable for vegetarians and vegans.

Prince Albert Vineyard
100 Lemmins Road, Waurn Ponds, Vic 3216
Tel:+61 3 5241 8091
Fax:+61 3 5241 8091
Email: hyettba@bigpond.com
Stockist: The Wine Treasury

The history of Victoria broadly mirrors that of the oldest of its three certified organic vineyards, Prince Albert Vineyard. This comprises two hectares of Pinot Noir and has been certified organic by OVAA since 1998. It was planted from 1840 onwards by John Tetaz. Pioneers like him contributed to a golden age of viticulture and the state of Victoria became known as 'John Bull's Vineyard' because the state's wines were so popular in Queen Victoria's England – why else would you call a vineyard Prince Albert? Disaster struck however in 1882 when Prince Albert Vineyard closed, its vines having succumbed to the vine louse phylloxera. Prince Albert was one of a number of old Victorian vineyards purchased and replanted by new owners searching for cooler climate wine-growing regions. Its current owner is a native of nearby Geelong called Bruce Hyett, who purchased the vineyard in 1975.

This part of Victoria is amongst the most renowned in Australia for producing red wines from the fussy Pinot Noir grape. A relatively cool climate coupled with limestone soils encourages Pinot's heady aroma and exotic flavour.

● Pinot Noir, Prince Albert Vineyard: dry red wine, made from hand picked fruit, fermented on the skins in open concrete-lined tanks and matured in new French oak (four new barrels are purchased each year), 600 cases average production; the first vintage of this wine to be made from organic grapes will be released only in 2000–2001. 🍶🍶🍶

The Murray River

Vineyards were first developed along the Murray River, North Eastern Victoria only from the end of the 19th century when irrigation projects were begun. The largest biodynamic producer in Australia (and in the Southern Hemisphere) is located here, 470 km from Melbourne.

Robinvale Wines

Sea Lake Road, PO Box 314, Robinvale, Vic 3549
Tel:+61 3 5026 3955/+61 3 5026 1955
Fax:+61 3 5026 1123
Email: demeter@mildura.net.au
Internet: http://cybermall.ozland.net.au/food/prices.html
Cellar Door Sales: yes
Mail Order: yes
Visitors: Welcome. The winery is listed among the tourist attractions of the district and is designed to resemble a Greek Temple, built in ancient Mt. Gambier stone
Stockist: Vintage Roots

Robinvale Wines was converted to biodynamics from 1980 when it consisted of a single vineyard, and now consists of two Demeter-certified vineyards covering over 50 hectares (40 hectares at Robinvale and 11 hectares near Swan Hill, which were acquired in the late 1980s). Robinvale's owners, the Caractsanoudis family, are Australia's equivalent of the Lolonis family in Mendocino in California. The atmosphere is homely, and the pace as fast as you want it to be. Current managers are brothers Bill (the winemaking) and Steven (the rest). Wines labelled 'Preservative Free' contain no added sulphur dioxide preservative but are made with a preserving powder (an enzyme called 'Endozyme').

- Chenin/Chardonnay/Sauvignon: dry white blend of Chenin Blanc, Chardonnay and Sauvignon Blanc; very broad, thick style of fruit which here is assuredly rendered; suitable for vegans. ⚑
- Oak Chardonnay: dry white, full buttery fruit beneath a thick coating of wood and alcohol. ⚑
- Sauternes: sweet white wine made in the style of sweet white Bordeaux but for sale under this label only in Australia. This is because European law prevents this Australian wine from being labelled as 'Sauternes' within the EU. See Sauternes AC (Bordeaux) (*page 21*) for more on the significance of this 'Australian Sauternes'. ⚑
- Cabernet Rosé, Preservative Free: off-dry pink; simple, thick, violet fruit; look for the most recent vintage. ⚐
- Cabernet Dry Red, Preservative Free: dry red, a blend of Cabernet Sauvignon, Merlot and Cabernet Franc, no added sulphur dioxide. Dense style of red made from thick and well-sunned grape skins. Decant six hours before drinking to give it air to 'cool off' and develop aromatically. ⚑
- Zinfandel Merlot: dry red, a rare combination in Australia. Zinfandel works here as a grape variety because winters are cool enough for the vines to shut down (achieve dormancy), unlike in Western Australia when the country's only other Zinfandel originates (that one is non-organic though). ⚑

Robinvale also produces fortified wines made from Brown Muscat and Mavrodaphne (a Greek variety), as well as non-alcoholic wines (Passion, Strawberry and Ginger), fruit juices and fruit wines (Plum). The biodynamic sultanas and raisins are worth finding too.

WESTERN AUSTRALIA

Western Australia's two certified organic growers contribute around 100 tonnes of grapes to the state's annual crush of nearly one million. Both are found in Western Australia's most fashionable region, Margaret River.

Margaret River

The Margaret River region lies 240km south of Perth. None of the educated, urban professionals who established vineyards here in the 1960s changed to organic methods as their peers have done in Mendocino County in California. Although Western Australia appears to be the perfect place to grow grapes organically – fungal diseases of the vine like downy mildew are rare and vine moth, apple moth and phylloxera (which all cause serious pest damage to vineyards elsewhere in Australia) are absent – Western Australia's proximity to the Indian Ocean means average temperatures during winter are too high for the vine to go into dormancy, which in turn affects bud break in spring. (Warm winter weather means some buds on the middle of the vine shoot never open, leaving empty spaces where there should be grapes at harvest.) Organic methods to encourage more complete bud break include pruning the vine twice to force it to direct its energy onto its buds rather than its shoots. Changing the way the vine shoots grow (by re-trellising the vine canopy) can also have the same effect. However, regulating how quickly the vine shoots grow at bud burst with non-organic growth regulators ensures optimum crop levels for minimal cost.

The two organic growers here make the point that the region's soils are severely phosphate deficient. Fertilising the soil with natural as opposed to chemical manure, including mulch from cover crops, allows phosphate locked up in the soil to be released. This helps the vine enough for the grapes to ripen without burning up their vital acids in the heat. Chemical fertilisers used by other Margaret River growers leave the wines reliant on artificial acidification in the cellar, and less able to express their taste.

Serventy Wines

Valley Home Vineyard, Witchcliffe, WA 6286

Tel:+61 8 9757 7534

Fax:+61 8 9757 3541

Email: serventy@netserv.net.au

Overall Price Rating: 🍷🍷🍷

Serventy Wines is named after its founders, Peter and Lyn Serventy. Originally they operated a small tin mine in the Northern Territory. However the day after the birth of their first child, Cyclone Tracy destroyed their Darwin home. They rebuilt and sold up, moving to Witchcliffe, Margaret River in 1984. The vineyard covers nearly three hectares and is certified organic by NASAA. All the wines are suitable for vegetarians.

- Chardonnay: dry white, made from vines planted in 1984.
- Sauvignon Blanc: dry white, made from the youngest vines, planted in 1997.
- Pinot Noir: dry red, made from vines planted in 1984; matured in French oak barrels.
- Pinot Noir Sparkling: red sparkling wine made by the traditional method from vines planted in 1984.
- Shiraz: dry red, made from vines planted in 1984; matured in French oak barrels.

Settlers Ridge (Organic Wines)

PO Box 121, Cowaramup, WA 6284

Tel:+61 8 9755 5388

Fax:+61 8 9755 5388

Overall Price Rating: 🍷

Settlers Ridge was certified organic by OVAA until August 1997, since when its vineyard and winery have been certified by NASAA. There are 40 hectares of land in total, of which eight are set aside for vineyard, although not all of this was producing in 1999. A settlement house remains on the property, which was originally part of a dairy farm. Settlers Ridge became organic after its owners, Wayne and Kaye Nobbs, enrolled on an organic gardening course and realised 'just how good organic produce could be'. The wines made include:

- Settlers Ridge Chenin Blanc: semi-sweet white.
- Settlers Ridge Chenin/Sauvignon Blanc: semi-sweet white first made in 1997.
- Settlers Ridge Sauvignon Blanc: semi-sweet white.
- Settlers Ridge Shiraz/Cabinet Sauvignon: dry red first made in 1997 from vines planted in 1994, oak aged.

New Zealand

In no other wine producing country featured in this book are the differences between organic and conventional methods so clearly marked as in New Zealand. Think of 'Cloudy Bay', the most famous New Zealand wine brand, and one has a clue as to the dominant feature of the country's climate and situation. None of the country's vineyards are located more than 110 km from the coast. Overcast, humid and wet, especially around vintage, New Zealand doesn't just attract the major vine fungal disease threats like the two mildews and bunch rot, but positively panders to them. Add to this sometimes extremely fertile soils that weaken the vines and life is made difficult for growers. Perhaps it is no wonder that, out of New Zealand's 8,200 hectares of vineyards, only 56.35 hectares were certified organic by New Zealand Biological Producers Council (BioGro NZ) in 1999.

The major commitment the organic growers here make to stave off vine fungal diseases is sustained 'canopy management'. This is a buzz wine term for tasks that must be performed every year on the vines, mainly during the period of vine growth (from bud break to ripening). These include removing excess buds and leaves to give the grapes the maximum amount of sunlight and air. This work must be done by hand to be most effective, and is thus a more labour intensive and expensive way of discouraging vine fungal diseases than using chemical sprays. This may account for why none of New Zealand's four biggest wine producers has yet to throw their hat into the organic ring, unlike in California (Fetzer Vineyards-Brown Forman) and Australia (Penfolds/Southcorp). In fact, wines from one of New Zealand's big four producers were impounded by Canadian customs in 1998 because traces of illegal bird repellent were detected. This has left the field clear for smaller producers to dominate the organic headlines. They belong to the following body:

New Zealand Biological Producers Council (BioGro NZ)

PO Box 9693 Marion Square, Wellington 6031

Tel:+64 4 801 9741

Fax:+64 4 801 9742

Email: enquiries@bio-gro.co.nz

BioGro NZ is the country's organic certification body with IFOAM accreditation and sets the criteria for organic wines in New Zealand. Since 1983 it has awarded the 'BioGro NZ' symbol to wineries whose annual vineyard management plans are approved. The system is reliant a great deal on trust because although BioGro takes soil samples and other such analyses when visiting the property, inspections are not annual. This reflects the practical difficulties in checking wine producers located on two separate islands spanning 1,200 km and 9° of latitude – the equivalent of North Africa to Paris.

A Note on Trust

Trust is not something New Zealand's conventional growers seem particularly good at. In 1998 Coopers Creek Vineyard admitted in a New Zealand court that some of its white wines, which were exported to the UK labelled 'Sauvignon Blanc', contained less than the legal minimum required of the grape (75 per cent) for this variety to feature on the bottle label under New Zealand wine labelling laws. No exact figure could be given by the owner of Coopers Creek, Andrew Hendry, regarding the contents of the bottles in question – i.e., how much Sauvignon Blanc variety they contained and how much of the wine was made from other, less renowned grape varieties.

In November 1998 another conventional New Zealand winery found itself having to answer embarrassing questions about exactly what its wines contained. Lintz had entered its 1997 Shiraz dry red wine in the Air New Zealand (Wine) Awards, the most prestigious wine competition in the country. The competition tasting was held in November 1998 and the Lintz wine was awarded 'the best red in the competition, other than Merlot, Cabernet and Pinot Noir'. When the wine was served to the judges – amongst whom was British wine writer Oz Clarke – they called 'foul'. It tasted nothing like as good as the blind tasting sample served to them during the competition. An investigation by the New Zealand Wine

Institute concluded that 'no breach of the rules occurred, but the blending and bottling techniques Lintz used resulted in marked differences between bottles of the same wine'. Even though it was exonerated Lintz returned the Air New Zealand award. The New Zealand Wine Institute's investigation did not reveal exactly why the two Shiraz wines were so different, or in what exact quantities they were made. Lintz had transitional BioGro status in the mid-1990s but, like Rippon Vineyard below, never made the transition to full organic status.

NORTH ISLAND

North Island is home to 70 per cent of the country's vineyards (and 70 per cent of the population).

Gisborne

Gisborne is located on the east coast and accounts for 20 per cent of the New Zealand vineyard (1,500 hectares), but 30 per cent of its production. Yields can be pushed up by rain here during harvest (which swells the grapes) and this has led to Gisborne being labelled a bulk-wine only producer. Others would argue that in the Millton Vineyard (below) the region possesses one of the finest domaines in the country.

The Millton Vineyard

Papatu Road, Manutuke, Gisborne, PO Box 63
Tel:+64 6.862.8680
Fax:+64 6.862.8869
Email: Millton@bpc.co.nz
Sales: retail, mail order and cellar door
Tours: by appointment only
Stockists: Vinceremos; Organic Wine Company

The Millton Vineyard in Gisborne on the eastern coast of North Island became the first New Zealand vineyard to be certified organic in 1984. It consists of four named vineyard sites. One of these, Opou, is the name of a wine estate founded in Gisborne from the 1960s by John Clark. His daughter, Annie runs the domaine with her husband James Millton. James worked in Rheinhessen, Germany. He returned to work for Corbans, one of

New Zealand's big four producers and exporters, but wanted to take the organic route. The four sites in the Millton Vineyard consist of 22 hectares and are:

- Naboths Vineyard, Gisborne; two hectares of Chardonnay and Pinot Noir on slopes so steep they have to be worked almost entirely by hand, which is exceptional for New Zealand where most vineyards are on table flat, fertile river valleys. Planted with Chardonnay and Pinot Noir, Naboths is said to be one of the first vineyards in the world to see the morning sun.
- Opou Vineyard; 10 hectares of Chenin Blanc, Sauvignon Blanc, Sémillon, Riesling, Cabernet Sauvignon and Cabernet Franc, located near where the first vines were planted in Poverty Bay.
- Riverpoint Vineyard; seven hectares of Chardonnay.
- Winery Vineyard; three hectares of Chardonnay, Chenin Blanc, Merlot, Malbec, July Muscat and Gewurztraminer.

In 1994 Millton lost the distinction of having the country's longest certified organic vineyard when a banned synthetic insect growth regulator was applied to six rows of vines to protect them against an aphid called the New Zealand Bronze Beetle, which grows from a grub in the grass and damages vines in newly planted plots. Millton used this instead of the organic treatment approved by BioGro, a plant extract called pyrethrum. The Milltons felt that this approved treatment is overly toxic to beneficial insects like lacewings and bees, even when it is used at night when these beneficial insects are dormant. Pyrethrums are an approved organic treatment in the EU, New Zealand, Australia, California and Canada, because they degrade easily in the atmosphere and leave a residue free soil. The Milltons could have sprayed nothing at all of course, and suffered the potential loss of their crop. Using a non-approved treatment meant the Millton vines had to pass through the compulsory transition phase of three years to regain certified organic status. This was duly granted again by BioGro NZ from 1997.

The 1999 vintage produced a tiny crop of excellent quality grapes. The shortfall in grapes on the vines meant the harvest lasted less than four weeks, the shortest on record (it generally lasts two and a half months at

Millton). One wine is produced here from bought in, non-organic grapes called Chardonnay, Gisborne Vineyards.

- Traminer Riesling: a white appetiser wine (only 10.5 per cent and a little sweetness), suitable for vegans (Organic Wine Company, 🍶).
- Chenin Blanc Barrel Fermented: dry white, made from the most widely planted variety in this part of the North Island; only 11.5 per cent alcohol (compared to 13 per cent minimum for the Chardonnays below); partly fermented in older wood to give the Chenin a resinous tweak. See Vouvray for French Chenin Blanc (*page 98*) (Vinceremos, Organic Wine Company, Safeway, 🍶).
- Sémillon/Chardonnay: dry white, lightly oaked and thus buttery, suitable for vegans. Modern style of white which resembles Graves Blanc Sec. (Vinceremos, Organic Wine Company, 🍶).
- Sauvignon Blanc, Te Arai River Oak Aged: dry white, spends only a couple of months in oak after fermentation; the 1996 vintage was made from two separate grape selections, shows nectarine and stone fruit; drink from 1–4 years of the vintage; suitable for vegans. 🍶
- Chardonnay Estate: dry white, hand picked, aged several months in French oak, shows clean, well-honed melon fruit; suitable for vegans (Organic Wine Company, 🍶).
- Chardonnay Barrel Fermented: dry white, hand picked, fermented in French oak; papaya fruit blends well with the wood if you give it time; suitable for vegans. The 1995 was more classic in texture but less intense than the 1996, which had to be picked in three stages due to a difficult vintage (Vinceremos, 🍶).
- Riesling, Opou Vineyards: sometimes sweet white, the result of late picking of selected, over ripe bunches, but designed to be drunk in its youth (Vinceremos, 🍶).
- Chardonnay, Botrytis, Clos de Ste Anne: sweet white sourced from grapes which are left to over-ripen; small volumes made, highly sought after. 🍶🍶
- Pinot Noir, Clos de Ste Anne: dry red, sourced from Naboths Vineyard, shows a mix of bright berries and undergrowth, southern Burgundy weight. 🍶🍶
- Merlot Reserve: dry red, first made in 1989 and then next in 1994. The 1994 spent 28 months in French oak (longer than most Bordeaux

wine), was fined with free-range egg whites and bottled unfiltered; suitable for vegetarians. ♨

- Cabernet/Merlot, Te Arai River: dry red, Bordeaux-style blend in which each variety is fermented apart; spends 21 months in French and American oak, shows bold tannin and clear, minty fruit. The 1994 contained 40 per cent Merlot, 40 per cent Cabernet Sauvignon, 10 per cent Malbec and 10 per cent Cabernet Franc. Suitable for vegetarians. Its equivalent in Bordeaux might be Château Falfas in Côtes de Bourg AC (*page 24*) (Vinceremos, ♨).

Hawke's Bay

Hawke's Bay lies on east side of North Island on gravelly soils that are some of the finest for Bordeaux-style red wines in New Zealand. There are two emerging producers here – one organic, one biodynamic – both free spirits.

Kingsley Estate

PO Box 1100, Hastings
Tel:+64 06 877 0355
Fax:+64 06 877 0355
Email: kingsley.estate@clear.net.nz
Internet: www.kingsley.co.nz
Stockists: refer to internet site above for updates on stockists worldwide
Overall Price Rating: ♨

Kingsley Estate is named after its founder, Kingsley Tobin, a native of the North Island town of Napier. Tobin studied sociology and political science at the University of Auckland before heading off to manage a restaurant in Newport Beach, California, where his interest in wine took root. Upon his return home in 1990 Tobin enrolled on a course in grape growing. He completed a research project on the feasibility of doing this using organic methods. He then planted six hectares of Merlot and Cabernet Sauvignon and has never used anything on the vines considered non-organic by BioGro. The site lies in the part of Hawkes Bay known as Gimblett Road. This area is viewed as the equivalent of Bordeaux's Left Bank for the elegant, intense red wines it produces. The vineyard has BioGro NZ transitional certified organic status, and gained full status from the 1999 vintage.

Tobin planted his vines four metres apart – twice the distance considered normal in New Zealand. The extra width gives Tobin's vines the opportunity to develop thick trunks and long permanent woody branches (from these grow the shoots each year upon which form the grapes). Called the 'big vine theory', this helps keep the vines in balance and leads to healthier, more concentrated grapes (they have more permanent woody vine from which to grow). The way the vines are trained is also unique. From the side the vines form a dovetail, alternating one above the other in the form of a 'Z'. Each vine can be picked individually, at maximum ripeness, because no vine is in direct competition for the sun with its neighbour. This is a fairly revolutionary way of growing, but already the grapes from these vines are arousing considerable interest for their velvet texture and rich plum perfumes. This is a pioneering estate to follow. Two red wines are made: a single varietal and a blend.

- Kingsley Estate Gimblett Road Cabernet Sauvignon.
- Kingsley Estate Gimblett Road Cabernet Sauvignon/Merlot.

Settler's Vineyard & Winery
Crownthorpe Settlement Road
PO Box 1414, RD 9, Hastings
Email: settler@clear.net.nz
Overall Price Rating: 𝝐

Settler's Vineyard & Winery belongs to Evert Nijzink, a Dutchman, and is the first New Zealand vineyard with biodynamic certification from Demeter (although New Zealand's first biodynamic arable farms date from the late 1970s). Only wines bearing the 1998 vintage and later are made entirely from estate-grown fruit. Previous releases in 1996 and 1997 were crushed from estate-grown grapes blended with purchased grapes. Nijzink began by planting 2.5 hectares of Chardonnay, Cabernet Sauvignon and Merlot from 1994. Production is tiny, and exports seem confined to the Low Countries. This is another small pioneering estate to follow.

SOUTH ISLAND

South Island contains a third of the New Zealand vineyard. Harvest begins in late February in Nelson and finishes late May in Central Otago.

Nelson

This is South Island's most northerly vineyard sub-region, and is a patchwork of small farms and vineyards on uneven grassland.

Holmes Brothers/Richmond Plains

McShane Road, Richmond, Nelson
Tel:+64 3 544 4230
Fax:+64 3 544 4231
Email: wine@hbd.co.nz
Internet: www.nzwine.com/holmes
Stockists: mail order available direct from the winery for delivery anywhere in New Zealand, or from the winery restaurant The Grape Escape Winery & Cellar; also from Commonsense Organics, and Untouched World (NZ); Vintage Roots, Vinceremos (UK); Peter Riegel Weinimport GmbH (Germany); Fuji Sequence Service Co. (Japan)
Overall Price Rating: ♦♦

Richmond Plains covers four hectares and was virgin land until 1991 when it was planted. It is the oldest certified organic vineyard on South Island and has been organic since planting. Its creators, the Holmes family, come from Bradford, Yorkshire, in England where they maintained a successful organic vegetable garden.

Holmes Brothers and a neighbouring but non-certified organic winery called Te Mania have set the format for spray-drift agreements between neighbours that has had some quite far reaching effects. After negotiations with the BioGro inspector, Te Mania agreed to have a spray buffer-zone entirely on its side of the vineyard boundary. Normally, rows of vines in the organic vineyard – usually the first half dozen nearest the non-organic neighbour – are not certified organic because of the risk of spray drift (the grapes are either sold off in bulk, or simply left unpicked by the organic vineyard, which thus suffers an economic penalty through no fault of its own). Te Mania has agreed not to spray vines on its side of the boundary in exchange for irrigation water from Holmes Brothers – which gets to pick and use all of its organically managed grapes as a result.

The wines are made under contract in a neighbouring winery and are marketed under the Richmond Plains label. They show healthy, pure tasting, ripe fruit. Recommended.

- Sauvignon Blanc, Nelson, Richmond Plains: dry white, first made in 1995, shows light to medium-bodied natural stone fruit and is a benchmark for New Zealand Sauvignon Blanc in terms of flavour and weight. Drink within three years of the vintage (the 'weight' of a wine is important – one of the most famous New Zealand Sauvignon Blanc's from the Marlborough region relies on freeze concentration for what the critics describe as its 'pungency'); suitable for vegans (Vintage Roots, Vinceremos, Organic Wine Company).
- Chardonnay, Nelson, Richmond Plains: dry white, first made in 1995; medium bodied, fermented in barrel, clean figgy fruit, clear mineral texture, excellent value for the quality; suitable for vegans in 1995, 1996, and 1997 (Vintage Roots, Vinceremos).
- Pinot Noir, Nelson, Richmond Plains: dry red, first made in 1995, medium bodied, clean cherry fruit, velvet texture; opens quickly in the glass to reveal a lighter style than the Pinot Noir from Silver Thread Vineyard (see New York State, *page 337*). The vines here are ten years younger though. Suitable for vegetarians in 1996 (egg fined) and suitable for vegans in 1997 and 1998 (Vintage Roots, Vinceremos).

Central Otago

This wine region covers less than 100 hectares. It lies south of the 45th parallel and was first planted to vines by late 19th-century gold miners. There are two producers of interest.

Kawarau Estate

PO Box 43, Cromwell, Central Otago
Email: kawarau@southnet.co.nz
Stockists: mail order available direct from the winery for delivery anywhere in New Zealand, or Queenstown Wines & Spirits, Regional Wines & Spirits (NZ); Chartrand Imports (USA)
Overall Price Rating: 👭

Karawau Estate is the most southerly organic vineyard in the world. It was established in 1992, and originally consisted of two vineyards, some distance apart. The smaller vineyard at Lake Hayes was sold in late 1996. This has left Kawarau with a vineyard together with grazing land at Lowburn in Central Otago, six miles north of the town of Cromwell. The grazing land is given to organic cattle. The vines at Lake Hayes produced fruity, off-dry white Gewurztraminer in 1995 and 1996 before they were sold. The vines at Lowburn produced 20 tonnes of grapes in 1998. Karawau's owners also make a Chardonnay from non-organic Marlborough grapes here.

- Sauvignon Blanc: dry white, 170 cases in 1998 plus 233 cases of Reserve (oak aged).
- Chardonnay: dry white, a total of 400 cases overall made.
- Gewurztraminer: first vintage grown at Lowburn is that of 1999.
- Pinot Noir: a total of 96 cases produced in 1998, plus 290 cases of Reserve (oak aged).

Rippon

Mt Aspiring Road, PO Box 175, Wanaka
Tel:+64 3 443 8084
Fax:+64 3 443 8084
Stockist: Fine Wines of New Zealand (UK)

Rippon is New Zealand's highest vineyard, at over 300m (1,000 feet) above sea level, and probably New Zealand's most scenic too, with views over Lake Wanaka to the Buchanan Mountains. It is often described as Central Otago's leading organic wine producer. In fact it has never had any legal title to that claim. It gained transitional organic status in the mid-1990s from BioGro NZ. However it failed to convert completely to organic methods within the specified maximum allowed period of three years. Thus Rippon was withdrawn from BioGro NZ's list of producers in conversion and was never given full BioGro NZ status.

South Africa

South Africa is keen to export its wine, but has trouble convincing wine buyers in the most competitive markets that its flagship wines are up to the mark. Part of the reason for this is poorly maintained vineyard, and poor vinestock in those vineyards. As the worst is grubbed up and replaced, we may begin to see more complexity and clarity of flavour in the country's wines. However, we may also see a standardization in taste, because much of the new vine budwood that is getting through South Africa's laborious quarantine restrictions is technically healthy but unexciting – factory vinestock from France, Italy, Germany and California chosen for its productivity. South Africa's wine industry is also trying hard to convince the rest of the world that, post-apartheid, it is giving blacks a fair deal – by employing them in positions of responsibility in the winery rather than as labourers in the vineyards. However, you can count the number of non-white winemakers in South Africa on the fingers of two hands: those who are paid to fly abroad to the fancy wine shows, selling South Africa's wine, are as white as a glass of the country's trademark Chenin Blanc.

South Africa has yet to establish its own rules for organic wine production, and the country's only certified organic vineyard, Sonop, is certified by an EU-accredited German body: Gesellschaft für Ressourcenshutz mbh, Prinzenstrasse 4, 37073 Göttingen. There is also one unofficial organic grower in the country's Stellenbosch region.

Paarl

The Paarl or 'coastal' region is located about 50 miles (80km) from Cape Town.

Sonop Wine Farm

PO Box 2029, Windmeul, Paarl 7630

Tel:+27 221 163 8534

Fax:+27 221 163 8723

Email: SONOP@iafrica.com

Stockist: Vintage Roots

Overall Price Rating: 🍷

Sonop Wine Farm boasts an easterly aspect which allows it to be in full sun from morning onwards, hence the name Sonop or 'sun up'. Sonop has been in a process of renewal since 1992 when the Swiss holding company (SAVISA) that owns it instituted an organic vineyard conversion programme. Now nearly half the vineyard is fully certified organic, including Sauvignon Blanc and Chardonnay for dry white wine and Cabernet Sauvignon and Pinotage for red. They are fairly rudimentary in style, but should improve once the entirety of the Sonop vineyard establishes its organic bearings. Sonop's conventionally managed vineyards produce a non-organic range of still wines labelled 'Kumala'. Sometimes these wines are sold in the UK under supermarkets' own brand names.

Stellenbosch

Stellenbosch is South Africa's best known wine region. There is one unofficial organic vineyard.

Klawervlei Wine Estate

PO Box 144, Koelenhof 7605, South Africa

Tel:+27 21 882 2746

Fax:+27 21 882 2415

Overall Price Rating: 🍷🍷

This 44-hectare vineyard was purchased by an Austrian couple called Hermann and Inge Feichtenschlager in 1995. They claim the estate is organic, although it is not certified by any body recognized by the EU. The claim is based on the fact that no copper sulphate is used on the vines (to treat downy mildew). Downy mildew affects Chenin Blanc, which here accounts for 23 hectares (over half the vineyard). But the mildew strikes Chenin only at the end of the season, and usually not before the grapes have ripened enough to be picked. However mildew did strike the red Pinotage and Merlot planted here, which resulted in very small crops in both 1997 and 1999.

Copper is tolerated under EU rules for certified organic vineyards, but it is due to be outlawed within 10 years because of its toxic effect on the soil. The Feichtenschlagers say they have trouble obtaining organic sprays like nettle (which is used by biodynamic growers to counter mildew and other fungal diseases of the vine) and so adopt a policy of minimal intervention in the vineyards by default. Mealy bugs are repelled with garlic and water rather than with insecticides. The Feichtenschlagers admit the winemaking has been haphazard, with excess sulphuring a feature in 1996 and haziness in the whites a feature in 1997 after errors were made by contract winemakers. Hermann Feichtenschlager hoped to resolve some of the winemaking problems by taking charge of the winemaking himself during the 1999 vintage. This may well be the first vintage to appear from this winery on the UK market.

South America: Argentina

Argentina is the world's fourth largest wine producer. Unlike Chile on the other side of the Andes, Argentina has an organic certification body (Argencert) which is IFOAM accredited. It certifies the two organic producers listed below. Both are located in San Juan, a province some way to the north of the country's most famous wine region, Mendoza. The wines made by the two producers here are not nearly of the same standard as those made by the two commercial operations cited in the Canadian section (Hainle and Summerhill). This may be something for IFOAM to bear in mind if it considers a standard for quality rather than merely for production methods – the two producers here have IFOAM's blessing which the two in Canada do not.

Some of the heaviest vineyard investment in Argentina at the moment is being made by Californians. They are planting new vineyards and renovating old wineries. The irony is that, given Californians' current obsession for organic methods and the fact that Argentina has an expanding organic agricultural base, so far none of these projects are organic. Another irony is that this foreign investment may do little to directly improve Argentina's rather poor reputation as a quality wine producer – both of organic wine (as noted above) and non-organic, because Californians can ship the wines they make in Argentina to California where they can be labelled 'Product of California'. This translates as 'Made in California but not from Californian grapes'. (This practice is also carried on in Washington State with imported Bulgarian grapes, subsequently passed off as wine produced in that State.)

CERTIFICATION BODIES

Argencert is the IFOAM accredited organic certification body in Argentina. It certifies the winegrowers belonging to MAPO – the Movimiento Argentino para la Producción Organica – the Argentinean organic umbrella organization. The relevant addresses are:

Argencert

Instituto Argentino para a Certificação e Promoção de Produtos Orgânicos
Bernado de Irigoyen 760, 17 'D' (1072), Buenos Aires
Tel:+54 1 334 2943
Fax:+54 1 331 7185
Email: argencert@interlink.com.ar

Organic certification body recognized by the relevant government authority in Argentina, the Secretaria de Agricultura e Gado da Nação, which allows products certified by Argencert to enter the EU under Argentina's third country status. Argencert certified the two wine producers listed below, both of which belong to MAPO, below. Argencert is also recognized by IFOAM.

MAPO – Movimiento Argentino para la Producción Organica

Av Santa Fe 873, Entrepiso 1059, Buenos Aires
Tel:+54 1 314 928
Fax:+54 1 311 8898

Organic Wine Producers

As noted above, Argentina has two certified organic vineyards.

Bodegas Fabril Alto Verde SA

Catamarca 202 Norte, 5400 San Juan
Tel:+54 264 421 2683
Fax:+54 264 423 8548
Email: altoverde@arnet.com.ar
Stockists: contact Vintage Roots for details
Overall Price Rating: ♦

This *bodega* (cellar) produces the Nuestra Esencia organic wines. Two wines are made, but consistency here has been hampered by the effect the El Niño weather pattern had on the 1998 vintage. This caused severe dilution to the wines.

- Chenin Blanc: off-dry white, not suitable for vegetarians, fades rather quickly.
- Malbec: dry red, made by fermenting the grapes as whole berries ('carbonic maceration'); limited oak ageing; the 1996 and 1997 vintages were slightly rubbery; 1998 was weak; suitable for vegetarians.

The cellar also produces a range of non-organic wines under the Montgaillard label.

Punte del Monte
Remo da Rold E Hijos SRL, Boulogne Sue Mar 809 Este, 5400 San Juan
Stockists: contact Vintage Roots for details
Overall Price Rating: 🍷

Two still wines are made, but again consistency is problematic.

- Blanco: off-dry white, in 1998 a blend including Muscat for grapiness and flavour; shows more fruit than the white wine above, but drink upon purchase; not suitable for vegetarians.
- Cabernet Sauvignon, Punte del Monte: dry red, again a slightly rubbery Cabernet; sees some oak, dry aftertaste; suitable for vegetarians.

Chile

The shocking fact about Chile is that, despite its reputation as a producer of good, inexpensive wines, there is not a single vineyard growing internationally recognized certified organic grapes there.

There are a number of official organizations and committees keen to promote Chile's fruits and vegetables, and even more it seems to promote her wines. However, in 1999 there was no independent certification body for organic production. One Chilean wine producer, La Fortuna, was claiming organic status at the end of the 1990s. It was backing its claims with soil analyses dated August 1997. These purported to show that two of its Central Valley vineyards (San Jorge and El Semillero in the Curicó sub-region) contained no trace of synthetic weed-killers, chemical fertilisers or pesticides. Unfortunately, it appears that these tests were carried out by Fundación Chile – a promotional body funded in part by an American corporation called ITT. Both of these organizations have commercial vested interests in the sale of Chilean products such as La Fortuna's wine. On the basis of these tests, Chile's national body for organic produce, PROA (Corporación de Promoción Orgánica Agropecuaria) has determined the Gran Fortuna vineyards can describe themselves as organic. This is fine if these wines are for consumption in Chile, and not for export.

PROA has issued two certificates for the Gran Fortuna vineyards, dated 5 December 1997. On the basis of the soil analyses carried out by Fundación Chile in 1997, PROA then decreed that both the San Jorge and El Semillero vineyards belonging to La Fortuna could be considered as organic for the last 15 and 20 years respectively. This appears very generous, especially since PROA then goes on to say that the 'certificate is valid for one year from the date of issue'. Certification bodies working to EU or IFOAM-approved standards *never* backdate organic certification as the Chileans appear to do, but accord it year by year after an annual inspection.

CHILE'S ORGANIC VINEYARDS – THE FUTURE

Chile has yet to establish organic production standards for its vineyards but when it does the wines to look out for as organic will almost certainly come from a native, Alvaro Espinoza Durán. He has not limited himself to one or either of the organic or the biodynamic fields for, unusually, he has a foot in both. In his late 30s, Espinoza studied winemaking at the Catholic University in Santiago and then at the University of Bordeaux in Pessac-Léognan (see the Graves Region in Bordeaux, *page 15*). He returned to Chile to set up the county's first cooperative winemaking cellar to be geared to quality rather than bulk production. In 1992 he became winemaker for Viña Carmen. This is a medium-sized, non-organic wine producer making wines under its own label from both own-grown and purchased wine grapes.

Espinoza has convinced the powers that be at Viña Carmen to conduct organic trials on 45 hectares of the company's vineyards. Part of this involved Espinoza spending a sabbatical year in Mendocino, California. His hosts were Fetzer Vineyards-Brown Forman Corporation, which has an experimental organic vineyard called 'Blue Heron' (*see page 302*). As well as this, Espinoza has converted his own small family vineyard near his house in Chile to biodynamics. The first wines from both this site (to be called 'Nativa') and Viña Carmen are due in the early years of the millennium.

FOUR REASONS WHY CHILEAN WINES ARE SO CHEAP

1   **Low labour costs:** these are substantially cheaper in Chile than in Australia for example (which is one reason why Australia's vineyards are so heavily mechanized and the Chilean vineyards not).

2   **Irrigation:** this is unrestricted and provided free through snowmelt from the Andes. The water runs across the Central Valley in the form of four major rivers, the Maipo, Rapel, Mataquito and Maule. This is arguably the cheapest irrigation in the world. (Washington State farmers, in contrast, have to pay the Canadian government for snowmelt from the Rockies, although the price they pay is kept artificially low by the US Government which pays huge subsidies on their behalf.)

3   **Climate**: Chile's climate is said to be perfect for the vine. It is one of consistent warmth from bud break to picking, unlike in Europe where warmth during the vine growing season is much more sporadic (which is why 'knowing your vintage' is so much more important there).

4   **Yields**: these are huge. The benign climate and the ability to irrigate allows each vine to ripen big bunches of grapes, with a sometimes incredible numbers of bunches per vine. For example in 1994, when I worked vintages on non-organic vineyards in both Chile and Bordeaux, I recorded a yield of 30,000 litres per hectare for Chilean Sauvignon Blanc (Maipo region), pruned May 1993 and picked March 1994. The level of sugar in the grapes was enough for 13.5 per cent alcohol – too much for Sauvignon so some of the tanks had to have water added to them so the bottled wine would contain 12.9 per cent permitted alcohol level. Incredible I know, but I saw it with my own eyes. In contrast, the yield in Bordeaux for Sauvignon Blanc (Entre Deux Mers region) which had been pruned in December 1993 and picked September 1994 was 6,000 litres per hectare. The level of sugar in the grapes was enough for 11 per cent alcohol and had to be boosted with sacks of beet sugar trucked down from the north of France. The final wine contained 12.3 per cent alcohol.

Appendix 1:
Organic Wine Stockists

Canada

Liberty Wine Merchants
Branches in Alberta and British Columbia (West Vancouver, Vancouver, North Vancouver and Victoria). For further details on the availability of domestically produced and imported wines made from organically grown grapes, call Liberty on:

+1 604 739 7801

Marquis Wine Cellars
1034 Davies St, Vancouver, BC V6E 1M3
Tel:+1 604 720 1260
Fax:+1 604 720 1260

Germany

As mentioned in the Country introduction, many German producers rely on farm gate sales for the majority of their turnover. This encourages German wine shops to stock imported organic wines. Organic wine specialists include:

Behringer Weinhandlung
Kobergerstr. 35, 90408 Nurnberg
Tel:+49 911 365 9340
Fax:+49 911 365 9293
Organic wine wholesaler.

Gerald Barkte GmbH

Hengdorfer Str. 12, 91189 Regelsbach

Tel:+49 912 283 6988

Fax:+49 912 283 9695

Email: bartkegmbh@t-online.de

Organic wine wholesaler, with organic olive and dairy products too.

Lambrecht W Weinhandel

Hauptstrasse 12, 63897 Miltenberg

Tel:+49 937 168 885

Fax:+49 937 165 514

Peter Riegel Weinimport GmbH

Steinäcker 12, 78359 Orsingen-Nenzingen

Tel:+49 777 493 13-0

Fax:+49 777 493 13-12

Email: Riegel.Weinimport@t-online.de

Probably the most influential wholesaler of organic wine in mainland Europe. A good contact to have if your favourite organic wine is out of stock in your local (European) market. Especially strong on wines from the French Midi and Switzerland.

TUF (Berlin)

Charlottemstr. 2, 10969 Berlin

Independent wine shop with another branch in Münster.

TUF (Münster)

Weinhandel Münster GmbH, Am Mittelhafen 43-45, 48155 Münster

Independent wine shop with another branch in Berlin.

Veritas

Haupstr. 30, 26122 Oldenburg

Independent wine shop with a strong selection of organic wine.

VivoLo Vin oGH
Duckwitzstraße 54/56, 28199 Bremen
Tel:+49 421 518 02-0
Fax:+49 421 518 02-34
Email: vivolovin@t-online.de
Wholesaler offering an expanding range of organic wine.

Weinblatt
Köln-Berliner-Strasse 87, 44287 Dortmund
Independent wine shop offering a mainly European organic selection.

Weinhandlung am Kleinen Platz
Kleiner Platz 3, 76829 Landau
Tel:+49 634 191 9593
Fax:+49 634 191 9594
Independent wine shop offering organic wines from around the world.

Japan

Fuji Sequence Service Co. Ltd
115–21 Sagami, Koka-cho, Koka-gun, Shiga 520-34, Japan
Tel:+81 748 88-3916
Fax:+81 778 88-2470
Email: renton-j@mx.biwa.ne.jp

New Zealand

Commonsense Organics
267 Wakefield Street, Wellington, New Zealand
Tel:+64 4 384 3314
Fax:+64 4 385 3383

The Grape Escape Winery & Cellar
McShane Road, Richmond, Nelson, New Zealand
Tel:+64 3 544 4254
Fax:+64 3 544 4054
Email: escape@hbd.co.nz

Queenstown Wines & Spirits
Shotover Street, Queenstown, New Zealand
Tel:+64 3 442 7697

Regional Wines & Spirits
Basin Reserve, Wellington, New Zealand
Tel:+64 4 385 6952

Untouched World
155 Roydvale Ave, Christchurch 5, New Zealand
Tel:+64 3 357 9399 (retail)/+64 3 357 9499 (café)
Fax:+64 3 358 9309

United Kingdom

Adnams
Sole Bay Brewery, Southwold, Suffolk IP13 9NE
Tel:+44 1502 727 220
Fax:+44 1502 727 252
Email: info@adnams.co.uk

Described by wine trade insiders as 'the thinking man's wine merchant' due to its intelligently written list. Small but developing range of wines made from organically grown grapes. Not cited in main text.

Anthony Byrne Fine Wines
Ramsey Business Park, Stocking Fen Road, Ramsey,
Cambridgeshire PE17 1UR
Tel:+44 1487 814 555
Fax:+44 1487 814 962

John Armit Wines Ltd

5 Royalty Studios, 105 Lancaster Road, London W11 1QF
Tel:+44 171 727 6846
Fax:+44 171 727 7133
Email: info@armit.co.uk
Internet: www.armit.co.uk
Prestigious but pricey independent fine wine merchant and broker with occasional organic listings.

Australian Wine Club

21A Southlea Road, Datchet SL3 9BH
Tel:+44 1753 594 925
Fax:+44 1753 591 369
Email: austwine.demon.co.uk
Mainly mail order, but if they don't have the Australian wine you are after they will tell you where to get it. Not cited in main text.

Balkan Business Ltd

Wolsey Hall, 66 Banbury Rd, Oxford OX2 6PR
Tel:+44 1865 311 883
Fax:+33 1865 310 407
Email: bozoukov@ocx.com
Internet: www.ocx.com.wine

Barratt, Proctor & Co

28 Recreation Ground Road, Stamford, Lincs PE9 1EW
Tel:+44 1780 755 810

Bibendum

113 Regents Park Rd, London NW1 8UR
Tel:+44 171 722 5577
Fax:+44 171 722 7354

Independent fine wine and mail order specialist with organic/biodynamic producers listed.

Booth's Supermarkets (Head Office)

4–6 Fishergate, Preston, Lancs PR1 3LJ

Tel:+44 1772 251 701

Fax:+44 1772 204 316

Email: cdee@booths-supermarkets.co.uk

Internet: booths-supermarkets.co.uk

Supermarket chain based in Cumbria and Lancashire.

Brown-Forman Wines International

Cavendish House, 51–55 Mortimer St, London W1N 8JE

Tel:+44 171 323 9332

The UK importer for Fetzer Vineyards-Brown Forman, California, which makes the 'Bonterra' range of wines. This address is the one certified by the Soil Association, which enables the Bonterra wines to be marketed in the UK as organic. For the purposes of this book the last vintage of Bonterra which was certified for import to the UK with the Soil Association logo was 1998.

The Bulgarian Vintners Company

Nazdrave House, 154 Caledonian Road, London N1 9RD

Tel:+44 171 278 8047

Fax:+44 171 833 3127

This was established in 1979 to market Bulgarian wine throughout Western Europe and was wholly state owned until the fall of Communism. Now privately run.

Classic Wines & Spirits Ltd

Vintner House, 28 Parkway, Deeside Industrial Park, Chester CH5 2NS

Tel:+44 1244 288 444

Fax:+44 1244 280 008

The Co-op (supermarket chain)

CWS, nr Century House, Manchester M60 4ES

Tel:+44 161 834 1212

Domaine Direct

10 Hardwick Street, London EC1R 4 RB
Tel:+44 171 837 1142
Fax:+44 171 837 8605

Durney Vineyards UK

PO Box 3660, London SW1Y 4AF
Tel:+44 171 930 9910
Fax:+44. 171 930 6213

The UK contact address for the Californian winery of the same name.

Farr Vintners

19 Sussex Street, Pimlico, London SW1V 4RR
Tel:+44 171 821 2000
Fax:+44 171 821 2020

Specialist independent fine wine broker with worldwide contacts to access older vintages of ♛-rated organic/biodynamic producers.

Fine Wines of New Zealand

PO Box 476, London NW5 2NZ
Tel:+44 171 482 0093
Fax:+44 171 267 8400

Pioneering independent importer of New Zealand wine into the UK.

Gauntley's of Nottingham

4 High Street, Nottingham NG1 2ET
Tel:+44 115 911 0555
Fax:+44 115 911 0557

Independent merchant noted for its Rhône selections.

Gelston Castle Fine Wines Ltd

Tel:+44 171 821 6841
Fax:+44 171 821 6350

or

Castle Douglas, Scotland DG7 1QE
Tel:+44 1556 503 012
Fax:+44 1556 504 183
Independent merchant with a very readable list featuring organic/bio-dynamic producers.

Georges Barbier

261 Lee High Road, London SE12 8RU
Tel:+44 181 852 5801
Fax:+44 181 463 0398

Haynes Hanson & Clark

25 Ecclestone St, London SW1W 9NP
Tel:+44 171 259 0102
Fax:+44 171 259 0103
Email: london@hhandc.co.uk

    or

Sheep Street, Stow on the Wold, Glos GL54 1AA
Tel:+44 1451 870 808
Fax:+44 1451 870 508
Email: stow@hhandc.co.uk
Independent fine wine retailer and mail order specialist featuring organic/biodynamic producers.

Howells of Bristol

The Old Brewery, Station Rd, Wickwar, Glos GL12 8NB
Tel:+44 1454 294 085
Fax:+44 1454 294 090

The International Exhibition Cooperative Wine Society Ltd

Gunnels Wood Road, Stevenage, Herts SG1 2BG
Tel:+44 1438 741 177 (switchboard)
Fax:+44 1438 726 485
Non profit-making wine merchant, featuring organic/biodynamic producers, that specializes in mail order delivery. To purchase from the Wine Society you must become a life member. This entails buying one share (currently £20).

Justerini & Brooks (London)

61 St James's Street, London SW1A 1LZ

Tel:+44 171 493 8721

Fax:+44 171 499 4653

   or

Justerini & Brooks (Scotland)

45 George Street, Edinburgh EH2 2HT

Tel:+44 131 226 4202

Fax:+44 131 225 2351

Fine wine retailer and mail order specialist.

Lauriston Wines Ltd

Effingham, Surrey

Tel:+44 1737 814 188

Majestic Wine Warehouses Ltd

Odhams Trading Estate, St Albans Road, Watford, Herts WD2 5RE

Tel:+44 1923 298 200

Fax:+44 1923 819 105

   or

Mail Order

Tel:+44 1727 847 935

Fax:+44 1727 810 884

Independent nationwide wine warehouse which leads the field in selling by the case (cases contain 12 bottles, the equivalent of 9 litres, and may be mixed).

Marks & Spencer

47 Baker St, London W1A 1DN

Tel:+44 171 268 3825

Fax:+44 171 268 2674

The first retailer in the UK to begin work on synthetic cork (in 1993) due to problems of cork taint from natural cork. Featured no organic/biodynamic producers in early 1999.

Mentzendorff

8th Floor, Prince Consort House, 27–29 Albert Embankment, London
SE1 7TJ
Tel:+44 171 415 3200
Fax:+44 171 415 3232

Oddbins (Head Office)

31–33 Weir Road, Wimbledon, London SW19 8UG
Tel:+44 181 944 4604
Fax:+44 181 944 4411

Nationwide retail specialist owned by Seagram. Set the pace for New
World wines a decade ago; will it do the same for organically grown
grapes? Featured one organic producer in early 1999.

Organic Wine Company

PO Box 81, High Wycombe, Bucks. HP13 5QN
Tel:+44 1494 446 557
Fax:+44 1494 713 030
Email: afm@lineone.net

Specialist independent shipper of wines from organic/biodynamic producers with one of the most readable wine lists around, complete with
detailed producer profiles, (sensible) food recommendations and high-
lighting the vegetarian and vegan status of its wines. Organizes tours to
European wine regions on its 'wine bus' (subscribers obtain discounts on
the wines listed).

Raeburn Fine Wines

23 Comely Bank Road, Edinburgh EH4 1DS, Scotland
Tel:+44 131 343 1159

Independent fine wine specialist with solid organic range.

Richards Walford

Manor House, Pickworth, Stamford, Lincs PE9 4DJ
Tel:+44 1780 460 451
Fax:+44 1780 460 276

This company deals direct with more biodynamic growers than any other
wine company currently operating, and supplies restaurants, hotels and

wine shops. It organized a Biodynamic Seminar at London's Kew Gardens in November 1995 with two Loire growers, Nicholas Joly (Clos de la Coulée de Serrant) and Noel Pinguet (Domaine Huet) as speakers. The event appeared to convince some leading commentators in the wine media that biodynamic winegrowing had left the fringe for the mainstream.

Roberson Wine Merchant Ltd

348 Kensington High Street, London W14 8NS
Tel:+44 171 371 2121
Fax:+44 171 371 4010
Email: wines@roberson.co.uk

Independent fine wine retail specialist with an innovative, futuristic building design that places correct wine storage at a premium.

Safeway Stores plc

6 Millington Road, Hayes, Middx UB3 4AY
Tel:+44 181 848 8744

The first UK supermarket to list a wide range of organically grown wines but it has now, to some extent, been caught up by others. Still lists a sound range of own label wines (Safeway Organic Red, for instance). Sponsors its own Organic Wine Fair (details on the above number) although a press release in 1998 on cork said Safeway was looking to synthetic and screw cap closures 'to tackle a world in which natural cork can never be relied upon again'. (Natural cork is the most sustainable form of bottle closure – cork oak trees are never cut down, for the cork bark is stripped from them every seven years, for up to 200 years.) We await the press release announcing Safeway's first 'Organic wine bottled with a plastic "cork"' with interest.

J Sainsbury plc

Stamford House, Stamford St, London SE1 9LL
Tel:+44 171 695 7926 / 0800 636 262 (Customer Careline)
Fax:+44 171 695 7925
Internet: www.sainsburys.co.uk

Vies with Tesco as the most powerful supermarket chain in the UK. Has an expanding organic range. Not mentioned in text.

Southcorp Wines Europe Ltd (Penfolds)

12 King St, Richmond, Surrey TW9 1ND
Tel:+44 181 334 2000
Fax:+44 181 334 2010
The UK contact address for the Australian winery, Penfolds.

T&W

51 King St, Thetford, Norfolk, IP24 2AU
Tel:+44 1842 765 646
Fax:+44 1842 766 407
Independent fine wine specialist.

Tesco Stores

PO Box 18, Delamare Road, Cheshunt, Herts EN8 9SL
Tel:+44 1992 632 222
Fax:+44 1992 658 225
Compared to its supermarket competitors, Tesco appeared slower off the mark as far as listing wine from organically grown grapes was concerned. Now catching up with bulk wines from Southern France and Northern Italy styled by Australian 'flying winemakers'. Flying winemakers are often employed by wine importers on a contract basis to ferment and bottle agreed amounts of wine for a set price point, specifically for a supermarket order – and they tend to stick to the winemaking handbook given to them during their time at wine college in their home countries. Their reliance on winemaking aids (packet yeast, enzymes, various acids, sugar) may account for why they have been described as 'Winemakers who kill local winemaking traditions.' A more positive view is that they make cheap silk purse wines out of sow's ear grapes by placing an emphasis on hygiene in the winery.

Vinceremos Wines & Spirits Ltd/Bottle Green

261 Upper Town St., Bramley, Leeds LS13 3JT
Tel:+44 113 257 7545
Fax:+44 113 257 6906
Email: vinceremos@aol.com
Specialist independent importer of wines from organic/biodynamic producers offering mail order, as well as non-organic wines. Non-certified

producers do creep onto the Vinceremos list – so order with care. The vegetarian and vegan status of all its wines are highlighted. Vinceremos has a sister company or 'supermarket arm' called Bottle Green Ltd. This provides supermarkets with the option of buying bulk wines and bottling them under their own label (ie Safeway Organic Red – a 'BOB' or Buyer's Own Brand).

Vintage Roots

Farley Farms, Bridge Farm, Reading Road, Arborfield, Berkshire RG2 9HT
Tel:+44 118 976 1999/+44 800 980 4992 (freephone)
Fax:+44 118 976 1998
Email: roots@ptop.demon.co.uk
Internet: www.vintageroots.co.uk

Independent wine merchant specializing in wines from organic/biodynamic producers. Organizes organic wine tours to wine regions. Produces an attractive, readable, easy-to-understand list. Wines bearing the 'Vintage Roots' label (i.e., BOBs) can offer excellent quality/price value. The list highlights the vegetarian and vegan status of its wines.

Yapp

Mere, Wilts BA12 6DY
Tel:+44 1747 860 423
Fax:+44 1747 860 929

Specialist independent importer with a sprinkling of organic growers and a few non-certified but sustainable ones on its list.

United States

Many of the companies here work as distributors, selling wines on to wine shops, restaurants and hotels. They will be able to put you in contact with the local stockist in your state if they are unable to sell to you direct.

Alabama

Grand Cru Wine Merchants
Alabama
Tel:+1 205 536 8966

Arizona

Mountain Peoples (Arizona)
Arizona
Tel:+1 530 265 3662

California

Golden Valley
170 Rucker Ave, Gilroy, CA 95020
Tel:+1 831 842 4893
Fax:+1 831 842 5036
Email: gvnc@safemail.com
Sales agents rather than distributors for Organic Wine Works wines.

Matagrano, Inc.
California
Tel:+1 650 246 3770

Mountain Peoples Wholesale (California)
California
Tel:+1 530 265 3662 / 800 679 8755

North Berkeley Wine
1505 Shattuck Avenue, Berkeley, CA 94709-9923
Tel:+1 510 848 8910
Fax:+1 510 848 0841

Organic Wine Co Inc.
1592 Union St, Suite 350, San Francisco CA 94123
Tel:+1 415 256 8888
Fax:+1 415 256 8883
Email: organic@ecowine.com   Internet: ecowine.com
This is not to be confused with the Organic Wine Company that is listed
under the UK stockists.

Transat Trade Co (California)
California
Tel:+1 310 672 1930

Young's Market Co
California
Tel:+1 510 475 2250

Colorado
Chez Suez Imports
Colorado
Tel:+1 303 499 1025

National Distributing Co
Colorado
Tel:+1 303 734 2400

Schott's & Company
Colorado
Tel:+1 303 773 1529

Connecticut
New England Wine & Spirits
Connecticut
Tel:+1 203 488 7155

Slocum & Sons
25 Industry Road, West Haven, CT 06516
Tel:+1 203 932 3688
Fax:+1 203 937 6430

Delaware
Constantine Wines (Delaware)
Delaware
Tel:+1 410 992 1400

District of Columbia

Constantine Wines (DC)
District of Columbia
Tel:+1 410 992 1400

Schneider's Liquors
300 Mass Ave, NE, Washington DC 20002
Tel:+1 800 377 1461
Fax:+1 202 546 6289

The Wine Source
5760 Second St. NE, Washington DC 20011
Tel:+1 202 832 6576
Fax:+1 202 832 2786

Florida

Apple A Day
Sarasto, Florida
Tel:+1 800 250 9463/+1 941 359 1048

Southern Wines & Spirits
c/o Transatlantic, 1605 NW. 159th Street, Miami, FL 33169
Tel:+1 305 884 6144
Fax:+1 305 628 0447

Georgia

Grapefields, Inc.
6050 N. McDonough Dr., Norcross, GA 30093
Tel:+1 770 416 8556
Fax:+1 770 416 9160

Prestige Wine Wholesalers
Georgia
Tel:+1 770 955 2876

Hawaii

Fine Wine Imports
500 Ala Kawa St, Honolulu, HI 96817
Tel:+1 808 841 7302
Fax:+1 808 842 3996

Idaho

Noveaux Beverage
Idaho
Tel:+1 208 377 4343

Illinois

Fine Wine Brokers
Illinois
Tel:+1 773 989 8166

Heritage Wine Cellars
6600 West Howard St, Niles, IL 60714
Tel:+1 847 965 3625
Fax:+1 847 965 3644

Organic Connection
Illinois
Tel:+1 773 989 8166 (toll free, nationwide mail order)

Romano Bros
Chicago, Illinois
Tel:+1 773 767 9500

Kentucky

Party Source
Kentucky
Tel:+1 606 291 4007

Vertner Smith Co. Inc.
Kentucky
Tel:+1 502 361 8421

Maine

Chartrand Imports
PO Box 1319, Rockland, ME 04841
Tel:+1 207 594 7300/+1 800 473 7307
Fax:+1 207 594 8098
Email: chartran@midcoast.com
Internet: www.midcoast.com/~chartran
Chartrand has been importing wines from organic and biodynamic producers since 1985 and was one of the first American companies to do so.

Colonial Distributing
Maine
Tel:+1 207 873 1143

Maryland

Boston Wine Co Ltd (Maryland)
Maryland
Tel:+1 617 666 5939

Constantine Wines (Maryland)
Maryland
Tel:+1 410 992 1400

Cray Burke Co (Maryland)
Maryland
Tel:+1 800 486 2729

Franklin Selections
12011 Guilford Road, ste 109, Annapolis Junction, MD 20701-1202
Tel:+1 410 880 4790
Fax:+1 410 880 6129

M. S. Walker (Maryland)
Maryland
Tel:+1 617 766 6700

Massachusetts
Carolina Wine & Spirits
99 Rivermore St., West Roxbury, MA 02132
Tel:+1 617 327 1600
Fax:+1 617 327 1486

M. S. Walker
Massachusetts
Tel:+1 617 776 6700

Michigan
AHD Vintners Limited
Michigan
Tel:+1 248 588 1414

Bellino's Quality Beverage
Michigan
Tel:+1 734 947 0920

Minnesota
Paustis & Sons
3500 Holy Ln North, ste. 30, Plymouth, MN 55441
Tel:+1 612 550 9545
Fax:+1 612 550 3944

Missouri
A. Bommarito Wines
2909 South Brentwood Blvd., St Louis, MO 63144
Tel:+1 314 961 8996
Fax:+1 314 961 5661

New Hampshire
United Beverage
New Hampshire
Tel:+1 603 228 6530

United Liquor Ltd
New Hampshire
Tel:+1 508 588 2300

New Jersey
Organic Vintages (NJ)
New Jersey
Tel:+1 707 463 2304/+1 800 877 6655 (toll free, nationwide mail order)

New Mexico
Mountain Peoples (New Mexico)
New Mexico
Tel:+1 530 265 3662

New York State/New Jersey
Charmer
New York City
Tel:+1 718 726 1329

Lauber Imports
24 Columbia Rd., ste. 100, Somerville, NJ 08876
Tel:+1 908 725 2100
Fax:+1 908 725 0317

Organic Vintages (NY)
New York
Tel:+1 707 463 2304/+1 800 877 6655 (toll free, nationwide mail order)

North Carolina
Hart Distributing
North Carolina
Tel:+1 800 786 9395

Ohio
Natural State Wines
Ohio
Tel:+1 614 487 9236

Oregon

Orang Special
Oregon
Tel:+1 503 288 9558

Vintage House Merchants
Oregon
Tel:+1 503 230 1020

Rhode Island

Copley Distributors
121 Hopkin Hills Rd., West Greenwich, RI 02817
Tel:+1 401 392 3580 ext 144
Fax:+1 401 397 3840

South Carolina

Champagne & Cotton
South Carolina
Tel:+1 864 242 0413

Texas

Glazer's Distributing
14860 Landmark Blvd., Dallas, TX 75240
Tel:+1 972 919 1777/+1 214 702 0900

Prestige Wine Cellars
Texas
Tel:+1 214 823 9272

Westcave Selections
Texas
Tel:+1 512 302 0151

Utah

Tsunami Wine Sellers
Utah
Tel:+1 801 328 1349

Vermont

Calmont Beverage
Vermont
Tel:+1 802 223 3281

DeWitt Beverage
Vermont
Tel:+1 802 254 4744

Virginia

National Distributors
Coast Virginia, Virginia
Tel:+1 804 550 1776/+1 800 432 0897 (toll free, nationwide mail order)

Roanoke Valley Wine Co.
South West Virginia, Virginia
Tel:+1 540 562 2078

Select Wines, Inc.
North Virginia, Virginia
Tel:+1 703 631 8100

Washington State

Frontier Distributing
Washington State
Tel:+1 509 332 1195

Lynch Distributing
Washington State
Tel:+1 509 248 0880

Noble Wines
Washington State
Tel:+1 206 326 5274

Northwest Purveyors
Washington State
Tel:+1 360 736 3375

Northwest Select
Washington State
Tel:+1 509 535 6233

Wisconsin

Import!
Wisconsin
Tel:+1 608 255 8622

Skip Brennan's
Wisconsin
Tel:+1 414 785 6606

Appendix 2:
Cover Crops

Cover crops are known as 'green manures' because they provide more desirable nutrients to the soil than plain weeds, and in greater quantities. They are used:

- to add biodiversity to vineyards, as the crops act as companion crops to the vineyards which, by their nature, are monocultural
- to attract beneficial flora and fauna into the vineyard, such as insects, spiders and predatory mites, by providing shelter and food (pollen, nectar, other bugs) to minimize the reliance on chemical insecticides. Growers need to know at which point in the vine cycle the cover crops will flower, and whether the flowers will attract desirable predators into the vineyard
- to 'fix' nitrogen and to act as a slow release, natural fertiliser. Leguminous cover crops draw nitrogen from the atmosphere and fix it to their roots. This is released slowly into the soil when the cover crops are mown and the roots are broken down by soil bacteria
- to provide a mat of vegetation when the cover crop is cut (mulching), which blocks sunlight out on the ground to prevent weed seeds from growing
- to prevent erosion and loss of soil moisture, and to reduce dust problems in New World vineyards, where dust-loving, non-beneficial spider mites congregate
- to provide organic matter and humus, and to allow rain to penetrate the soil by improving soil structure.

The following list details the types of cover crops available.

COVER CROP TYPES

Some cover crops work well in combination with others, and each grower has to observe which is the best combination for the types of soil present in his or her vineyard.

Austrian Winter Peas – Legume used to provide nitrogen.

Belle Beans – Legume which fixes nitrogen and, with its tall stalk, acts like a straw to get air into the soil. Belle beans are used in California to attract beneficial predatory mites that reproduce on the bean plants.

Cayuse Oats – Planted to provide structure for other legumes to climb up.

Chicory – Used in New Zealand to suck up rain water and excess nitrogen in the soils to prevent dilution in the grapes.

Clover – Widely used legume; called 'klee' in Austria. Low growing or 'sub-' clovers squeeze out weedseeds. Crimson clover blooms early to provide a thick stock for a good mat of vegetation; rose clover complements crimson clover by blooming later in the season.

Crown Vetch/Fescue – Nitrogen-fixing legume. Sowed every second or third row at Hainle Vineyards Estate Winery in Canada. Crown vetch can grow too high in vineyards with low trained vines.

Dycon Radishes – Have a long tap root, and so penetrate into the ground to help aerate the soil.

Lupins – Legume used to fix nitrogen.

Mustard Seed – Used widely in California; forms a yellow carpet between the vines – which attracts the photographers responsible for all those pretty pictures in wine magazines.

Phacelia – Planted to loosen compacted soil; called 'lockern' in Austria.

Rye – Used in California to build organic matter.

Timothy Grass – Used in New York State by Silver Thread Vineyard to make potassium available where it lacks in the soils around Finger Lakes.

Vetch – Common legume which provides nitrogen and a bed for overwintering insects; called 'wicke' in Austria.

Winter Wheat – Used in California for biomass, it forms a mat to keep down undesirable weeds.

Appendix 3:
Biodynamic Principles and Preparations

Demeter biodynamic standards tend to be stricter than those allowed by the EU for organic farmers; for example Demeter emphasizes the importance of local sources of manure – a neighbouring horse stable, rather than imported Peruvian bird droppings as is the fashion in California. Demeter also emphasizes primary rather than processed raw materials for composts (i.e., natural manure rather than processed textile or animal products such as bonemeal, which is allowed by California's CCOF for example). Biodynamic growers recycle all their leftover pressings (even in France, where these may be taken by the government to make a wash for distilling in spirit as a form of tax on all winegrowers; they are kept separate from conventional 'marc' in the distillery and are returned after washing to the growers).

Biodynamic preparations and composts have to be carefully prepared and used in order to get the most out of them. For example, biodynamists apply their rock powders after dynamizing them, i.e., stirring them in water and nothing else – no soya products are used for this. The main preparations are:

Dung Compost of Maria Thun: Dung compost is made like organic compost (animal manure mixed with straw and water) except that it is seasoned with a small amount of biodynamic compost preparations BD502–507 (see below for how these plant based preparations are made). Dung compost is applied in the autumn on 'root' days (see below) to support and reinforce the decomposition of organic matter. It should be full of bacteria so as to introduce life to the soil.

BD500 Horn Manure: This is made from dung placed in a cow's horn which is buried in the ground over winter. It has the texture of rolling tobacco, and is applied on root days at three separate times in the spring to halt winter decomposition and to bring energy and vitality to the roots to make them stronger. It is also applied once in the autumn to stimulate the germination of the cover crop seeds which are sown then. BD500 is applied as a liquid made up of warm water and 2.5oz (two-thirds of a cupful) per hectare of horn manure, stirred for one hour. Biodynamists view the horn as a natural energy captor (the Egyptians represented the bullock Apis with a sun between its horns, and we talk of a 'horn of plenty'), and they put their compost in one to allow it to fill up with vitalizing energy. However, some see the 'horn manure' preparation as sorcery, but it is no more unusual than storing a precious bottle of wine in a deep, dark cellar rather than in a bright, noisy thoroughfare for the effect the surroundings have on the wine inside. Remember, organic growers apply ground-up animals (in the form of bonemeal) to their vineyards, whereas biodynamists do not. They use their cow horns for life, to be passed on to the next generation.

Other benefits of Horn Manure include:

- stimulating activity in the roots, making roots grow thicker and longer and thus better able to absorb nutrients. This in turn means the vine is less susceptible to drought and disease. Its sap circulates more regularly.
- attracting planetary and earth forces into the vine sap (the complementary cosmic forces are provided by the Dung Compost as silica).
- stimulating soil micro-life and increasing beneficial bacteria growth in the soil.
- helping regulate levels of lime and nitrogen in the soil, and the release of trace elements (i.e., it makes the soil work so that it is neither too acid, too fertile or too stagnant).

BD501 Horn Silica/Silicum: Horn silica consists of finely ground/powdered quartz crystals, which are placed in a cow's horn and buried during summer (rather than in winter like BD 500 Horn Dung). This allows the quartz to capture the sun's live forces. When applied to the vine it enhances the way the plant metabolizes light, by enabling the leaves to assimilate the micro-nutrients found in the atmosphere. It is applied to the vine on leaf days around flowering and the moment the embryonic berries form, as well at as the moment the berries change colour (one month before harvest). It acts as a quality impulse to the vine and results in grapes with better colour, aroma, flavour and keeping qualities. Remember that in winter a vine which is pruned has little wood; by summer it has considerable fruit and growth upon it. Only 10 per cent of what is created by the vine comes from the root. The dynamised quartz stimulates photosynthesis (the transformation of invisible, intangible matter or light into matter like the blue-black colour in a Cabernet grape) and the formation of chlorophyll. Horn Silica is applied before picking, and also again after picking. Although at this point the vine has lost its fruit (the grapes are picked and in the vats) it is important that the vine hardens on into winter, but remains receptive to the light of the sun to ward off disease. Horn Silica is made from 2.5 grams, or one and a half teaspoons per hectare of ground quartz dynamized in cool water for one hour.

BD 502 Yarrow (Achillea millefolium or l'achillé or les milles feuilles in French): Yarrow is found in pastures, meadows and along roadsides in Europe and North America. One gram or 1 teaspoon of composted yarrow flowers is added per 10–15 tons of Dung Compost of Maria Thun, or as a dynamized spray. It revitalizes the vine by allowing the potassium present in the soil to combine with the sulphur present in the yarrow. It works in harmony with BD501 Horn Silica to attract cosmic forces. The Native Americans used Yarrow as a tonic for run-down conditions and indigestion. It is also known as Thousand Seal.

BD 503 Camomile (Chamomilla officinalis): Camomile enhances the decomposition of organic matter to provide humus. One 1 gram (1 teaspoon) of composted camomile is added per 10–15 tons of Dung Compost of Maria Thun, or is applied as a dynamized spray. It stabilizes nitrogen within the compost and increases soil life, so as to stimulate plant growth.

BD 504 Nettle (Urtica dioica, or l'ortie in French): Nettle can stimulate a flow of sap in the vine roots and trunk even under drought conditions, so that the vine keeps its 'bones' healthy. In the soil nettle activates iron to prevent chlorosis (iron deficiency, common in a chalk soil where iron becomes 'locked'). One 1 gram (1 teaspoon) of composted nettle is added per 10–15 tons of Dung Compost of Maria Thun, or is applied as a dynamized spray.

BD 505 Oak bark (l'écorce de chêne): The bark of the oak (Quercus robur) is hard and rich in calcium. It is used for its resistance to harmful plant diseases (it protects the oak tree from them after all). One gram (1 teaspoon) of composted oak bark is added per 10–15 tons of Dung Compost of Maria Thun, or is applied as a dynamized spray.

BD 506 Dandelion (Taraxacum officinale, or le pissenlit in French): Dandelion is a bright yellow flower resembling the sun. Its petals contain traces of silica crystal which indicate its affinity to light. When the silica in the dandelion combines with the potassium in the soil, cosmic forces are attracted to the vineyard. One gram (1 teaspoon) of composted dandelion is added per 10–15 tons of Dung Compost of Maria Thun, or is applied as a dynamized spray.

BD 507 Valerian (Valerian officinalis, or la valériane): Valerian is native to Europe and Asia, and is widely cultivated in Holland, Belgium, France and the US for its sedative properties. It is a source of phosphorus and acts as heat blanket. It attracts and intensifies warmth into the vineyard, which increases protection against frost and augments the chances of the grapes ripening. However it is not a miracle cure or quick fix because this is one of the treatments the vineyard take several years to acclimatize to. When composted, valerian flowers stimulate the Dung Compost when it is added. Half the valerian is inserted into the compost pile, and the other half is applied by spray onto the pile (the spray is prepared with 1ml or 20–30 drops per gallon of water, stirred for 10 minutes). Valerian enables the phosphorus components already present within the Dung Compost to be properly used by the soil.

BD 508 Horsetail (or equesetum or arvense): Horsetail is a fern-like plant which has the highest concentration of silica (light) in the vegetable kingdom (think about how bright the forest floor can be, even though shaded from the sun). It draws in light, the main scourge of powdery mildew and other shade-dependent fungal dieseases of the vine (downy mildew, grey rot), discouraging their spores from establishing. Horsetail is picked on the summer solstice and boiled into a tea (it is *not* added to the Dung Compost). Horsetail would be applied to vines during bloom, preferably mid-morning, when the flowers are open and receptive to solar forces.

Dynamizing

Liquids and solids are dynamized by stirring in water both clockwise and anti-clockwise, to mimic the effect of water at the earth's two poles. The stirring tank is usually made of wood (in Europe) or metal (in the New World) and is two-thirds the height of a human. The water spins from between 10 minutes to one hour (most stirrers are rigged to automatic timers, so whilst one lot is being dynamized another can be applied in the field by a single person). The wall or vortex of water which this stirring process creates is the manifestation of the transfer of energy from matter to water. Some producers use flow form fountains instead of tubs. Solutions of only 30 litres per hectare are needed.

Cosmic Influences: Leaf, Root, Flower and Fruit

Biodynamic growers recognize that the passage of the moon through the different constellations exerts four distinct elemental influences on the vineyard which are shown by:

- the leaf, which breathes in minute droplets of water and exhales litres of it especially under the influence of water signs Cancer, Scorpio and Pisces
- the root, which takes up mineral elements from the soil especially under the influence of earth signs Taurus, Capricorn and Virgo
- the flower, which opens itself to the atmosphere under the influence of air signs like Gemini, Libra and Aquarius (those organizing wine tastings should note that flower days are when the wines show most aroma)
- the fruit and its seed (the pip), which are linked to to the heat of the sun, especially under the influence of fire signs Aries, Sagittarius and Leo.

As biodynamic growers intervene in the vineyard only if the natural forces which are at work in and around the site are optimal, they must consult the Seedling Calendar.

Seedling Calendar – Maximizing the Four Elements

A Seedling Calendar is used by biodynamic growers to decide when they are going to plant vines (root and fruit days), when they are going to pick the grapes (fruit days) or even when they are going to rack the wine (fire days allow the wine to absorb sun energy, which is why biodynamic wine-makers rack the wines off the sediment in the casks during fruit days, opening the cellar doors to get the sun's influence onto the wine at the same time – one biodynamist in Bordeaux even reads poetry to his wines while doing this). Fruit days are also important for cultivating and treating the vines.

Working to the seedling calendar must be maintained irrespective of long weekends or holidays, but it encourages the symbiosis between the different organisms – the plant, the earth and the cosmos – and of course the grower. If harmony is achieved the plant will defend itself better or, rather, will not attract its enemies (fungi such as mildew , or insects, grape moths, vine moths or mites).

Appendix 4:
Making Wine Vegetarian or Vegan Suitable

As outlined in 'How to Use this Book', it is the agents used during the fining process which determines the suitability of wine for vegetarians or vegans. Fining works by electrostatic attraction — if the element in the wine that needs to be removed has a negative charge, then a fining agent with a positive charge will be added. The fining agent thus acts as a magnet, and collects the unwanted matter in the wine, which sinks to the bottom of the tank. Then the clear wine is racked or decanted off the sediment into a clean tank. A list of common fining agents includes:

- **Bentonite clay:** tolerated by vegetarians and vegans, bentonite is used to stop white wines turning cloudy in warm weather.
- **Casein (skim milk):** tolerated by vegetarians, casein is used to soften bitterness, and is the main protein of milk.
- **Diatomaceous earth:** tolerated by vegetarians and vegans even though diatomaceous earth (a fine, white powder) is the result of the crushing of tiny, fossilized shells which once contained living creatures. The reasoning is that as the animals inside the shells have been dead for millions of years this fining agent is vegetarian and vegan suitable. Diatomaceous earth is a filtration agent, rather than a fining agent per se.
- **Carbon:** tolerated by vegetarians and vegans, carbon is used to strip off flavours from rotten grapes when pressed.
- **Egg white or egg albumin:** tolerated by vegetarians, egg albumin is used to soften bitterness (usually in red wines) and is a protein soluble in water. Organic growers are encouraged to use fresh organic eggs from a local source by most certifiers. Biodynamic growers are encouraged to keep their own chickens in the vineyard.

- **Gelatin**: tolerated neither by vegetarians nor vegans because gelatin is derived from animal bones.
- **Isinglass**: tolerated neither by vegetarians nor vegans, isinglass is derived from the swim bladder of certain exotic fish. Manufactured isinglass (a polymer) is not allowed for organic winemaking.
- **Kaolin**: similar to bentonite (a clay), and thus tolerated by vegetarians and vegans.

FRIENDS *of the*
earth
for the planet for people

Friends of the Earth works to protect and improve the conditions for life on Earth, now and for the future.

Friends of the Earth is:

- the most extensive international environmental network in the world, with almost one million supporters across five continents
- the UK's most influential national environmental pressure group
- a unique network of campaigning local groups, working in 240 communities throughout England, Wales and Northern Ireland.

Friends of the Earth
26–28 Underwood Street
London N1 7JQ
Tel: 0171 490 1555
Fax: 0171 490 0881
Email: info@foe.co.uk
www.foe.co.uk

In the US, Friends of the Earth can be contacted at:

Friends of the Earth
1025 Vermont Ave, Suite 300, NW
Washington DC 20005
Tel: 202 783 7400
Email: foe@foe.org
www.foe.org

Other Friends of the Earth groups include:

FOE Australia: www.foe.org.au
FOE Canada: www.foecanada.org

There are also FOE groups in most European countries.

Friends of the Earth's Real Food campaign is for food which is safe — free from genetically modified ingredients, pesticides and other contaminants — as well as nutritious, tasty, and produced in a way that respects the environment.